THE NEW BOOK OF KNOWLEDGE ANNUAL

THE
NEW BOOK
OF
KNOWLEDGE
ANNUAL

The Young People's Book of the Year

Grolier Incorporated, Danbury, Connecticut

1998

Highlighting Events of 1997

ISBN 0-7172-0631-9

ISSN 0196-0148

The Library of Congress Catalog Card Number: 79-26807

 COPYRIGHT © 1998 BY GROLIER INCORPORATED

Copyright © in Canada 1998 by GROLIER LIMITED

STAFF

CONTENTS

CONTRIBUTORS

DAVIS, Francis
Contributing Editor, *The Atlantic Monthly;*
Author, *In the Moment; Outcats; The
History of the Blues; Bebop* and *Nothingness*

JAZZ

DIERKS, Carrie
Science writer; Editor, *Ask Isaac Asimov*
series

LLAMAS

GAY, David E.
Folklore Institute, Indiana University

FAIRIES

GODFREY, Laurie
Professor, Department of Anthropology,
University of Massachusetts; Author, *Scientists Confront Creationism;* Associate
Editor, *Journal of Human Evolution;*
Associate Editor, *Journal of Physical
Anthropology*

HUMAN BEINGS

KAUFMAN, Michael
Assistant Professor, Department of English,
Temple University

PURITANS

KURTZ, Henry I.
Author, *John and Sebastian Cabot;
Defending Our Country: The U.S. Army;
Captain John Smith; The Art of the Toy
Soldier*

JOHN CABOT

PASCOE, Elaine
Author, *South Africa: Troubled Land;
Neighbors at Odds: U.S. Policy in Latin
America; Racial Prejudice; The Horse
Owner's Preventive Maintenance Handbook; Freedom of Expression: The Right
to Speak Out in America*

AROUND THE WORLD
HUMAN RIGHTS

SILVERSTEIN, Alvin
Professor of Biology, College of Staten Island, CUNY; Author, *Human Anatomy and Physiology;* Coauthor, *The Circulatory System; The Digestive System; The Sense Organs; The Story of Your Ears*
HEART

SILVERSTEIN, Virginia
Translator of Russian and Scientific Literature; Coauthor, *The Circulatory System; The Digestive System; So You're Getting Braces; The Sense Organs; The Story of Your Ears*
HEART

STEPHANI, Julie
Editor, *Crafts 'n Things* magazine
POPULAR CRAFTS

STERNBERG, Robert J.
IBM Professor of Psychology and Education, Yale University; Author, *Pathways to Psychology; Introduction to Psychology; In Search of the Human Mind*
PSYCHOLOGY

TESAR, Jenny
Author, *Endangered Habitats; Global Warming; Scientific Crime Investigation; The Waste Crisis; Shrinking Forests; The New Webster's Computer Handbook; What on Earth Is a Meerkat?; Spiders*
EARTH WATCH
SPACE BRIEFS

VAN RYZIN, Robert
Managing Editor, *Numismatic News,* Krause Publications; Author, *Striking Impressions: A Visual Guide to Collecting U.S. Coins*
COIN COLLECTING

WEBB, Kempton E.
Chairman, Department of Geography, Columbia University; Author, *Latin America*
LATIN AMERICA

IN THE PAGES OF THIS BOOK . . .

How closely did you follow the events of 1997? Do you remember the people who made news during the year? What about the trends—what was in and what was out? Who won in sports? What were the top songs, films, and television shows? What important anniversaries were celebrated? All these helped make up your world in 1997—a year that was like no other.

Here's a quiz that will tell you how much you know about your world—about what took place during the past year and about other things, as well. If you're stumped by a question, don't worry. You'll find all the answers in the pages of this book. (The page numbers after the questions will tell you where to look.)

On January 20, Vice President Al Gore was inaugurated to a second term by Supreme Court Justice (Sandra Day O'Connor/Ruth Bader Ginsburg/Janet Reno), the first woman to administer an inaugural oath. (*16*)

Sky watchers enjoyed a rare sight in 1997 when Comet _____ blazed across the night sky. (*98*)

What film won the 1997 Academy Award for best motion picture? (*248*)

Unlike other (lambs/puppies/cubs), Dolly didn't result from a mating between a male and a female; she was cloned. (*106*)

Millions of people throughout the world mourned the death of _____, who was killed in a car accident in Paris, France, in August. (*13, 30, 40*)

September marked the 100th anniversary of a famous newspaper editorial that was written in response to an 8-year-old girl's question. What did she ask? (*33*)

U.S. President Bill Clinton's daughter Chelsea graduated from high school and left the White House for (Yale/Harvard/Stanford) University in September. (*234*)

In only their fifth season of play, the Florida _____ defeated the Cleveland Indians in seven games to capture the World Series in October. (*162*)

Name the hit summer movie that starred Will Smith and Tommy Lee Jones as a pair of secret agents keeping tabs on hundreds of extraterrestrials living on Earth. (*261*)

One of our favorite desserts—(pudding/Jell-O/ice cream)—celebrated its 100th birthday in March. (*21*)

President Clinton named _____ as his new Secretary of State. She was the first woman to hold the post. (*60*)

What TV shows won 1997 Emmy Awards as best comedy and drama series? (*264*)

In May, a memorial dedicated to President (Harry S. Truman/ Abraham Lincoln/Franklin D. Roosevelt) was opened in Washington, D.C. This president was the only one to serve four terms. (*25*)

Fourteen-year-old _____ became the youngest-ever figure-skating champion when she won both the U.S. and world women's figure-skating championships early in the year. (*174*)

The year 1997 marked the 150th birthdays of two men whose work made possible such modern conveniences as the telephone and recorded music. Who were these two great inventors? (*185, 214*)

On July 4, a robotic rover named *Sojourner* rolled onto the Red Planet and met up with some "Martians" called Yogi, Casper, and Barnacle Bill. What were they? (*120*)

The British pop music quintet, _____, took the music world by storm with their catchy singles, "Wannabe" and "Say You'll Be There." (*268*)

November marked the 75th anniversary of the discovery of the tomb of a teenage king who lived in ancient Egypt more than three thousand years ago. What was his name? (*186*)

A team of marine archeologists announced in March that they had discovered a wreck off the coast of North Carolina that they believed was the remains of the flagship of the notorious pirate (Blackbeard/Captain Kidd/Long John Silver). (*204*)

Fans were thrilled when the science-fiction movie _____ and its sequels returned to theaters with souped-up special effects and entire new scenes. (*254*)

The U.S. Air Force released a detailed report about the mysterious Roswell Incident, which marked its 50th anniversary during the summer. What took place near Roswell, New Mexico, in 1947? (*27*)

In August, the Guinness Book of Records declared that Marie-Louise Febronie Meilleur of Canada was the world's (tallest/oldest/shortest) person. (*30*)

On April 15, a tribute for baseball legend _____ was held at New York's Shea Stadium. The event marked the 50th anniversary of his becoming the first African American to play in modern major-league baseball. (*181*)

One of the top television stars of 1997 was a Jack Russell terrier named Soccer, who played a pooch that imagines himself the hero of classic literary tales. Name this children's TV series. (*91*)

The world's oldest national park, (Zion/Yosemite/Yellowstone) marked its 125th birthday in August. (*31*)

The _____ downed the Utah Jazz four games to two to win their fifth NBA title in seven years. (*166*)

Comic-book superhero (Superman/Batman/Spiderman) was given a new look that turned him into a sort of energy-based cyberman. (*259*)

In September, in Oslo, Norway, about 100 countries endorsed a treaty to ban _____, deadly explosive weapons that lie hidden in the ground. (*32*)

A new era began in Hong Kong on July 1, when the former British colony once again came under the rule of what Communist country? (*29, 55*)

Bobbi McCaughey of Iowa gave birth to four boys and three girls in November. The babies were the first (quintuplets/septuplets/octuplets) to be born to an American woman. (*36*)

The year's top teen music idols were three young boys who formed the group _____. Their bouncy pop sound propelled their album, *Middle of Nowhere,* to the top of the charts. (*267*)

In March, at the age of 16 years, 6 months, Martina Hingis became the youngest woman to gain the number-one ranking in her sport. Name that sport. (*177*)

In December, delegates from 161 countries met in Kyoto, Japan, and agreed to reduce Earth's "greenhouse" gases. Greenhouse gases cause (nuclear radiation/plant diseases/global warming). (*38*)

THE WORLD IN 1997

People worldwide were saddened by the death of Diana, Princess of Wales, on August 31, 1997. Diana, 36, was the former wife of Prince Charles, heir to the British throne. Her warmth and beauty had made her one of the best-loved public figures in Great Britain and the world, and her sudden death in a car crash prompted an overwhelming outpouring of grief. Thousands of mourners placed flowers outside her home at Kensington Palace in London, to honor her memory and show sympathy for her sons, princes William and Harry.

THE YEAR IN REVIEW

Elections, wars and rebellions, chilling terrorist threats—all were in the news in 1997. But some of the year's biggest news stories took place outside the realm of politics and international relations. This was the year that scientists showed that the impossible was possible—by producing the first clone of an adult animal, a sheep. It was a year in which an unmanned spacecraft sent back close-up pictures of Martian rocks, and a brilliant comet with three tails glowed in the night sky.

It was also a year in which people mourned the deaths of several world figures. When Diana, Princess of Wales, died in a Paris car crash on August 31, people around the world were saddened. The former wife of Prince Charles, heir to the British throne, Diana, 36, was widely admired for her glamorous image, her warm personality, and her charitable work. Some 2.5 billion people worldwide watched her moving funeral on television. While the world was still mourning Diana, news came of the death of Mother Teresa of Calcutta, the legendary Roman Catholic nun. Mother Teresa, who had devoted her life to helping the poor and sick of India, died on September 5, at age 87.

China also lost one of its most important citizens in 1997. Deng Xiaoping, the nation's supreme leader for many years, died on February 19, at age 92. Deng had come to power in 1978 and had remained an important figure even after retiring from his official posts. He had led the country through sweeping economic reforms, while keeping a tight rein on political dissent. A second event made 1997 a historic year for the Chinese. The territory of Hong Kong was returned to China on July 1, after more than 150 years of British rule. While the Chinese celebrated the transfer, many people in the West worried that limits on free speech and other restrictions would soon change Hong Kong's Westernized way of life.

A confrontation between Iraq and the United Nations raised new fears of war in the Persian Gulf region. Iraq had been under U.N. economic sanctions since the end of the Persian Gulf war of 1991, to ensure that it would live up to the agreement ending that conflict. Part of the agreement called for Iraq to destroy supplies of chemical and biological weapons and to cease making such weapons. But Iraq didn't cooperate fully with U.N. inspectors sent to follow up on this provision, repeatedly hindering their work.

In November 1997, Iraq ordered American members of the U.N. inspection teams to leave the country. In response, nearly all the U.N. inspectors pulled out. Iraq began to prepare for war. But then, in an agreement brokered by Russia, Iraq allowed the inspectors to return. The United Nations Security council voted to keep economic sanctions in place, neither increasing them (which the United States urged) nor easing them (which Iraq requested). The question of what chemical and biological weapons Iraq might be hiding was still unanswered. Such weapons are a great source of concern, not only because of their devastating effects in war but also because they might fall into the hands of terrorists. And the world had plenty of examples of terrorist violence in 1997.

In Algeria, where Islamic extremists have been waging a campaign of terror since 1991, violence reached new heights. Terrorist bands attacked villages, killing civilians by the score. Although the Algerian government negotiated a truce with the main Islamic group, the most extreme terrorists were not part of the agreement. In Egypt, meanwhile, Islamic terrorists targeted foreign tourists at the ancient Temple of Hatshepsut, near Luxor, on November 17. Fifty-eight tourists, four Egyptians, and six terrorists died in the assault.

Terrorism colored events in the Middle East, where the dispute between Israel and the Palestinian Arabs approached its 50th year. Under past agreements, Palestinians had achieved a measure of self-rule in the West Bank and the Gaza Strip, territories Israel had occupied since 1967. But with negotiations suspended for much of 1997, Israeli and Palestinian authorities made little progress in agreeing on a timetable for Israeli withdrawal from more West Bank territory. Militant Islamic groups staged a number of terrorist attacks, including several deadly suicide bombings in Jerusalem. And Israel drew sharp criticism when its agents attempted to assassinate a leader of one of those groups in neighboring Jordan. Talks between Israelis and Palestinians resumed in the fall.

In Africa, Mobutu Sese Seko, who had ruled Zaire since 1965, was driven from power by a rebel group in May. Known for his iron-handed rule and lavish lifestyle, Mobutu had been ill, and he died in exile in the fall. The rebellion that ousted him began with ethnic violence in the east, along the border with Rwanda, and then swept the country. Its leader, guerrilla fighter Laurent Kabila, declared himself head of state and changed the country's name to Congo. Although Kabila denied it, there was evidence that his soldiers, on their way to victory, had murdered hundreds of refugees, mostly members of the Hutu ethnic group.

In contrast, 1997 was a quiet year for Western nations. In the United States, scandals and controversy over campaign financing made news. Congressional Republicans charged that Democrats had been guilty of a range of fund-raising abuses, including accepting money from foreign businessmen, during the 1996 election campaign. Democrats countered that Republicans were guilty of even greater abuses. As investigations into the charges and counter-charges continued, a bill to reform the campaign-financing system failed in Congress.

The year saw important elections in several countries. In Britain, the Labour Party defeated the Conservative Party in general elections on May 1. The Conservatives had been in power for eighteen years, but now Tony Blair, the 43-year-old Labour Party leader, replaced Conservative John Major as prime minister. A month later, elections shifted control of the French Parliament from conservatives to a coalition of leftist parties, led by the Socialists. Socialist Party leader Lionel Jospin, 59, replaced conservative Alain Juppé as prime minister. And in Canada, the Liberal Party held onto power with a narrow victory in parliamentary elections on June 2. Jean Chrétien thus remained prime minister. But the vote was split along regional lines, raising questions about Canadian unity.

The nations that belong to the North Atlantic Treaty Organization (NATO) decided to invite some new members into their club in 1997. NATO was originally formed after World War II to defend Europe from the threat posed by the Soviet Union and its Communist allies in Eastern Europe. But in the 1990s, after the collapse of communism and the break-up of the Soviet Union, Eastern European countries adopted democracy and asked to enter NATO. After overcoming objections from Russia, the alliance invited Poland, Hungary, and the Czech Republic to join by 1999. Many people saw an encouraging sign in the fact that former enemies would now work together to ensure the stability of Europe.

JANUARY

4 Floodwaters began to recede in the northwestern United States, following a week of heavy rains and snow. Parts of California, Idaho, Nevada, Oregon, and Washington were battered by some of the region's worst flooding in decades. In California alone, the wild weather caused nearly $2 billion in damage. At least 29 deaths were blamed on the storms, and more than 100,000 people were forced to leave their homes.

21 The U.S. House of Representatives voted, 395 to 28, to reprimand Speaker Newt Gingrich, a Republican, for bringing discredit upon the House. He was accused of using tax-exempt donations for political purposes and then providing false information to the House Ethics Committee. Gingrich was also fined $300,000. It was the first time in the history of the House of Representatives that it imposed a sanction against its Speaker.

22 The U.S. space shuttle *Atlantis* completed a ten-day mission. The primary objective of the mission was to link up with the Russian space station *Mir* and bring home U.S. astronaut John E. Blaha, who had been stationed aboard *Mir* for more than four months. The *Atlantis*

On January 20, U.S. President Bill Clinton was inaugurated to a second term. Chief Justice William H. Rehnquist administered the oath of office as the president placed his hand on a family Bible held by his wife, Hillary Rodham Clinton. Moments earlier, Vice President Al Gore had been sworn in by Supreme Court Justice Ruth Bader Ginsburg, the first woman to administer an inaugural oath.

Up, Up, and Away

In January, three teams competed to become the first to fly nonstop around the world in a hot-air balloon. Two of the three balloons landed less than a day after launching because of technical problems. But the third balloon, piloted by American Steve Fossett (right), sailed on and on.

Fossett took off from St. Louis, Missouri, on January 13 in his silver-colored balloon *Solo Spirit.* The balloon consisted of a polyester and mylar bag that was 150 feet (46 meters) high, and an unpressurized cabin. It was fueled by a combination of helium gas and hot air heated by propane gas.

The entire voyage around the world was expected to take eighteen days. Throughout the trip, the *Solo Spirit* performed well. Four days after liftoff, Fossett crossed the Atlantic Ocean. He had planned to fly over Europe, but winds forced him southward, over Africa and the Middle East. However, Fossett was burning fuel faster than expected. And on January 20 he was forced to land in India—halfway around the world from where he had started.

Although Fossett didn't reach his goal, he did set new world records in ballooning—for the longest distance traveled and for the longest time spent in the air. His record-breaking flight covered 9,672 miles (15,566 kilometers) and lasted 146 hours, 54 minutes.

crew consisted of Michael A. Baker, John M. Grunsfeld, Marsha S. Ivins, Brent Jett, Peter J. K. Wisoff, and Jerry L. Linenger, who replaced Blaha aboard *Mir.*

23 Scientists reported that they had found the oldest stone tools known to have been made by human ancestors. The nearly 3,000 objects, found in Ethiopia, were more than 2.5 million years old. They included fist-size stones and small sharp-edged flakes, which were probably used to crack nuts and sharpen sticks for digging.

Government changes in January: In **Austria,** Viktor Klima was named chancellor. He succeeded Franz Vranitzky, who had been chancellor since 1986.

FEBRUARY

4 A civil jury in Santa Monica, California, unanimously found former professional football player O. J. Simpson liable in the 1994 slayings of his ex-wife, Nicole Brown Simpson, and her friend Ronald L. Goldman. A civil lawsuit is a dispute between citizens—in this case, a suit was brought against Simpson (the accused) by relatives of the deceased (the plaintiffs). If found liable, the accused can be ordered to pay money in compensation but cannot be sent to jail. During a 1995 criminal trial, Simpson had been found not guilty of the crime. The two verdicts reflected the differing standards of proofs required in civil and criminal trials. In a civil trial, a jury can determine a defendant's liability based on a preponderance—or more than 50 percent—of the evidence. In a criminal trial, the jury must find evidence of guilt beyond a reasonable doubt to reach a conviction. (On February 10, the jury ordered Simpson to pay $25 million in damages to the plaintiffs.)

14 Nearly four years after some 300 Chinese immigrants had illegally entered the United States, the government ordered the release of 53 of them from prison. The immigrants had paid smugglers to take them to the United States and had been passengers on the freighter *Golden Venture.* In June 1993 their ship ran aground a few miles from the Statue of Liberty, and the passengers swam ashore and were detained by officials. Some were allowed to remain in the United States legally, some were sent back to China, and some were imprisoned while immigration authorities handled their cases. The fate of the 53 immigrants was still uncertain, but they were placed on parole and allowed to live with families that had agreed to sponsor them.

21 The U.S. space shuttle *Discovery* completed a ten-day mission. The objective of the mission was to make repairs to the Hubble Space Telescope that would allow it to peer even deeper into the universe. During five spacewalks, the astronauts raised the telescope into a higher orbiting position, installed new observation equipment, and repaired tears in its insulation panels. The crew consisted of Kenneth D. Bowersox, Gregory J. Harbaugh, Steven A. Hawley, Scott J. Horowitz, Mark C. Lee, Steven L. Smith, and Joseph R. Tanner.

26 A major earthquake measuring 6.1 on the Richter scale of ground motion struck northwestern Iran. About 1,000 people were killed, 2,600 were injured, and more than 40,000 were left homeless by the quake.

Government changes in February: In **Bulgaria,** Stefan Sofiyanski was named premier. He succeeded Zhan Videnov, who had been premier since 1995. . . .In **China,** Deng Xiaoping, one of the founders of the nation's Communist government, died. He led China from 1978 until 1989, and thereafter continued to exert great political power. . . .In **Ecuador,** Fabián Alarcón was named presi-

Viking Life in Ancient Greenland

In February, archeologists reported that they had uncovered the remains of a 1,000-year-old Viking settlement in Greenland (above). Located near Nuuk, Greenland's capital city, the site is known as Vesterbygden, or "western settlement."

The Vikings (inset) were a Scandinavian people who built powerful ships and sailed on long voyages far from home. Some voyages were for plunder, some for trade, and some for exploration. In the year 982, Vikings began to settle along the coast of Greenland. They lived there for several hundred years, but abandoned their colonies by the early 1400s.

After the Vesterbygden settlement was abandoned, it became buried in sand and permafrost—thus becoming preserved with its contents intact. It's the first Viking settlement in Greenland to be studied layer by layer, down to its original foundations. The archeologists found six interconnected buildings made of stone and peat. Each building had up to 30 rooms, and inside each room were objects from the people's everyday lives. There were useful items such as tools, kitchen utensils, storage barrels, and wooden bowls. And there were items that showed that the Vikings also had time for pleasure—necklaces made of reindeer bone, dice made from walrus teeth, and miniature boats that may have been children's toys.

dent. He succeeded Abdalá Bucaram, who had been president since August 1996 and Rosalia Arteaga who was in office for two days. . . .In **North Korea,** Hong Song Nam was named premier. He succeeded Kang Song San, who had been premier since 1993. . . .In **Pakistan,** Nawaz Sharif was named prime minister. He succeeded Malik Meraj Khalid, who had been prime minister since late 1996.

MARCH

1-10 Powerful tornadoes and thunderstorms tore across seven states— Arkansas, Indiana, Kentucky, Ohio, Mississippi, Pennsylvania, and West Virginia. About 58 people died and thousands were driven from their homes as a result of the severe weather. Among the hardest hit areas was Arkadelphia, Arkansas, where tornadoes leveled much of the town. And residents of the Ohio River Valley experienced some of the worst flooding in more than 30 years.

20 The Liggett Group, a major cigarette manufacturer, acknowledged that tobacco is addictive and causes cancer. It was the first time that a U.S. tobacco company admitted that it knew that tobacco was addictive. The company also said that cigarette makers had consciously marketed their products to teenagers. Liggett made these statements as part of an agreement to settle lawsuits brought against it by 22 states trying to recover costs in treating smoking-related illnesses.

26 In Rancho Santa Fe, California, authorities discovered the bodies of 39 people who had committed suicide. The 21 women and 18 men were members of a religious cult called Heaven's Gate. They believed that by killing themselves they would be able to join an alien spacecraft that would carry them to heaven. It was one of the largest mass suicides in U.S. history.

A family of cats is safely rafted through a flooded street in New Richmond, Ohio.

Happy Birthday, Jell-O

It wobbles. . .it bobbles. . .it jiggles. . .it shimmers. It's Jell-O! And in March, this best-selling dessert celebrated its 100th birthday. The dessert—a mixture of fruit flavoring and powdered gelatin—was invented in 1897 by Pearle Wait, a young carpenter who lived in Le Roy, New York. Wait's wife gave the colorful concoction its name.

Jell-O wasn't an immediate hit. Wait went door-to-door trying to sell it, but without much success. In 1899 he sold the formula to Orator Woodward, the wealthiest man in town, for $450. Within eight years, Woodward had built Jell-O into a $1 million dollar business. One of Woodward's best sales tactics was giving away thousands of free samples. Jell-O's popularity grew as people discovered that the easy-to-prepare treat could be used in countless ways—not only as a dessert, but also in snacks, salads, and even drinks. Today, Jell-O is owned by Kraft Foods, and there are 22 flavors. The dessert is so popular that about thirteen boxes are purchased every second.

To mark the 100th anniversary, a new cookbook filled with Jell-O recipes was published. And a Jell-O museum opened in Le Roy. Also, a new Jell-O flavor was introduced—sparkling white grape. The flavor may become popular, but its pale color will probably prevent it from becoming number-one. When it comes to Jell-O, most people seem to like strawberry best!

Government changes in March: In **Albania,** Bashkim Fino was named premier. He succeeded Aleksander Meksi, who had been premier since 1992. . . .In **Guyana,** Samuel Hinds became president. He succeeded Cheddi Jagan, who died on March 6 after more than four years in office. . . .In **South Korea,** Koh Kun was named premier. He succeeded Lee Soo Sung, who had been premier since 1994.

APRIL

8 The U.S. space shuttle *Columbia* ended a four-day mission. The mission had been planned to last sixteen days, but it was ended early because of problems with the shuttle's power supply. The crew consisted of Roger K. Crouch, Michael L. Gernhardt, James D. Halsell, Gregory T. Linteris, Susan L. Still, Donald A. Thomas, and Janice Voss.

15 In Saudi Arabia, more than 300 Muslim pilgrims died and 1,300 were injured when a fire swept through a camp of some 70,000 tents near the holy city of Mecca. Many of the people died in a stampede as they tried to escape the flames. The accident occurred during the annual *hajj,* or pilgrimage, that marks the high point of the Islamic year. Every Muslim is expected to make the pilgrimage at least once in his or her lifetime, and some two million Muslims from all over the world were in Mecca at the time of the accident.

24 The U.S. Senate approved the Chemical Weapons Convention, by a vote of 74–26. The treaty bans the use, development, production, and stockpiling of all poison-gas weapons. It also requires nations to destroy all existing stockpiles of such weapons by the year 2007. (The treaty, which was ratified by 88 countries, went into effect on April 29.)

27-29 The Presidents' Summit for America's Future, designed to encourage volunteer work, was held in Philadelphia, Pennsylvania. The three-day event, led by President Bill Clinton, former President George Bush, and summit chairman General Colin L. Powell, focused on the needs of children. Its main objective was to inspire people to become mentors or act in other ways to help two million at-risk children by the year 2000.

On April 24, scientists announced the discovery of a spectacular fossil ground in northeastern China. The specimens recovered at the site included many kinds of animals and plants that lived about 140 million years ago. In dinosaur fossils such as the one shown at right, scientists saw internal organs—the first fossilized internal organs of dinosaurs ever found. The stomach of one dinosaur contained the remains of a mammal, which was the first proof that dinosaurs sometimes ate mammals.

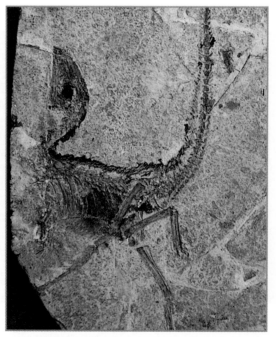

A Rescue in Peru

On April 22, Peruvian soldiers (right) stormed the residence of the Japanese ambassador in Lima, rescuing 72 hostages and ending a four-month standoff with leftist guerrillas.

The guerrillas, members of the Túpac Amaru Revolutionary Movement, had seized control of the residence on December 17, 1996. More than 500 people who were attending a party there were taken hostage, including ambassadors from a dozen countries and scores of other foreign dignitaries. In the days following the attack, negotiations between the guerrillas and the Peruvian government led to the release of several hundred hostages. But the guerrillas refused to release the remaining captives unless hundreds of their comrades were freed from Peruvian prisons, a condition that Peru's president, Alberto Fujimori, was unwilling to meet.

The rescue operation took less than an hour. It began when soldiers exploded a bomb in a tunnel that had been dug underneath the ambassador's residence. Within minutes, other soldiers blasted their way through the front door and through a second-story door opened by the hostages. All fourteen of the guerrillas were killed during the raid. Two soldiers were also killed, and one hostage died after suffering a heart attack.

30 During the month, communities along the Red River of the North—especially parts of North Dakota, Minnesota, and the Canadian province of Manitoba—experienced some of the region's worst flooding in hundreds of years. Record snowfall, topped off by an April blizzard, caused the river and its tributaries to overflow. About 100,000 people had to leave their homes. The hardest-hit community was Grand Forks, North Dakota, where half the houses were either damaged or destroyed.

Government changes in April: Following national elections in **Bulgaria,** Ivan Kostov was named premier. He succeeded Stefan Sofiyanksi, who had been premier since February. . . .In **India,** Inder Kumar Gujral became prime minister. He succeeded H. D. Deve Gowda, who had been in office for less than a year.

MAY

10 A powerful earthquake measuring 7.1 on the Richter scale of ground motion struck northeastern Iran. About 2,400 people were killed, and 6,000 were injured. The quake destroyed some 200 villages, leaving 50,000 people homeless.

20 Scientists from Argentina reported the discovery of fossils of the most birdlike dinosaur ever found. The new species was named *Unenlagia comahuensis,* which means "half bird from northwest Patagonia" (Patagonia is a region of Argentina.) *Unenlagia,* which lived about 90 million years ago, was a meat-eating dinosaur that stood nearly 4 feet (1.2 meters) tall. Its shoulder and upper arm bones were very similar to those of birds, and allowed the dinosaur to move its small forelimbs in an up-and-down flapping motion. *Unenlagia* couldn't fly, but it may have used its winglike arms to maintain its balance when chasing prey. Scientists believe that the creature may have shared a common ancestor with the first birds.

24 The U.S. space shuttle *Atlantis* completed a nine-day mission that included a link-up with the Russian space station *Mir.* The crew consisted of Eileen M. Collins, C. Michael Foale, Edward T. Lu, Carlos I. Noriega, Charles J. Precourt, Jean-François Clervoy of France, and Elena V. Kondakova of Russia. Foale remained on *Mir;* U.S. astronaut Jerry Linenger, who had been on the space station for four months, returned to Earth.

27 At least six tornadoes roared through central Texas, killing 30 people. Hardest hit was Jarrell, a small town north of Austin. About fifty homes there were destroyed by a tornado that packed winds of more than 260 miles (420 kilometers) per hour. The twisters were the most destructive tornadoes to hit Texas in ten years.

Government changes in May: In national elections in **Great Britain,** Tony Blair of the Labour Party was elected prime minister. He succeeded John Major of the Conservative Party, who had been prime minister since 1990. . . .In national elections in **Iran,** Mohammed Khatami, a moderate, was elected president. He succeeded Ali Hashemi Rafsanjani, who took office in 1989. . . .In national elections in **Mongolia,** Natsagiin Bagabandi was elected president. He succeeded Punsalmaagiyn Ochirbat, who had been in office since 1990. . . .In **Sierra Leone,** President Ahmad Tejan Kabbah was overthrown in a coup. He was succeeded by a military council led by Major Johnny Paul Koromah. . . .In **Zaire,** Laurent Kabila declared himself president and renamed the country Congo, which had been the country's name when it gained independence from Belgium in 1960. Kabila succeeded Mobutu Sese Seko, who had been president since 1965.

THEY (WHO) SEEK TO ESTABLISH
SYSTEMS OF GOVERNMENT BASED ON
THE REGIMENTATION OF ALL HUMAN
BEINGS BY A HANDFUL OF INDIVIDUAL
RULERS... CALL THIS A NEW ORDER.
IT IS NOT NEW AND IT IS NOT ORDER

A Memorial for FDR

On May 2, in Washington, D.C., President Bill Clinton opened a memorial dedicated to Franklin Delano Roosevelt, the 32nd president of the United States. Roosevelt held office from 1933 until his death in 1945—the only president elected to serve four terms. Known for his confidence and optimism, FDR led the nation through the Great Depression of the 1930s and World War II.

The granite memorial has four open-air galleries, one for each of FDR's presidential terms. Using sculptures and FDR's own words, the memorial traces his impact on his times. For instance, in one area, there's a sculpture showing hungry people standing in a breadline during the Depression. FDR started many social and job programs to help people hurt by the Depression.

The memorial includes sculptures of both FDR and his wife, Eleanor. Some people criticized the sculpture of FDR because it didn't show him in the wheelchair he often used after he was stricken with polio in 1921. However, others pointed out that during his lifetime, FDR's inability to walk unaided wasn't widely known by the public. He wanted people to focus on his enormous abilities, not on his disability. At the opening ceremonies, President Clinton paid tribute to FDR's leadership. He hailed Roosevelt for his "open, American spirit, with a fine sense for the possible."

JUNE

2 A federal jury in Denver, Colorado, found Timothy J. McVeigh guilty of conspiracy and murder in the bombing of the Alfred P. Murrah Federal Building in Oklahoma City, Oklahoma, on April 19, 1995. McVeigh, a former soldier with strong antigovernment beliefs, had been charged with conspiring to detonate a truck bomb in the incident that killed 168 people, including nineteen children, and injured hundreds of others. It was the deadliest terrorist attack ever to occur on U.S. soil. (On June 13, the jury unanimously recommended that McVeigh be sentenced to death for the bombing. A second defendant in the case, Terry L. Nichols, went on trial in November.)

22 In Denver, Colorado, the leaders of the major industrial nations ended their 23rd annual summit meeting on world economic issues. The countries represented were Canada, France, Germany, Great Britain, Italy, Japan, the United States, and Russia. It was the first time that Russia participated as an equal member of the group, which changed its name from the Group of Seven to the Summit of the Eight. Among the issues discussed were the planned expansion of the North Atlantic Treaty Organization (NATO) into Eastern Europe, aid to Africa, and global warming.

Government changes in June: Following national elections in **France,** Lionel Jospin of the Socialist Party became premier. He succeeded Alain Juppé, a Conservative, who had been premier since 1995. . . .Following national elections in **Ireland,** Bertie Ahern became the youngest prime minister in the country's history. He succeeded John Bruton, who had been prime minister since 1994. . . .In **Turkey,** Mesut Yilmaz was named prime minister. He succeeded Necmettin Erbakan, the nation's first leader from a religious party, who had resigned after one year in office.

A guilty verdict for Timothy McVeigh made headlines around the country. McVeigh was charged with the 1995 bombing of a federal building in Oklahoma City, resulting in the deaths of 168 people.

The Roswell Incident

What fell from the sky near Roswell, New Mexico, in the summer of 1947? Strange pieces of metal foil were found on a sheep ranch. Officials at a nearby Air Force base said the debris was the remains of a weather balloon. But some people didn't believe it. They said that the metallic material was part of a UFO—an unidentified flying object. An alien spacecraft had crashed to Earth, they claimed, and the U.S. government had hidden the wreckage—and the bodies of extraterrestrials on board.

The supposed crash and cover-up became known as the Roswell Incident. Over the years, stories about the strange events grew. People claimed to have seen alien bodies and actual alien spacecraft. Under pressure to explain the claims, the Air Force admitted in 1994 that the wreckage came not from a weather balloon but from a high-altitude balloon that was part of a secret nuclear espionage program. But that didn't stop talk about the Roswell Incident, which inspired books, television shows, and movies.

On June 24, 1997, as the 50th anniversary of the incident neared, the Air Force released a detailed report. In 231 pages, it explained how secret military work may have given rise to the UFO stories. "Alien bodies," for example, were probably test dummies dropped from high altitudes. "UFO's" were secret spy planes.

The report didn't change the minds of true believers in UFO's. Nor did it dampen Roswell's six-day anniversary celebration in early July 1997. Thousands of people toured the alleged crash site, visited UFO museums (above), ate glow-in-the-dark "alien" lollipops, and took home T-shirts and other out-of-this-world souvenirs.

JULY

4   *Mars Pathfinder,* an unmanned U.S. spaceship, landed on Mars. *Sojourner,* a small robotic vehicle, left *Pathfinder* and began exploring the planet's surface. It gathered data on the climate and atmosphere, and sent detailed photographs of the Martian landscape back to Earth. The mission was the first to Mars since two U.S. *Viking* spacecraft landed there in 1976.

17   The U.S. space shuttle *Columbia* completed a sixteen-day mission. The goal of the mission was to complete scientific experiments that had begun during the shuttle's April mission, which had been cut short because of technical problems. The crew consisted of Roger K. Crouch, Michael L. Gernhardt, James D. Halsell, Gregory T. Linteris, Susan L. Still, Donald A. Thomas, and Janice E. Voss.

29   Paul Cellucci became governor of Massachusetts. He succeeded William F. Weld, who had resigned.

30   In Jerusalem, Israel, two suicide bombers set off explosions in a busy marketplace, killing themselves and thirteen other people. More than 150 people were injured. Hamas, the militant Palestinian organization, claimed responsibility for the attack.

On July 21, the U.S.S. *Constitution*—the nation's oldest commissioned warship—celebrated its 200th anniversary by sailing without assistance for the first time since 1881. Known as "Old Ironsides," the *Constitution* was ordered built by President George Washington and was launched in 1797. The ship, which was never defeated in 42 battles, underwent a four-year restoration that once again made it seaworthy.

A New Era Begins in Hong Kong

On July 1, the British colony of Hong Kong once again came under the rule of China. China had leased the territory to Great Britain in the 1800s. During the 156 years of British rule, Hong Kong had grown to become a lively center of world trade and finance. China pledged that Hong Kong would be a self-governing unit, able to keep its own economic system and way of life for the next 50 years.

As June 30th ended and July 1st began, leaders from around the world watched as Great Britain's Union Jack flag was lowered and the Chinese flag and a new Hong Kong flag were raised. Then Chinese President Jiang Zemin welcomed Hong Kong's residents "to the embrace of the motherland"; and a new legislature headed by Hong Kong businessman Tung Chee-hwa was sworn in.

Throughout the day, there were parties and celebrations in Hong Kong (above) and the rest of China. Fireworks, dragon dances, concerts, and sound-and-light shows were enjoyed by millions of people. In the evening, a colorful boat parade sailed through Hong Kong's harbor.

However, despite the festivities, it remained uncertain how the Chinese government would treat Hong Kong. Communist China has long restricted the political freedom of its own people. And many Hong Kong citizens were afraid that the new government would place rigid controls on many of their rights.

Government changes in July: Following national elections in **Albania,** Rexhep Mejdani was named president. He succeeded Sali Berisha, who had been president since 1992. Fatos Nano was named premier. . . .In **Cambodia,** Prime Minister Norodom Ranariddh was ousted in a coup. Ung Huot was named to succeed Ranariddh, who had been prime minister since 1993. . . .In **India,** Kocheril Raman Narayanan was chosen president. He succeeded Shankar Dayal Sharma, who had been president since 1992. . . .In national elections that followed seven years of civil war in **Liberia,** Charles G. Taylor was elected president. He succeeded Ruth Perry who had been president for less than a year. . . .In **Yugoslavia,** Slobodan Milosevic was named president. He succeeded Zoran Lilic, who had been president since 1993.

AUGUST

5 U.S. President Bill Clinton signed legislation to balance the federal budget by the year 2002. The plan combined spending cuts that would save about $263 billion over five years with tax cuts worth about $95 billion over the period. Included were cuts in personal income taxes, but also tax increases on items such as cigarettes and airline tickets. The plan would balance the federal budget for the first time since 1969.

14 The Guinness Book of Records declared that 117-year-old Marie-Louise Febronie Meilleur of Ontario, Canada, was the world's oldest living person. The previous holder of the title was Jeanne Calment of France, who died earlier in the month at the age of 122.

19 The U.S. space shuttle *Discovery* completed a twelve-day mission. The mission had three major objectives: to release and retrieve an environmental satellite that monitored the Earth's ozone layer; to observe Comet Hale-Bopp; and to test a miniature robotic arm that would be used for the future international space station. The crew consisted of Curtis L. Brown, Jr., Robert L. Curbeam, Jr., N. Jan Davis, Stephen K. Robinson, Kent V. Rominger, and Bjarni V. Tryggvason of Canada.

31 Diana, Princess of Wales, was fatally injured in a car accident in Paris, France, and died several hours later at a nearby hospital. Also killed were her companion, Emad Mohamed (Dodi) al-Fayed and the driver

Diana, Princess of Wales, died on August 31. Here, Prince Charles, Prince Harry, Diana's brother Earl Spencer, Prince William, and Prince Philip follow Diana's coffin as it is carried into Westminster Abbey for her funeral on September 6.

Yellowstone at 125

On August 25, Yellowstone National Park—the oldest national park in the world—celebrated its 125th birthday. The park was established on March 1, 1872, but most observances of the anniversary were held during August, when milder weather allowed more people to visit the park and enjoy the gala celebration.

Yellowstone covers 2.2 million acres (890,310 hectares) in Wyoming, Montana, and Idaho. Named after the yellow rocks that lie along part of the Yellowstone River, the park is best known for its geysers and hot springs, spectacular scenery, and abundant wildlife. It has about 300 active geysers—more than any other area in the world. The most famous of these is Old Faithful, which erupts about every 78 minutes. Another spectacular landmark is Minerva Terrace (above), part of Yellowstone's Mammoth Hot Springs. Yellowstone is also one of the largest wildlife preserves in the United States. Among the animals roaming the park are bear, bison, elk, deer, and wolves, as well as bald eagles and trumpeter swans. More than 3 million people visit Yellowstone each year.

of the car. A fourth passenger, bodyguard Trevor Rees-Jones, survived the crash. Millions of people everywhere mourned the death of Diana, the former wife of Britain's Prince Charles. She was one of the world's most admired public figures, known for her beauty, compassion, and support of many charitable causes.

Government changes in August: In **Bolivia,** Hugo Banzer was named president. He succeeded Gonzalo Sanchez de Lozada, who had been president since 1993. . . .In **Taiwan,** Vincent Siew was appointed premier. He succeeded Lien Chan, who had been premier since 1993.

SEPTEMBER

3 A federal jury convicted J. Fife Symington III, Governor of Arizona, of fraud. Symington, a Republican, was found guilty of defrauding investors in his real estate business before becoming governor. (On September 5, Symington resigned from office and was succeeded by Arizona's Secretary of State, Jane Dee Hull, a Republican.)

4 In Jerusalem, Israel, three Arab suicide bombers detonated bombs in a crowded shopping mall, killing themselves and four Israelis. About 190 people were injured by the blasts. The militant Palestinian group Hamas claimed responsibility for the attack. (On September 5, twelve Israeli naval commandos on a raid into Lebanon were ambushed and killed by Muslim guerrillas. Two Lebanese civilians were also killed in the fighting.)

8 In Haiti, a ferry capsized and sank about 50 yards (45 meters) from the port of Montrouis. At least 200 people drowned. The accident apparently occurred when most of the ferry's passengers rushed to one side of the vessel to get into rowboats that were to transfer them ashore.

17 In Oslo, Norway, more than 120 nations approved a treaty to ban land mines. An estimated 100 million such mines are deployed in some 30 countries around the world; in addition, many countries have large stockpiles

In September, more than 120 nations approved a treaty that would ban land mines. These deadly explosive weapons lie hidden in the ground and kill or injure about 25,000 people—many of them children—each year. The issue had gained greater attention following the death of Diana, Princess of Wales, who had visited young land mine victims and supported the ban. (At left, United Nations soldiers are disarming land mines in Bosnia.)

Is There a Santa Claus?

September marked the 100th anniversary of the publication of one of the most famous newspaper editorials of all time—an essay written in response to an 8-year-old girl's question: "Is there a Santa Claus?"

Like many children, Virginia O'Hanlon of New York City (right) believed in Santa Claus. But some of her friends had told her that Santa didn't exist. When she asked her father, he avoided giving her an answer. So she told him that she was going to write to *The New York Sun,* a popular newspaper of that time. Her father replied, "If you see it in *The Sun,* it's so."

Virginia's letter was answered by Francis Pharcellus Church, a writer who handled religious and controversial subjects for *The Sun.* In what is widely regarded today as a literary masterpiece, Church assured her, "Yes, Virginia, there is a Santa Claus."

Since the editorial first appeared on September 21, 1897, it has been translated into many languages. Its fame is due to the hope it gives not only to children but to grownups too. The ability of people to have faith and believe in "unseen and unseeable" wonders is a glorious gift that gives life beauty and joy, noted Church. Santa Claus, he wrote, "lives and he lives forever."

The world has changed in many ways since 1897. But even today, those timeless words—"Yes, Virginia, there is a Santa Claus"— still speak to people who hope that their dreams will come true.

Merry Christmas to you.

of the mines. About 25,000 people are killed or maimed by the devices each year. The treaty was the first international agreement to ban a widely used weapon since the end of World War I. The United States was among a small group of nations that said they wouldn't sign the treaty. The United States based its decision on its need to use land mines to help guard South Korea from an invasion by North Korea.

Government changes in September: Following national elections in **Norway,** Kjell Magne Bondevik became premier. He succeeded Thorbjoern Jagland, who had been premier for less than a year. . . .In **Vietnam,** Phan Van Khai was named premier. He succeeded Vo Van Kiet, who had been premier since 1991.

OCTOBER

4 Hundreds of thousands of men gathered in Washington, D.C., to attend a religious rally organized by Promise Keepers, a controversial all-male evangelical Christian group. During the rally, the men listened to speakers, prayed for spiritual renewal, and repented their failures in fulfilling their responsibilities to their families.

6 The U.S. space shuttle *Atlantis* completed an eleven-day mission that included a link-up with the Russian space station *Mir.* The highlight of the mission was the first shuttle-based U.S.-Russian space walk. The crew consisted of Michael J. Bloomfield, Wendy B. Lawrence, Scott E. Parazynski, James D. Wetherbee, David A. Wolf, Jean-Loup Chretien of France, and Vladimir G. Titov of Russia. Wolf remained on *Mir;* U.S. astronaut C. Michael Foale, who had been on the space station for four months, returned to Earth.

8-9 Hurricane Pauline battered the Pacific coast of Mexico with heavy rains and winds of up to 115 miles (185 kilometers) per hour. At least 230 people were killed and hundreds more injured, mostly by floods and landslides unleashed by the storm. Among the most heavily damaged communities was the popular resort town of Acapulco.

13 In Black Rock Desert in Nevada, a jet-powered car became the first vehicle to break the sound barrier on land. The *Thrust* SuperSonic Car, which was powered by two engines taken from a fighter jet plane, was

In the Nevada desert, Great Britain's jet-powered *Thrust* SuperSonic Car breaks the sound barrier—thus becoming the first vehicle to accomplish the feat on land.

The 1997 Nobel Prizes

Chemistry: Paul D. Boyer of the United States, John E. Walker of Great Britain, and Jens C. Skou of Denmark, for their independent research on how living cells store and release energy. Their work focused on how the body uses adenosine triphosphate (ATP), a chemical molecule that stores energy for such tasks as building proteins, transmitting nerve impulses, and contracting muscles.

Economics: Myron S. Scholes, a Canadian-born American, and Robert C. Merton of the United States (working together), for creating a formula to determine the worth of stock options. A stock option is a type of financial investment that allows a person to buy stock or other assets at a prearranged price within a specified period of time.

Literature: Dario Fo of Italy, for his plays, which use satire to comment on politics, religion, and other aspects of society. The prize committee compared him to "the jesters of the Middle Ages," who used humor to poke fun at authority and uphold "the dignity of the downtrodden."

Peace: The International Campaign to Ban Landmines, and its coordinator, Jody Williams of the United States, for efforts to outlaw land mines, which kill or injure about 25,000 people each year.

Physics: Steven Chu and William D. Phillips of the United States, and Claude Cohen-Tannoudji of France, for their independent work in developing a method to trap atoms. Atoms, tiny particles that make up all matter, normally move so quickly that they are difficult for scientists to study. The researchers discovered a technique to slow atoms down by trapping them in a "syrup" of laser light, making them easier to observe.

Physiology or Medicine: Stanley B. Prusiner of the United States, for his discovery of a type of protein called prions. Prusiner and many other researchers believe that prions cause certain infectious brain diseases, such as bovine spongiform encephalopathy ("mad-cow disease") and its human counterpart, Creutzfeldt-Jakob disease.

---

designed by Richard Noble and driven by Andy Green, both of Great Britain. It reached 764.168 miles (1,229.852 kilometers) per hour, and crew members said they heard a sonic boom signaling the breaking of the sound barrier.

Government changes in October: After winning a four-month civil war in **Congo Republic,** Denis Sassou-Nguesso became president. He succeeded Pascal Lissouba, who had been president since 1992. Sassou-Nguesso had previously been president from 1979 until 1991. . . .In national elections in **Ireland,** Mary McAleese was elected president. She succeeded Mary Robinson, who had been president since 1990. . . .In **Poland,** Jerzy Buzek was named premier. He succeeded Wlodzimierz Cimoszewicz, who had held the position since early 1996.

NOVEMBER

17   In Luxor, Egypt, six members of the militant Islamic Group opened fire on people visiting the ancient temple of Queen Hatshepsut, killing 62 people, including 58 foreign tourists. It was the deadliest attack by the militants in their five-year campaign to overthrow the Egyptian government and install an Islamic state. All six gunmen were killed in the ensuing battle with police.

19   Bobbi McCaughey, of Carlisle, Iowa, gave birth to four boys and three girls—the first time that an American woman gave birth to septuplets and only the second time that septuplets were known to be born alive. McCaughey had taken fertility drugs, which can help a woman conceive; however, the drugs raise the chances of multiple births. Although two months premature, the babies were all doing well after birth. News of the births attracted worldwide attention, prompting much discussion on the risks involved with fertility drugs.

25   In Vancouver, British Columbia, leaders of eighteen Pacific Rim nations concluded their annual Asia-Pacific Economic Cooperation summit meeting. The major topic of discussion was the economic crisis facing several Asian nations, especially South Korea, Indonesia, and Thailand. The financial turmoil was severe enough to cause a slump in U.S. and European stock markets.

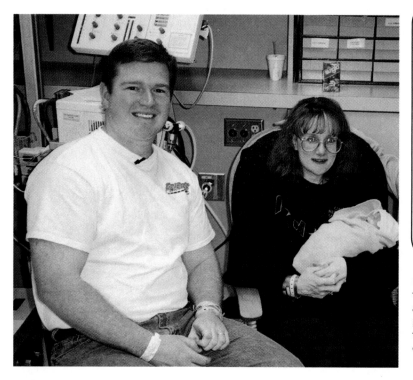

Dear Bobbi McCaughey,
Taking care of seven little ones can be trying at times. If you ever need help, please call.

Yours truly,
Snow White

Bobbi and Kenny McCaughey with the first of their septuplets, four boys and three girls. Many corporations pledged their help with everything from a van to a lifetime supply of diapers (about 31,500!).

Schoolboys try to protect themselves from the air pollution caused by Indonesia's forest fires.

Darkness Over Southeast Asia

On November 19, monsoon rains began to clear the air over Southeast Asia. For months, the area had been hidden under a thick haze caused by vast forest fires that burned out of control in Indonesia. It was believed to be the region's worst environmental disaster ever.

The haze from the fires reduced visibility and sent air-pollution levels soaring in Indonesia, Brunei, Malaysia, Singapore, the Philippines, and Thailand. Tens of thousands of people became ill with respiratory ailments. In many classrooms, the smoke was so thick that students couldn't see the blackboards. The haze forced businesses and airports to close and disrupted shipping. And an Indonesian airplane apparently lost its way in the haze and crashed, killing 234 people—the deadliest air disaster in Indonesia's history.

At least 1.5 million acres (600,000 hectares) of Indonesian forest were burned, killing orangutans and other endangered animals. Most of the forest fires had been deliberately set by large agricultural and logging companies as a cheap way to clear land. Peasants and farmers also set fires to clear land—a centuries-old practice in Indonesia that continues despite laws banning it. Usually, monsoon rains arrive in September and put out the fires. But changing weather patterns caused by El Niño resulted in a prolonged drought, which added to the problem.

Government changes in November: In **Thailand,** Chuan Leekpai was named premier. He succeeded Chavalit Yongchaiyudh, who resigned after less than a year in office.

DECEMBER

5 The U.S. space shuttle *Columbia* completed a sixteen-day mission. During the mission, an astronomy satellite was accidentally sent into a spin after it was released; it was retrieved by astronauts in a daring space walk. The crew consisted of Kalpana Chawla, Kevin R. Kregel, Steven W. Lindsey, Winston E. Scott, Takao Doi of Japan, and Leonid K. Kadenyuk of Ukraine.

11 An eleven-day United Nations summit on global warming ended in Kyoto, Japan. Delegates from 161 nations adopted the Kyoto Protocol, an international treaty that sets limits on industrial countries' emissions of "greenhouse gases." These polluting gases include carbon dioxide and other gases given off by motor vehicles, factories, and power plants. Greenhouse gases are a major cause of global warming—the gradual heating up of Earth's atmosphere. The treaty would take effect after ratification by at least 55 nations that are responsible for major carbon dioxide emissions.

23 A federal jury in Denver, Colorado, found Terry L. Nichols guilty of conspiracy and involuntary manslaughter in the 1995 bombing of the Alfred P. Murrah Federal Building in Oklahoma City, Oklahoma. Nichols was acquitted of the charge of murder.

As the year ended, crowds were flocking to New York City to see the smash musical version of *The Lion King*, which was based on the Disney animated film. In the Broadway production, the performers wore colorful masks and handled life-sized puppets to create the jungle of animal characters.

...and Looking Ahead to 1998

Here are a few of the many anniversaries that will be celebrated in 1998:

- The 500th anniversary of the completion of **The Last Supper,** the famous fresco created by Italian artist Leonardo da Vinci.

- The 150th anniversary of the **discovery of gold** at Sutter's Mill in California, on January 24, 1848, which led to the California Gold Rush.

- The 150th anniversary of the **birth of Paul Gauguin,** the French painter best known for his brilliant paintings of Tahitian natives and scenes.

- The 100th anniversary of the **Spanish-American War,** which began on April 21, 1898. The war made the United States a world power and cost Spain the last important colonies of its empire.

- The 25th anniversary of the launch of the U.S. space station **Skylab,** on May 14, 1973. During 1973 and 1974, Skylab was visited by three teams of astronauts.

Government changes in December: In national elections in **Guyana,** Janet Jagan was elected president. She succeeded Samuel Hinds, who had held the position since March. . . .In national elections in **Honduras,** Carlos Flores was elected president (effective January 1998). He would succeed Carlos Roberto Reina, who had been president since 1994. . . .In **New Zealand,** Jenny Shipley became the nation's first woman prime minister. She succeeded Jim Bolger, who had been prime minister since 1990. . . .In national elections in **South Korea,** Kim Dae Jung was elected president (effective February 1998). He would succeed Kim Young Sam, who had been president since 1993.

Diana's brother, Earl Spencer; and others who had known and loved the princess. More than a million onlookers stood silent as the solemn procession wound from Kensington Palace, Diana's home, to Westminster Abbey. Some 2.5 billion people, in 60 countries, watched on television.

To the mourners, Diana's life seemed like a fairy tale gone sadly wrong—from her storybook marriage to Prince Charles, heir to the British throne, through estrangement and divorce, to her tragic death at age 36. Beautiful and glamorous, but also caring and very human, Diana was one of the most well-known and admired women in the world. British Prime Minister Tony Blair summed up the feelings of many when he said: "She was the people's princess, and that's how she will stay, how she will remain, in our hearts and in our memories forever."

THE GIRL NEXT DOOR

Diana Frances Spencer grew up as a member of the British aristocracy. She was born on July 1, 1961, the daughter of the eighth Earl Spencer and his first wife, Frances. The Spencers trace their lineage back to the Stuart kings of England. They moved in the same circles as the royal family, and Diana spent part of her childhood at Park House, next to the royal retreat at Sandringham. There her playmates included her future husband's younger brothers, Andrew and Edward.

Although Diana was surrounded by wealth and privilege, her childhood wasn't entirely happy. Her parents divorced when she was 6. Along with her younger brother and two older sisters, she divided her time between their homes. At 12, she went off to an exclusive private girls' school. She was a mediocre student—and so shy that she would take only nonspeaking roles in school plays. She left school at 16 and, after a short time at a Swiss finishing school, took a job with an American couple, caring for their young child. Later, she worked at a kindergarten in London. Love of children was a trait she carried all her life.

A FAREWELL FOR THE PEOPLE'S PRINCESS

On September 6, 1997, a horse-drawn gun carriage moved slowly through the streets of London, escorted by red-coated Welsh Guards. It bore the coffin of Diana, Princess of Wales, killed in a car crash in Paris on August 31. The casket was draped with the British royal standard and topped by three white bouquets, one bearing a card with the word "Mummy" printed in a child's hand.

Behind the carriage walked Diana's two sons, William and Harry; their father, Prince Charles; their grandfather, Prince Philip;

Diana and Charles were married in a fairy-tale wedding in 1981. The couple had two sons, William and Harry, and Diana was devoted to them.

In London, where Diana shared an apartment with three other young women, she began to date Charles. She was 19, and he was 32. Despite the difference in their ages, they seemed perfect for each other when they announced their engagement in February 1981. She was beautiful, charming, and full of life. He was the most eligible bachelor in the world—the future King of England. And they were in love.

A FAIRY-TALE WEDDING

The wedding of Charles and Diana—in London on July 29, 1981—was a magnificent event. Hundreds of thousands of people waited in the streets to catch a glimpse of the royal family as a procession of antique carriages took them to St. Paul's Cathedral. Diana arrived in a glass coach, wearing a diamond tiara and silk gown with a long train. Inside the cathedral, more than 2,500 guests—including heads of state from around the world—witnessed the wedding. Some 700 million people watched on television.

The ceremony was performed by the Archbishop of Canterbury. He captured the feeling of the day when he said: "Here is the stuff of which fairy tales are made: the Prince and Princess on their wedding day." But, he noted, fairy tales end with the phrase "they lived happily ever after"—but in real life a wedding is "the place where the adventure really begins."

Diana was very active in an international campaign to end the use of land mines. Here she chats with a youngster who was maimed by a land mine in Angola.

The adventure seemed to begin well for Charles and Diana. Their son William was born in 1982, and Harry in 1984. The prince and princess were seen smiling and waving as they traveled abroad as goodwill ambassadors for Britain and officiated at ceremonies and charitable events. Often Diana drew the largest crowds and loudest cheers. She was a glamorous figure, and millions of women copied her elegant style. But she also doted on her sons and loved to do things with them—skiing, bike riding, going to amusement parks and hamburger joints, even visiting a shelter for the homeless. She showed genuine sympathy for victims of AIDS and others she met through her involvement in charity work. Charles seemed aloof and aristocratic, even a bit eccentric. Diana seemed warm, one of the people—and the people loved her for it.

In fact, there were growing strains in the marriage. Charles and Diana had little in common. He liked gardening and architecture; she liked buying clothes and gossiping with friends. He liked classical music and played the cello; she liked pop. He liked to hunt; she hated it. More seriously, Diana felt deeply insecure. She was overwhelmed by the publicity that followed her every move. And, she would later disclose, she felt unloved by her husband and rejected by the other members of the royal family. By the mid-1980s, she was suffering from the eating disorder bulimia and had tried several times to kill herself.

These sad facts were unknown to the public. But in time, signs of the strain between Charles and Diana began to show. They spent less time together. When they appeared in public as a couple, they spoke little and looked unhappy. Rumors swirled around them. Would the royal couple split? The answer came late in 1992, when they officially separated.

ON HER OWN

The idea of a divorce in the royal family shocked many people. But after three-and-a-half years of separation, bitterness, and continuing gossip, divorce seemed to be the best course. Charles and Diana ended their marriage in August 1996. Under the terms of the divorce agreement, they were to share the upbringing of their sons. Diana gave up the right to be called "Her Royal Highness," but retained the title "Princess of Wales." She could continue to live at Kensington Palace, and she received a $22.5-million settlement to maintain her way of life.

After the divorce, Diana involved herself even more seriously with charities. She auctioned off dozens of her fabulous gowns to raise some $3.25 million for the fight against AIDS and cancer. She also helped organizations working against leprosy and homelessness and for children's medical care. She became especially active in an international campaign to end the use of land mines, which have killed or maimed countless civilians worldwide. Diana was a polished and self-assured spokesperson for these causes, a far cry from the shy schoolgirl she once had been.

In the summer of 1997, Diana began a new romance, with Emad Mohamed al-Fayed, known as Dodi. Dodi, 41, was the son of a wealthy Egyptian businessman. The media loved the story, and freelance photographers—the "paparazzi"—followed the couple wherever they went, which bothered Diana.

On August 30, Diana and Dodi had a late dinner at the Ritz Hotel in Paris. They left after midnight, in a limousine driven by a hotel security officer. Photographers on motorcycles gave chase. The limousine picked up speed and entered a tunnel. Traveling perhaps 85 miles (135 kilometers) an hour, it crashed into a pillar, spun out of control, and hit the tunnel wall. Dodi and the driver were killed instantly. Diana and a bodyguard were rushed to the hospital, where she was pronounced dead a few hours later.

Diana's casket was topped with three white bouquets. In one bouquet was a card with the word "Mummy" printed in a child's hand.

QUEEN OF HEARTS

Many people blamed the paparazzi for causing the accident. But there was evidence that the driver had been drinking and that a second car might have been involved. The bodyguard survived but remembered little of the ordeal.

As the investigation continued, so too did the mourning. Even Diana's greatest admirers were amazed at how many people were touched by her death. At British embassies worldwide, people waited on line to sign condolence books. In London, thousands of people piled bouquets of flowers in front of the gates of Kensington Palace and camped out on London sidewalks the night before her funeral, to be sure of catching a glimpse of the procession.

The funeral itself was a mixture of royal tradition and popular culture that suited Diana's memory. Inside Westminster Abbey, a church where 39 English monarchs have been crowned, Diana's brother, Charles, delivered the eulogy. And the pop star Elton John, a longtime friend of the princess, performed a version of his song "Candle in the Wind," with new lyrics honoring Diana as "England's rose."

Recorded soon after, that song quickly became the biggest-selling single in history. Profits went to the charities Diana had supported. Direct donations also poured into those charities.

Change in the royal family was expected to be another part of Diana's legacy. When she died, many people criticized the royals for being out of touch with the public. Queen Elizabeth II, in an unprecedented television speech, acknowledged the criticism, saying that there were "lessons to be drawn from [Diana's] life and from the extraordinary and moving reaction to her death."

Diana's appeal went beyond her beauty and charm. She was royalty, and yet she was an ordinary person, with strengths and weaknesses many people shared. She struggled with a poor self-image. She married young, and the marriage didn't work. Yet she always had room in her heart for others, and she emerged from her difficulties a stronger and more independent person. Divorce cost her the chance to be queen of England. But she became, as she once said she hoped she would, the queen of people's hearts.

U.S. President Bill Clinton applauds a speaker at a Democratic Party fund-raising dinner. In 1997, questions about Clinton's fund-raising activities were part of a growing debate over campaign finance.

CAMPAIGN FINANCE REFORM

Do you think you might run for the U.S. Congress someday? Better start saving money. Campaign costs—travel, staff, print and television advertising, and more—are expensive. And the higher the office, it seems, the more costly the campaign. Winning candidates for the U.S. House of Representatives spent more than $680,000, on average, in the 1996 election. A winning Senate race cost almost $4 million. And that was pocket change compared to the 1996 presidential campaign, in which the major parties spent hundreds of millions of dollars.

Where do politicians get these huge sums? Mostly from donors—individuals, corporations, and organizations—who support the candidates. Fund-raising has become a very big, and very controversial, part of political life.

Much of the recent controversy has centered on President Bill Clinton's 1996 re-election effort. After Clinton defeated the Republican challenger, Senator Robert Dole of Kansas, the Republicans charged that the Democrats had broken numerous campaign finance regulations. In 1997, Congress held hearings on the allegations, and the Justice Department conducted an investigation. Neither the hearings nor the investigation turned up evidence that Clinton had broken the law. However, the charges threw a spotlight on some shady—and common—campaign finance practices.

PLAYING BY THE RULES

This wasn't the first time that people have questioned how campaign funds are raised and spent. Most people agree that the system has built-in problems. Time spent drumming up contributions takes politicians away from the jobs to which they're elected. And if politicians feel obligated to the people who donate money, and donors expect favorable treatment in return, the money chase creates opportunities for corruption.

In 1974, prompted partly by abuses in the election of 1972, Congress passed new regulations on campaign financing. Candidates must disclose the source of money they receive, and individuals can't give more than $1,000 per candidate. Groups of people who share an interest—anything from environmental preservation to automobile travel—can form a political action committee (PAC), which can donate $5,000 per candidate.

Individuals and groups can also donate up to $20,000 a year to national political parties. The party can use these donations—called "hard money"—to help any of its candidates. In addition, individuals and groups can give national political parties unlimited amounts of "soft money"—donations earmarked for general activities, such as voter registration and "get-out-the vote" drives.

The law originally set limits on campaign spending, too. But the Supreme Court later ruled that mandatory limits were unconstitutional. However, the regulations provide an incentive for presidential candidates to meet voluntary spending limits: They can qualify for funds from the government if they do. In 1996, Clinton and Dole received close to $100 million in government funds under this provision.

BENDING THE RULES

In 1974, lawmakers hoped that these regulations would rein in campaign costs, help equalize spending by candidates, and keep donors from having undue influence over elected officials. It hasn't worked that way. Campaign spending has grown, and both parties have found dozens of ways to get around the rules. "Soft money" donations have increased enormously, and critics charge that much of this money helps candidates indirectly. Individuals and groups also spend their own money directly on ads and activities that support candidates. These independent expenditures, as they are called, aren't linked to the candidates' campaigns, so they don't count as donations.

So the Washington money chase has continued, and politicians remain under pressure to raise more and more money. Much was made in 1997 of the fact that Clinton entertained donors at the White House, even inviting some to spend the night there. In itself, this didn't break the law—the president didn't actually solicit donations at the White House, nor did he promise favors in exchange for money. But many people thought it was inappropriate.

More disturbing were disclosures that Chinese and Indonesian businessmen had attempted to make donations to the 1996 campaign, in violation of rules that bar contributions from abroad. However, the donations were returned when their source was discovered, and there was no evidence that they affected U.S. policy.

Campaign finance laws were broken in 1996, though. In the most notable case, a Pennsylvania landfill company was fined $8 million for making illegal contributions to federal candidates, including both Dole and Clinton. The company had funneled money through "straw" (phony) donors to get around the limits, a clear violation of the law. It was the largest such fine ever, but it was far from the first time that an abuse like this had been uncovered.

PROPOSALS FOR REFORM

Most people agree that the campaign finance system needs reform. But they disagree about how the system should be changed. Here are some of the ideas that have been put forward.

● Limit donations from political action committees. Many people mistrust PACs on the grounds that, because these groups represent interest groups, they may try to influence policy on specific issues.

● Ban "soft money" contributions. Many critics of the system think these contributions are a huge loophole, because they allow interest groups to donate unlimited amounts of money.

● Increase the amount of public financing for election campaigns. Some people would like to see public funding for all federal elections. That, they argue, would end the need for private donations and create an equal chance for all candidates.

● Provide free television and radio time to candidates. The huge cost of TV advertising is one of the main reasons running for office is so expensive. TV stations could donate the time, or it could be purchased with public funds and distributed among candidates.

● Strengthen the Federal Election Commission (FEC), which enforces campaign finance laws. Critics say that the FEC is underfunded, badly structured, and ineffective at rooting out abuses.

A campaign finance reform bill was introduced in Congress in 1997 but failed to pass. However, supporters of reform vowed to try again. Cleaning up campaign financing was essential, they believed, if Americans were to keep their faith in democracy.

Great Britain: Prime Minister Tony Blair and family.

WESTERN ELECTIONS: WINDS OF CHANGE

Three major Western democracies held important elections in 1997, and the outcome was change for two out of three. Voters in Great Britain and France chose new leaders who rejected the conservative stands of past governments. In Canada, the Liberal Party held onto power—but the vote was very close.

GREAT BRITAIN

The British election marked the greatest shift. Led by prime ministers Margaret Thatcher and John Major, her successor, the Conservative Party had held power in Britain for eighteen years. But in general elections on May 1, 1997, the Labour Party trounced the Conservatives. Tony Blair, the 43-year-old Labour Party leader, replaced Major to become the youngest prime minister in 185

years. As leader of the Labour Party since 1994, Blair had convinced party members to drop some proposals that they had long supported, such as nationalizing utilities. That helped broaden Labour's appeal and roughly double its membership. During the six-week 1997 campaign, he emphasized the need to narrow the gap between rich and poor, while encouraging free enterprise. Major campaigned on the Conservatives' record of economic prosperity. British voters liked the "New Labour" message. They also liked the energetic, Scottish-born Blair and his wife, Cherie, a prominent attorney. In the vote, Labour candidates took 419 of the 659 seats in Parliament, compared to 165 for the Conservatives. The Liberal Democrats won 46 seats, and the rest went to smaller parties. Blair's first actions in office included steps to revive peace talks in Northern Ireland and to give more self-government to Scotland and Wales. He was also expected to review Britain's role in the European Community.

France: Prime Minister Lionel Jospin.

46

FRANCE

A month after the British elections, control of the French Parliament shifted to a coalition of leftist parties, led by the Socialists. Socialist Party leader Lionel Jospin, 59, replaced conservative Alain Juppé as prime minister. Just four years earlier, French voters had given a huge majority in Parliament to a conservative coalition. And in 1995, Jospin had lost to conservative Jacques Chirac in a race for the presidency. Under Chirac and Juppé, the government cut spending and reduced budget deficits. A major goal of these reforms was to meet criteria for a single European currency, to be adopted in 1999. Hoping to demonstrate support for these policies, President Chirac called for new parliamentary elections in 1997. But the mood of the country had changed. Unemployment was rising, and many French voters feared that continued economic reforms would only lead to more job losses. They gave their votes to the Socialist and Communist parties, which together promised to create 700,000 new jobs. In two rounds of voting, on May 25 and June 1, the Socialists won 274 of the 577 seats in Parliament, and the Communists 38. Together, they had enough for a majority. The election left France with an odd political situation called "cohabitation": The two top government jobs were held by different parties. Jospin was prime minister, but Chirac was still president—and his term would run until 2002. How they would work together, and how the election would affect France's role in Europe, remained to be seen.

CANADA

With a narrow Liberal Party victory in parliamentary elections on June 2, 1997, Jean Chrétien remained prime minister of Canada. But the vote revealed deep regional divisions among Canadians and raised questions about the country's future. Chrétien called the election a year-and-a-half ahead of schedule, and he campaigned on his record. Since winning a strong majority in Parliament in 1993, the Liberals had slashed budget deficits and accomplished other reforms. But they lost ground in the 1997 vote, winning 155 seats out of 301 in Parliament. That was a loss

Canada: Prime Minister Jean Chrétien.

of 19 seats, and barely enough for a majority. The Bloc Québécois (BQ), the leading opposition group since 1993, also lost seats. The BQ holds that Quebec warrants special treatment because of its French-speaking culture and its history as a former colony of France. Ultimately, the party wants Quebec to be independent. But this idea has been put to voters in several referendums, most recently in 1995, and failed to pass. And in 1997, the Bloc Québécois lost six seats in Parliament. It held on to just 44, all in Quebec. The greatest gains were made by the Reform Party, which won a total of 60 seats, all in western Canada. Reform Party leader Preston Manning appealed to conservative voters by denouncing concessions made to Quebec and calling for equal treatment for all provinces. The New Democratic and Progressive Conservative parties also showed gains, winning 21 and 20 seats respectively. Reform's second-place finish in the election made it the new official opposition party. Canadians expected some lively debates in Parliament as a result. And with regional differences heightened by the elections, there was growing concern about the prospects for Canadian unity.

In April, former U.S. Presidents George Bush and Jimmy Carter joined President Bill Clinton and Vice President Al Gore in Philadelphia (right), for the Presidents' Summit for America's Future—a three-day meeting to encourage volunteerism. While there, they all pitched in to help clean up a rundown neighborhood. Above: President Carter paints over graffiti on an abandoned building.

A CALL FOR VOLUNTEERS

The President of the United States, wearing a baseball cap and a bright yellow T-shirt, was painting a cinder-block wall at a community pool. The Vice President, in faded jeans, was assembling equipment at a neighborhood playground. Why were the nation's leaders in Philadelphia, Pennsylvania, working in a rundown neighborhood on a sunny April Sunday? They had volunteered their time in the hope of inspiring others to do the same.

Along with three former presidents, 30 state governors, 100 mayors, and several thousand ordinary citizens, President Bill Clinton and Vice President Al Gore were in Philadelphia for a three-day meeting called the Presidents' Summit for America's Future.

Held April 27 through April 29, 1997, the meeting was designed to encourage people to volunteer their time and skills in their communities. The message of the conference was this: Volunteers can help solve problems in ways that government can't—especially the problems faced by young people.

Why was such a meeting necessary? The number of children who live in poverty has grown in recent years. So has the rate of violent juvenile crime. Poverty, gangs, illegal drugs—kids today face many risks, and often they face those risks alone. In many poor families, only one parent is present, and that parent is working. Kids are on their own much of the time, and many drop out of school.

While these problems have grown, the ability of government to deal with them has not. The federal and state governments have cut spending on social programs in an effort to balance their budgets and avoid raising taxes. Government funding for many programs designed to help kids has been shrinking just as the need for such programs has increased.

Volunteers, many people believe, can help close the gap. As President Clinton put it: "The era of big government may be over, but the era of big challenges for our country is not. And so we need an era of big citizenship."

STAR VOLUNTEERS

The Presidents' Summit for America's Future was the idea of George W. Romney, a former governor of Michigan. Romney proposed the meeting in July 1995, shortly before his death. Others picked up the idea and organized the conference. Retired army general Colin L. Powell, former head of the Joint Chiefs of Staff, served as its chairman. Besides Clinton and Gore and their wives, the guest list included former presidents George Bush, Jimmy Carter, and Gerald Ford. Former president Ronald Reagan, who was ill, was represented by Nancy Reagan, his wife.

The event began with a rally at Philadelphia's Marcus Foster Stadium. Some 5,000 people gathered to hear Clinton, the former presidents, and Powell speak. "We're still losing too many kids to crime, to drugs, to not having a decent income in their home and to not having a bright future," Clinton told the crowd. "And we're here because. . .we believe that together we can change it."

When the speeches were over, the group rolled up their sleeves and went to work. They split up in brigades to clean up a city neighborhood plagued by crime and drug abuse, picking up trash and painting over graffiti. Although the work they did was important for its own sake, its real value was the message it sent. Television and newspapers showed pictures of Clinton and the others at work. Each picture said, more clearly than any speech, how important it was to serve in the community.

The next day, delegates to the conference met in small groups for roundtable discussions. At these "breakout" sessions, they exchanged ideas on ways to meet the conference's primary goal—helping two million children by the year 2000. The highlight of the conference was an April 28 rally in front of

Retired army general Colin Powell, chairman of the Summit, speaks to a youth group about the importance of volunteering.

teers who work with church and charitable groups. Powell was to lead an organization called America's Promise: Alliance for Youth. It would call on individuals and businesses for funds, services, and volunteers to help kids in five key ways:

● **Mentors:** An adult mentor spends a few hours each week with a child who's at risk of dropping out of school, using drugs, or getting into trouble in other ways. Those few hours can make a big difference. Mentors can help with homework, offer advice, and listen to the kids' concerns. Just knowing that someone cares helps kids feel better about themselves and their future. The conference organizers estimated that as many as fifteen million kids could be helped by mentors. Finding ways to link caring adults with needy kids became one of the most important follow-up goals.

Independence Hall, where TV talk-show host Oprah Winfrey acted as master of ceremonies. Clinton and other leaders again spoke. Powell told the crowd: "All of us can spare thirty minutes a week or an hour a week. All of us can give an extra dollar. All of us can touch someone who doesn't look like us, who doesn't speak like us, who may not dress like us, but, by God, needs us in their lives."

A PLAN OF ACTION

The rallies were exciting, the speeches were inspiring—but would they produce results? The organizers of the conference planned a follow up campaign to make sure they would. Clinton proposed expanding the government volunteer program called AmeriCorps, which was started in 1993. His plan would create 50,000 scholarships for volun-

A mentor can make a big difference in a young person's life by helping with homework and showing care and concern.

Count Me In!

Maybe you spent a Saturday morning pitching in to clean up a trash-filled vacant lot in your neighborhood. Maybe you washed cars to raise funds for charity. Or maybe you baked cookies for a church bake sale. If you did any sort of community service work last year, you can count yourself among some 93 million American volunteers. Together, Americans donate about twenty billion hours of their time each year to help each other and their communities.

According to a study conducted by the U.S. Department of Education, almost 50 percent of kids in grades 6 through 12 are involved in some kind of community service, more than 25 percent on a regular basis. In many cases, schools help set up opportunities for volunteer work. Kids who are involved in these programs benefit intellectually and emotionally, educators say.

Other research shows that volunteering is the latest college craze. Nearly 75 percent of U.S. college freshmen do some sort of public service work today, an all-time high.

• **Safe places for kids after school:** Kids who have no place but the streets to play, and no adult supervision after school, are more likely to get in trouble. Volunteers can donate time and money to build and maintain playgrounds and to run after-school programs that offer field trips and other activities. With government funds running low, such projects rely more and more on private donations. In one example of the kind of volunteer effort the group hoped to inspire, Kimberly-Clark, a major paper manufacturing company, is spending $2 million to build 37 playgrounds.

• **Health care:** Many poor children don't have access to good health care. Individuals and businesses can donate time, funds, and supplies to help solve this problem. For example, Pfizer, a drug manufacturer, is giving medicines worth $5 million to help poor children.

• **Skills:** To earn a living, everyone needs job skills. Children in poor families and those who drop out of school early often don't learn the skills they need to find work—and that can mean a life of poverty. Volunteers can help by teaching skills, and businesses can donate equipment and funds. For example, the telecommunications firm AT&T is spending $150 million to connect 110,000 schools to the Internet, the worldwide computer network.

• **A chance to volunteer:** The benefits of volunteering work both ways. Volunteers help others, and they get a sense of satisfaction from doing so. One goal of the conference was to provide kids with a chance to volunteer themselves. It was hoped that once kids were bitten by the community service bug and learned the value of helping others, volunteering would become second nature for them.

Some people criticized the conference for suggesting that volunteers could solve big problems like poverty and juvenile crime. Private efforts, the critics said, can never take the place of government assistance. In his keynote speech at the conference, Clinton acknowledged government's role. But, he said, many of the problems children face "can only be resolved when there is a one-on-one connection" with someone who cares.

Would people answer the call? Jimmy Carter summed up the hope at the end of the presidents' meeting: "The real revolution will take place only if we carry this spirit of Philadelphia back to our neighborhoods."

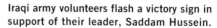
Iraqi army volunteers flash a victory sign in support of their leader, Saddam Hussein.

AROUND THE WORLD

Reminders of old conflicts in the Middle East, Southeast Asia, and other regions troubled the world in 1997. Following is an overview of some of the developments that made news during the year.

IRAQ AND THE UNITED NATIONS

Iraq staged a confrontation with the United Nations in 1997, recalling the trouble that led to the Persian Gulf War of 1991 and leading many people to worry that war might once again break out. In the Persian Gulf War, an international coalition led by the United States had driven Iraqi forces out of Kuwait, which Iraq had invaded and attempted to annex. At the time, there was great concern over the efforts of Iraqi leader Saddam Hussein to acquire weapons of mass destruction, especially chemical and biological weapons. So, as part of the accord that ended the conflict, Iraq was required to destroy its supplies of such weapons. U.N. inspectors were to make sure this was done—and that no more deadly chemical or biological agents were produced. The United Nations also imposed strict economic sanctions on Iraq, to ensure that it met the terms of the agreement.

But Iraq didn't fully live up to the agreement. U.N. inspectors were denied access to some sites. At others, they were delayed long enough for the Iraqis to remove evidence of weapons production. The inspections were supposed to be finished in months; instead, they dragged on for years, and Iraq's defiance of the United Nations became increasingly bold. The United States proposed tightening sanctions to get the Iraqis to comply, but other members of the U.N. Security Council didn't agree. Iraq, for its part, claimed that the sanctions had caused thousands of children to die from malnutrition and disease, even though it was allowed to sell some of its oil in exchange for food and medicine.

Matters came to a head in November 1997, when Saddam Hussein ordered American members of the U.N. inspection teams to leave the country. Nearly all the U.N. inspectors left with the Americans, and the world wondered if the standoff would lead to war. Saddam Hussein even placed Iraqi civilians, including women and children, at likely bombing targets, to serve as "human shields."

Finally, Russian diplomats helped convince Iraq to allow the inspectors to return. By November 25 they were back on the job—and still having trouble finding evidence of hidden weapons. Just what weapons Saddam Hussein might be hiding, and how they might be used, were causes for great concern.

ISRAEL AND THE PALESTINIANS

There was little progress in the effort to forge peace between Israel and the Palestinian Arabs in 1997. Palestinians, many of whom were displaced when Israel was created as a Jewish homeland in 1948, have long demanded a state of their own. They have fought Israel, often with terrorist tactics. But in 1993 and 1995, negotiations brought a measure of self-rule to Palestinian Arabs in parts of the West Bank and Gaza Strip, territories occupied by Israel since 1967.

Israel was to give the Palestinians more control, and talks were to determine the final status of these territories by 1999. But the peace process ground to a halt after Benjamin Netanyahu, leader of the conservative Likud bloc, was elected prime minister of Israel in May 1996. Although Netanyahu promised to honor the existing agreement, talks between Israel and the Palestinians ended. Riots broke out in Arab sections.

Early in 1997, Netanyahu met with Yasir Arafat, leader of the Palestinian National Authority (PNA), the governing authority for Palestinian self-rule. They agreed on terms for Israeli withdrawal from the West Bank city of Hebron. That raised hope that the process would get back on track. But in March, an Israeli decision to build Jewish housing in Arab East Jerusalem inflamed the situation.

Terrorist violence increased, spearheaded by Hamas and Islamic Holy War, two militant Arab groups. Among the most serious incidents were suicide bombings in Jerusalem on July 30 and September 4, which together killed seventeen Israelis and injured several hundred others. Palestinian leader Yasir Arafat denounced the violence, but Israeli officials said that the Palestinians had done less than they might have to bring the terrorists to justice.

On September 25, Israeli agents attempted to assassinate a Hamas leader in Jordan. The attack drew outraged reactions from many nations. The captured Israeli agents were later exchanged for 23 Palestinian and Jordanian prisoners. Among them was Sheik Ahmed Yassin, the founder of Hamas, who vowed to continue to fight Israel.

In the aftermath of that incident, Israeli-Palestinian talks resumed on October 8. Israel indicated that it was ready to pull out of parts of the West Bank if the Palestinians would then negotiate the final status and boundaries of the territory. Palestinians objected that the pullout

Israeli prime minister Benjamin Netanyahu waves to the crowd in Jerusalem.

still left Israel in control of far too much of the West Bank, while conservative Israelis objected that any pullout was too much. The Israeli-Palestinian conflict headed into its 50th year, with no clear solution in sight.

TERRORISM IN NORTH AFRICA

Two North African nations were the targets of radical Islamic terrorist groups in 1997. The most serious violence was in Algeria, where civil war had been simmering since 1991. In that year, Algeria held its first free elections, and the

Islamic Salvation Front, an extreme fundamentalist group, emerged as the winner in the first round of voting. The Algerian military promptly declared the results void, and civil war broke out.

At first, Islamic groups attacked soldiers and police. But in 1993, a terrorist band called the Armed Islamic Group began to target officials, journalists, intellectuals, and foreigners. The government responded by rounding up and executing suspected terrorists. In 1995, the terrorists changed their tactics and began to target ordinary people, using bombs and night attacks. Despite government reprisals, the violence spread. Terrorist bands grew bolder, entering neighborhoods and villages and murdering everyone they could find. The death toll mounted. By some estimates, the violence had claimed 60,000 lives by fall 1997.

The Algerian government rejected the idea that outside mediators might help end the conflict. But the government did begin peace talks with the Islamic Salvation Front, and in late September that group's military wing called for a truce. Even so, violence seemed likely to continue—because the worst attacks were carried out by the Armed Islamic Group, which had not taken part in the talks.

The other North African nation that experienced terrorism in 1997 was Egypt. There, foreigners were the targets of a devastating terrorist attack on November 17. At the 3,400-year-old Temple of Hatshepsut, near Luxor, six gunmen opened fire on crowds of tourists, killing 58. Most of the victims were Swiss. Four Egyptians were also killed.

The attack was the worst incident in a five-year-long campaign by Islamic militants to undermine the Egyptian government. Despite harsh government reprisals, 1,200 people had died in terrorist violence since 1992. Of those, 34 were foreigners, including nine German tourists killed in Cairo in September 1997. The terrorists targeted foreigners with the idea that destroying Egypt's profitable tourist industry would somehow weaken the government.

All six gunmen at the temple were killed by policemen, who pursued them into the hills nearby. The terrorists were believed to be members of the Islamic Group, the largest of Egypt's militant Islamic organizations. Sheik Omar Abdel Rahman, the spiritual leader of the group, was in prison in the United States, serving a life sentence for plotting to blow up the World Trade Center in New York City in 1993.

REBELLION IN CENTRAL AFRICA

One of Africa's longest-ruling dictators, Mobutu Sese Seko of Zaire, was ousted by rebels in May 1997. When he took power in 1965, the country was known as Congo. Mobutu changed the name to Zaire. He suppressed political opposition, put down several rebellions, and enriched himself and his cronies at the country's expense. He became one of the world's wealthiest men, known for his lavish lifestyle and his trademark leopard-skin cap. But by 1997, Mobutu was seriously ill. And after 32 years of his government, many Zairians were tired of poverty, corruption, and repression.

The trigger for the rebellion was ethnic violence in eastern Zaire. The Hutus and the Tutsis, two groups who live there and in neighboring Rwanda and Burundi, have a long history of conflict. Since 1993, their bitter rivalry has killed hundreds of thousands of people in Rwanda and Burundi. The upheaval sent more than one million refugees, mostly Hutus, fleeing into Zaire. Many returned to their homes after the fighting died down, but several hundred thousand Hutu refugees stayed in Zaire. Some were guerrilla fighters, and they brought ethnic conflict with them.

Zaire's Hutus and Tutsis had previously lived peacefully, but now Hutu fighters began to attack Tutsis and others, hoping to carve out a homeland in the region. Zaire's government did little to stop them. But in October 1996, Tutsis in Zaire rebelled and began to attack the Hutu fighters and refugees. A rebel army, led by guerrilla fighter Laurent Kabila and helped by Rwanda, swept the last of the Hutu fighters from eastern Zaire. Refugees poured over the border into Rwanda or fled into the countryside.

By 1997, the rebellion had widened. Kabila set his sights on toppling Mobutu, who was in France for medical treatment. When Mobutu returned in March, he couldn't muster enough support to stop Kabila's advance. He gave up

Zairians celebrate the overthrow of dictator Mobutu Sese Seko by guerrilla fighter Laurent Kabila. Kabila declared himself president and changed the country's name to Congo.

power and fled the country on May 16. The next day, Kabila declared himself president and changed the country's name back to Congo. Mobutu died in exile in Morocco on September 7.

In the months after Kabila's takeover, stories of terrible events emerged. Witnesses reported that during the rebellion, Kabila's troops had massacred hundreds, perhaps thousands, of Hutu refugees. Kabila claimed that those killed were Hutu guerrillas, but human-rights investigators said that many were innocent people, including women and children. It was impossible to say how many had died, partly because no one knew how many Hutu refugees had been in Zaire at the start of the rebellion.

A NEW ERA FOR CHINA

Two events made 1997 an important year for China. The first was the death of Deng Xiaoping, China's longtime supreme leader, on February 19. Deng, 92, had been part of the Communist movement that brought Mao Zedong to power in 1949. Under Mao, he was twice driven out of government, only to be restored to power later. In 1978, two years after Mao's death, he emerged as China's top leader. Deng then began a sweeping program of eco-nomic reforms, rejecting state control of industry in favor of increased trade and private enterprise. China's economy boomed. But at the same time, Deng suppressed political opposition and squelched demands for democracy.

Deng retired from his last official post in 1989. But he remained a powerful force behind the scenes in China's government for several years after that. China's current leaders, President Jiang Zemin and Prime Minister Li Peng, pledged to continue his policies. They faced problems: Economic change had brought corruption, inflation, unemployment, and other ills along with benefits.

The second major event of 1997 was the return of Hong Kong to China on July 1, after more than 150 years of British rule. As a British colony, this territory on China's south coast had become a thriving financial center. Under the agreement for the transfer, worked out by Deng in the mid-1980s, Hong Kong was to keep its free-market system and a measure of self-government for at least 50 years. Hong Kong residents and people in the rest of China celebrated the transfer. But some people in Hong Kong and in Western nations were concerned by signs that China would limit democracy. Hong Kong's elected Legislative Council was replaced by a new legislature whose

Mourners place flowers alongside a portrait of Deng Xiaoping, China's longtime supreme leader, following his death in February. Deng brought economic reform to China, but squelched democracy during his rule.

members were chosen by a special committee. And a new chief executive, Tung Chee-hwa, placed restrictions on political activities and protests.

These steps made many people worry that Hong Kong would soon follow China's policies, outlawing dissent and jailing people if they criticized the government. In fact, China's record on human rights was a major source of strain with the United States and other Western countries. In the fall of 1997, Chinese president Jiang visited the United States and met with President Bill Clinton. They discussed trade issues as well as the treatment of China's dissidents.

Then, in November, China paroled one of its most prominent political prisoners, Wei Jingsheng. An advocate of democracy, Wei had been imprisoned since 1979. He was flown to Detroit, Michigan, where he entered a hospital for medical evaluation. It wasn't clear whether his release was a token gesture or the start of a new, more relaxed policy.

TROUBLE RETURNS TO CAMBODIA

The people of Cambodia have endured more than their share of violence. In 1997, it seemed that they would have to endure still more, as civil war once again broke out.

Cambodia's troubles stretched back to 1970, when Prince Norodom Sihanouk, the country's ruler, was ousted in a coup. After a long civil war, the Khmer Rouge, a Communist guerrilla group led by Pol Pot, took power in 1975. In the next four years, more than one million people died of disease or starvation or were killed by the Khmer Rouge. In 1979, Vietnam invaded Cambodia and drove the Khmer Rouge from power. The Vietnamese installed a new government, but civil war continued.

In 1991 the warring factions finally agreed to a U.N. peace plan. Two years later, elections were held. Parties led by Sihanouk and his son Norodom Ranariddh won the most votes. But the former Communist party, led by Hun Sen, wouldn't accept the results. At Hun Sen's insistence, the others agreed to form a coalition government. Sihanouk returned as king of a constitutional monarchy, with little real power. Norodom Ranariddh became first prime minister, while Hun Sen was named second prime minister. The Khmer Rouge, which refused to take part in the voting, kept fighting from bases in Cambodia's northwestern forests.

The new government was in trouble from the start. Ranariddh and Hun Sen, who had been prime minister under the Vietnamese, didn't share power well. They even maintained separate military forces. The rivalry burst into the open after Ranariddh started negotiations with members of the Khmer Rouge in 1996. Apparently, Hun Sen feared that his rival might get support from the guerrilla group. In July, he staged a coup. Ranariddh fled the country, and several of his top aides were executed. Once again, factional fighting erupted.

Meanwhile, the Khmer Rouge was also torn by divisions. Pol Pot attempted to crush a splinter movement in 1996 by ordering the deaths of its leaders. But in 1997 the tables were turned. Rival Khmer Rouge forces captured Pol Pot and, in July, staged a show trial at a site in the jungle. Pol Pot was sentenced to life imprisonment for the murders—ironically, not for the million or more deaths he was responsible for as Cambodia's ruler from 1975 to 1979.

No one outside the guerrilla group recognized this trial as legal. Most observers thought it was staged to improve the Khmer Rouge's image, perhaps so the group could change its focus to politics. The rebellion was making little progress. And Khmer Rouge fighters, weary of life in the malaria-infested forests, were deserting in droves.

In July, Khmer Rouge forces staged a show trial of their brutal former leader, Pol Pot, in the Cambodian jungle.

INDIA AND PAKISTAN

For India and Pakistan, 1997 marked a milestone—the 50th anniversary of independence. It was a time for celebration, and for a look back at history.

From 1858 to 1947, Britain ruled the Indian subcontinent, including the areas that form India and Pakistan today. But from the 1880s on, the people of the subcontinent began demanding independence. Heading the independence movement were Mohandas Gandhi, who became world famous for his nonviolent protests; leaders of the Indian National Congress; and Mohammed Ali Jinnah, head of the Muslim League. Great Britain finally agreed to independence after World War II. At first, it balked at Jinnah's demand that India be split into two states—one Hindu and one Muslim. But after religious violence swept the country, the British agreed. On August 15, 1947, two nations were born.

Today, Indians point with pride to their democratic government, while acknowledging that Indian politics are often filled with turmoil. Despite several rebellions, clashes with Pakistan, and periodic ethnic and religious violence, the country has stayed together. It has made great strides against poverty and disease, although many of its 944 million people are still desperately poor.

Pakistan has seen its share of troubles, too. Originally, it was made up of two parts—West Pakistan, north and west of India, and East Pakistan, east of India. In 1971, East Pakistan rebelled. Helped by India, it won independence as Bangladesh. Since then, Pakistan's fragile democracy has survived a period of military rule

U.S. President Bill Clinton greets Polish troops during a visit to Warsaw in July. Poland, Hungary, and the Czech Republic were invited to join NATO by 1999.

NATO: Expanding the Alliance

The North Atlantic Treaty Organization (NATO) was formed in 1949 to protect Western Europe from communism. Its original members were the United States, Canada, and ten Western European nations. More countries joined later, bringing membership in the military alliance to sixteen. For nearly 50 years, through the Cold War, NATO troops helped ward off the threat of invasion from the Soviet Union and the Communist nations of Eastern Europe. Then in the 1990s, after the break-up of the Soviet Union, the mission changed. NATO became a bulwark against *any* threat to stability in Europe, not just communism. And as the countries of Eastern Europe adopted democracy, they asked to come under NATO's protective umbrella.

NATO members agreed that expanding the alliance would help maintain peace in Europe, but there were important questions to answer first.

● Which countries should be allowed to join, and when? The United States favored admitting Poland, Hungary, and the Czech Republic, which had good records of democratic reform. Other members, especially France, favored including Romania and Slovenia as well.

● How would expansion affect relations with Russia? The former Soviet Union once held sway over the very nations that now wanted to join the West. Many people in Russia saw the expansion of NATO as a threat to their national security. In 1997, NATO answered those fears by setting up a joint council to give Russia a voice in matters that might affect it.

● How much would it cost to expand the alliance? Many of the would-be members were relatively poor nations and didn't have strong, well-equipped armies. Much of the cost of upgrading their forces would fall on the United States, which contributes the most to NATO. That was one reason why NATO's expansion was less popular in the United States than in Europe.

Despite some misgivings, in July the alliance formally invited Poland, Hungary, and the Czech Republic to join by 1999, while leaving the door open for others to join later. Soldiers from nations that had once been enemies would now work side by side.

and a series of scandals, as well as conflict between Muslim groups. Still, Pakistan has built thriving industries and trade links with other countries.

As August 14, 1997, approached, people in both countries put their troubles aside to celebrate with parades, flags, and fireworks. They had much to be proud of, and much to look forward to.

A SCANDAL IN SWITZERLAND

Quiet, conservative Switzerland suddenly found itself in the center of an international uproar in 1997. The controversy stemmed from events that had taken place more than 50 years earlier, during World War II. Although the Swiss were officially neutral in the war, they helped the Allies in several ways, such as allowing their country to serve as a base for spying. But in 1997, evidence showed that the Swiss had also been helpful to Nazi Germany—by accepting millions of dollars worth of stolen gold.

The revelations came after two years of efforts by the United States and Jewish groups to trace gold stolen by the Nazis. By some estimates, the Nazis acquired gold worth more than $900 million at 1945 prices during the war. More than half came from the central banks of countries the Nazis had conquered. The rest came from businesses and individuals—including an estimated $146 million from victims of the Holocaust, the Nazi program that killed six million Jews.

The Nazis sold much of this gold to foreign banks, especially Swiss banks, in exchange for currency that they used to buy goods abroad. As much as $400 million in Nazi gold was in Swiss banks at the end of the war. Only $58 million was returned, and that, along with Nazi gold held in Germany and other places, went to the European central banks the Nazis had raided. At the time, there was no effort to figure out how much of the gold came from individuals.

Switzerland wasn't the only nation to hold onto some Nazi gold—Portugal, Spain, and Turkey were among others. Attention focused on the Swiss, however, because they had played an important role as bankers for the

Indians remembered the legacy of Mohandas Gandhi as they celebrated 50 years of independence in 1997.

Nazis. Research also turned up more than 1,700 dormant Swiss bank accounts dating from the war years. Many were opened by Jews hoping to safeguard their money as the Nazis stepped up their anti-Semitic attacks. Swiss banks are famous for protecting the privacy of their depositors. In this case, however, they were criticized for doing too little to find survivors and restore their money.

In December 1997, an international conference in London, England, met to review the question of the Nazi gold and to figure out what to do with the gold that remained in Allied bank vaults. One leading proposal was to use this gold as the basis for a fund that would compensate survivors of the Holocaust.

ELAINE PASCOE
Author, *South Africa: Troubled Land*

NEWSMAKERS

When U.S. President Bill Clinton started his second term in 1997, he named a new Secretary of State: **Madeleine K. Albright.** Albright, 59, was the first woman to hold the post, and the highest-ranking woman ever in the U.S. government. She was well qualified to be the nation's top diplomat. Fluent in five languages—Russian, French, Polish, Czech, and English—she had been the U.S. ambassador to the United Nations during Clinton's first term. She was known as a strong advocate of human rights and a tough negotiator.

Albright's personal history was linked to some of the most important events in the 20th century. She was born in Czechoslovakia, where her father, Josef Korbel, was a diplomat. The Korbels fled to England before World War II to escape Nazism, and they returned to Czechoslovakia after the war. But when Communists took control in 1948, they fled again, this time to the United States. Madeleine was raised as a Roman Catholic. Her parents didn't tell her that they had converted from Judaism to Catholicism before she was born—in fact, she didn't even discover this until 1997, when reporters uncovered the secret. In America, she studied political science, married (and later divorced) Joseph Albright, and began her career. Before her U.N. appointment in 1993, she worked at top research institutions, on the Senate staff, at the National Security Council, and as a professor of international affairs at Georgetown University.

In January 1997, **Kofi Annan** of Ghana became the seventh Secretary General of the United Nations, replacing Boutros Boutros-Ghali of Egypt. Annan, 58, was the first black African ever elected to the post, and he was well known and respected internationally. He had worked at the United Nations for most of his career, rising to the position of undersecretary general for peacekeeping operations. In his youth, Annan had studied in the United States, and he had close ties to the African-American community. Among the goals he set for his five-year term as Secretary General were improving the efficiency of the United Nations and getting member nations to pay their back dues—especially the United States, which owed $1.2 billion.

When people are married for 25 years, they celebrate a silver anniversary. At 50 years, the anniversary is golden. And 81 years? That's a record. **George Couron and Gaynel Emery** of Orangevale, California, were married on April 10, 1916. In 1997, George, 100, and Gaynel, 97, celebrated their 81st wedding anniversary and became the longest-married living couple in the United States. (Some couples had been married as long as 86 years, but they were no longer living.) The secret to their happiness? "We still tell each other we love each other." George said.

In 1945, serving with the U.S. Army in Italy, **Joseph Vernon Baker** wiped out four enemy machine-gun nests and drew fire so that his comrades could escape. Fifty years later, in January 1997, he received the Medal of Honor—the highest U.S. award for bravery—from President Bill Clinton. The medal also went to six other black soldiers, all deceased. They were the first African Americans so honored for service in World War II.

Mother Teresa of Calcutta worked for 50 years to build the Missionaries of Charity, a worldwide Roman Catholic order that cares for the poor, sick, and dying. In March 1997, six months before her death, members of the order chose her successor: **Sister Nirmala Joshi**, 62 (shown standing behind Mother Teresa). Sister Nirmala was born in Bihar, India, and was raised as a Hindu. Over the objections of her family, she converted to Catholicism at age 24, after learning of Mother Teresa's work among the poor of Calcutta. She joined the Missionaries of Charity and eventually became head of the order's Contemplative Wing, which oversees the spiritual life of members.

This is no ordinary skydiver. It's former U.S. President **George Bush,** parachuting through the blue skies over Arizona in March 1997. Bush, 72, made the jump partly to put a bad memory to rest. As a pilot in the Pacific during World War II, he had been forced to bail out when his plane was hit by ground fire. Two crew members were killed. Bush himself narrowly escaped death when his parachute opened too soon and was almost snared by the plane. He was determined to parachute again someday, to "do it again and do it right." In 1997 he got the chance. First, Bush was coached by experts from the U.S. Parachute Association and the Army's Golden Knights parachute team. Then he took off in a plane and—some 12,500 feet (3,810 meters) over the desert— jumped out. For about one minute, he was in free fall, but he wasn't alone. Coaches were at his sides, and other jumpers circled around, snapping pictures. At 4,500 feet (1,370 meters) Bush pulled the rip cord, and his chute opened. He steered it to a safe landing. It was a thrilling experience. "I'm a new man," the former president said.

In 1997, pilot **Linda Finch** successfully completed the round-the-world journey begun by famed aviator Amelia Earhart 60 years before. Earhart disappeared over the Pacific Ocean in 1937, on the last leg of her flight. To this day, her fate remains a mystery. Finch, a 46-year-old Texas businesswoman, set out to duplicate that flight precisely—and finish it. She flew a refurbished Lockheed Electra 10E, the same type of plane used by Earhart. But she took along modern navigation and computer equipment. That allowed her journey to be tracked precisely, and thousands of people used the Internet to follow her progress. Finch took off from Oakland, California, on March 17, leaving on the same date and from the same hangar as Earhart. After 26,000 miles (41,800 kilometers) and stops in eighteen countries, she returned safely to Oakland on May 28.

On May 25, 1997, **Strom Thurmond** of South Carolina completed 41 years and 10 months in the Senate and reached a milestone: He became the longest serving senator in history. At 94, he was already the oldest serving member of Congress. Thurmond, a Republican, was governor of South Carolina before his first Senate term began in 1956. At that time, he was known for opposing the civil rights movement, a stand he later eased. Thurmond planned to serve out his latest term, which runs to 2003.

When **Harold E. Ford, Jr.,** took his seat in the U.S. House of Representatives in January 1997, he became the youngest serving member of Congress. Ford, 26, a Democrat from Tennessee, was elected to the seat previously held by his father, Harold Ford, who retired in 1996. Still, he wasn't the youngest Congressman ever. William Claiborne, who was elected in 1797, was just 22—below the constitutional age limit.

ANIMALS

What's so funny? Maybe these orangutans are laughing at a funny joke. But it's more likely that they're just having fun and playing around. Many kinds of animals like to play. Primates—monkeys, apes, and especially humans—are among the most playful animals of all. Some young monkeys and apes spend as much as half their waking hours playing. And often adults can't resist joining in the fun. But humans are the only animals that laugh at jokes—at least as far as anyone knows, that is!

Anybody home? Wild animals, like this moose, are becoming common visitors to suburban backyards.

SUBURBAN WILDLIFE

Picture this: You're waiting for the school bus one morning when you hear something rustling the leaves and branches behind you. You turn, just in time to see the noise maker disappear into the bushes: It's a moose!

Ridiculous? Not at all, if you live in the northern United States or Canada. Moose sightings are becoming more and more common. And moose are just one of many wild animals that are popping up in suburban backyards. Bats, bears, beavers, coyotes, deer, foxes, geese, raccoons, skunks—what's going on?

For years, towns and cities have been growing. They've taken over more and more land that was once wild or used only for farming. Housing developments, shopping centers, and office parks now stand where once there were only woods and fields. At first, the wild animals that lived in those woods and fields moved on, finding homes in other open areas. But as the amount of open land has shrunk, wildlife has

begun to adapt. The suburbs—with lawns, small ponds, and carefully tended gardens—are an artificial habitat. But many wild animals are learning to live there, at close quarters with people. And for people, the animals are a source of both pleasure and problems.

OH, DEER!

A deer in the middle of New York City? The report was no hoax. In June 1996, a female white-tailed deer turned up in Manhattan, the heart of New York. She was spotted outside a subway station and tracked to a park. There she was captured and taken to open spaces north of the city.

White-tailed deer are turning up everywhere, it seems. One jumped through the window of a store in Northampton, Massachusetts. Another cantered through an airport in Washington, D.C. Of all the animals in the suburban wildlife boom, they have increased the most dramatically.

By some estimates, there are 25 million white-tailed deer in the United States south of the Canadian border. That's about the same number that roamed the woods when European settlers arrived in the 1600s. By 1900, hunting and land-clearing had reduced the white-tailed population to half a million. But now the deer are back.

These adaptable creatures live in small bands in the wooded areas and fields that dot the suburbs. For deer, it's a great life. There's plenty to eat—including shrubs and flowers that suburban gardeners plant. There are no predators, and hunting isn't allowed in populated suburban areas. So the deer population has boomed.

The deer are delicate, graceful, and charming. They're also a problem. Homeowners are outraged when deer devour flowers and expensive shrubs. And car accidents involving deer are common and often serious. Each year such accidents kill about 100 people—and about 350,000 deer. That's led wildlife officials to search for solutions to the deer boom. Fencing is one option. But fences must be high to stop deer—they can jump up to 7 feet (2.1 meters).

WILDLIFE GALORE

Will moose be the next visitors in suburban backyards? These big relatives of deer are spreading south from the forests of the far north. They're already a common sight in Canada and parts of the United States that border that country. Now they're being sighted in wooded areas as far south as Connecticut. One even turned up in Boston, Massachusetts! A moose sighting is an event. These animals can stand 6 feet (2 meters) tall and weigh 1,200 pounds (544 kilograms). But when a car hits a moose, the results are devastating. Such accidents are becoming more frequent.

In Nevada, people are running into problems with wild horses. Nevada has more than 22,000 wild horses, descendants of mounts brought to America by the Spanish hundreds of years ago. Most of the horses live on public range land. But in Hidden Valley, near Reno, houses are being built in an area that's a winter grazing ground for three bands of wild horses. Now wild horses are nibbling suburban lawns and playing in the streets. Some residents love it. Others want to run the horses out of town.

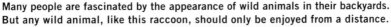

Many people are fascinated by the appearance of wild animals in their backyards. But any wild animal, like this raccoon, should only be enjoyed from a distance.

Moose and horses are still unusual in backyards, however. Smaller animals are much more common. Chipmunks, skunks, cottontail rabbits, and opossums thrive in suburbia. Raccoons break into people's garbage cans to feast, and squirrels rob bird feeders. Sometimes these animals get into suburban attics or drop down chimneys into living rooms.

Beavers are making a comeback in some areas. When they build their dams and block streams, they can affect water wells and sewage disposal. Beavers also damage trees. In Chicago, a beaver cut down a tree along North Lake Shore Drive—and blocked traffic.

Birds such as crows and jays, which are clever and eat just about anything, are also doing well. And Canada geese are everywhere. Some towns employ trained border collies to chase them out of parks, ballfields, golf courses, and beaches, where the birds (and their messy droppings) aren't welcome.

PREDATORS, TOO

As animals such as chipmunks, rabbits, and deer have increased in number, predators that kill and eat them have begun to move into the suburbs. Coyotes have been common in the West for many years, even around big cities like Los Angeles. Now

A black bear raids a backyard bird feeder, hoping to find a tasty treat. Black bears will eat almost anything, and they often search for food close to people's homes.

their eerie howls are heard in the East, too. Coyotes hunt small animals; they don't attack people. But they don't draw the line between wildlife and household pets. House cats and even small dogs have fallen victim to suburban coyote packs.

Black bears are also showing up in populated areas. Bears are most common in the West. There, many new houses have been built in areas where bears live, and the bears don't always move out right away. But bears are turning up in the East, too—even in the suburbs of New York City. Black bears will eat just about anything, and they go into people's yards to get garbage, birdseed in feeders, or pet food that's been left outside. In New Jersey, one bear even broke into a house in search of food! Bears also hunt small animals, so they are a danger to pets. And while they don't usually bother people, they are extremely dangerous if cornered or frightened.

People in California and other parts of the West have an even more serious predator in their midst: the mountain lion. In Colorado, for example, there are several thousand mountain lions. When people build homes in "lion country," they aren't always aware that these predators are around. They leave garbage or food outside, and that attracts raccoons. Then a mountain lion comes, hunting the raccoons. Mountain lions can easily kill cats and dogs, even big dogs. Attacks on people are rare, but they happen. In 1991, for example, a lion killed a jogger not far from Denver, Colorado.

GETTING ALONG

Large predators like bears and mountain lions aren't vicious. They're just acting naturally—trying to survive while their habitat is changing. Sometimes their need to survive puts them in conflict with people.

As wildlife has moved into the suburbs—and the suburbs have spread into wild areas—many other conflicts have arisen. There are car accidents and property damage. Health worries are another problem: Goose droppings can foul water supplies. Some animals carry diseases that can affect people. For example, deer and mice are hosts to ticks that carry Lyme disease. In parts of the country, rabies is a serious problem among raccoons, skunks, foxes, and some other wild animals.

Wildlife experts worry that animals that take up suburban life may be crowding out other animals that can't adapt so quickly. For example, deer devour the woodland understory—the shrubs and low growth—where many songbirds nest. That makes it harder for songbirds to find nesting places. Then crows and raccoons prey on songbird nests, eating the eggs.

To keep wild animals from becoming a problem, experts say, it's best not to attract them. For example, don't leave garbage cans or pet food outside, and don't feed deer in winter. Where animals are already a problem, people don't always agree about what to do. Some favor hunting or "thinning" the growing populations of deer and geese, for example. That upsets other people, who don't like to see animals killed. They prefer different methods, such as contraception. Animals like bears and mountain lions can sometimes be captured and relocated to wild areas.

Often, people adjust to having wild animals in their midst—just as animals adjust to people. That's what happened in Austin, Texas, after a colony of 1.5 million bats moved into the crevices under a highway bridge. At first, newspaper headlines screamed "Bats Invade Austin," and people were afraid. But Austin-

Deer are lovely and graceful—but they are a problem in many areas. However, people disagree about how to control their growing numbers. Some people are in favor of hunting; others don't like to see animals killed and prefer different methods, such as contraception.

ers came to know the bats and understand the good they do (they eat thousands of pounds of insects every night). Now, when the bats emerge from their roost at twilight, people gather to watch. In fact, Austin's bats are a big tourist attraction.

Will man and beast ever become peaceful backyard neighbors? Only time will tell.

Young animals, like these wrestling lion cubs, have a great time playing with each other. But their rough-and-tumble play is also teaching them important skills that will help them survive as adults.

ANIMAL ANTICS

Lion cubs wrestle outside their den, pretending to bite without hurting each other. A cheetah cub pounces on a stick and begins to bat it around. A young antelope bounds into the air, runs, and leaps up in the air again. A mother gorilla covers her face, playing peek-a-boo with her baby.

What are these animals doing? They're all playing, and having a wonderful time at it. But animal play is more than fun. Play serves a serious purpose: It helps animals develop skills they need to live in the wild.

Rough-and-tumble antics help animals grow strong and develop quick reflexes. Scientists think play may even help animals' brains develop, especially the parts of the brain involved in coordination. Play also helps animals learn patterns of behavior that they'll use throughout their lives—hunting, fleeing from predators, courting a mate, besting a rival. Among some animals, play helps form bonds among members of a group.

Not all animals play. No one has yet seen snails frolicking, or ants playing tag. With very few exceptions, all playful animals are mammals and birds. Some adult animals play, especially among species that are generally considered intelligent, such as dolphins and primates. But most of the fooling around is done by youngsters. That makes sense, in light of play's role as a sort of natural survival school. And different kinds of animals play in different ways—ways that, in each case, will help them survive.

RUN-AWAY PLAY

Have you ever seen young horses playing in a field? They race back and forth, chasing each other, leaping, bucking, and kicking up their heels. Even though they're safe in the field, they are practicing moves that will help them escape from predators in the wild.

Horses, sheep, goats, antelopes, and other herbivores (plant-eaters) instinctively run away at the first hint of danger. But that instinct to run away isn't enough. In the wild, most animals must also be quick on their feet, or they'll wind up as dinner for wolves, lions, or other predators. That's where play comes in. High-speed chase games help the youngsters develop strong running muscles and stamina. As they dodge this way and that, they fine-tune their reflexes and learn to run evasive patterns, like a football player running down field. Bucking and kicking are defensive actions that would help drive away a predator that was getting too close.

Some animals are famous for this kind of "run-away" play. Pronghorns, for example, race in circles and make fantastic leaps. Mountain goats and their relatives, chamois and ibexes, scamper across steep, rocky slopes. They jump from ledge to ledge and vault straight up into the air, just for the fun of it. All the while, they're developing the keen balance and coordination they must have to stay alive in their rugged mountain homes.

Small animals play chase games, too. Maybe you've seen squirrels or chipmunks racing around, playing their own version of tag. Mice and rats play in the same way. They're practicing moves that will help them evade their enemies—predators such as cats, owls, and hawks. A little extra speed, a slightly bigger leap, or a turn that's just a bit quicker can make the difference between life and death for prey animals.

Through its playful leaps, a mountain goat develops the balance it needs to stay alive in its rugged mountain home.

Toys and Games

Animals not only play with each other—they also play with toys. A young wolf (below) will use a stick to start a chase game, "daring" another wolf to take it and then running away with it. Naturalists have seen whales playing with balls of kelp, and elephants hurling clods of earth with their trunks. A raven will carry a stick into the air, drop it, and dive to catch it before the stick hits the ground. In New Zealand, people sometimes wake up to the sound of stones landing on their roofs. The culprits are parrots called keas, which toss rocks for fun and sometimes drop them on rooftops below.

Dolphins are famous for playing with toys in the water. But visitors to the Amsterdam zoo were amazed one day to see a hippopotamus playing with a leaf that had landed on the surface of its pond. The hippo went underwater and blew the leaf into the air with a blast from its nostrils. As soon as the leaf floated back down to the water surface, the hippo went down and blew it up again. Lethargic on land, hippos can really cavort in water. They've even been seen doing underwater back flips.

The naturalist Dian Fossey, who studied gorillas in Africa, saw these big animals playing a version of football by tossing and kicking fruit. Sometimes primates even *make* toys. A chimp will poke a hole in a leaf and peer through it, for a new view of the world. Young Japanese macaques—the snow monkeys of Japan—make snowballs. The monkeys carry the snowballs around as toys but, so far as anyone knows, they don't throw them.

GOTCHA!

Predators have their own kinds of play. If you've watched a kitten or a puppy, you've seen some of these games. Toss a stick, and a puppy will be off and running, racing after it. The puppy pounces on the stick, grasps it in its teeth, and shakes its head. Wiggle a string or a feather in front of a kitten, and the little animal can't resist the game—it pounces on the moving object or reaches out to bat at it with its paws. Wolf cubs, lion cubs, and other wild members of the cat and dog families play similar games. They stalk, chase, pounce, bat, and "catch" sticks, stones, feathers, leaves, grasshoppers, and whatever else catches their eye—including their tails. Often, litter mates stalk and chase each other. It's great fun, but it's also a way for these young animals to sharpen essential hunting skills. When they grow up, they'll have to stalk and capture prey to survive.

Adult predators are generally too busy finding food to spend much time in play. But they'll tolerate a lot of playful nipping, swatting, and freshness from their youngsters, and sometimes they get in the act. Lionesses twitch their tails to give their cubs something to chase. Cheetahs and other hunting cats sometimes bring their offspring small prey before it's killed. The kittens play with the still-living prey, getting paws-on practice for the hunt.

Dolphins sharpen their fishing skills as they frolic in the waves and play underwater tag.

You might be surprised at some of the other animals that play hunting games. When young dolphins frolic in the waves and play underwater tag with each other, they're honing skills that will help them catch fish. Bears go play-fishing, too, splashing in mountain streams where, later, they'll catch dinner. When young bats start to fly, they chase each other through the air, learning to make the loops and dives they'll need to catch flying insects.

SOCIAL PLAY

When lion cubs wrestle and tumble around with each other, they're doing more than practicing hunting skills. Many kinds of play serve important social purposes, especially for animals that live in groups. Through play, young animals bond with other members of their group and learn to get along. They also learn to understand body language and other cues that group members use to communicate.

A playful baby rhino runs rings around its mother and butts her until she lets out a grunt that means "Stop that!"

The Language of Play

Are these hippos fighting or playing? Animal play mimics serious behavior—fleeing, hunting, fighting. But animals can tell each other that they're just having fun! Animal play has its own language, made up of special signals called play markers. Here are some examples of the many ways animals have to say "let's play!"

- Mountain goats rear up on their hind legs or lean to one side.
- Horses leap, buck, or shake their heads.
- A dog or wolf does a play bow, crouching down in front with its tail waving in the air.
- A kitten taps another kitten with its paw.
- A weasel arches its back and hops.
- A playful panda turns a somersault to let others know that it wants to romp.
- A frolicsome rat flips over on its back.
- Animals of many species, including dogs and primates, have a special play face, usu-

ally a relaxed, open-mouthed grin. When they're play-fighting, the grin says, "I'm not really angry—I'm just kidding around!" However, chimpanzees, baby gorillas, and baby orangutans are the only animals (other than people) that actually laugh.

Mock fighting can help establish rank in the group. It can help youngsters learn how and when to give in, and how to control aggression. Wrestling matches, butting contests, and other games teach these skills. In Africa, lion cubs play "king of the hill" on termite mounds. Elephants bump heads and wrestle with their trunks. Sheep and goats play butting games, too. When they grow up, they'll use the same moves to fight off rivals during breeding season. And young rhinos, who don't have too many play-mates, still find a way to play. A young rhino will run rings around its mother and then suddenly butt her—until she lets out a grunt that means "Stop that!"

Bears are also known for their playful ways. There's nothing a brown bear likes better than giving a big bear hug—to another brown bear. Litter mates and even mothers and cubs hug tight and roll around, having a great time. Ani-

An orangutan tumbles in the treetops. Apes and monkeys are among the most playful of all animals.

mals that most people don't think of as playful also kick up their heels at times. The collared peccary, a wild pig that lives in the southwestern United States, is best known for its quick temper. But bands of peccaries have frantic play sessions. All the members of the group tumble and leap around until they're exhausted; then they pile up together and nap. Naturalists think these group games help forge tight bonds within the band.

young mountain goats that leap for joy, can fall and be injured. An animal may be so distracted while playing that it falls victim to a predator. But the skills that animals learn through play are important. Animal games look like fun—but they're really serious business.

And it seems that some animals just *have* to play, even in the most unlikely ways. No one knows, for example, why dolphins often

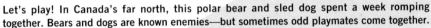

Let's play! In Canada's far north, this polar bear and sled dog spent a week romping together. Bears and dogs are known enemies—but sometimes odd playmates come together.

Monkeys and other primates are among the most playful animals of all. Some monkey youngsters spend half their waking hours in play. They race through the treetops, playing hide and seek or follow the leader. They spin and twirl and wrestle with each other. Often adults get into the act, too. For example, chimpanzee moms make funny faces at their babies and tickle them under the chin or on the toes. Young chimps tickle back.

SERIOUS BUSINESS

Play can be pretty risky in the wild. Monkeys that scamper through the trees, and

seek out boats and even swimmers, and frolic alongside in the water. Some playmates are even odder. In Alaska, a naturalist watched a bear and a raven play tag.

From Canada's far north comes the unusual story of a polar bear that played with sled dogs. Polar bears and dogs are sworn enemies, and this big bear was definitely hungry. But for more than a week, the bear lumbered over to a place where about 40 dogs were tethered and romped with them. The two species seemed to understand each other—through the universal language of play.

The multi-colored MANTIS SHRIMP spends most of its time in a hole it digs on the ocean floor. But the shrimp moves like lightning when it spots a tasty-looking fish or mollusk, and it captures the prey with its large, strong claws. Should danger threaten, the mantis shrimp swims backward by rapidly flipping its large fanlike tail. The bright spots on its tail are used to attract a mate.

The CANDYCANE SHRIMP might look like a delicious dessert to some fish. But like all other shrimp, the candycane won't be eaten as long as it sits among the poisonous tentacles of a sea anemone. The shrimp's shell protects it from the poison. But the shrimp's enemies have no such protection. So they would rather give up "dessert" than be killed by the sea anemone.

THE SHRIMP SQUAD

Shrimp may be small in size, but they are big in beauty and variety. Some are pale pink, light gray, or pure white. Others are bright red, blue, yellow, or green. Some are covered with decorative spots and stripes. Many kinds are luminescent, with special organs that produce a pale, glowing light. Some shrimp can even change their colors to match their surroundings.

There are about 2,500 known kinds, or species, of shrimp. They range in size from less than ½ inch (1 centimeter) to more than 8 inches (20 centimeters). Shrimp belong to a group of invertebrates called crustaceans, which also includes crabs, lobsters, and crayfish. The name crustacean comes from *crusta,* the Latin word for "shell." Shrimp have a hard, stiff shell called an exoskeleton that encloses and protects the soft body. As a shrimp grows, it periodically sheds its shell and grows a new, larger shell.

A shrimp's body has three parts: the head, thorax (trunk), and abdomen. On the head are long feelers and a pair of eyes on stalks. The thorax bears five pairs of walking legs. Some shrimp have large, sharp claws on the two front legs. The abdomen, which ends in a fan-shaped tail, has tiny flattened

The red-blotched HARLEQUIN SHRIMP uses its large, powerful claws to tear apart its favorite food: sea stars (starfish). The shrimp may eat only one arm of a sea star before wandering off to rest (a sea star can regrow its arms). But if the shrimp is really hungry, it will eat the whole creature. A harlequin shrimp needs about two days to eat a sea star that's twice its size.

The exotic-looking HUMPBACK SHRIMP lives in coral reefs in warm tropical seas. Its colorful, mottled pattern allows it to blend into the surroundings, making the shrimp nearly invisible to hungry enemies. The many hairs on the shrimp's body are thought to be used as sensing organs or to attract mates. Female humpback shrimp are much more hairy than the males.

limbs called swimmerets, or "swimming paddles." The shrimp uses the paddles to swim forward. By quickly flipping the tail, it can swim backward.

Most species of shrimp live in the sea— some in shallow waters along coasts, some at medium depths, and some in deep, cold waters. Shrimp also inhabit rivers and other freshwater environments. Some colorless species live in caves.

Many shrimp feed quietly on tiny drifting organisms. But some are fierce predators, grabbing fish and other prey with their claws. And some shrimp have unique eating habits. For example, cleaner shrimp feed on parasites that live on fish; the shrimp get a meal and the fish get rid of harmful pests.

To avoid being eaten by other sea animals, shrimp tend to hide. Many live in cracks in coral reefs or among underwater plants. Some burrow into the ocean bottom or even into solid coral. The pearl oyster shrimp lives inside an oyster's shell—and steals some of the oyster's food.

Most of the shrimp eaten by people are raised commercially on large shrimp farms. They are often called "common shrimp." But, as you can see from the pictures shown here, they have lots of uncommon, truly extraordinary relatives!

A kinkajou from Central America licks its chops. But tongues are meant for more than just licking!

TERRIFIC TONGUES

A chameleon sits motionless on a branch. Only its bulging eyes move—in two different directions at once! When one eye sees an insect, the other eye swivels and also focuses on the unsuspecting victim. In less than a second, the chameleon judges the distance to the insect. Then, almost faster than your eyes can see, it flicks its muscular tongue forward. The insect is caught on the sticky clublike tip and pulled into the chameleon's mouth.

Unlike the tongues of most animals, the chameleon's tongue is attached to the front of its mouth. When it shoots out of the mouth, the tongue expands and can reach prey that's more than a body's length away.

The size of the prey depends on the size of the chameleon. Small chameleons catch mainly insects. Large chameleons feed on lizards, birds, and small mammals, as well as on insects.

Frogs and toads also have tongues that are attached to the front of the lower jaw and are loose at the back. They use their tongues in much the same way as the chameleon. But their tongues can't be extended as far as the tongue of a chameleon. Frogs and toads feed mainly on insects, although some will eat almost anything that moves and is the right size.

AN EATING UTENSIL

Getting food and eating are the main functions of an animal's tongue. There are many different sizes and shapes of tongues in the animal world, and each is adapted for a certain type of food. Anteaters, like chameleons and frogs, eat insects. But they don't try to catch quick-moving flies and moths. Rather, they capture ants and termites that live in large nests. An anteater uses its sharp claws to tear open a nest. Then it sticks its long snout into the opening. Its sticky, wormlike tongue moves in and out of the mouth, licking up insects by the hundreds. A giant anteater—whose tongue may be 2 feet (60 centimeters) long—eats as many as 30,000 ants and termites in a day to satisfy its great appetite.

The honey possum, a tiny mammal that lives in Australia, has a tongue that looks like a bristle brush. It uses its tongue to lap up nectar and pollen from flowers. When the tongue is retracted, ridges on the roof of the mouth scrape off the food.

Another animal that feeds on nectar is the honeybee. It has a tongue that's a hollow tube. When the bee finds a nice source of nectar, it sucks up the liquid much as you draw up soda through a drinking straw.

The hummingbird, another nectar feeder, has a long, slender tongue that's forked at the end. The bird curls its tongue inward, to form a tubelike structure, and drinks the nectar. The hummingbird often takes in tiny insects at the same time.

OTHER USES, TOO

Tongues are used for other activities besides catching food and eating. The gecko uses its tongue as a windshield wiper. This lizard has transparent eyelids. Unlike your eyelids, they don't move. The upper and lower lids are fused together, over the surface of the eye. This protects the eye from dust and other particles. If the covering becomes dirty, the gecko licks it clean with the tip of its tongue.

The okapi, a short-necked relative of the giraffe, can also stretch out its tongue far enough to lick dust from its eyes— and even from its ears. The giraffe may

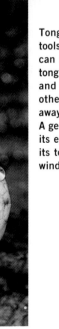

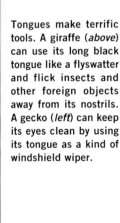

Tongues make terrific tools. A giraffe (*above*) can use its long black tongue like a flyswatter and flick insects and other foreign objects away from its nostrils. A gecko (*left*) can keep its eyes clean by using its tongue as a kind of windshield wiper.

81

A hedgehog (*above*) uses its tongue to toss saliva over its spines in order to conceal its scent. A rattlesnake (*right*) can detect the smell of prey through its forked tongue. And a lorikeet (*far right*) has a tongue like a little brush to help it gather pollen.

even lick the inside of its nostrils to remove insects and other foreign objects. Its tongue, which may be more than 20 inches (50 centimeters) long, is nearly black in color. Scientists think that this dark coloring protects the tongue from being burned by the hot African sun.

Some animals use their tongues as a cooling device. Cats are good examples. A cat pants when its body temperature is too high. This increases the evaporation of water from the tongue and tissues lining the mouth. As the water evaporates, heat is removed from the body. In addition, the cat cools off by licking itself with saliva. If extremely hot, it licks every part of its body that can be reached by the tongue, to the point where it's dripping wet.

A cat does other things with its tongue, too. The surface of a cat's tongue is rough, like sandpaper. The cat makes use of this rough-ness as it grooms its fur—much as you use a brush to groom your hair. The cat uses its tongue to clean not only itself but also its children. It may also lick other animals and the human beings with whom it shares its home. Such licking is a sign of affection.

The hedgehog has a peculiar behavior called self-anointing. When a hedgehog comes upon an object that has a stimulating smell, it licks the object. Or, if the object is small enough, the hedgehog takes it into its mouth and chews it. (Stimulating objects may include flowers, soap, earthworms, rotten meat, books, and cigarette stubs.) As it licks or chews the object, the hedgehog produces great amounts of saliva. It turns its head to the side and, using its tongue, tosses the foamy saliva over its spines. It does this three or four times before spitting out the object. The saliva dries on the spines. Scientists believe that the smell of the saliva conceals the

tongue into its mouth and places the tips to two small holes, or pits, called Jacobson's organs. These are located in the roof of the mouth, and they have the same function as your nose. When the snake smells an approaching mouse or other animal, it prepares to strike. The sensory system also helps the snake track down an animal that it has bitten and that has crawled away to die. By continuously testing the air with its tongue, the snake can follow the trail of the victim.

Your tongue also has many uses. It helps you chew and swallow food. It tells you how the

hedgehog's true scent, thus protecting it from enemies that might otherwise find it.

The rattlesnake uses its forked tongue to detect the odor of prey. It flicks its tongue back and forth, picking up molecules of scent from the air. Then the rattlesnake draws its

food tastes and whether it's hot or cold. And it does something that no animal tongue can do. It enables you to speak. Without your tongue, you wouldn't be able to form many of the words that are part of your everyday speech. So you see, you too have a terrific tongue!

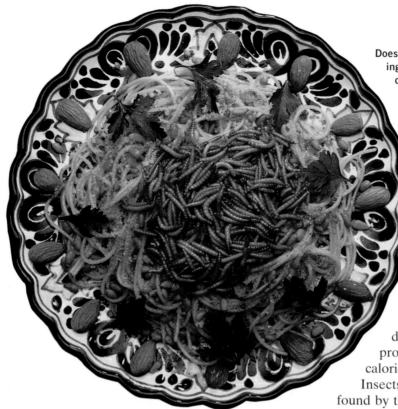

Does pasta with mealworms sound appetizing to you? In many countries, insects are considered tasty and healthful foods.

INCREDIBLE EDIBLE BUGS

What's your favorite pizza topping? Let's see, now. . .meatballs, green peppers, sausage, extra cheese, bugs. . . .

BUGS? Most people in North America and Europe would send a pizza back to the kitchen faster than you can say "pepperoni" if it arrived at the table with even one insect on it. But in many parts of the world, diners would be delighted with a buggy topping.

In regions of Asia, Africa, and Central and South America, certain insects and other creepy crawlies such as spiders and worms are considered good food, even gourmet delicacies. Strange? It just depends on what you're used to. Many foods that Americans eat—milk, cottage cheese, corn on the cob—are considered strange and even revolting by people in other parts of the world.

Would you eat insects? Read on before you answer no. When you learn all the benefits of this food source—and some of the tasty ways insects are prepared—you just might change your mind. (But NEVER eat a bug without making sure it's safe. Some bugs are poisonous.)

GOOD—AND GOOD FOR YOU

Why would people eat bugs? Insects, as it happens, are a nutritious, healthful food. They're high in protein, and they're a great source of energy. In fact, roasted termites (a popular dish in Africa) have twice as much protein and more than twice as many calories, ounce for ounce, as ground beef.

Insects are certainly plentiful. They're found by the billions all over the world. That makes common insects such as grasshoppers an inexpensive source of good nutrition. These insects are an important food in places where meat, fish, and other protein sources are costly or difficult to obtain.

It's hard for many people in Western countries to think of insects as "healthful" because insects are often associated with dirt and disease. In fact, most insects probably carry no more germs than many of the other foods we eat. Cooking kills the germs and makes the insects safe to eat, as it does with other foods.

People who eat bugs say they taste great. A traveler who sampled some local specialties in Laos gave this description: "A toasted dung-beetle or soft-bodied spider has a nice crisp exterior and soft interior of soufflé consistency, which is by no means unpleasant." Sweet, nutty, spicy—flavors vary, depending on the insect. Locusts, for example, are said to taste a bit like shrimp. Some caterpillars reportedly taste just like bacon.

INSECT TREATS

People all over the world have their favorite insect snacks, and their favorite ways of preparing these critters. Here are a few examples.

• A gourmet restaurant in Singapore specializes in foods that are valued as medicines in traditional Chinese medicine. Among the most popular items on the menu are ants. The chefs prepare an elegant dish called "Ants Climbing Up the Tree." The "tree" is made of potatoes and lettuce, and it's topped with fried black ants. Scorpions are also popular with diners at this restaurant. The restaurant marinates scorpions in wine, deep fries them, and serves them, stingers and all, with asparagus on the side.

wasps, red ants, mealworms (the larvae of beetles) and the eggs of water bugs are popular ingredients in other Mexican recipes.

• In central Australia, native people who crave a sweet snack head for a honey ant colony. They dig up the underground nest and collect ants that have a special sac filled with sweet nectar. To eat an ant, a snacker holds the insect by its head, and bites off the sac. The liquid tastes just like molasses, they say.

• In southern Africa, mopane trees provide people with a delicious snack—and it's not fruit. Caterpillars that feed on the leaves of these trees are a favorite taste treat. People

Left: In southern Africa, mopane caterpillars canned in tomato sauce are a super snack. Above: Grasshoppers broiled in soy sauce are a popular treat in Japan.

• In parts of Japan, cicadas are boiled and then used like shrimp in stir-fry recipes. The Japanese are also fond of a crunchy snack sold in food stalls—grasshoppers boiled in soy sauce. Insect larvae, especially the larvae of water insects, are also a favorite there. Larvae are easy to eat because they're soft, with no tough wings or long legs.

• Bugs are big in Mexico. In some areas, people make a special salsa with stink bugs. They toast the bugs (which gets rid of the stinky odor), grind them up, and mix them in a spicy sauce that's spread on corn tostados. Beetles,

collect the caterpillars, which are then dried and fried or canned in tomato sauce.

Will insects become a food fad in North America? Maybe. Insect treats are turning up in fancy restaurants and gourmet shops. A California company makes lollipops with mealworms in the middle, toffees with insect-larva centers, and salty larva-cheese snacks. In 1997, there were insect food festivals in several cities. Visitors had a chance to taste such dishes as cricket fritters and three-bug salad.

Who knows? One day you just may enjoy a dinner of steaming pasta with mealworms or cricket Marsala, followed by honey-glazed ants over ice cream for dessert. Yum!

SNOW MONKEYS—JAPAN'S TREASURES

An icy wind sends snow swirling across the forested mountains, piling it into deep drifts. It's cold—15°F (−9°C)—and getting colder. And right in the middle of this chilly winter scene, a band of monkeys is scampering through the woods.

Monkeys romping in the snow? If you think that's strange, you're right: Nearly all monkeys live in warm places, such as the tropical rain forests that lie near the Equator. But these monkeys are different. They are Japanese macaques (muh-KAKS). And their home is farther north, and far colder, than the home of any other monkey species.

Snow monkeys, as these macaques are often called, have lived in the mountains of Japan for thousands of years. They know how to survive the harsh winters there. As clever as they are cute, they are still finding new ways to cope with the cold. But today they face other challenges in their mountain homeland.

EQUIPPED FOR COLD WEATHER

The macaques are a large family, so the Japanese snow monkeys have relatives in many parts of the world. Macaques probably originated in Africa and spread from

Japanese macaques live farther north than any other monkeys, and they have learned many ways to survive in their cold mountain home.

there through Asia. Scientists think they may have reached Japan during the Ice Age, when land bridges linked the Japanese islands to the Asian mainland.

Today there are about 50,000 snow monkeys in Japan. They live in troops, or bands, that number anywhere from 30 to several hundred members. Each troop has its own territory. Japanese macaques have no permanent nests or dens. Instead, they move from place to place within their territory, in a constant hunt for food.

Adult snow monkeys weigh more than 30 pounds (14 kilograms), and they are well designed for keeping warm in winter. They are stockier and have shorter tails than many other kinds of monkeys. As a result, they don't lose as much body heat into the air. Except for a pink face and a patch of pink skin on the rumps, snow monkeys are covered from head to toe with luxuriously thick reddish-brown and gray fur. The macaques' fur is thickest in the cold months. That's when they grow a special long winter coat, with long whiskers that protect the face. The winter coat is also light in color, helping the monkeys blend with the snow.

This young snow monkey made his own snowball. But the snowball's not for throwing—it's for nibbling on to get a drink of water.

A troop of snow monkeys spends most of the day on the ground, searching for food. During summer they eat fruit, leaves, bamboo shoots, seeds, insects, and, near the seashore, crabs.

The search is much more difficult in winter when plant foods are scarce and there are no insects to be found. The monkeys may dig in the snow to find grass, chew leaf buds or pine needles, and even eat tree bark.

Males act as leaders and guards while the troop searches for food. They lead the troop to food sources, and they keep watch for danger. If a male sees an intruder, he screeches and waves his arms to warn the group. Like other monkeys, Japanese macaques are very social. Youngsters play with each other, and adults and children enjoy grooming each other. At night, the whole troop heads for the trees and sleeps in the branches. In winter, they huddle close together and turn their backs to the cold wind as they try to stay warm through the long night.

Hot-tub happiness: A troop of snow monkeys escapes the frigid winter air by taking a dip in the waters of a hot spring.

Young macaques are born in spring, after the snow is gone. Newborns are tiny—they weigh less than 1 pound (.5 kilograms). At first, the mother monkey holds the baby to her chest as she ambles along on three legs. She's very protective of her new baby and sometimes won't let other monkeys come too near. When the baby is bigger, it will ride on its mother's back, clinging tightly to her fur.

MONKEY SEE, MONKEY DO

In the 1960s, scientists who were studying Japanese macaques decided to help them through winter by providing foods such as sweet potatoes, wheat, and soybeans. That led the scientists to discover what may be the most remarkable trait of the snow monkeys: Individual monkeys can learn new behaviors and then pass on their knowledge to others.

Here are some examples:

● In the mountains of central Honshu, Japan's main island, hot springs rise and form pools. Even in winter, the pools are as warm as a bath. One cold day in 1963, a young female monkey waded into one of these pools to get some soybeans that had fallen in. Mukubili, as the researchers called her, discovered that the hot springs were a great way to escape the cold. Before long other monkeys were following her lead. Today, a good hot soak is part of the daily routine for snow monkeys in this area. Most of the troop piles into the water for 20 to 30 minutes at a time. Youngsters splash and play, while adults relax and warm up.

● On a beach on the small, mountainous island of Koshima, scientists watched as a young female monkey picked up a sweet potato that was covered with sand. The monkey, whom the researchers called Imo, dipped the potato in water to wash it. No one had ever seen a macaque wash food before. But within several months, other members of Imo's band were washing their sweet potatoes, too. Eventually, only the oldest monkeys in the band—those who were already grown when Imo made her discovery—weren't washing their potatoes.

● A few years later, Imo made another discovery. When researchers put wheat on the beach, the wheat kernels often became mixed with sand. One day, Imo tossed a handful of sandy wheat into the water. The sand sank, and the wheat floated. Imo could scoop the clean grain out of the water and eat it. Other macaques soon copied this trick, too. Scientists once thought that only people could pass along knowledge in this way, which is called "cultural transmission." Now they know better. As in these examples, it's usually the young monkeys who try new ways of doing things. Others then copy them, and the new behavior is passed on from one generation to the next. But there are always some older monkeys that, like some people, are too set in their ways to change.

SNOW MONKEYS IN DANGER

Despite their survival skills, snow monkeys are finding life more and more difficult these days. Logging, farming, and development have destroyed forests in many places where they once lived. New highways and ski slopes cut through the remaining woodlands, splitting up the monkeys' territories. The snow monkeys are slowly being squeezed into smaller and smaller sections of forest, and this has put them in conflict with people. When forests don't provide enough food for a troop, the monkeys come down from the mountains and raid farmers' fields and orchards. The farmers don't take this lightly—a band of hungry macaques can devour a season's crops very quickly. In some places, the problem is so bad that farmers have called in hunters and trappers to control the situation and protect their livelihood. Under attack from farmers, with their natural habitat shrinking, snow monkeys may be in danger of dying out. They have already disappeared from some areas

Monkey Tales

The Japanese have always been especially fond of their clever snow monkeys. The monkeys are often portrayed in Japanese art. They were the models for the famous three wise monkeys of Buddhist teachings—the monkeys that "see no evil, hear no evil, speak no evil" (as shown in the photo below).

Snow monkeys also appear as characters in stories and legends, sometimes as comical blunderers and sometimes as helpers. Folk wisdom once held that they would protect children and horses from harm.

There are superstitions about the monkeys, too. Gamblers try never to say the Japanese word for monkey, *saru*. This word also means "go away"—and gamblers are afraid that if they say it, their luck will disappear. For the same reason, monkeys are unwelcome guests at weddings. According to an old superstition, a monkey might make the bride run away!

where they once lived. To ensure the survival of its treasured snow monkeys, Japan will need to protect its mountain forests. Then there will be new hope for these resourceful and adaptable creatures

Everybody needs a buddy—but nobody would expect a grizzly bear weighing 650 pounds (295 kilograms) to team up with a house cat. Nevertheless, **Griz the bear and Cat the cat** are inseparable. Both live at an animal rescue center near Grants Pass, Oregon. Griz was orphaned as a cub and is blind in one eye, so he can't live in the wild. Cat was abandoned at the center as a 6-week-old kitten, in 1995. He was so afraid of people that he wouldn't let the center's staff near him. After roaming loose for several days, he wandered into the bear's enclosure—just as Griz was having lunch. The hungry kitten went right up to the huge bear and begged for food—and, to the complete amazement of the staff, Griz gently placed a piece of chicken in front of him. Now they're best friends. Griz lets Cat ride on his back and swat at his nose, and Cat lets Griz carry him in his mouth, by the scruff of his neck. At night, Cat follows Griz into his den box and sleeps curled up under his bear buddy's chin.

What does it take to be a star? Poise, talent, training, the ability to look great in lots of different outfits. In 1997, a Jack Russell terrier named **Soccer** showed that he had it all. Soccer had the title role on *Wishbone,* a PBS children's television series about a pup who imagines himself as the hero of classic literary tales. The series premiered in late 1995, and each episode features a modern-day story based on the classic one. Playful off camera, Soccer was all business on the set, looking perfectly natural as Robin Hood and Romeo. The little dog kept his cool even when the script called for horseback riding.

Here's a bird that stands out in a crowd. A scientist studying Emperor penguins in Antarctica spotted this **all-white Emperor chick** in December 1996. As a rule, emperor penguins have white bellies and dark heads and backs, with a bit of orange at the throat. This was the first white one ever sighted. The scientist almost missed it—it looked like a lump of snow.

Shown here sitting on a coin the size of a nickel, the newly discovered **"microfrog"** is the tiniest frog in the Northern Hemisphere—and one of the tiniest four-legged creatures anywhere. In 1993, scientists found four of these mini-amphibians living among leaf litter on Monte Iberia in Cuba, which is probably the frogs' only home. Just ⅓ inch (10 millimeters) long when full grown—about the size of a fingernail—the micro just misses setting the record as the world's smallest frog. That honor belongs to an even tinier frog found in Brazil.

This furry, pudgy-faced little animal is another recent discovery. The **Panay cloudrunner** was found in the Philippines, in a remote mountain area on the island of Panay. Like squirrels, cloudrunners live in trees. They sleep during the day and climb around at night, looking for bananas and other fruits. Scientists think they may once have been common in the Philippines. But most of their forest homeland has been cut down, and they are now very rare.

It's exciting to watch wild animals such as gorillas at the zoo. It would be really exciting to go in the pens and walk around with the animals—but that would be much too dangerous. Zoo Atlanta came up with the next best thing in 1997. Visitors to the Georgia park can put on a virtual reality helmet, grasp a joystick, and take a walk through a computer simulation of a gorilla habitat. The simulation was modeled on one of five real habitats at the zoo. Its **virtual gorillas** include a dominant male silverback, lower-ranking males, females, and youngsters. Each gorilla is programmed to respond with a set of typical gorilla behaviors, grunts, and screams. Visitors enter the gorilla band as low-ranking adolescents, and they get firsthand experience in what life in gorilla society is like. They have to be careful—if they walk too close to the cyber-silverback, he may charge! Programmers hope to improve the simulation. They would like to give the gorillas facial expressions and more complex behaviors, such as the ability to play. Eventually, they hope to create simulations of other species habitats, so visitors can stroll with elephants and tigers in a complete virtual zoo.

A standard schnauzer topped some 2,500 entries at the 1997 Westminster Kennel Club Show in New York City. **Champion Parsifal Di Casa Netzer,** who answers to the simple name "Pa," was the first of his breed to win top honors at Westminster, the premier dog show in the United States. But standard schnauzers are an old breed. They date back to the 1400s, when they were used as guard dogs and rat catchers in the castles of German nobility. Pa was bred in Italy and brought to the United States in 1994. He had hundreds of show victories to his credit. Among his rewards for being named top dog at Westminster was one he could really enjoy: a plate of chopped sirloin, served on a silver platter at a New York steak house.

What could be cuter than a baby koala? **Twin baby koalas.** Euca and Lyptus are only the second set of koala twins to survive in captivity. They were born in April 1996 at a preserve in Western Australia. It was an exciting event because, even in the wild, female koalas usually give birth to only one baby every other year. But there wasn't much to see at first. Like all baby koalas, the twins spent several months riding around in their mother's pouch, hidden from view, until they were big and strong enough to venture out. The twins were named for eucalyptus leaves, the favorite food of koalas. Koalas spend most of their lives in eucalyptus trees. As the twins demonstrate here, they are expert climbers.

Here's another reason to enjoy chocolate: The **pink-legged graveteiro,** a bird so rare it wasn't discovered until 1996, lives only in the tall trees that shade cocoa plantations in eastern Brazil. (Cocoa is the source of chocolate.) The bird's name means "twig gatherer" in Portuguese. The graveteiro is a type of ovenbird and, like other ovenbirds, builds an elaborate nest—a domed structure made of twigs, with a long entrance tunnel and sometimes several rooms. It's not surprising that the bird was only found recently. It spends its entire life in the forest canopy, 140 feet (43 meters) above the ground. Brazilians call the bird "acrobata" because it climbs around the treetops like an acrobat, swinging upside down among the leaves as it hunts for insects to eat. But the bird's habitat is threatened. Cocoa production has dropped, and many trees that shaded former plantations have been cut. Conservationists hope to preserve enough forested land to save the species.

SCIENCE

These kids are "wired!" Their third-grade classroom is equipped with computers and hooked up to the worldwide group of computer networks known as the Internet. Schools are rushing to go "on line" and connect up with these computer networks, sending and receiving information over telephone lines. Educators already know that computers are great tools for teaching. Now, with network links to sources of information all over the world, classroom computers are becoming more important than ever.

Yamadano
Japan

The Flower Drum Song
China

Show Ha Mo (Frogs)
China

Hey La La La
China

Leron, Leron, Sinta
Philippines

Atin Cu Pung Singsing
Philippines

Tinikling
Philippines

Kookaburra
Australia

Titi Torea
New Zealand

Ka Mate
New Zealand

Haka
New Zealand

Arabian Nights: Aladdin
Arabia

THE WORLD

A Ram Sam Sam
Morocco

Kum Ba Yah
Africa

Wonto Dwom
Ghana

HALE-BOPP:
THE "WOW" COMET!

Sky watchers were treated to a rare sight in 1997. Comet Hale-Bopp appeared in the night sky for the first time in about 4,200 years. This bright comet—which looked like a big blurry star with a hazy, glowing tail—was visible to the naked eye for several months as it streaked past Earth and swung around the sun.

A visit from a bright comet is always exciting. In 1996, another comet, Hyakutake, came within 9 million miles (15 million kilometers) of Earth. Hale-Bopp was much farther away—122 million miles (196 million kilometers) at its closest. But it was a huge comet, about 25 miles (40 kilometers) across. And it glowed especially brightly in the sky. People in the Northern Hemisphere were treated to the Hale-Bopp sky show in March and April. People in the Southern Hemisphere saw the comet in May and June, on its way back to the edge of the solar system. Thanks to its brightness, Hale-Bopp was one of the most watched and most studied comets ever.

DIRTY SNOWBALLS

Billions of comets orbit the sun, far out on the fringes of the solar system. Out there, they are nothing more than dirty snowballs—dark chunks of ice, rock, and dust, probably left over from the formation of the solar system. But every so often, a comet is tugged by the gravitational pull of a planet or a nearby star. It falls into a new orbit that brings it nearer to the sun.

The sun's heat warms the comet as it approaches. Its ice begins to vaporize, or turn to gas. As the comet gets closer to the sun, more material evaporates from the frozen center, or nucleus. The gases spread out into a hazy cloud called a coma, which together with the nucleus forms the head of the comet. The solar wind, a stream of electrically charged particles emitted by the sun, "blows" some of the dust from the nucleus and gases from the coma into long shimmering tails. The tails may sweep out behind the

Comet Hale-Bopp blazes through the night sky over Arizona.

comet for millions of miles, and they always point away from the sun. We are able to see the comet for two reasons: The solar wind causes the gases to glow, and sunlight is reflected by the dust.

Comets that pass close to the sun follow elliptical orbits—long, narrow ovals. Some comets have fairly short orbits. A speedy little comet called Encke whips around Jupiter and back toward the sun every 3½ years. Halley's comet travels beyond Neptune and orbits the sun every 76 years. It's due to pass by Earth again in 2061. Other comets follow longer orbits, so that thousands of years pass between sightings. Comet Hale-Bopp

was one of those. It last visited Earth when the pharaohs ruled ancient Egypt. Then there's Comet West, six times as bright as Hale-Bopp. Its orbit is so enormous that it won't pass near Earth for another 6.5 million years.

After many trips around the sun, a comet begins to fizzle. Most of its frozen gases have vaporized, so it no longer glows brightly. Often old comets break up into many small fragments, called meteoroids. Sometimes the Earth passes through a group of meteoroids. The fragments burn up as they enter the Earth's atmosphere, creating brief fiery streaks in the sky—a meteor shower.

The Comet Hunters

About a dozen new comets are discovered each year, many by amateur astronomers. Comet hunters search the night sky as a hobby, hoping to be the first to spot a comet. If they are, the comet may be named for them. That's what happened to Alan Hale and Thomas Bopp.

On July 22, 1995, working separately, both men noticed a faint, blurry object in the night sky. Hale, who has a doctorate in astronomy, spotted it while scanning the skies from the driveway of his home in New Mexico, as he often did on clear nights. When he checked his telescope an hour later, the fuzzy dot had moved—a sure sign of a comet. At the same time, in the Arizona desert, Bopp sighted the blurry object through a friend's telescope. An amateur stargazer, he also recognized it as a new comet.

Both astronomers reported their discovery to the Central Bureau for Astronomical Telegrams at Harvard University, which acts as a clearinghouse for new comet sightings. Hale's e-mail message arrived just before Bopp's telegram. But because they saw the comet at the same time, it was named for both of them.

Alan Hale and Thomas Bopp

At the time it was first sighted, Comet Hale-Bopp was farther from Earth than the planet Jupiter. The fact that it could be seen so far away gave scientists their first clue that this was an exceptionally bright comet—and a rare and exciting visitor.

BRIGHT VISITOR

Comet sightings are far more common than you might think. But most comets can be seen only with a telescope. Bright comets like Hale-Bopp are quite rare—only three or four comets a century can be seen easily, and even then few are as bright as Hale-Bopp. Hale-Bopp's nucleus was four times as big as Halley's comet, and as it neared the sun it spewed out 40 times as much dust. "It's a WOW comet," one astronomer said.

Naturally, Hale-Bopp's visit was a great event. Even over cities, where artificial light makes stargazing difficult, it could be seen easily without a telescope. Still, many people used binoculars or telescopes just to get a better look. Others lined up for a chance to peer through more powerful telescopes at schools and colleges. Although the comet was actually speeding toward the sun at 27 miles (44 kilometers) per second, it seemed to stand still in the night sky.

Scientists hoped that Comet Hale-Bopp would answer many questions about comets and even about the origins of the solar system 4.5 billion years ago. Of all the objects in the solar system, comets have probably changed least. Thus, they may hold clues to the materials that were present when the sun and the solar system formed.

To learn what Hale-Bopp was made of, scientists used instruments called spectroscopes and spectrographs, which analyzed the light from the comet. In this way, they were able to identify various chemical elements. They found substances they expected, including lots of water vapor, and some they didn't, including unusual carbon molecules and chemical compounds. Some of their findings seemed to support the idea that the chemical building blocks of life might have been carried to Earth on comets.

Hale-Bopp produced another surprise. Scientists have long known that most comets have two tails. A bright, narrow tail of gases stretches straight out behind the comet. A wide, even brighter tail of dust flares out at a slightly different angle. On clear nights, Hale-Bopp's dust and gas tails could be seen even without a telescope. But when scientists trained their spectroscopes on the comet, they discovered that it had a *third* tail, formed entirely of sodium atoms. A sodium tail had never been observed before.

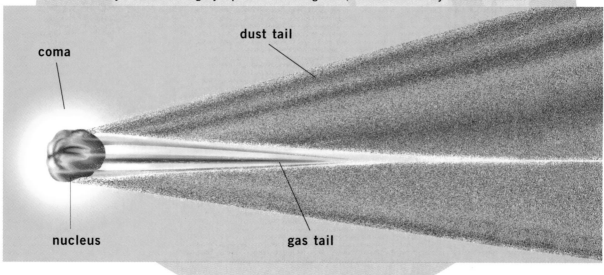

Most comets are made up of a nucleus, a coma, and two tails (as shown in this diagram). The nucleus, consisting of chunks of ice, rock, and dust, is the solid center of the comet. As the comet approaches the sun, some of the ice vaporizes, or turns to gas. The gases spread out into a hazy cloud surrounding the nucleus, called the coma. The solar wind "blows" some of the gases and dust from the nucleus and coma into long tails: a narrow gas tail and a wide dust tail. Scientists studying Hale-Bopp were surprised to discover that it had a third tail—a nearly invisible one slightly separated from the gas tail, and formed entirely of sodium atoms.

coma

dust tail

nucleus

gas tail

Comet Tales

Before people knew much about astronomy, comets amazed and frightened them. The sudden appearance of a new "star" in the sky was thought to mean certain disaster. The ancient Chinese thought comets were "broom stars," used by the gods to sweep evil from the heavens. The evil then fell to Earth, bringing misfortune. In other times and places, comets were linked to the assassination of the Roman ruler Julius Caesar, the fall of Jerusalem to Roman armies in A.D. 70, the Norman conquest of England in 1066, and the fall of Constantinople to the Turks in 1453.

In the 1700s, the English astronomer Edmund Halley proved that comets orbit the sun. He did this by correctly predicting the return of the comet that now bears his name. But that didn't stop people from worrying about comets. In 1910, after astronomers announced that Earth would pass through the tail of Halley's comet, people rushed out to buy gas masks and "comet pills" for protection.

Even in 1997, wild stories circulated about Comet Hale-Bopp. The comet was said to fit an ancient Hopi prophesy, in which the appearance of a "yellow star" signals the "end of time." Some people thought Hale-Bopp fit a similar prophesy in the biblical book of Revelation. Still others claimed that the comet was being shadowed by an alien spaceship four times the size of Earth.

As Hale-Bopp headed back out to the edge of the solar system, these wild rumors disappeared with it. But most probably, the next time a comet appears in the night sky, old superstitions will spring to life again.

Hale-Bopp's visit seemed to raise as many questions as it answered. Scientists will be analyzing and discussing the information they collected for years to come. They'll also be gearing up for the next close encounter with a comet. Comet Wild-2 is expected to pass near Earth in 2004. Researchers hope to send up a spacecraft that will capture particles from that comet's tail and bring them back to Earth.

GARLIC, GLORIOUS GARLIC!

Would you ever wear a garlic necklace? In medieval Europe, some people did—and they didn't do it to make a fashion statement. Hundreds of years ago, people thought that this flavorful herb had magical powers, and they wore cloves of garlic around their necks to ward off vampires!

Today that belief survives only in Hollywood horror movies. No one wears garlic. But as a food, garlic is more popular than ever. In fact, a sort of garlic craze is sweeping North America. Garlic has long been used to add robust flavor to all sorts of dishes—soups, stews, sauces, and more. Now it's gaining new respect as a food that may help people stay healthy.

THE "STINKING ROSE"

Garlic is a close relative of onions, chives, and leeks. All these plants are members of the lily family. The garlic plant grows from an underground bulb, and it's the bulb that's used in cooking. Each bulb is made up of a number of individual pieces called cloves. There are ten to twelve cloves in an average bulb, each enclosed in papery skin that must be peeled off. Mincing or crushing a garlic clove releases oils that carry the familiar garlicky scent and taste. It doesn't take much garlic to enhance food—this plant's odor and flavor make it by far the most pungent member of its family. In fact, garlic is sometimes called the "stinking rose."

Garlic was one of the first cultivated plants. Ancient records show that people were growing it as long as 5,000 years ago. The plant probably originated in Siberia. From there it spread around the world. And from the beginning, it seems, people believed that garlic had special powers.

In ancient Egypt, garlic was thought to cure heart disease, bites, worms, tumors, and headaches. According to one story, laborers who built the Egyptian pyramids refused to work without a daily ration of garlic. In ancient Greece, athletes ate garlic to increase their strength. In ancient Rome, soldiers ate

The Gilroy Garlic Festival

More than 90 percent of the U.S. garlic crop is grown in California. And no place grows more garlic than the California town of Gilroy. Gilroy is so proud of this, it has proclaimed itself the garlic capital of the world. Each July since 1979, the town has thrown a party—the Gilroy Garlic Festival—for its favorite product. Drawn by the love of garlic, as many as 135,000 people travel to Gilroy for the annual festival.

Attractions at the garlic festival include bands, jugglers, and balloon rides. Booths sell garlic remedies and crafts and clothing with garlic motifs. There's a contest for the best garlic recipe and a pageant in which a Miss Garlic is chosen. But the main reason people go to the festival is to smell and eat garlic. Garlic sausage, snails in garlic butter, spaghetti with garlic sauce, garlic-stuffed mushrooms, pickled garlic, roasted garlic—visitors can feast on these and many other garlicky gourmet treats at more than 90 food booths. Over the festival's three days, garlic lovers gobble up more than a ton of their favorite treat.

it to increase their courage. They also rubbed it on their bodies to ward off illness. (Perhaps the smell of garlic drove off their enemies, too.) In ancient China, garlic was used to fight infections and heart disease.

Garlic was considered a cure-all in medieval Europe, and it was widely used by peasants. An English herbal published in the 1650s claimed that garlic would heal dog bites and snakebites, cure plagues and ulcers, clear chest congestion, and rid children of worms. Two hundred years later, in 1858, the chemist Louis Pasteur discovered that garlic could kill bacteria, microscopic organisms that can cause disease. Scientists began to wonder: Could there be a kernel of truth in the old claims about garlic's medicinal powers?

CRAZY FOR GARLIC

In North America, garlic's popularity has been steadily growing since the 1980s. This is partly the result of a food trend. More North Americans are interested in new foods, especially foods that are strongly seasoned with herbs and spices. They're enjoying pestos, salsas, and other garlicky dishes from Italy, Mexico, and Asian countries. In 1975, the average American ate about ½ pound (0.2 kilograms) of garlic a year. By 1994, the amount had jumped to more than 1½ pounds (0.7 kilograms). U.S. farmers grow almost

People long thought that garlic had magical powers. One of the most enduring legends about the herb was the belief that its pungent odor could keep vampires away.

500 million pounds (226 million kilograms) of garlic each year to meet the demand—and even so, more garlic is imported. In Canada, where most garlic is imported, more farmers have begun to plant this popular food crop.

More than taste is behind the surge in garlic consumption. There's growing evidence that garlic is good for you. New research suggests that garlic actually *may* help fight infections, just as people in ancient and medieval times believed. Scientists are studying chemicals in garlic that can kill disease-causing bacteria in the lab. These are some of the same chemicals that give garlic its odor and strong taste, and they are enhanced, not destroyed, by cooking. Do they really act to fight disease inside the human body? Some scientists think so, and they're trying to confirm that hunch through research.

In addition, garlic seems to help lower blood levels of cholesterol, a fatty substance that's linked to heart disease. It may also help lower blood pressure and prevent blood clots from forming, thus reducing the risk of strokes as well as heart disease. Scientists also want to investigate some other reported benefits of garlic—that the herb may ease arthritis and improve memory, for example. Researchers are also trying to figure out if garlic can even help prevent cancer. They have noticed that

Delicious Garlic Bread

Garlic bread is an easy—and delicious—way to enjoy the flavor of this herb. Here's what you need:

- 1 loaf of French or Italian bread
- ¼ pound of butter or margarine, softened
- 2 cloves of garlic
  knife
  aluminum foil

1. Remove the papery skin from the garlic cloves.
2. Carefully chop the cloves. The smaller the pieces, the better.
3. Mix the chopped garlic with the butter or margarine. Let this mixture stand at room temperature for about half an hour.
4. Preheat the oven to 350°F.
5. Cut the bread lengthwise. Spread the butter-garlic mixture on the inside of both the top and bottom halves. If you wish, you can also sprinkle grated Parmesan cheese and a little paprika on the bread.

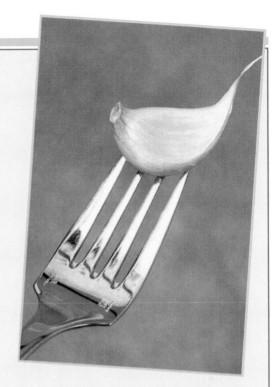

6. Put the two halves back together, and slice the loaf into serving pieces.
7. Wrap the bread in aluminum foil, being sure to seal it completely.
8. Put the bread in the oven for about 15 minutes. Serve it warm.

fewer people get stomach or colon cancer in areas where garlic is often found on the menu.

TAKE TWO CLOVES. . .

Scientists are sure to learn more about the health benefits of garlic in years to come. Meanwhile, many people have already decided that eating garlic is an easy, and tasty, way to stay healthy. But how much garlic should you eat? Scientists don't agree. Some suggest a clove a day; others recommend as much as five or six cloves daily. That's a lot, even for garlic lovers.

Eating lots of garlic can have some pretty negative effects. For one thing, it does terrible things to your breath. It's almost impossible to eat garlic without ending up with garlic breath. You can reduce bad breath by chewing a sprig of parsley sprinkled with lemon juice or eating strawberries right after you eat garlic, but that's not often convenient. And garlic, especially raw garlic, can irritate the stomach. For that reason, you should always eat it as part of a meal that includes other foods.

Many people take garlic supplements—capsules filled with garlic oil, and tablets made from dried garlic. The supplements, which vary in strength, are popular, and they're sold in supermarkets, pharmacies, and health-food stores. They leave less odor on the breath, but they're more expensive than either fresh garlic or garlic powder (a bottled seasoning that's made from dried garlic).

And, of course, taking a supplement doesn't give you a chance to enjoy the delicious flavor and aroma of fresh garlic. For true garlic lovers, good taste and good health go hand in hand.

Science fiction come to life: Dolly—the first clone (exact copy) of an adult mammal.

HELLO, DOLLY

She didn't look special. She was just a little woolly lamb, like any other in the flock. But the lamb named Dolly caused an international uproar in 1997. Unlike other lambs, Dolly didn't result from a mating between a ram and a ewe. She was a clone (an exact copy), and she was the first clone ever created from an adult animal.

Dolly was cloned by a team of scientists in Edinburgh, Scotland. Until they announced their success in February 1997, most people—even most scientists—didn't think an adult animal could be cloned. Dolly's birth thus marked an exciting new threshold for science.

It also created controversy because it raised some troubling questions. If scientists could clone sheep, could they also clone humans? Should research into cloning humans be allowed?

SHEEP COPY

New scientific knowledge made Dolly possible. In recent years, scientists have discovered a lot about heredity and the ways in which cells function. At the same time, new laboratory methods have allowed them to manipulate microscopic structures inside cells. Among those structures are genes, chains of chemical DNA that act like coded instructions. Genes determine whether an animal is a bat or a bird, whether a bird is a hawk or a robin, and whether your eyes are blue or brown. Genes are arranged in strings called chromosomes inside the nucleus of each body cell. And every cell in an adult animal carries a full set of genes, a complete blueprint for all the traits of an individual.

Normally, a lamb gets half its genes from each of its parents. That's true for all creatures that reproduce sexually. A sperm cell from the male fuses with an egg cell from the female, and their genetic material is combined. Then the fertilized egg begins to divide, forming a many-celled embryo. As the embryo continues to grow, the cells "differentiate"; that is, they take on different properties. Some become muscle cells, some nerve cells, some bone cells, and so on. The offspring that results is unique—like both parents, but not identical to either.

A clone, in contrast, has only one "parent." The clone grows from a single cell, with no mating and no mixing of genetic material. It's identical in every way to its parent. With the exception of certain invertebrates, animals don't reproduce this way in nature. And until recent times, no one thought that clones could be created by people. The first cloning experiments were done with frogs in

The Birth of Dolly

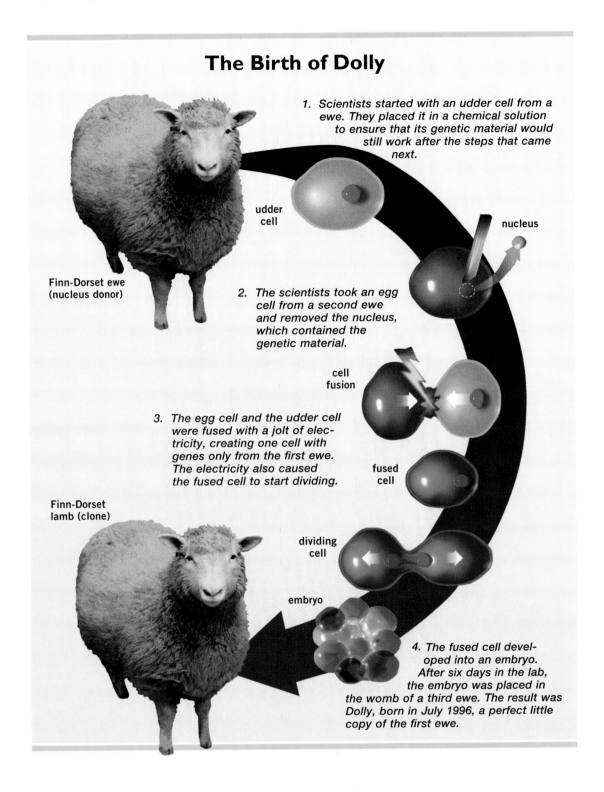

1. Scientists started with an udder cell from a ewe. They placed it in a chemical solution to ensure that its genetic material would still work after the steps that came next.

udder cell

nucleus

Finn-Dorset ewe (nucleus donor)

2. The scientists took an egg cell from a second ewe and removed the nucleus, which contained the genetic material.

cell fusion

3. The egg cell and the udder cell were fused with a jolt of electricity, creating one cell with genes only from the first ewe. The electricity also caused the fused cell to start dividing.

fused cell

Finn-Dorset lamb (clone)

dividing cell

embryo

4. The fused cell developed into an embryo. After six days in the lab, the embryo was placed in the womb of a third ewe. The result was Dolly, born in July 1996, a perfect little copy of the first ewe.

the 1950s, and they failed. In the 1970s, scientists had better luck with frogs, but the clones didn't develop past the tadpole stage.

In the 1980s, researchers came up with a cloning method that seemed to work. They started with a cell taken from a sheep embryo at an early stage, before the embryo's cells started to differentiate. They took the nucleus from this cell, and transferred it into an egg cell of an adult sheep. That cell then began to develop into a new embryo. Implanted in another sheep that served as a surrogate mother, this embryo developed into a lamb—a perfect clone of the original.

This method worked well with other mammals, too—cattle, goats, pigs, rabbits, even rhesus monkeys. But it worked only when cells were taken from embryos at very early stages of development. Scientists thought that adult cells couldn't be cloned, because the cells had differentiated and most of the genetic code they carried was switched off.

Dolly proved them wrong. Ian Wilmut, a British scientist, led the team of researchers who cloned her. They began with a single cell, with the genetic material intact, taken from the udder of a six-year-old Finn-Dorset ewe. Then they obtained an egg cell from a Scottish blackface ewe and removed its nucleus, which contained the blackface's genes. They used a pulse of electricity to fuse the two cells. The fused cell carried only genes from the Finn-Dorset ewe, and it began to grow into an embryo. The embryo was transferred to another blackface ewe.

Down on the Pharm

In July, the same team of British scientists that cloned Dolly announced the birth of another remarkable lamb, Polly. Like Dolly, Polly was a clone. But she was special in yet another way: She was a product of genetic engineering, and she was the first cloned animal whose cells contained human genes. This was the first time that the technique of cloning had been used in combination with genetic engineering, in which scientists actually change the genetic code inside a cell.

Polly started with a sheep embryo cell. In the laboratory, the scientists grafted a human gene onto the sheep DNA in this cell. Then they fused the embryo cell with an egg cell, just as they had done in creating Dolly. The fused cell developed into an embryo and then into a lamb—Polly (shown here with her surrogate mother). The researchers created four other lambs through the same method.

Why put human genes in a sheep? The genes that the scientists insert prompt the animals to produce certain key proteins and chemicals in their milk—substances that can be extracted and used as medicines. By combining gene transfer (also called transgenics) and cloning, scientists hope they'll one day be able to produce herds of animals that can turn out limitless quantities of human medicines, or pharmaceuticals. They've even coined a term for this high-tech agriculture—"pharming."

Using embryo cells, scientists cloned this pair of Rhesus monkeys (named Neti and Ditto)—the first time a species so close to humans was cloned.

Five months later, in July 1996, a lamb that was genetically identical to the original Finn-Dorset was born. She was named Dolly—for the country singer Dolly Parton. She was a perfect little copy of the adult sheep, just six years younger.

THE DOLLY DEBATE

Dolly's birth was kept secret for months, while the scientists obtained a patent for the process they used. When the news was finally released, it made headlines worldwide. The little sheep was shown on television, and her picture was on the front pages of newspapers everywhere. Reporters rushed to interview the scientists who had created her.

The scientists explained that their goal went beyond simply creating clones. They hoped to combine cloning with techniques of genetic engineering, to create animals with special traits that would be useful in agriculture or in human medicine. The cloning method used to create Dolly was far from perfect, they acknowledged. They had tried it unsuccessfully 276 times before they succeeded.

Other scientists immediately set about trying to duplicate the work that led to Dolly. That's one of the ways that scientists test results. If it turned out that the method worked reliably, chances seemed good that one day it could be used to clone any adult animal—even humans. Suddenly cloning—a subject that had seemed like science fiction—was the focus of serious debate. And the debate heated up when scientists in Oregon announced that they had cloned rhesus monkeys, using embryo cells. It was the first time a species so close to humans had been cloned.

Many people were alarmed by the possibility that humans might be cloned sometime in the future. The idea raised lots of questions. What would the world be like if people were no longer individuals, each one of a kind? What if there were a dozen, or a thousand, people exactly like you? What if your mother was actually your "original" and thus also your twin? Who would decide which people would be cloned? What standards would be used? What if anyone—even criminals and dictators—could order clones of themselves?

With unanswered questions like these in the air, it wasn't surprising that people were concerned. Polls showed that more than 85 percent of Americans opposed human cloning. The U.S. government announced that it wouldn't fund human cloning research. Some people urged government leaders to ban human cloning. And a government commission agreed that such a ban should be imposed.

If humans are ever cloned, scientists agree, it won't happen for many years. But with or without government funding or approval, whether the world is ready or not, research into cloning seems certain to go forward. The little sheep named Dolly brought the world into a new era in 1997—the era of clones.

Schools across North America are getting hooked up to the world with computers—making classroom walls disappear.

"WIRED" TO THE WORLD

The fourth grade is visiting the White House. Fifth graders are chatting with some new friends—in Italy. Sixth graders are collecting pictures, sounds, and information for a report on endangered animals. A seventh-grade science class is discussing the results of an experiment with a professor at a university hundreds of miles away.

All these activities are taking place right in the classroom. This school is "wired"—it's linked to the worldwide assembly of computer networks known as the Internet. Computers are opening up new worlds for kids in school. And with network links, the possibilities seem almost endless.

Schools across North America are rushing to install classroom computers and go "on line," connecting with computer networks by sending and receiving information over telephone lines. According to one survey, by 1997 more than 80 percent of U.S. elementary and high-school students were using computers in school, and 60 percent had access to the Internet. President Bill Clinton made it a goal of his administration to connect all the nation's schools to the Internet by the year 2000. Similar efforts are underway in Canada, where about half the public schools are linked to the Internet and to each other through a program called SchoolNet.

Computerizing classrooms is a big job, and it costs a lot of money. Some states have earmarked hundreds of millions of dollars for the task. In many schools, businesses have donated or offered discounts on personal computers (PC's) and other equipment, and volunteers have pitched in to install them. California has one of the biggest volunteer programs. On March 9, 1996—dubbed NetDay—more than 20,000 volunteers laid 6 million feet

(1.8 million meters) of cable to wire schools there. President Clinton and Vice President Al Gore came to help. The program was so successful that more NetDays were scheduled in California, as well as in other states.

But wiring schools is just the first step. Once computers are installed and on line, how are they being used?

COMPUTERS IN THE CLASSROOM

Computers have much to offer in the classroom. With self-help programs that let students learn at their own speed, computers can help teach math, reading, science, and just about any other subject. These programs are especially helpful for special education and for disabled students. With encyclopedias and other reference works on CD-ROM, computers also become reference tools. And word-processing programs help students create polished reports.

Linked to the Internet, computers open the door to countless new uses in the schoolroom. Kids who are researching a report, for example, can browse library collections all over the country—or all over the world. They can get in touch with organizations, government agencies, and businesses that provide information. And they can tap into computer databases—huge collections of information stored by computers. From the World Wide Web, a section of the Internet that includes lots of graphics, they can view pictures as well as read text. They can use their computers to combine pictures and text and create multimedia reports.

On-line discussion groups and electronic mail, or e-mail (messages sent over computer networks), give students a chance to "chat" with young people in distant places, even in

A Rat in the Wall!

Linking a school to the Internet is a difficult task. Wires and cables must be run to every classroom that's connected; and they must be run right through existing walls, floors, and ceilings. How can it be done without tearing the school apart? One way is to call Rattie!

Rattie (shown at right) is a female white rat that's been trained by Judy Reavis, an executive at a California company that brings new technology to schools. Reavis taught the rat to run through PVC pipe, which is often used to hold wires and cables in walls. Rattie also learned to squeeze through insulation, chicken wire, even gaps between boards and concrete blocks—whatever she might find inside a wall.

When Rattie wires a school, she wears a special type of harness. A string is attached to the harness, and cable is attached to the string. The rat runs through the wall or ceiling where the cable is needed, while the trainer taps on the surface to let her know where to go. When Rattie finally comes out at the other end, volunteers pull the string to feed the cable through the space. Then Rattie gets a well-deserved reward. Green Gummy Bears are her favorite treat.

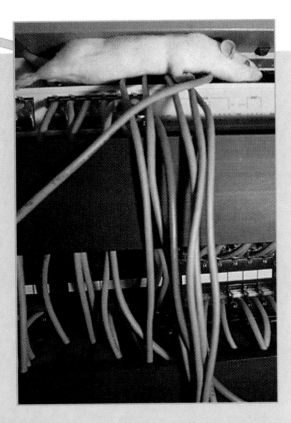

By mid-1997, Rattie had wired eight schools and was becoming something of a celebrity. Reavis began training an understudy for her star rat, Rattie Junior. And she was getting many inquries from schools that wanted to train their own rat wirers.

Students in North East, Maryland, use computers to study the decline of oysters in Chesapeake Bay.

other countries. They can exchange greetings and ideas. Students may also confer on line with experts on subjects that they are studying. They can also take electronic "field trips" to museums and famous places, such as the Eiffel Tower in Paris, by visiting sites on the Web.

Here are a few examples of other ways schools are using their computers:

• In North East, Maryland, biology students are using computers to analyze a serious problem in their region: the health of oyster beds in Chesapeake Bay. They use a program designed by their teacher to study the declining numbers of oysters and to search for reasons for the decline. The program has animation and video clips. But at its core are statistics that let the students analyze everything from oxygen levels to pollutants.

• High-school seniors link up and learn negotiating skills in a project developed by the University of Connecticut. The Connecticut Project in International Negotiation is a sort of model United Nations. Schools all around the United States take part, each representing a different country. E-mail messages flash back and forth for six weeks, as they hash out issues such as arms control, drug trafficking, human rights, and environmental protection. The students have to do lots of research, on and off the computer, to learn about the issues and about the countries they represent.

• In Casper, Wyoming, high-school students can enter a Roman villa, an Egyptian pyramid, even a living cell—all through virtual reality. In the school computer lab, students learn to write programs (instructions for the computer) that create virtual "worlds," which exist only on the computer. First, they draw objects, by plotting points on the screen. Then they use mathematical formulas to give the drawing depth and dimension. The computer uses this information to figure out how the object will look from various angles. To enter the virtual world, the students use 3-D goggles, a joy stick, and a PowerGlove, a device that lets them control the computer images with hand movements. They can reach out to "touch" an image, for example, and it will change or turn.

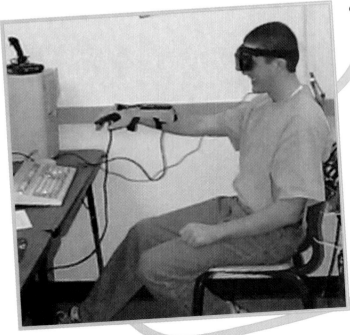

Wearing 3-D goggles and a PowerGlove, a student in Casper, Wyoming, explores a virtual "world" that exists only on the computer.

- In Tenafly, New Jersey, students took samples from a local pond and studied them to find out what kinds of microscopic creatures lived in the water. Then they exchanged their information, via computer, with students in Akita, Japan, who were studying samples from a river in their town. The results? Similar microorganisms were found in both places. More important, the students had a chance to share their experiences with kids in a completely different part of the world.

- Virtual High is a private school in Vancouver, Canada, that relies almost entirely on computer links. The founders of this institution prefer to think of it as a "learning center" rather than a school because there are no traditional classes and teachers. Nearly all the 35 students have their own PC's. They work with staff members on site, and with dozens of specialists in every subject on line.

- A San Francisco, California, high school found a new use for some outdated PC's that were donated by local businesses. The computers became key equipment in a class on robotics. Students in this class learn to write programs that control robots put together from Lego blocks. If they make a mistake in the program, they see the results right away—the robot does something bizarre.

FAD OR FABULOUS?

Some parents and educators are worried by the growing use of computers in schools. Computers are exciting, they say, but they may be only an educational fad. Computer technology accounts for a growing share of school budgets. School budgets are tight—and when money is spent on computers, there's less available for books and other basics. And no one knows if kids will really learn more from computers.

Critics say that flashy multimedia presentations don't teach students to think logically and critically. There are other problems: The Internet has lots of information, but a great deal of the information that's posted is misleading, incomplete, or just plain wrong. And spending hours in front of a computer limits the time kids spend with each other. That means they're less likely to develop good social skills.

Still, most educators like the idea of wired schools. Kids love computers—they're fun and entertaining, and students who use them in school get involved with their studies. At

San Francisco students use computers to program robots built from Lego blocks.

one junior high in Newfoundland, Canada, absentee rates dropped 40 percent after computers were installed. In most schools, students team up and work on computers in groups, so they still have opportunities to interact with their classmates. And they have new opportunities to interact with other students around the world on the Internet.

The key to making wired schools work, educators agree, is creativity. Classroom computers are wasted when they're only used for skill drills. But when teachers and students use them to solve problems and expand horizons, they can make classroom walls disappear.

A visitor to a tropical rain forest enters a mysterious emerald world teeming with plant and animal life. Yet these vital forests are in danger of vanishing forever—and taking their secrets with them.

NATURE'S VANISHING RAIN FORESTS

Enter the dim, green world of the tropical rain forest. As you walk down the forest trail, huge trees surround you. Tropical vines hang from their limbs, and far above you their leafy branches form a rooflike canopy that blocks out the sun. The air is warm, damp, and heavy.

High in the treetops, you hear the calls of howler monkeys and parrots and other exotic birds. But on the forest floor, you see few signs of life. Every so often you hear a soft rustle as a toad or some other small creature hops away, startled by your footsteps. And now and then you spot a brilliant blue butterfly fluttering through the dim light. Be careful to stay on the trail—the tree trunks look so much alike that it's easy to get lost. And keep your eyes open for snakes.

Tropical rain forests like the one you have entered cover a narrow band of the Earth near the equator. They are found in Africa, South and Central America, Asia, and Oceania. (The world's largest rain forest is around the Amazon River, in Brazil.) They get their name from the fact that it rains there almost every day, which also accounts for the heavy, damp air. And, although you may see few animals as you walk along the forest floor, rain forests actually teem with life. More than a third of the world's animal and plant species live there—and nowhere else on Earth. Scientists believe that the tropical habitat is home to many other species that haven't even been discovered yet.

But the rain forests are disappearing at an alarming rate:

The passion flower is an exotic rain-forest plant.

More than 50 acres (20 hectares) of forest are cut every minute, as people take the trees for lumber and the land for farms, roads, and other types of development. Thus scientists are rushing to study these exotic living laboratories before they vanish. And conservationists are working on plans to save as much of the rain forests as they can.

THE RAIN-FOREST FLOOR

Tropical rain forests are one of the world's last great wilderness areas. Few people live in them, and many regions of the forests have never been explored. The forests took centuries to develop—some of the tropical trees that now tower hundreds of feet above the ground were saplings when Columbus sailed to the New World. Unlike northern forests, where you will see many trees of the same species grouped together in clumps and stands, the tropical rain forest contains a seemingly endless variety of different types of trees.

The dense shade cast by the canopy of the treetops means that there's no tangle of underbrush on the forest floor—without sunlight, plants can't grow. Instead, just a few species of ferns and similar plants survive in the open spaces between the tree trunks. Some trees have huge "buttress" roots that flare out from the trunks 20 feet (6 meters) above the ground. The roots extend down into the soil, and scientists think they help anchor the trees in the thin leaf mold that carpets the forest floor.

A Hidden Habitat

The rain-forest canopy is a hidden habitat. Scientists who study it face special risks and problems in their work. The first problem is getting up to the treetops.

Climbing the trees isn't a good solution—snakes and scorpions lie in wait along the branches. Some researchers build towers up to treetop level. Others use "cherrypickers"—the mechanical lifts often used in tree work and fruit harvesting. Some are lowered into the trees from helicopters or dirigibles. And some hoist themselves up with ropes and pulleys. Researchers in Panama survey the canopy from a gondola that hangs from a giant construction crane (right).

Once aloft, researchers construct platforms in the trees, linked by rope bridges that run from one tree to the next. This allows them to observe canopy life firsthand. A scientist working in Costa Rica uses a different method. He glides along a network of steel cables, wearing a harness that clips to the cables. He also developed a sort of canopy cable car that runs through the trees.

It's dangerous up in the canopy. Violent storms can uproot the trees, and there's always the risk of a fall. Still, dedicated researchers continue to climb into the canopy, to see firsthand one of the least-studied habitats on Earth.

Medicine from the Rain Forest

Some scientists believe that the rain forests hold life-saving secrets—plants that could provide cures for diseases such as cancer and AIDS. Plants have been an important source of medicines since ancient times. Today about 25 percent of prescription medicines originally came from plants, and many of those plants grow in the tropical rain forests. Extracts made from plants can be powerful drugs—in fact, many plant extracts can be poisonous. But in the right formulas, and the right amount, they can also heal.

To unlock the secret of rain-forest plants, scientists called ethnobotanists are turning to native people who have lived in the forests for generations. The forest has provided these people with food, with shelter—and with medicine, from plants that cure their infections and help heal their wounds. To find out which plants work best in curing disease, the scientists work alongside traditional healers deep in the rain forest. They collect samples of plants and learn the ancient lore that tells which plants heal certain illnesses. Then the scientists return to their laboratories, to analyze their samples and, they hope, find plant chemicals that act against disease. These scientists have an important mission. Their work may save not only the rain forest, but countless lives as well.

The soil of the floor isn't rich, and some trees and plants have developed other ways of getting the nutrients they need. For example, special types of fungi grow around the tree roots and help the trees break down the few nutrients that the soil does contain. And some trees have developed above-ground roots that trap water and minerals in the air. The soil is so poor, in fact, that when land has been cleared for farming, people often find that it will support crops for only a year or two.

Sometimes there's a break in the canopy because a tree has fallen, or because a stream has cut its way through the forest. Then sunlight can enter, and the forest produces a riot of vines, shrubs, and flowering plants. Animals congregate in these spots, too—monkeys, iridescent butterflies, and brightly colored birds such as parrots, toucans, and orioles. In the South American forests, there are brilliant red and blue dart-poison frogs, whose bright colors warn predators of the deadly poison secreted by their skin. And always, there are snakes that hang like vines from tree limbs.

Forest streams also teem with life. In many places, there are strange species of fish. In the forests around the Amazon, for example, one type of fish has flat-topped teeth like those found in cows and other grazing animals. The teeth have a purpose—for two to four months a year, when the Amazon's waters are high, the river spills over its banks and floods the forest floor. Then the fish can swim out through the forest and eat the seeds, fruit, and nuts that they find there. Other fish have the remarkable ability to breathe air during the brief dry seasons when forest ponds shrink. They do this through a special collection of blood vessels in their foreheads. These vessels work much like human lungs, pumping oxygen directly into the bloodstream.

One reason you see so few signs of life as you walk through the forest is that many of the animals are nocturnal—they sleep during the day and come out to hunt for food at night. But the biggest reason is that most of the life of the forest is found far above the ground, in the treetop canopy.

Macaws, the largest of the parrots, sparkle like jewels in this Peruvian rain forest. The birds dwell high in the rain-forest canopy, feeding on fruits and nuts that they crack with their powerful beaks.

THE TREETOP CANOPY

The rain-forest canopy is a completely different world. Here, in the sunlight 50 to 200 feet (15 to 60 meters) above the ground, the huge trees send out massive horizontal branches. And they support an almost endless variety of life forms—from birds, bats, and butterflies to mice, monkeys, and countless other, more exotic animals. Many of the creatures that live here spend their entire lives in the treetops, rarely or never setting foot on the ground.

The key to life high above the ground is interdependence: The plants and animals of the canopy depend on each other to stay alive. For example, a strange plant called the trashbasket plant anchors itself to tree limbs. It traps debris that falls from higher in the canopy and turns this material

A red-eyed leaf frog clings to a spiky-topped bromeliad. These rain-forest plants trap water in their leaves, becoming an ideal nursery for tadpoles and baby frogs.

into nutrient-rich humus. The humus supports not only the plant but also insects like earthworms and centipedes.

Many other plants grow in the treetops, too. Most of these are epiphytes—plants that grow on tree limbs and take the moisture and nutrients they need from the air rather than from the soil. There are countless epiphytic varieties of orchids, mosses, lichens, and ferns. One epiphyte, a spiky-topped plant called the bromeliad, helps nurture baby frogs. The leaves of this plant trap water, and tree frogs place their eggs there. When the eggs hatch, the tadpoles can swim about in the water caught by the plant.

A few of the mightiest trees depend on single species of insects to reproduce. The flower of the Brazil nut, for example, is so tightly closed that only one bee, the carpenter bee, is able to open it. Without this bee, the flowers couldn't be pollinated, and no

117

Using its strong limbs and long tail for balance, the raccoonlike coati skillfully scampers among the treetops of a rain forest in Costa Rica.

follow army ants as they march across the floor looking for food. The birds eat insects that the army ants flush out, and they in turn are followed by butterflies that feed on their droppings.

One of the best-known treetop dwellers is the sloth—a mammal that hangs upside-down from the tree limbs and sleeps most of the time. More than twenty species of insects, including several moths and beetles, live in the sloth's furry coat. A type of algae also grows on the coat, giving the animal a greenish tint that helps it stay camouflaged among the leaves.

Like other tree-living animals, the sloth is specially adapted to its home: It has long limbs and grasping hands that help it reach and hold vines and tree branches, and its eyes are positioned looking forward, for good depth perception. The many species of monkeys that live in the canopy also have these traits. Treetop animals seem to share still another trait—intelligence. Parrots, which are said to be among the smartest of birds, live in the rain-forest canopy. And the coati, a raccoonlike animal that also lives in the treetops, uses basic reasoning to get its food, much as a chimpanzee does.

seeds would be produced. Most of the many species of tropical fig trees in the rain forest depend on tiny fig wasps for pollination. The wasps in turn lay their eggs in the tree's fruit.

Some species of insects also depend on each other. In South America, for example, wasps bore holes in the long hanging nests of Azteca ants. The Azteca ants then protect the wasps from their main predators, the army ants. And the stinging wasps in turn protect the Azteca ants from anteaters that climb into the trees in search of food.

Sometimes the chain of interdependence extends back down to the forest floor. Several species of birds, for example,

THE FUTURE OF THE RAIN FORESTS

It seems likely that as more acres of forest are cut, many of the rain-forest plants and animals will become extinct. This is because so many of these plants and animals depend

A hungry rhinoceros hornbill feasts on the fruit of a strangler fig tree in a lowland rain forest in Borneo.

High schoolers taking part in the Forman Rain Forest Project try to calculate how fast a basilisk lizard runs across the water.

The Ultimate Field Trip

Your science class is studying ecology and the environment. As part of the course, you'll be making a field trip to a nature preserve. Ho hum? Not when the nature preserve is a slice of rain forest in Central America or the Amazon Basin.

Kids have been in the forefront of efforts to preserve the world's tropical rain forests. And as travel and tourism in rain-forest areas has increased, more kids have had the opportunity to visit them. High schools in particular are combining classroom studies of ecology with field trips that let students observe for themselves the variety of plants and animals they contain.

One such program is the Forman Rain Forest Project, in Connecticut. In 1997, eleven high-school students traveled to a preserve in Costa Rica as part of this program. For two weeks, they studied rare plants and wildlife—including dart-poison frogs, scorpions, stinging ants, and basilisk lizards, which can run across water. When they returned home, they shared their experiences with scientists and with other schools nationwide. Programs like this are exciting. They are helping to create a new generation of scientists—scientists who may solve the problem of the endangered rain forests.

closely on each other. Yet the outlook for saving the forests isn't good. Most of the forests are in developing countries that badly need both farmland and the income from lumber that cutting the forests provides.

But there are ways in which the uncut forests can provide income. Brazil nuts already are an important crop in South America. And some countries have started to experiment with other means of producing crops from the rain forest—oil from oil palms, for example, and certain fast-growing trees that can be raised and harvested for lumber. Other tropical plants provide valuable chemicals that can be used in medicines and insecticides, and they might be grown for those purposes. With careful planning and good conservation, the tropical rain forests may yet be saved.

The U.S. spacecraft *Mars Pathfinder* landed on Mars on July 4, 1997, and released the robotic rover *Sojourner* (above). Among the information collected by the minicraft was this picture of a bear-shaped rock that scientists nicknamed Yogi.

SPACE BRIEFS

The news from space was filled with excitement during 1997. There were fascinating close-ups of rocks on Mars, extraordinary pictures of an invisible star, scary encounters with fire and fumes aboard a space station, and a daring rescue of a wandering satellite.

MISSIONS TO MARS

The biggest space event of 1997 featured a rock festival, with headliners named Barnacle Bill, Yogi, Casper, Scooby Doo, Flat Top, and The Couch. The festival took place on Mars, but the "headliners" weren't the kinds of Martians you would expect to see in a science-fiction movie. They were rocks, and they were found by the first of two unmanned space probes that reached Mars in 1997.

Mars Pathfinder, the first probe—and the first spacecraft to reach Mars since the 1976 *Viking* missions—was launched on December 4, 1996. After landing on a rocky plain called Ares Vallis on July 4, it sent out a small six-wheeled robotic vehicle named *Sojourner.* Two feet (0.6 meter) long, 1 foot (0.3 meter) high, and weighing about 22 pounds (10 kilograms), *Sojourner* used laser technology to navigate. It explored and photographed the area near the landing vehicle, and it chemically analyzed rocks and soil. Each rock it visited was given a playful nickname by Earthbound scientists. The first rock, a bumpy lump, was called Barnacle Bill; a bear-shaped rock was named Yogi; a ghostly white rock was dubbed Casper; and so on.

Pathfinder was also equipped with a camera, and weather instruments to measure wind speed, temperature, and other conditions. The probe was designed to work about thirty days. Instead, *Pathfinder* operated nearly three times as long, transmitting data to Earth until late September. During that time it sent 16,000 pictures, plus the data collected by *Sojourner.* All this material will help scientists determine what conditions are like on Mars today, and what they were like in the past.

Some of the data supported earlier findings. For example, the soil on Ares Vallis was rich in iron, and similar to the soil at the places where the *Viking* probes had landed. This iron, combined with oxygen, gives Mars its reddish color. Conditions on Ares Vallis also supported the long-held belief that vast floods of water once washed over the surface of the planet.

There were new discoveries, too. Barnacle Bill seemed to contain a lot of quartz— the first time that evidence of quartz was ever found in extraterrestrial material. Three kinds of soil were found: powdery, grainy, and dense. And temperatures on Ares Vallis fluctuated tremendously, which could explain why towering dust devils spiraled across the plain in the afternoons.

Mars Global Surveyor, the second Mars probe, was launched on November 7, 1996, and reached Mars on Sep-

tember 11, for a two-year mission. By January 1998, the probe is expected to settle into an orbit 235 miles (378 kilometers) above the planet. Then it will use cameras and other remote-sensing instruments to gather data on the Martian atmosphere and climate. It will also begin mapping the planet's entire surface, a task that will help scientists identify areas on Mars that were or are most likely to support life.

The United States planned to send at least three more probes to Mars in the coming years. If all goes well, in 2005 it will launch the first round-trip spacecraft to Mars, which will bring Martian rocks and soil back to Earth.

THE NEWS FROM HUBBLE

Launched by the United States in 1990, the Hubble Space Telescope was primarily designed to look at distant stars and galaxies. Its list of fabulous discoveries continued to grow during 1997 when it found the brightest star yet discovered in the Milky Way, the galaxy that is the home of our solar system. Named the Pistol Star because it is surrounded by a pistol-shaped nebula of dust and gas, this star burns with the brightness of ten million suns. The star is only about 25,000 light-years from Earth; however, it can't be

In October, the Hubble Space Telescope discovered the brightest star ever found in the Milky Way—the Pistol Star. The star shines with the brightness of ten million suns.

A Fish in Space

"Space flight is a dangerous business," said U.S. astronaut Jerry Linenger. He spoke from experience. During his 132-day mission in space—from January 12 to May 24, 1997—he had to contend with one problem after another aboard the Russian space station *Mir*. First there were shooting flames from a fire. Then

oxygen problems. Then antifreeze fumes and soaring heat and humidity. It was the toughest, roughest visit to *Mir* ever for an American astronaut.

But nothing stopped Linenger. He exercised like mad, conducted science experiments, and joined cosmonaut Vasily Tsibliyev in a space walk. During the space walk Linenger was attached to the end of a long, thin pole, which was controlled by Tsibliyev. "I felt like a fish on the end of a long fly-fishing rod, getting whipped back and forth," he said.

Despite all the problems, Linenger said it was the adventure of a lifetime. He also said he'd do it all again. But not right away. First he planned to sit by a quiet lake. This time, though, *he* would be the one holding a fishing rod.

seen by the human eye because it's hidden within its huge nebula. But the light the Pistol Star emits can be detected by infrared instruments aboard Hubble.

Far beyond the Milky Way—some 60 million light-years away—Hubble also detected homeless stars. Previously, all known stars belonged to galaxies. But when Hubble looked at the Virgo cluster of galaxies, it found as many as 600 stars that didn't belong to any galaxy. Astronomers suggested that the isolated stars were originally parts of galaxies but for some reason broke free.

What would happen if the Milky Way collided with Andromeda? These two galaxies are moving closer together, at a speed of 300,000 miles (483,000 kilometers) an hour. Fortunately, they are still 2.2 million light-years apart, so they aren't likely to collide for another five billion years. Photographs from Hubble of the collision of two galaxies—known as the Antennae and some 63 million light-years away—showed what might happen. In a brilliant burst of fireworks, millions of new stars were being born in the Antennae, as clouds of hydrogen gas and dust were compressed into dense spheres.

REPAIRING AN AGING *MIR*

When the Russian space station *Mir* was launched in 1986, it was designed to last five years. But it was still occupied and orbiting Earth more than eleven years later. By 1997, however, it was showing its age. In February, a fire broke out in a faulty air-purification unit. In March, the main oxygen generators broke. In April, the cooling system began leaking. In June, *Mir* collided with a space cargo vessel. In August, the main computer system began malfunctioning, forcing the

Russian cosmonaut Vasily Tsibliyev checks scientific equipment outside the space station *Mir* in April. The successful space walk was a bright spot in a trouble-filled year for the aging Russian craft.

crew to disable some of *Mir*'s electrical systems. All these incidents made life difficult and sometimes dangerous for the crews aboard the station. However, they always had the option of returning to Earth aboard a *Soyuz* spacecraft kept moored to *Mir*.

Russian cosmonauts have been living and working on *Mir* almost continuously since 1986, with most of them staying for periods of several months. In recent years, American astronauts have joined the Russians. Three times during 1997—in January, May, and September—the U.S. space shuttle *Atlantis* linked up with *Mir*. Each time, it picked up an astronaut who had lived aboard *Mir* for about three months, and left behind another astronaut.

Atlantis and Russian spaceships delivered fire extinguishers, generators, a computer, and other parts to *Mir*, and crew members were kept busy making repairs and installing new equipment. All this work was excellent training for assembling an international space station—a mammoth project that was scheduled to begin in 1998.

SHUTTLE SCIENCE MISSIONS

In addition to the three missions to *Mir*, there were five space shuttle missions devoted to science during 1997. The first of these, in February, focused on repairing and upgrading the Hubble Space Telescope. The other four missions included experiments and observations on a variety of subjects, from the influence of gravity to the composition of Earth's ozone layer. Various satellites were sent into orbit, not always without difficulty. For example, in November, the *Columbia* crew released a satellite that was to observe the sun's atmosphere. The satellite went into a spin after it was accidentally given a push by the shuttle's robot arm. This caused it to go out of control and stop functioning. During a space walk several days later, two astronauts grabbed the tumbling satellite with their gloved hands and maneuvered it back aboard the shuttle, to be released on a future mission.

JENNY TESAR
Author, *Global Warming*

123

A CASE OF THE GIGGLES

You have a math test tomorrow, and a book report is due the same day. You're sneezing—is that a cold coming on? And you can't miss soccer practice; there's a big game Saturday. Wow, you're really under pressure! What should you do?

You might start by laughing. As strange as it seems, laughter is a good response to serious pressure. Laughing helps you get rid of tension and anxiety. After a good laugh, you can tackle your problems with a fresh outlook.

Laughter can help in other ways, too. Scientists who have studied laughter's physical and mental effects think that the old saying "laughter is the best medicine" has more than a grain of truth. Laughter, they say, can actually make you a happier, healthier person.

WHAT IS LAUGHTER?

Scientists who study laughter can't tell a comedian which jokes will make an audience laugh. But they have turned up some interesting facts about laughter. For example, humans are the only animals that can laugh at some-thing that strikes them as funny. Chimpanzees and some other apes laugh, but only when they're tickled.

Babies start to laugh when they are about ten weeks old. By the time they are four months old, they laugh an average of once an hour. Six-year-olds laugh an average of 300 times a day. Adults, as you have probably noticed, are more serious. They laugh any-where from 15 to 100 times a day, with each laugh lasting about half a second to a minute. You also may have noticed that laughter is con-tagious. If one person in your classroom starts to laugh, it isn't long before everyone cracks up. That's why so many television shows use laugh tracks.

Everyone's laugh is different. Yours may be a cackle or a roar. Your chest capacity and vocal power are among the factors that deter-mine how you laugh. Most people's laughs get deeper as they get older. Eventually, though, vocal cords become less elastic. That's why elderly people often have high-pitched laughs.

Almost every part of your body gets into the act when you laugh: When you see or hear something that strikes you as funny, your brain immediately sends signals along nerves throughout your body. Some of these signals prompt your body to produce chemicals that make you more alert and stimulate your heart and lungs. The chemicals also cause your arteries to contract, so your blood pressure starts to go up.

At the same time, your muscles spring into action. Your face muscles contract, drawing your features into a grimace. Your lips pull back, and your nostrils flare. Your stomach and chest muscles tighten up. Your diaphragm—the sheet of muscle between your lungs and abdomen that contracts when you inhale—tenses. Air starts to build up in your lungs. Meanwhile, the muscles that control your vocal cords go into spasms, and you can't speak.

Suddenly your stomach and chest muscles contract in a spasm, forcing the air out of your lungs as fast as 70 miles (113 kilometers) an hour. It rushes past your vocal cords in a burst of quick sounds—ha-ha-ha, or heh-heh-heh. While you roar with laughter, tear glands release tears from your eyes.

The body chemicals that are released when you start to laugh also prompt you to keep laughing. That's why you sometimes feel as if you'll never stop giggling. As your heart keeps working harder, increasing your circulation, your face gets red. Your temperature may go up half a degree.

As the laughing fit ends, your muscles start to relax. Gradually your blood pressure and your heart rate drop. In fact, they drop below normal, a sign of relaxation and reduced stress.

INNER EXERCISE

The effects of laughter on your body are a lot like the effects of exercise. In fact, one scientist calls laughter "inner jogging." When laugh-

ter increases your heart rate, it helps strengthen your heart and circulation, the same way jogging does. And laughter vibrates through your whole body and gives a good workout to the muscles of your chest and stomach, as well as to your diaphragm. That muscular effort burns up calories. All in all, laughing 100 times a day gives your body as much exercise as ten minutes of rowing.

Anatomy of a Laugh

Almost every part of your body gets into the act when you laugh.

tear glands release tears from your eyes

your face muscles contract

your lips pull back, and your nostrils flare

your stomach and chest muscles tighten and then contract in a spasm

your face turns red

your heart works harder, increasing your circulation

125

chemicals that make you alert and speed your heart rate, laughter may also stimulate the release of body chemicals that dull pain and give you a feeling of well-being. Some studies show that the right side of the brain, believed to be the creative side, is more active when people laugh.

There are psychological benefits as well as physical ones. Laughter distracts you from things that may be worrying or upsetting you. It can relieve emotional stress and pressure, and it can make you feel less anxious in tense situations. In fact, scientists think laughter may have developed as a

The good effects of laughter go on long after the chuckling stops. Your muscles are more relaxed than they were before you laughed. Because your blood pressure and heart rate drop below normal after laughter, the heart is less stressed than it was before. There's also evidence that a good laugh prompts the stomach to secrete enzymes that aid digestion. And several studies show that laughter helps the body's immune system function better, aiding in the ability to fight infection and disease.

A case of the giggles has other effects, too. In addition to

way of dealing with just such situations—by providing an outlet for tension and fear. And shared laughter is a sort of social glue. When you and your friends laugh at something together, your laughter helps cement your friendship.

LAUGHTER AS MEDICINE

"A merry heart does good like a medicine," says a proverb from the Bible. Doctors have long known that happy patients get well faster. In the 1400s, a surgeon named Henri de Mondeville told jokes to his patients as they left the operating room, to speed their recovery. In the 1700s, Richard Mulcaster, an English educator, advised tickling under the armpits as a treatment for colds and melancholy. Among certain North American Indian tribes, medicine men performed tricks and stunts to help their patients laugh away their illnesses.

Today, doctors are giving new weight to the idea of laughter as medicine. Laughter seems to help many physical problems—headaches, infections, and high blood pressure among them. People with the respiratory condition emphysema, who have difficulty breathing, find that laughing helps clear stale air from the lungs. Laughter can also lessen pain, helping people with conditions such as arthritis.

Some hospitals and medical centers have made humor a regular part of therapy. They have set up special humor rooms and "laughmobiles"—carts stocked with humorous books, tapes, and games for patients to enjoy. There's even an organization, the International Center for Humor and Health, devoted to spreading the healing art of laughter. Laughter can't replace medicine, of course. And getting sick is no joke. But humor can work together with medicine to speed recovery from illness.

Psychologists and other mental health workers use humor in therapy, too. A good laugh helps people release painful emotions and see their problems from a new point of view. Laughter lifts the spirits of people who are lonely and depressed. And more and more employers are learning that laughter can help relieve stress and tension in the workplace. As one psychologist said, "We don't laugh because we're happy—we're happy because we laugh."

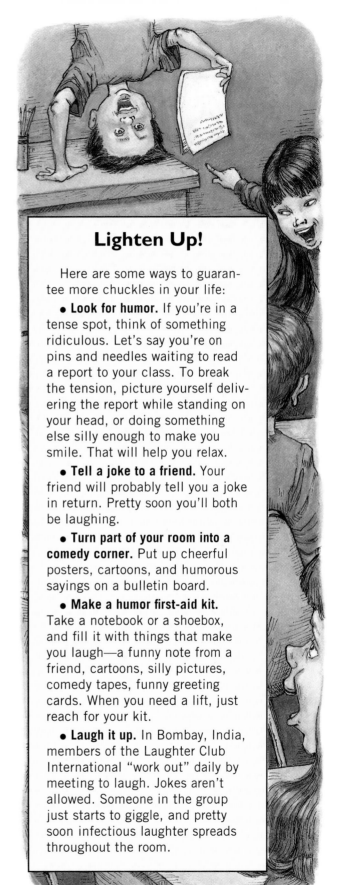

Lighten Up!

Here are some ways to guarantee more chuckles in your life:

● **Look for humor.** If you're in a tense spot, think of something ridiculous. Let's say you're on pins and needles waiting to read a report to your class. To break the tension, picture yourself delivering the report while standing on your head, or doing something else silly enough to make you smile. That will help you relax.

● **Tell a joke to a friend.** Your friend will probably tell you a joke in return. Pretty soon you'll both be laughing.

● **Turn part of your room into a comedy corner.** Put up cheerful posters, cartoons, and humorous sayings on a bulletin board.

● **Make a humor first-aid kit.** Take a notebook or a shoebox, and fill it with things that make you laugh—a funny note from a friend, cartoons, silly pictures, comedy tapes, funny greeting cards. When you need a lift, just reach for your kit.

● **Laugh it up.** In Bombay, India, members of the Laughter Club International "work out" daily by meeting to laugh. Jokes aren't allowed. Someone in the group just starts to giggle, and pretty soon infectious laughter spreads throughout the room.

El Niño arrived in 1997, creating all kinds of weather havoc throughout the world—including Hurricane Nora, shown swirling off the Pacific coast of Mexico in this satellite photo.

EARTH WATCH

No part of Earth's environment exists in isolation. Thus, a change in one part of the environment can have dramatic consequences on other parts. An ocean current can disrupt weather patterns around the world. Plants introduced into a new home can battle native species for turf. Human activities can lead to the disappearance of coral reefs. Mysterious diseases can devastate frogs, manatees, and bees. During 1997, much attention was focused on these particular environmental changes and their effects.

Here Comes El Niño. A hurricane off Mexico, a drought in Indonesia, an autumn snowstorm in Colorado. All these disasters of 1997 had something in common. They were linked to El Niño. Given the Spanish name "the child" because the phenomenon usually happens in early winter, around Christmas, El Niño is a climate disturbance that occurs when surface waters of the eastern Pacific Ocean become unusually warm. It begins when the trade winds—which normally blow from east to west across the Pacific—weaken or reverse direction. This pushes warm water toward the west coast of South America, bringing heavy precipitation that would normally fall in the western Pacific. El Niño disrupts weather all over the world. It causes drier weather than normal in Brazil, and it stops the formation of hurricanes in the Atlantic Ocean. Deprived of rain, places like Indonesia and Australia suffer droughts. The disturbance has even been linked to droughts as far away as southern Africa.

In the past, El Niños occurred once or twice a decade. But there were several El Niños in the early 1990s. These were mild, however, compared to the El Niño that began in 1997—when temperatures in the eastern Pacific rose to unusually high levels. Weather forecasters have made all sorts of predictions about what may happen. For example, they expect southern California to have one of its wettest winters ever in 1997–98, while the northeastern United States and southern Canada may be drier and warmer than usual. Some researchers have even predicted that this El Niño might be "the climatic event of the century."

One of the biggest concerns is how El Niño's warm ocean currents will affect marine life on the west coast of North America. The warmer waters will force cold-water fish to dive deeper or go elsewhere to find food. Semitropical fish, such as marlin, yellowfin tuna, and Pacific mackerel, will move northward toward Alaska. In 1997, such fish were being caught in waters off the coast of Washington, far from their usual habitats off Mexico and southern California. This isn't good for local species. For example, Pacific mackerel feed on young salmon, thus reducing already threatened populations.

Scientists don't understand what triggers El Niños or why they are occurring more frequently. Whatever the causes, scientists expect the current El Niño to create lots of mayhem before it disappears.

Insects to the Rescue. Many plants and animals live where nature didn't intend them to be. For example, American box elders grow in China, African killer bees live in Mexico, and Norway rats are found almost everywhere. In their original homes, these organisms have natural enemies that limit their populations. In their new homes, there are no natural enemies, and populations soar. The newcomers battle native species for food and living space. Usually, the natives lose— they die out and the newcomers take over.

Two plants that have caused big problems in their new environments are purple loosestrife and melaleuca. Now, some of their natural enemies have been called to the rescue!

Purple loosestrife is an attractive plant that bears long spikes covered with hundreds of tiny purplish flowers. It grows in wetlands, such as marshes and swamps. A native of Europe, it arrived in North America early in the 19th century. No one is certain how it crossed the Atlantic Ocean; perhaps its seeds were carried in bales of hay or in a ship's ballast water. But before long, it was crowding out native grasses and other plants.

In Europe, there are two little beetles that feed only on purple loosestrife. The beetles were studied for many years because scientists wanted to be sure that the beetles wouldn't become a nuisance if they were imported into North America. Then, in the summer of 1997, about half a million of the beetles were released in parts of North America where

This little beetle was one of two European beetles released in North America to combat the spread of the beautiful but rampant purple loosestrife (*right*).

purple loosestrife has become a pest. Scientists expect that the beetles will have the plant under control within fifteen years.

Another type of beetle was imported to fight melaleuca. This Australian tree was introduced into Florida in the early 20th century, to protect against soil erosion. Without enemies, it spread rapidly and began to choke out native plants in Florida's Everglades. In 1997, scientists waded into the Everglades and released a little Australian snout beetle that eats only melaleuca. It's hoped that the beetle will munch lots of melaleuca flower buds, thereby preventing the trees from producing seeds.

Reef Relief. Concerned by threats to coral reefs around the world, governments and scientists declared 1997 the International Year of the Reef. The purpose of this global effort was to increase people's awareness about the importance of coral reefs and to support projects that protect the reefs.

Coral reefs grow in clean, shallow tropical waters. They are built by tiny sea animals called coral polyps. It takes hundreds or even thousands of years for these animals to build a coral reef. In the process, they create one of the most diverse habitats on Earth. A single reef may be home to thousands of different kinds of ocean plants and animals, which depend on the reef for food, shelter, and protected places in which to reproduce and raise their young. If a reef dies, the community within it also dies.

Reefs around the world, including those in the Florida Keys and the Caribbean, are dying or being destroyed. Mysterious diseases and sewage are killing the coral polyps. Sediment from coastal development and agricultural runoff smothers the animals. Careless boaters ram their vessels into reefs. In Southeast Asia, fishermen use dynamite to break apart reefs so they can catch fish hidden within. Divers remove rare black coral and other species used as souvenirs and for making jewelry.

It's estimated that 30 percent of the world's reefs have been severely harmed, and may die within the next 10 to 20 years. But with everyone's help, the tide may be reversed. People are encouraged not to collect coral or buy coral jewelry. Divers and snorkelers should avoid touching coral reefs. Communities and businesses should take care not to pollute reefs with sewage, oil, or sediment.

New Hazards for Wildlife. Mutant frogs, sick manatees, disappearing honeybees—what's happening to these beautiful and valuable animals?

The year 1997 was declared the International Year of the Reef, to call attention to the dangers facing coral reefs and the many creatures that live among them.

Threats to North America's wildlife: Manatees are being killed by poisonous algae and a strange virus. . .pesticides and other chemicles may be causing terrible deformities in frogs. . .and mites are killing huge numbers of honeybees.

In recent years, more and more deformed frogs have been found in North America. Some have extra legs, or no legs at all. Some are missing eyes, or grow extra eyes on their backs. Studies of the genetic material of these frogs don't indicate any mutations in the genes. This suggests that the abnormalities developed during the early stages of life. No one knows what's causing the problem, although many scientists suspect pesticides or other chemicals in the water.

Manatees are an endangered species. Many have died after colliding with boats or being cut by boat propellers. In recent years, however, manatees seemed to be making a comeback. But in 1996, more than 400 manatees were found dead off the coast of Florida. Scientists discovered that they had died from a poison produced by reddish-brown algae known as "red tide." Yet another threat faced by manatees was one discovered in 1997: a virus that causes skin lesions. Scientists are collecting manatee blood samples and doing other tests in the hope of finding ways to combat these poisons and viruses.

Across North America, populations of honeybees have plummeted. In some places, 90 percent of wild honeybees have been destroyed, and many commercial honeybee colonies have also died out. The main culprits are tiny parasitic mites that suck the blood from bees, eventually killing them. The massive loss of honeybees is of great concern because it threatens food supplies. As honeybees fly from flower to flower, they transfer pollen. This leads to the formation of fruits and seeds. About 15 percent of U.S. crops are pollinated by honeybees, including alfalfa, apples, squash, cranberries, and almonds. Scientists are looking for ways to fight the mites. They are also studying other types of bees—such as the bumblebee and the blue orchard bee—that might be used as crop pollinators.

JENNY TESAR
Author, *Endangered Habitats*

Use lots of imagination—and have lots of fun—as you make a colorful collage like this one out of many scraps of fabric. Begin by drawing a picture on a piece of heavy paper, such as posterboard. Then glue on the background fabrics—the sky and grass. Glue on the remaining fabrics, working with the larger pieces first, and then the smaller ones. Decorate your picture with bits of lace, tiny buttons, and bright sequins. You can also paint details onto your picture. Then frame it, and wait for the ooohs and aaahs!

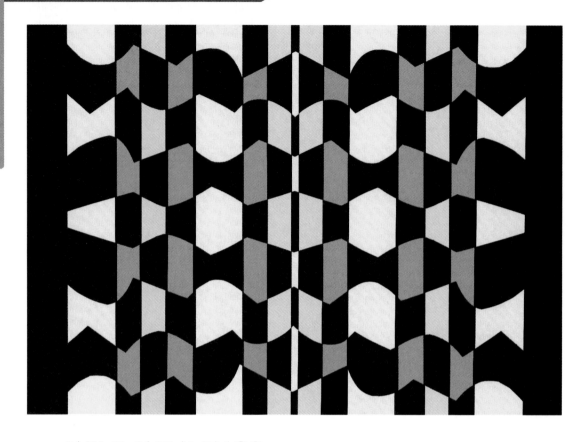

WILD WEAVINGS

Wild and wonderful paper weavings are fun and easy to make. You'll need a sheet of colored paper for the base (background), plus long strips of other colored papers for weaving. You'll also need scissors and tape or glue.

Begin by folding the base paper in half. Starting at the fold, cut a series of lines to about 1 inch (2.5 centimeters) from the edges of the paper. The lines can be parallel to one another and evenly spaced, or they can zigzag, curve, and wiggle. But they can't cross one another.

Now cut strips of different colored papers that are longer than the base paper. The strips can all be the same width, or they can be a mix of thick and thin widths. You can create multicolor strips by gluing a narrow strip of one color atop a wider strip of another color.

Open the base paper so that it lies flat. Starting at one end of the paper,

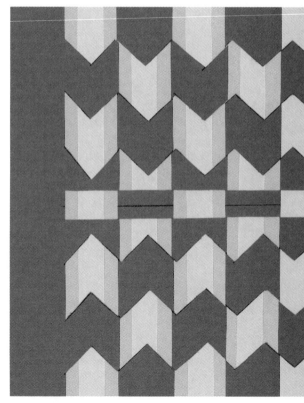

weave a paper strip over and under, through the cuts you've made. Tape or glue the ends of the strip to the back of the base paper, so that it will stay in place. Alternate colors of strips. Continue to weave until you've covered the entire area with strips. To avoid "holes" in your weaving, keep the strips close together.

When you are finished, you can add glitter, stickers, or small cut-out designs such as hearts and stars. To protect your art, glue a sheet of paper to the back of the weaving.

Paper weaving offers almost unlimited possibilities. You can create an informal, aimless design, ending with a random—but nonetheless exciting—pattern. Or you can have a design with carefully measured and balanced distances and angles, thus creating a classical pattern that's similar to those seen on beautiful Indian rugs.

STAMP COLLECTING

Stamp collectors looked back to the past and ahead to the future in 1997. For the U.S. Postal Service, the year marked an important milestone. It was the 150th anniversary of the nation's first postage stamps, which were issued in 1847. Hobbyists looked back over those years and noted how much has changed since then.

U.S. STAMPS

The first U.S. stamps were 5-cent and 10-cent issues featuring portraits of Benjamin Franklin and George Washington. For the 150th anniversary of these stamps, replicas were printed in special souvenir sheets and issued at Pacific 97, a worldwide stamp exhibition held in San Francisco in May and June. Back in 1847, the stamps were remarkable. But their dull dark designs are a far cry from the colorful variety of stamps today.

Among the most unusual U.S. releases of 1997 was a pair of triangular 32-cent stamps, also honoring Pacific 97. They were the first tri-

angular stamps ever issued by the U.S. Postal Service. One of the stamps showed a clipper ship, and the other a stagecoach—two popular ways of traveling to California in the 1800s.

Many of the year's issues had special appeal for young collectors. A favorite cartoon character, Bugs Bunny, turned up on a self-adhesive 32-cent stamp. In a typical smart-aleck pose, Bugs was shown leaning against a mailbox, munching a carrot. This was the first time that the Postal Service had featured a commercial cartoon character on a stamp.

Children's book author and illustrator Chris Van Allsburg designed a stamp on the theme of "helping children learn," using cut paper to create a colorful picture of an adult and a child reading together. Another colorful design was created by artist Synthia Saint James for a stamp honoring Kwanzaa, the African-American festival held in late December.

Swans were the theme for the 1997 U.S. Love stamp, issued for Valentine's Day. The

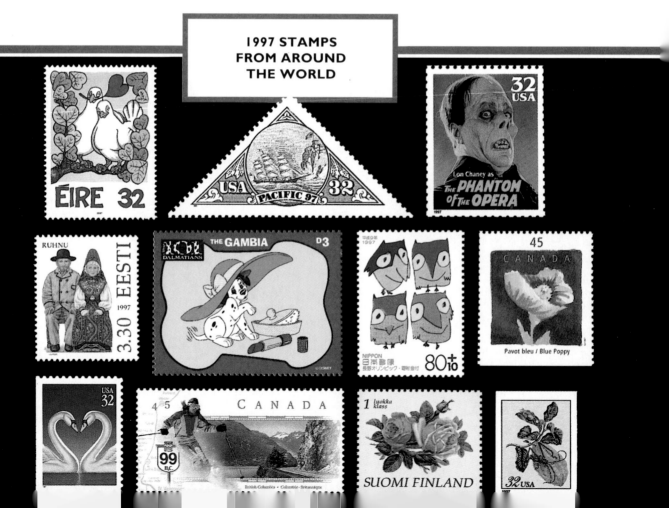

1997 STAMPS FROM AROUND THE WORLD

design, featured on a 32-cent stamp and a 20-cent postal card, showed two birds forming a heart with their graceful necks. And two 32-cent self-adhesive stamps featured the botanical prints of 17th-century American artist Anna Maria Sibylla Merian.

Dinosaurs and other prehistoric creatures came back to life in one of the year's most popular issues. Fifteen stamps formed a pane that featured two panoramic scenes. One, with eight stamps, showed Colorado 150 million years ago, with huge creatures such as *Allosaurus* prowling around. The second, with seven stamps, showed Montana as it may have looked about 75 million years ago. Included were baby dinosaurs hatching from eggs.

Just in time for Halloween, the Postal Service released five stamps showing movie monsters as portrayed by famous actors. They were Dracula (Bela Lugosi), Frankenstein (Boris Karloff), the Mummy (also Boris Karloff), the Phantom of the Opera (Lon Chaney, Sr.), and the Wolf Man (Lon Chaney, Jr.). The stamps had a mysterious secret, too—images that could

be seen only with a special decoder. The images were meant to deter counterfeiters, but lots of people had fun finding bats flying around Dracula's head and other hidden pictures.

The last stamp released in 1997 was a whopper—in fact, it was the largest U.S. stamp ever issued. Honoring the Mars landing in July, the $3 stamp showed the *Mars Pathfinder,* along with the robotic vehicle *Sojourner,* on the surface of the "red planet."

STAMPS AROUND THE WORLD

The United States wasn't the only country to issue "monster" stamps in 1997. Canada greeted Halloween with four spine-tingling 45-cent designs, showing a vampire, a werewolf, a frightening ghost, and a nasty-looking goblin.

Great Britain showed Dracula, Frankenstein, the Hound of the Baskervilles, and Dr. Jekyll and Mr. Hyde—all horrors that sprang from the pens of British writers—on four stamps. The stamps were printed with special ink, so that they glowed in ultraviolet light. They were part of the 1997 Europa series, which

included stamps from many European countries on the theme of stories and legends.

Most of the year's other stamps took cheerier themes. Canada began a series on its scenic highways with four 45-cent stamps showing famous routes from different parts of the country: the Cabot Trail, which follows the coast on Cape Breton Island in Nova Scotia; the Wine Route, which passes through vineyards in Ontario; Highway 34, in the Big Muddy badlands of Saskatchewan, and the Sea to Sky Highway in coastal British Columbia.

Marking a ten-day flower festival in Quebec, Canada released a 45-cent commemorative and a postal card showing a watercolor painting of a blue poppy. A 45-cent stamp honoring Highland Games featured photographs of actual participants in recent Games. The Games include strenuous events such as tossing the caber (a massive pole), along with traditional Scottish music and dance. Brought to Canada by Scottish settlers in the early 1800s, Highland Games are held in many communities today.

Wildlife was the theme of several Canadian stamps. New designs in the Birds of Canada series showed the western grebe, mountain bluebird, northern gannet, and scarlet tanager. Ocean fish—the great white shark, bluefin tuna, Pacific halibut, and Atlantic sturgeon—appeared on another group of 45-cent stamps. And an $8 stamp, the first in a new series of high-value stamps, showed a grizzly bear.

Wild creatures were showcased on stamps from many other nations. They ranged from Magellanic penguins, from the Falkland Islands, to tropical butterflies, from Antigua and Barbuda. The United Nations continued its series on endangered species with twelve letter-rate stamps, four each in U.S., Swiss, and Austrian denominations. The 32-cent group showed the cougar, African elephant, black-footed ferret, and Major Mitchell's cockatoo.

Cartoon puppies from the Walt Disney film *101 Dalmations* frolicked across a sheet of stamps from the African nation of the Gambia. Disney stamps, always-popular with collectors, were released by many other countries, too.

A TOPICAL COLLECTION OF TOYS AND GAMES

Roses were featured on Valentine's Day stamps from several countries. In Sweden's design, roses formed a heart. Finland issued a booklet of eight "friendship" stamps with old-fashioned designs of roses, cherubs, and children holding hands. Ireland's 1997 Love stamp took a different theme. It showed a pair of doves in a tree, surrounded by heart-shaped leaves. And a stamp from the Netherlands had a silvery heart that could be scratched away to reveal one of ten secret messages.

Colorful 19th-century folk costumes were featured on a pair of stamps from Estonia, on the Baltic Sea. Neighboring Latvia also showed traditional costumes. Colombia, Suriname, and Cuba were among nations of the Americas to depict traditional dress on stamps.

The spectacular 1997 visit of Comet Hale-Bopp was celebrated on two stamps from the Dominican Republic. Both showed the comet against a glowing sunset, with a palm tree and a building in the foreground.

Japan released two new stamps for the 1998 Winter Olympics, to be held in Nagano. One showed the emblem of the Games, the "snowflower," which looked like a cross between a snowflake and a flower. The other showed four "snowlets"—comical, owl-like cartoon creatures that are the Games' mascots.

In the Chinese lunar calendar, 1997 was the Year of the Ox, and many countries issued stamps on that theme. The return of Hong Kong to Chinese rule also produced several stamps. On June 30, the last day of British rule, Hong Kong issued a stamp that was valid for that day only. It was the last to show the emblem of Queen Elizabeth II of England. Then, on July 1, the first stamps to bear the words "Hong Kong, China" were released.

A TOPICAL COLLECTION OF TOYS AND GAMES

Do you love toys? Then create a topical collection—a collection built around a single theme—with stamps that feature toys and games. You'll find plenty to choose from. For example, in 1997, classic American dolls were featured on U.S. stamps, while Australia showed dolls and teddy bears. Keep hunting for stamps like these, and before long your "toy collection" will be the envy of your friends!

IT'S GAME TIME...

BATTER UP!

In 1997, sports fans celebrated the 50th anniversary of one of the most important days in the history of baseball. On April 11, 1947, Jackie Robinson became the first African American to play in a major league baseball game. For the next ten years, until he retired in 1957, Robinson was one of baseball's most exciting players.

Which National League team brought Robinson onto the playing field? To learn the answer, you need a pencil and a sheet of paper. Carefully follow the directions given below. Hint: It will be easier if you rewrite the complete words at each step. (The solution is on page 414.)

1. Print the words JACKIE ROBINSON. Leave the words separated.

2. Change the A to an O.

3. Remove the third letter from the left.

4. Replace every I with the letter that comes after C in the alphabet.

5. Find the fifth consonant from the left. Move it to the beginning of the second word.

6. Put a G between the D-E combination.

7. Find the fourth letter from the right. Make it the fourth letter from the left.

8. Change the last letter of the second word to an R.

9. Reverse the S-O combination.

10. Change the J to an L. Move it between K and N.

11. Move the last three letters of the first word in front of the S.

12. Insert a Y between L and N.

13. Reverse the S-R combination.

14. Move the first three letters of the second word to the beginning of the first word.

In 1962, Jackie Robinson was elected to the Baseball Hall of Fame—the first black ever to achieve this honor.

TWO HEADS...

. . .are better than one. This is an old proverb—a saying that makes a comment about situations people encounter in everyday life.

Trying to solve problems by yourself can be difficult. Two heads— two minds, that is—can more easily find solutions to problems. So, this proverb says, if you have a problem, discuss it with another person.

Some proverbs express accepted truths: "Seeing is believing." Other proverbs have morals: "Haste makes waste." Still others give general advice: "An apple a day keeps the doctor away."

Here are some broken proverbs. You can complete them by putting the part in the left column together with the correct part in the right column. Then think about what each proverb means.

1. Don't bite the hand	**a.** before they hatch
2. You can't teach an old dog	**b.** when the well runs dry
3. Beauty	**c.** is better than none
4. You only miss the water	**d.** but it pours
5. Too many cooks	**e.** never boils
6. A man's home	**f.** has its puddle
7. It never rains	**g.** over spilled milk
8. Practice	**h.** new tricks
9. Actions	**i.** spoil the broth
10. A watched pot	**j.** is only skin deep
11. Every path	**k.** is his castle
12. When the cat's away	**l.** there's fire
13. He who hesitates	**m.** speak louder than words
14. Half a loaf	**n.** is lost
15. Nothing ventured	**o.** the mice will play
16. Don't count your chickens	**p.** that feeds you
17. Seeing	**q.** makes perfect
18. Where there's smoke	**r.** is believing
19. Don't cry	**s.** nothing gained

ANSWERS: 1.p; 2.h; 3.j; 4.b; 5.i; 6.k; 7.d; 8.q; 9.m; 10.e; 11.f; 12.o; 13.n; 14.c; 15.s; 16.a; 17.r; 18.l; 19.g.

MAKING FACES

Paint your face and become a black-masked raccoon or a goofy clown! Or turn yourself into a hissing wildcat, a spotted ladybug, or a green witch with a spider crawling up your cheek. Paint hearts on your face for Valentine's Day, balloons for a birthday party, and rainbows for Earth Day.

Carefully follow the directions below. But before you begin, cover your clothes with a towel, or wear old clothes. Hold your hair back with a headband. And be very careful not to put paint or makeup too close to your eyes.

WHAT YOU NEED:

Facepaints or makeup	Tissues
Paintbrushes	Towel
Cold cream	Headband
Small sponges	Mirror

1. If you are going to use regular makeup, first rub cold cream on your skin. This will make it easier to remove the makeup.

2. Use your fingers or a small damp sponge to spread the paint or makeup on your skin. Apply the base color first. Let it dry.

3. Use a paintbrush to make fine lines. If the design has both light and dark colors, apply the light colors first.

Just Clowning Around

Professional clowns begin with white and then add darker colors one by one. Be careful not to smear the colors together.

4. To make a happy clown, start by painting your face white. Make a bright red smile and a red nose.

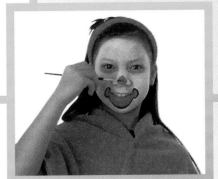

5. Then add red freckles. Use black to make high, half-moon eyebrows and little sparkle lines near your eyes.

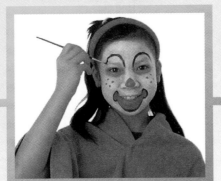

6. A sad "hobo" clown has a gray patch around the mouth, a big red frown, and a red nose. Add a teardrop or two.

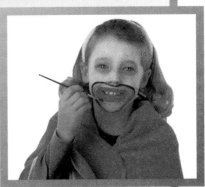

From delivering newspapers to baking cookies, you can find many ways to start your own business—and make $$$.

WE'RE IN THE MONEY!

One thing just about everyone can use more of is money. And that probably includes you. Many young people are discovering that there are lots of ways to earn money. One of the best ways is to start your own business.

"But what should I do?" you ask. The answer is simple: Provide people with anything they need. . .or want. Some kids bake cookies to sell at local fairs. Some have newspaper routes. Some kids have a snow shoveling service. Others create worm farms and sell the worms for bait. Still others help vacationing neighbors by feeding pets, watering plants, and bringing in mail and newspapers. Here are some guidelines that may help you decide what kind of business would be best for you.

1. What can you do well? A business will be successful only if the product or service you sell is of good quality. Make a list of the things that you do well. Do you have a green

thumb? Then raise and sell house plants. Do you speak fluent French or Spanish? Begin a tutoring service.

2. What do you like to do? A business is generally more successful if it revolves around something you enjoy doing. Do you like young children? Open a baby-sitting service. Do you love parties? How about starting a party business—help people create party themes, and then set up and serve at the parties.

3. Do your neighbors need any special service that you might be able to provide? The best way to learn your neighbors' needs is to ask them. For instance, if you have elderly neighbors who don't get out much, ask if they're interested in a grocery shopping service.

4. How will competition affect you? Even if you're providing a desired service or product, your chances of having a successful business will improve if you don't have a lot of competition. Consider, for example, a business involving crafts. Many people make and sell such items as bookmarks, wreaths, placemats, and potholders. Therefore, you should try to create products that are unique—maybe personalized T-shirts.

5. How much money do you need to spend to get started? Most businesses require some start-up money. For example, if you are going to create posters for people, you'll need to buy posterboard, construction paper, and paints and brushes. If you're planning to make placemats, you'll have to buy fabric and thread.

Once you've decided what type of business you'll have, you must figure out what to charge for your work. One way to do this is to find out what other people are charging for the same service or product and perhaps price your work slightly lower. But remember: If you want to make a profit, you have to charge more than what it costs you to make and sell your product.

A business is usually more successful if you enjoy the work. Mowing lawns is a great job for someone who likes being outdoors. If you enjoy being around small children, a baby-sitting service is a terrific opportunity.

Sometimes, instead of charging less than your competition, you may want to give your customers something extra. If you have a lawn-service business, give people a coupon each time you mow their lawn. Tell them that you'll provide a free plant trimming when they've collected ten coupons.

Now it's time to let people know about your business. Advertise! Make lively announcements that can be hung in local stores (be sure to first get the store manager's permission). Distribute flyers in your neighborhood. Make up business cards. (You

Before you start a business, find out what people need. Grocery shopping might provide a welcome service for elderly neighbors.

can write them out on ordinary file cards. Just make sure that each card lists your name and telephone number and clearly indicates what service you provide.)

For some businesses, you may want to make appointments with potential customers. Dress neatly. People are more likely to listen to you—and buy your product or service—if you look professional. Smile when you introduce yourself, and shake hands. Explain why you're there. If the person isn't interested, keep smiling! Offer one of your cards and say something like, "Please call me if you need this work done in the future."

Many people will say "no" to you. But some will say "yes." And if you do a good job, they'll become satisfied customers. They'll call on you again, and they'll recommend you to their friends. That's the way a business—any business—grows and becomes successful.

Put your creativity to work by designing and selling unique items—like nifty T-shirts.

you bring the dog back early, customers may feel they aren't getting what they're paying for. If you keep the dog out longer, customers may worry that there was an accident. Remember, too, that there's value in offering a little extra—an occasional bonus walk or a free brushing.

Sometimes you may not be able to get to your job, perhaps because you're sick or out of town. Try to have someone else available to walk the dog when you can't. It's a good idea to introduce this person to your customers and their pets ahead of time. Go over the route you follow, point out do's and

If you're an animal lover, you can earn money by caring for pets. You could begin with a dog-walking service, and then expand your business to include dog grooming.

Let's take a closer look at three areas in which you might start a business.

A PASSION FOR PETS

If you like animals and if there are lots of animal owners in your community, start a business that involves caring for pets. A dog-walking service is a good way to begin.

You don't need any money to start a dog-walking service. You do, however, have to be a very responsible person. Dog owners will probably want you to walk their dogs on a regular schedule. Be sure to stick to the schedule, and always arrive on time.

Agree ahead of time on how long you are to walk the dog. Try to be exact about this. If

You can have a successful car-washing service if your customers see that you do a better job than the local car wash. So scrub, clean, and shine!

business—simply because many people hate to clean. They dislike cleaning windows and garages and cars and floors and yards. So offer to do it for them!

In planning your business, decide who will provide the cleaning supplies. If you provide them, you can charge more but you'll have to spend money in advance. If the customers provide the cleaning supplies, you don't have to spend money and you'll know that you'll be using the products they prefer.

Before offering to clean something, be sure you know how to do it. Cleaning a window is different from cleaning a floor. And cleaning a boat is different from cleaning a car. Your best bet is to learn the job by helping someone who already knows how to do it. If you want to learn how to clean cars, for example, learn from people who keep their own cars shining.

don't's (such as areas where it's illegal to walk dogs), and in general familiarize the person with your routine—and your professional standards.

After a while, you may wish to expand the services you provide. Let customers know that you will groom dogs or take care of them for extended periods of time, such as when owners are on vacation.

You can even sell items related to your service. Pet identification tags, collars, toys, and pet placemats are popular. You can make these yourself. Or you can sell them for a friend who makes them—and collect a commission (a percentage of the sale) on every item you sell.

THE CLEAN SCENE

Cleaning may not be your favorite activity, but it can be the basis of a very profitable

A successful car-washing service can bring in steady money. Try to line up customers by leaving flyers under windshield wipers of cars. Once you have your customers, you can keep them by doing a better job than the local car wash. Scrub the tires, clean the mud flaps, and shine the chrome.

Start small and with a service that you can do really well. Then expand. You might consider offering to clean the interior for an additional fee. (You should vacuum the inside, empty ashtrays, dust the dash, and wash the windows.) Then why not add a waxing service to your car-wash business?

COMPUTER SERVICES

If you enjoy using computers, there are many creative ways in which you can turn this talent into money-making opportunities. For example, many people want to learn how to use a computer or specific computer programs. You can earn money simply by teaching them how to do this.

If you have a computer at home with a word-processing or desktop publishing program, you may want to become a publisher. You could publish a neighborhood paper, with stories about the people who live and work in your area. Include information on local events, such as soccer games, art shows, and public meetings. Sell the newspaper door-to-door. After you've published several issues and people are familiar with the paper, try to get subscriptions. Ask local store owners if they would like to advertise in the paper. Neighbors who are planning tag sales may wish to place an ad. So may friends who offer baby-sitting, lawn-cutting, and other services.

With a desktop publishing program, you can create business cards, letterhead stationery, and other printed matter for parents, friends, teachers, and store owners. Make sure to get feedback from them: Would they prefer different styles of type? A border or other graphic design? A slogan? It's important to create a card or stationery that matches people's specific needs and preferences. For large orders, you'll probably want to take the design to a professional printer; that would be quicker and easier than using your own printer. You then bill the cost—plus your design fee—to the clients.

Perhaps someone you know would like a special birthday card for her father, or wants

to send congratulations to a friend who just won his first tennis tournament. If you have an artistic flair—plus a color printer and a desktop publishing program—you can offer to create personalized, one-of-a-kind greeting cards.

One of the hottest areas in computers is the Internet. Many people want to get on the bandwagon with their own site on the World Wide Web—a section of the Internet that includes lots of graphics as well as text. Such a site consists of one or more "pages" that are

If you're a whiz on the computer, use your talents to start a business at home. Your expertise in desktop publishing or creating Web sites will keep people knocking at your door.

usually highly designed. If you've designed your own Web site, offer your expertise to others.

With hard work and a little luck, you may soon find that your part-time business has grown too big for you to handle by yourself. Then it's time to look for assistants. You won't have to look far, because there are lots of kids out there looking for ways to earn some extra money!

A ROOT IN YOUR SOUP

The next time you eat vegetable soup, look closely. You'll find roots and stems and maybe even fruit in it. This is because we eat different parts of different plants.

Most plant foods are grouped as fruits or vegetables. But this doesn't necessarily tell us what part of the plant is being eaten. We eat the underground stem of a potato plant; the seeds of a pea plant; the fruit of an orange tree; the bark (stem covering) of a cinnamon tree; and the leaves of an onion plant. (Onions are leaves wrapped around one another, forming a bulb.)

The names of 33 plants are listed below. Match each to the part that you normally eat.

a. LEAF   **b.** STEM   **c.** ROOT   **d.** FLOWER   **e.** FRUIT   **f.** SEED

1. apple	**12.** coconut	**23.** potato
2. artichoke	**13.** collards	**24.** pumpkin
3. asparagus	**14.** corn	**25.** radish
4. banana	**15.** cucumber	**26.** rhubarb
5. beet	**16.** eggplant	**27.** spinach
6. broccoli	**17.** fig	**28.** squash
7. cabbage	**18.** green pepper	**29.** strawberry
8. carrot	**19.** lettuce	**30.** tomato
9. cauliflower	**20.** parsley	**31.** turnip
10. celery	**21.** pear	**32.** walnut
11. cherry	**22.** pineapple	**33.** watermelon

ANSWERS: 1.e; 2.d; 3.b; 4.e; 5.c; 6.d; 7.a; 8.c; 9.d; 10.a; 11.e; 12.f; 13.a; 14.f; 15.e,f; 16.e,f; 17.e,f; 18.e; 19.a; 20.a; 21.e; 22.e; 23.b; 24.e; 25.c; 26.a; 27.a; 28.e,f; 29.e,f; 30.e,f; 31.c; 32.f; 33.e.

Next, go on a hunt. All 33 plants are hidden in this word-search puzzle. Try to find them. Cover the puzzle with a sheet of tracing paper. Read forward, backward, up, down, and diagonally. Then draw a neat line through each plant as you find it.

B	R	A	B	U	H	R	W	A	T	E	R	M	E	L	O	N
R	O	S	E	A	E	G	A	B	B	A	C	T	I	N	G	I
O	T	P	R	Y	R	E	L	E	C	L	O	M	I	B	N	K
C	A	A	G	A	A	T	N	H	E	E	T	E	N	O	E	P
C	T	R	R	S	E	R	U	T	Z	B	A	G	A	E	G	M
O	O	A	E	F	C	B	T	J	L	E	M	T	O	P	G	U
L	P	G	E	C	A	U	L	I	F	L	O	W	E	R	P	P
I	T	U	N	O	C	O	C	O	C	R	T	A	P	P	L	E
D	T	S	P	E	G	I	R	U	R	H	R	B	F	D	A	H
N	U	S	E	H	T	O	D	A	M	H	O	I	E	N	N	S
O	R	S	P	I	N	A	C	H	I	B	G	K	A	E	T	I
V	N	Q	P	I	N	E	A	P	P	L	E	N	E	S	T	D
L	I	U	E	V	Y	R	R	E	B	W	A	R	T	S	N	A
Q	P	A	R	S	L	E	Y	E	R	B	C	O	R	N	A	R
Y	G	S	O	O	D	F	O	S	D	R	A	L	L	O	C	R
Y	C	H	E	R	R	Y	N	A	E	Z	A	M	O	L	V	O

MANY FRIENDS COOKING

GROUNDNUT CRUNCH
from Tanzania

East Africans rarely munch on sweets. But when they do, groundnuts, or peanuts as we call them, are always included. Groundnuts are the main ingredient of many African foods. If you and your friends like to munch, try sharing this groundnut crunch.

INGREDIENTS

⅔ cup chopped
   unsalted nuts
⅓ cup water
⅓ cup sugar
½ teaspoon cinnamon

EQUIPMENT

measuring cup
measuring spoons
heavy-bottomed saucepan
wooden spoon
waxed paper

HOW TO MAKE

1. In a heavy-bottomed saucepan heat the water and sugar over low heat, stirring constantly until the sugar dissolves.

2. Add the nuts and cinnamon and continue to stir for about 3 minutes until the mixture turns light brown. Be careful that the mixture doesn't burn.

3. Remove the pan from the heat and let cool about 10 minutes until cool enough to handle.

4. Pick up bits of the mixture and shape into little balls. Place on waxed paper.

5. Refrigerate several hours and serve immediately.

This receipe makes about 15 balls.

SESAME BEEF
from Korea

Koreans make this tasty barbecued beef outdoors over a small charcoal burner. However, it is just as delicious cooked indoors under a broiler. Either way, the sesame flavor, found in many Korean recipes, comes through—nutty and delicious. (Have an adult help you with this recipe.)

INGREDIENTS	EQUIPMENT
1 pound flank steak	sharp knife
2 scallions	small bowl
1 clove garlic	small frying pan
2 tablespoons toasted sesame seeds	wooden spoon
	measuring spoons
2 tablespoons sesame oil or vegetable oil	measuring cup
	shallow pan to hold steak
¼ cup soy sauce	4-6 metal skewers

HOW TO MAKE

1. Place sesame seeds in a small frying pan over medium heat. Cook, stirring constantly until golden brown. Don't let them burn.

2. Slice the steak very thin across the grain. Cut steak strips into 3-inch-long pieces.

3. Slice the scallions thinly into small rounds.

4. Peel the garlic clove and mince.

5. In the small bowl combine the scallions, garlic, sesame seeds, oil, and soy sauce.

6. Place the steak in a shallow pan and pour the seasoning over the meat. Turn the steak to coat with the marinade. Marinate at least 1 hour.

7. To cook, thread the pieces of steak on skewers. Grill or broil for 2 minutes on each side. The meat should be crisply browned but not burned.

This recipe serves 4 people.

153

Dressed in her finest, Miss Penelope Pig is so charming that she can sit with you at the breakfast table. And she's just one of the cool crafty characters that you can make.

CRAFTY CHARACTERS

Need something to do on a lazy afternoon? Here's a crew of amusing characters that you can create, using various techniques and materials. You'll have lots of fun while you're crafting—and lots of opportunities to use your imagination.

PENELOPE PIG

Did anyone ever warn you that if you ate too much you'd swell up like a balloon? Well, that's exactly what's happened to Penelope Pig. This chubby pink pig is made by blowing up balloons, and then covering them with lots and lots of thread.

You'll need a large balloon for Penelope's body, a medium one for the head, and four small ones for the feet. You'll also need pink crochet thread, thread stiffener, glue, a plastic cup, a large bowl, beads, pieces of pink and black felt, and a pink pipe cleaner.

Blow up and knot the ends of the balloons. For the body, tie one end of the thread to the knot of the large balloon. Wrap the thread around the balloon, crisscrossing it in all directions so that the balloon is completely covered. Tie the thread to the balloon knot, leaving a "tail" for hanging. Follow the same procedure for all the other balloons.

Make a snout from the bottom of the plastic cup. Wrap thread around the cup, just as you did around the balloons.

Now comes the messy part, so be sure your work surface is covered with a plastic bag or newspaper. One by one, hold each balloon and the snout over the large bowl and pour thread stiffener over it, repeating the process

Funky Fish Magnets

until all the threads are saturated. Hang the balloons and snout by their "tails" over a protected surface for one to two days, until the threads are completely dry. Then cut off the "tails" and puncture the balloons. Remove the plastic cup from the snout.

Gently press an indentation into one side of the body and glue on the head. Follow the same procedure for the feet. Glue the open end of the snout to the head. Glue felt nostrils onto the snout, beady eyes and felt ears onto the head, and the pipe-cleaner tail onto the body.

To turn Penelope into a perfect little pig, dress her in a lace collar and a little straw hat. Now she's ready to charm family and friends.

FUNKY FISH

Find a piece of fabric that's "swimming" with tropical fish and use it to create colorful fish magnets. In addition to the fabric you'll need felt, iron-on adhesive, glue, fiberfill stuffing, clear glitter fabric paint, clear fabric glitter, and round magnets.

Cut a fish shape from the fabric, leaving a bit of background fabric around the edges. Use this cutout as a pattern to cut a matching fish from a piece of felt.

Place the fabric fish, right side up, on the iron-on adhesive. Using an iron preheated at medium setting, press the fish onto the adhesive for about five seconds. Don't move the iron during pressing! When cool, trim the excess fabric around the fish.

Rollin' Rosie and Skateboard Sam

155

Glue a magnet to the center of one side of the felt fish. Place the felt fish, magnet side down, on the ironing board. Put a small amount of fiberfill stuffing in the center. Place the fabric fish on top. Press with the warm iron for a few seconds. Use the tip of the iron to press around the outside edges, to make certain the pieces are sealed together. Trim the excess felt, leaving a thin felt border around the outside of the fish.

Outline the fish, its fins, and other details with the fabric paint. While the paint is still wet, sprinkle on glitter. After the fish dries, it's ready to swim across your refrigerator!

ROLLIN' RACERS

With hair standing on end, Rollin' Rosie and Skateboard Sam (page 155) show off their nimble-footed skills. Each of these teenage speedsters is made from a miniature seagrass broom (hair), a wooden craft spoon (face and body), a pipe cleaner (arms), two wooden craft sticks (legs), and two wooden ovals (feet).

Paint the front and side edges of the spoon with flesh-colored paint. Add details to the face. Let dry. Place the broom on your work surface. Center the pipe cleaner on the back of the handle, just below the bristles; glue it on the handle to form the arms. Glue the spoon to the front of the broom handle, placing it so the face is centered in a halo of hair. Glue the craft sticks atop the lower part of the handle, so that they are even with the bottom of the spoon, to form the legs. Glue the oval feet to the bottoms of the craft sticks.

Make Rosie's skates from painted wooden circles, and Sam's skateboard from a jumbo craft stick, with four wooden circles for wheels. Dress the pair in clothes made from brightly colored felt or construction paper, and these kids will be ready to race!

SLIM 'N' JIM

These smilin' cowpokes look mighty cute in their ten-gallon hats and nifty bandannas. The hats can be purchased at a craft store, but the bandannas and other clothing can be made from old jeans and scraps of fabrics.

To make Slim—he's the tubby one—you'll need a wooden bead for the head, two craft spoons for the arms, a large foam ball for the body, and a large wooden heart for the feet. Skinny Jim is made from a head bead, two short dowels for the arms, a doll pin for the body, and a small wooden heart for the feet. You'll also need doll hair and glue.

Slim 'n' Jim Cowpokes

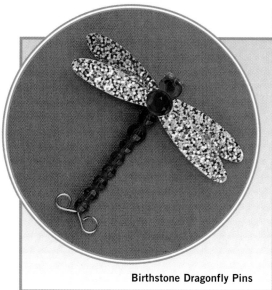

Birthstone Dragonfly Pins

January	February	March	April
May	June	July	August
September	October	November	December

Paint faces on the head beads, and paint the hearts brown. While these dry, make the cowboys' clothes. Begin with the shirt sleeves: Wrap pieces of fabric around the arms; glue the fabric edges together; and glue the fabric to the arms. In a similar fashion, attach fabric around each cowboy's body, first the shirt and then the pants.

Glue the arms, head, and heart onto each body. Glue doll hair and then a hat onto each head. Wrap a bandanna around each neck, and add button belt buckles. Your cowboys are gettin' ready to rustle up some fun!

DAZZLING DRAGONFLIES

Dragonflies are among nature's most beautiful insects. They look like sparkling jewels as sunlight reflects from their bodies. You can re-create this splendor by making a birthstone dragonfly pin—it's a great birthday present for friends or family.

Here are the birthstone colors for each month: January, dark red; February, purple; March, light blue; April, crystal; May, green; June, light purple; July, red; August, light green; September, blue; October, rosy pink; November, amber; and December, turquoise.

To make a pin you'll need eight faceted beads, two slightly larger than the others; and four faceted stones—a large round one, two small round ones, and a large heart-shaped one. You'll also need adhesive-backed glitter paper, posterboard, beading wire that's 8 inches (20 centimeters) long, jewelry glue, and a pin back.

Bend the wire in half and twist it two or three times to form a small loop, as shown in the diagram at right. This will be the body.

To make the dragonfly's tail, insert both wire ends through the eight beads, beginning with the two larger ones. Push the beads up to the loop, and then bend the bottom ends of the wire into small curls.

Remove the backing from the glitter paper and press the paper to the poster board. Cut out two pairs of wings. Glue the front wings onto the front of the wire loop. Glue the back wings so that they overlap the front wings and touch the first bead of the tail.

The heart-shaped stone is the dragonfly's head. Glue the two little round stones onto the curves of the heart, to create eyes. Glue the heart to the body so that it sligtly overlaps the wings. Glue the large round stone atop the wings. Glue the pin back on, and your dragonfly is ready to fly onto a jumper or sweater!

JULIE STEPHANI
Crafts 'n Things magazine

157

COIN COLLECTING

Innovative coins and sets, including many that were the first of their kind, provided coin collectors with plenty of exciting choices in 1997.

U.S. COINS

In 1947, Jackie Robinson broke the color barrier to become the first African-American player in modern major-league baseball. The U.S. Mint honored the 50th anniversary of that event with several coins and sets. One popular set teamed a reproduction of a 1952 baseball card of Robinson with a $5 gold coin depicting a full-face view of the famous Brooklyn Dodger. Collectors could also purchase proof or uncirculated versions of a Robinson silver dollar. The silver dollar's design was based on a photograph showing Robinson stealing home during Game 1 of the 1955 World Series. A portion of the proceeds from the sale of the Robinson coins was earmarked for the Jackie Robinson Foundation, a non-profit organization that awards scholarships to qualified young people.

U.S. $5 gold coin honoring Jackie Robinson, and silver dollar showing the National Botanic Garden.

One of the year's hottest coin sets featured a silver dollar authorized to raise funds for the National Botanic Garden, in Washington, D.C. Collector interest was heightened by the fact that the set also included a 1997 Jefferson nickel with a special matte (dull) surface, typical of the finish used on proof coins in the early 20th century. Collectors rushed to get the sets, which sold out quickly.

Two other commemorative coins were released by the U.S. Mint in 1997—a National Law Enforcement Officers Memorial silver dollar, which honored those officers who lost their lives in the line of duty, and a Franklin D. Roosevelt $5 gold coin, the first modern U.S. commemorative to be available only in gold.

The Mint also issued a group of American Eagles that were the first U.S. coins to be struck in platinum. They were issued in proof and bullion versions, valued by the amount of precious metal they contained, in weights rang-

U.S. $100 platinum coin in the American Eagles group.

ing from a tenth-ounce to one ounce. The one-ounce coin carried a denomination of $100, a first and the highest face value ever for a U.S. coin. The coins showed the Statue of Liberty on the obverse and a soaring eagle on the reverse.

WORLD COINS

Alexander Graham Bell was featured on the reverse of Canada's 1997 $100 coin. The coin marked the 150th anniversary of the birth of the Scottish-American inventor of the telephone. Bell made the first long-distance telephone call in Canada in 1876, from a store in Mount Pleasant, Ontario, to a telegraph office in Brantford, Ontario.

A 10-cent commemorative from Canada marked the 500th anniversary of the 1497 voyage of explorer Giovanni Caboto, or John Cabot. Cabot, an Italian-born navigator, sailed from England in search of a route to Asia and reached the North American coast at Newfoundland or Cape Breton Island. The coin showed his ship, the *Matthew*.

Canada's coins featuring Alexander Graham Bell, John Cabot, Team Canada, and a Haida Indian mask.

A Canadian silver dollar, in proof and uncirculated versions, honored the 25th anniversary of Team Canada's dramatic hockey victory over the Soviet Union in 1972. The coin's reverse showed the winning goal by Paul Henderson of Team Canada, making this the first Canadian coin to depict living people (other than the British monarch).

The Royal Canadian Mint also released only the second coin in its history with no inscription on the reverse. A dramatic Haida Indian mask covered the entire reverse of a $200 gold coin, the first in a planned series honoring native cultures. The mask depicted Raven, the mythical Haida hero, who brought sunlight to the world.

Canada's 1997 platinum commemoratives depicted the endangered wood bison, while new coins in the gold-on-silver aviation series showed the Canadian F-86 Sabre and the Canadian CT-114 Tutor. Dogs were featured on four 50-cent silver commemoratives.

The deaths of two widely admired women, Princess Diana of Britain and Mother Teresa of Calcutta, saddened the world in 1997. Several countries marked these losses with coins. Sierra Leone took an unusual approach by showing the two women together on gold coins issued in several denominations. It was the first time Mother Teresa, renowned for her work with the poor, had appeared on a coin.

As always, animals—from tame to ferocious—were featured on many coins. The history of cats was traced in five 1-crown coins from the Isle of Man. The Isle of Man also released a gold-on-silver 10-crown coin, marking the tenth anniversary of its cat-theme coin series. It showed a tailless Manx cat surrounded by images from other cat-theme crowns struck since 1988. Since 1997 was the Year of the Ox in the Chinese lunar calendar, several nations showed that beast on coins. A

The Isle of Man's gold-on-silver coin depicting numerous cats, and Gibraltar's 50-pence coin showing Santa Claus.

50-cent Year of the Ox coin from Hong Kong was among the first coins issued by that territory after it passed from British to Chinese rule on July 1.

The British-ruled territory of Gibraltar issued some of 1997's most whimsical coins. A group of gold, silver, platinum, and copper-nickel coins honored *The Tale of Peter Rabbit,* with a mischievous Peter on the reverse. For Christmas, a seven-sided 50-pence coin showed Santa Claus in his reindeer-powered sleigh, soaring over Gibraltar.

BOB VAN RYZIN
Editor, *Coins* magazine

Sierra Leone's gold coin honoring
Mother Teresa and Princess Diana.

Women's pro basketball was the hot sports ticket of 1997. The Women's National Basketball Association joined the eight-month-old American Basketball League as a second U.S. women's league, and games drew capacity crowds. With stars like New York Liberty forward-center Rebecca Lobo (below, with Catarina Pollini of the Houston Comets), play was fast—and good. Fans cheered the action and the attitude of the leagues. As one fan put it: "There are no big heads and no big salaries, and I love it!"

Florida pitcher Livan Hernandez was named MVP of the World Series. Florida defeated Cleveland 4 games to 3.

BASEBALL

For the Florida Marlins, 1997 was only their fifth season, yet they won the World Series by defeating the Cleveland Indians in seven games. No other expansion club had ever reached baseball's pinnacle in so short a time.

Manager Jim Leyland's Marlins were also the first "wild-card" team to take the Fall Classic. In the regular season, they came in second in the East Division of the National League (NL), following the Atlanta Braves. The Houston Astros finished atop the Central Division, and the San Francisco Giants led the West.

In the division series (the first round of playoffs), Florida swept San Francisco in three games, while Atlanta did the same to Houston. The Marlins then beat the Braves, 4 games to 2, in the National League Championship Series (NLCS). Livan Hernandez, Florida's rookie right-handed pitcher, was named the Most Valuable Player (MVP) of the NLCS.

Cleveland topped the Central Division in the American League (AL). The Seattle Mariners won the West, and the Baltimore Orioles finished just ahead of the wild-card New York Yankees in the East.

In the division series, the Indians ousted the Yankees, 3 games to 2, and the Orioles sank the Mariners in four games. Though underdogs to Baltimore in the American League Championship Series (ALCS), Cleveland won, 4 games to 2. Indian centerfielder Marquis Grissom was the MVP of the ALCS.

Game 1 of the Fall Classic—the first World Series game ever played in Florida—attracted more than 67,000 fans to Pro Player Stadium in Miami, and the home team came away with a 7–4 victory. Livan Hernandez pitched $5\frac{2}{3}$ innings; he was only the fifth rookie starter ever to win the opening game of a World Series.

In Game 2, the Indians won, 6–1. Cleveland starter Chad Ogea pitched $6\frac{2}{3}$ innings for the victory. So, having won one game apiece, the opponents left Florida and headed to chilly Jacobs Field in Cleveland for Games 3, 4, and 5.

The weather was indeed a factor in Game 3, contributing to all-around sloppy play. Cleveland and Florida pitchers issued a combined total of 17 walks. The Indians blew a four-run lead, and tied a World Series record by committing three errors in one inning. The Marlins won, 14–11. Florida's margin was 2 games to 1.

Snow flurries swirled about during Game 4; unperturbed, the Indians won, 10–3. Rookie pitcher Jaret Wright went six innings for the victory. The Series was tied, 2 games to 2.

In Game 5, Cleveland mounted a 4–2 lead. But propelled by Moises Alou's third home run of the Series, a three-run shot, Florida finally prevailed, 8–7. Livan Hernandez hurled eight innings; he became only the first rookie in half a century to win two games in a World Series. The Series now returned to Florida, with the Marlins up, 3 games to 2.

Chad Ogea pitched the first five innings of Game 6 to notch his second victory of the

1997 WORLD SERIES RESULTS

		R	H	E	Winning/Losing Pitcher
1	Cleveland	4	11	0	Orel Hershiser (L)
	Florida	7	7	1	Livan Hernandez (W)
2	Cleveland	6	14	0	Chad Ogea (W)
	Florida	1	8	0	Kevin Brown (L)
3	Florida	14	16	3	Dennis Cook (W)
	Cleveland	11	10	3	Eric Plunk (L)
4	Florida	3	6	2	Tony Saunders (L)
	Cleveland	10	15	0	Jaret Wright (W)
5	Florida	8	15	2	Livan Hernandez (W)
	Cleveland	7	9	0	Orel Hershiser(L)
6	Cleveland	4	7	0	Chad Ogea (W)
	Florida	1	8	0	Kevin Brown (L)
7	Cleveland	2	6	2	Charles Nagy (L)
	Florida	3	8	0	Jay Powell (W)

Visiting team listed first, home team second

Series, as the Indians won, 4–1. Equally important, Ogea knocked in two runs with a second-inning single; the runs batted in (RBIs) were the first for a Cleveland pitcher since 1972, the year before the AL instituted the designated hitter.

Game 7 was exciting and well-played; the teams battled into extra innings before the contest was decided. The Indians opened a 2–0 lead, but Florida third baseman Bobby Bonilla got one back with a homer in the seventh inning. Cleveland held its 2–1 lead until the last of the ninth, when Marlin second baseman Craig Counsell drove Moises Alou home from third with a sacrifice fly. Finally, in the last of the eleventh, Counsell scored on a single by shortstop Edgar Renteria. Score: 3–2; and the Florida Marlins were the world champions.

Livan Hernandez was named MVP of the Series, becoming only the second rookie ever to win the award.

The 1997 regular season saw some fine performances. Tony Gwynn of the San Diego Padres tied an NL record by capturing his eighth batting title. Mark McGwire and Ken Griffey, Jr., both went after the single-season home run record; both fell short. McGwire did, however, tie the record for right-handed hitters, with 58; he hit 34 for the AL Oakland A's and 24 for the NL St. Louis Cardinals. Seattle's Grif-

fey hit 56; he also had 147 RBIs and was named the AL's regular-season MVP.

The NL MVP was Larry Walker of the Colorado Rockies; he batted .366, smashed 49 homers, had 130 RBIs, and scored 143 runs.

Roger Clemens won his fourth Cy Young Award; in his first year with the Toronto Blue Jays after a superb career with the Boston Red Sox, he led the AL in victories (21), strikeouts (292), and earned run average (ERA) (2.05). Pedro Martinez of the Montreal Expos received the NL Cy Young Award; he won 17 games, led the league with a minuscule 1.90 ERA, and struck out 305 batters.

The AL Rookie-of-the-Year was shortstop Nomar Garciaparra of the Boston Red Sox. He batted .306, hit 30 homers, batted in 98 runs, and scored 122 times. The top rookie in the NL was Philadelphia Phillie third baseman Scott Rolen, who batted .283 with 21 home runs and 92 RBIs.

Seattle's Ken Griffey, Jr., was named the American League's regular-season MVP. He smacked 56 homers.

MAJOR LEAGUE BASEBALL FINAL STANDINGS

AMERICAN LEAGUE

Eastern Division

	W	L	Pct.	GB
Baltimore	98	64	.605	—
New York	96	66	.593	2
Detroit	79	83	.488	19
Boston	78	84	.481	20
Toronto	76	86	.469	22

Central Division

	W	L	Pct.	GB
*Cleveland	86	75	.534	—
Chicago	80	81	.497	6
Milwaukee	78	83	.484	8
Minnesota	68	94	.420	18½
Kansas City	67	94	.416	19

Western Division

	W	L	Pct.	GB
Seattle	90	72	.556	—
Anaheim	84	78	.519	6
Texas	77	85	.475	13
Oakland	65	97	.401	25

NATIONAL LEAGUE

Eastern Division

	W	L	Pct.	GB
Atlanta	101	61	.623	—
*Florida	92	70	.568	9
New York	88	74	.543	13
Montreal	78	84	.481	23
Philadelphia	68	94	.420	33

Central Division

	W	L	Pct.	GB
Houston	84	78	.519	—
Pittsburgh	79	83	.488	5
Cincinnati	76	86	.469	8
St. Louis	73	89	.451	11
Chicago	68	94	.420	16

Western Division

	W	L	Pct.	GB
San Francisco	90	72	.556	—
Los Angeles	88	74	.543	2
Colorado	83	79	.512	7
San Diego	76	86	.469	14

*League Championship Series winners

MAJOR LEAGUE LEADERS

AMERICAN LEAGUE

Batting
(top 10 qualifiers)

	AB	H	Avg.
F. Thomas, Chicago	530	184	.347
E. Martinez, Seattle	542	179	.330
Justice, Cleveland	495	163	.329
Ramirez, Cleveland	561	184	.328
Williams, New York	509	167	.328
O'Neill, New York	553	179	.324
Greer, Texas	601	193	.321
Jefferson, Boston	489	156	.319
Vaughn, Boston	527	166	.315
I. Rodriguez, Texas	597	187	.313

Home Runs

	HR
Griffey, Seattle	56
T. Martinez, New York	44
Gonzalez, Texas	42
Thorne, Cleveland	40
Buhner, Seattle	40

NATIONAL LEAGUE

Batting
(top 10 qualifiers)

	AB	H	Avg.
Gwynn, San Diego	592	220	.372
L. Walker, Colorado	568	208	.366
Piazza, Los Angeles	556	201	.362
Lofton, Atlanta	493	164	.333
Joyner, San Diego	455	149	.327
Grace, Chicago	555	177	.319
Galarraga, Colorado	600	191	.318
Alfonzo, New York	518	163	.315
Mondesi, Los Angeles	616	191	.310
Biggio, Houston	619	191	.309

Home Runs

	HR
L. Walker, Colorado	49
Bagwell, Houston	43
Galarraga, Colorado	41
Piazza, Los Angeles	40
Castilla, Colorado	40
Bonds, San Francisco	40

*Mark McGwire hit a total of 58 home runs—34 in the American League, and 24 in the National League

Pitching
(top qualifiers, based on number of wins)

	W	L	ERA
Clemens, Toronto	21	7	2.05
Johnson, Seattle	20	4	2.28
Radke, Minnesota	20	10	3.87
Pettitte, New York	18	7	2.88
Moyer, Seattle	17	5	3.86

Pitching
(top qualifiers, based on number of wins)

	W	L	ERA
Neagle, Atlanta	20	5	2.97
Maddux, Atlanta	19	4	2.20
Estes, San Francisco	19	5	3.18
Kile, Houston	19	7	2.57
Martinez, Montreal	17	8	1.90
Schilling, Philadelphia	17	11	2.97
Fernandez, Florida	17	12	3.59

Little Leaguers from Guadalupe, Mexico, won the 1997 World Series, defeating the U.S. champs, 5–4.

LITTLE LEAGUE BASEBALL

"It ain't over till it's over." That famous baseball saying, attributed to Hall of Famer Yogi Berra, was proven true yet again in the 1997 Little League World Series. A fine team from Guadalupe, Mexico, was behind by three runs going into the sixth—and last—inning of the final game. Refusing to fold, they scored four times to defeat the U.S. champs, from Mission Viejo, California, by the score of 5–4.

The U.S. pitcher, Gavin Fabian, was starting his third game in five days. And he didn't allow a hit by Mexico through five innings. But Fabian walked the first two batters in the sixth, and he was replaced on the mound. Mexico's Gabriel Alvarez was in the batter's box, and on one swing, he tied the score with a soaring three-run home run.

Javier De Isla then walked, and went to second on another base on balls. Pablo Torres followed with a single to center; the ball bounced off the U.S. centerfielder's glove, and De Isla raced home with the winning run.

Mexico's two hitting stars were also their pitchers. Gabriel Alvarez started the game.

Pablo Torres relieved him in the fourth inning, struck out six of the eight batters he faced, and was ultimately the winning hurler.

The only other Mexican team to win the Little League World Series was a club from Monterrey, which took the title twice, in 1957 and 1958. The legends that have grown about that Monterrey team in the intervening four decades helped inspire the 1997 champs in their quest for the Little League crown.

Guadalupe, Mexico, reached the final game by finishing first in the Little League tournament's International Division. The other International teams were from Yokohama, Japan (the Far Eastern champs); Dhahran, Saudi Arabia (representing Europe); and Surrey, British Columbia (the Canadian titlists). Mission Viejo, California, eliminated the three other U.S. teams, which hailed from Bradenton, Florida; Pottsville, Pennsylvania; and Dyer, Indiana.

The Little League World Series is held each August at Lamade Stadium in Williamsport, Pennsylvania.

Karl Malone of the Utah Jazz (with ball) was the NBA's MVP in 1997, but Michael Jordan (behind Malone) led the Chicago Bulls to the league title.

BASKETBALL

When the final history of basketball is written, the first and last paragraphs will probably contain the name Michael Jordan. In 1997, he led the Chicago Bulls to their fifth National Basketball Association (NBA) title in seven years, as they downed the Utah Jazz, four games to two, in the playoff finals.

Celebrating its 50th anniversary in 1997, the NBA named its all-time top 50 players. Joining Jordan on the list was teammate Scottie Pippen, plus two members of the Utah Jazz: power forward Karl Malone, who was honored as Most Valuable Player (MVP) of the 1997 regular season; and guard John Stockton, the league's all-time leader in assists.

Coach Phil Jackson's Bulls weren't just a two-man team. Valuable contributions all season long came from Ron Harper, Toni Kukoc, Luc Longley, Dennis Rodman, Steve Kerr, and Brian Williams.

The Bulls finished the regular season atop the Central Division of the Eastern Conference with the NBA's best record. In round one of the playoffs, they swept the Washington Bullets three games to none. Chicago then eliminated the Atlanta Hawks four games to one in round two. And Chicago beat the Miami Heat, also in five games, to win the Eastern Conference finals.

In the Western Conference playoffs, Utah defeated the Los Angeles Clippers in round one; the Los Angeles Lakers in round two; and the Houston Rockets in the conference finals. The Jazz thus reached the NBA finals for the first time in its history.

The first two games of the finals were played in United Center in Chicago. Game 1 was close throughout, and was tied with just seconds to play. But as he has so many times in the past, Jordan swished a jumper just before the buzzer. Chicago won, 84–82. Jordan had 31 points, Pippen added 27, and Malone led Utah with 23.

Game 2 was easier for the Bulls; they won 97–85. Jordan poured in 38 points while Malone had 20 for the Jazz.

Delta Center in Salt Lake City was the site of the next three games. Happy to be home, the Jazz won Game 3 by 104–93. Malone soared for 37 points, while Stockton passed for 12 assists.

Utah also won Game 4, sparked by Stockton's heroics in the last two minutes. The Jazz scored the game's final 9 points and won 78–73. The series was now tied at two games apiece.

Michael Jordan showed up with the flu for Game 5, and the Jazz charged off to an early lead. But Jordan shook off his illness and the Bulls battled back. In the fourth quarter, Jordan scored 15 points, including a 3-pointer with 25 seconds to play. He had 38 points overall, and Chicago won, 90–88.

The Bulls returned home with a 3–2 lead. In Game 6, down 44–37 at halftime, they rallied to tie the Jazz in the game's final minute.

NBA FINAL STANDINGS

EASTERN CONFERENCE

Atlantic Division

	W	L	Pct.
Miami	61	21	.744
New York	57	25	.695
Orlando	45	37	.549
Washington	44	38	.537
New Jersey	26	56	.317
Philadelphia	22	60	.268
Boston	15	67	.183

Central Division

	W	L	Pct.
Chicago	69	13	.841
Atlanta	56	26	.683
Detroit	54	28	.659
Charlotte	54	28	.659
Cleveland	42	40	.512
Indiana	39	43	.476
Milwaukee	33	49	.402
Toronto	30	52	.366

WESTERN CONFERENCE

Midwest Division

	W	L	Pct.
Utah	64	18	.780
Houston	57	25	.695
Minnesota	40	42	.488
Dallas	24	58	.293
Denver	21	61	.256
San Antonio	20	62	.244
Vancouver	14	68	.171

Pacific Division

	W	L	Pct.
Seattle	57	25	.695
L.A. Lakers	56	26	.683
Portland	49	33	.598
Phoenix	40	42	.488
L.A. Clippers	36	46	.439
Sacramento	34	48	.415
Golden State	30	52	.366

NBA Championship: Chicago Bulls

COLLEGE BASKETBALL

Conference	Winner
Atlantic Coast	Duke (regular season) North Carolina (tournament)
Atlantic Ten	St. Joseph's, Xavier (tied, regular season) St. Joseph's (tournament)
Big East	Georgetown, Villanova, Boston College (tied, regular season) Boston College (tournament)
Big Ten	Minnesota
Big Twelve	Kansas (regular season and tournament)
Big West	Utah State, Pacific (tied, regular season) Pacific (tournament)
Ivy League	Princeton
Missouri Valley	Illinois State (regular season and tournament)
Pacific-10	UCLA
Southeastern	South Carolina (regular season) Kentucky (tournament)
Southwest	Mississippi Valley (regular season) Jackson State (tournament)
Western Athletic	Utah (regular season)

NCAA, men: Arizona
women: Tennessee

NIT: Michigan

With five seconds left, Chicago sub Steve Kerr buried a 17-footer. Toni Kukoc added a dunk at the buzzer. Final score: 90–86. Michael Jordan scored 39 points; he was named MVP of the finals for the second year in a row and the fifth time in his career. He averaged 32.3 points per game in the finals.

During the regular season, Jordan won his ninth scoring title—an NBA record—averaging 29.6 points per game. Philadelphia 76er point guard Allen Iverson was named rookie of the year.

Women's Leagues. Two women's pro leagues began play in 1997. The Houston Comets won the championship of the NBA-sponsored Women's National Basketball Association. And the Columbus (Ohio) Quest captured the title of the independent American Basketball League.

College Play. The University of Tennessee, coached by Pat Summitt, won its second straight National Collegiate Athletic Association (NCAA) women's championship, defeating Old Dominion in the final, 68–59. Lady Vol All-American Chamique Holdsclaw scored 24 points and was named MVP.

Miles Simon was MVP for the University of Arizona's NCAA men's championship team. He scored 30 points for coach Lute Olson's Wildcats in their 84–79 final victory over Kentucky.

FOOTBALL

The Green Bay Packers—a team with a winning tradition in the National Football League (NFL)—won the first two Super Bowls ever played, and then waited 29 years, until 1997, to win another. In the Canadian Football League (CFL), the Toronto Argonauts captured their second consecutive Grey Cup. And the University of Michigan placed first in the regular-season college rankings, while its star player took home the Heisman Trophy.

THE NFL PLAYOFFS AND SUPER BOWL XXXI

Green Bay topped its division in 1996 with a 13–3 regular-season record, tied for the best in the NFL. The other National Conference division leaders were the Dallas Cowboys and the Carolina Panthers; the wild-card teams were the San Francisco 49ers, the Philadelphia Eagles, and the Minnesota Vikings.

Terrell Davis's rushing propelled the Denver Broncos to the playoffs in 1997. He led the American Conference.

In the first round of the playoffs, Dallas overwhelmed Minnesota, 40–15, while San Francisco shut out Philadelphia, 14–0.

The following week, though, both first-round winners were eliminated, as the Packers bested the 49ers by 35–14, and the Panthers upset the Cowboys (the defending Super Bowl champs), 26–17.

Green Bay's offense dominated the National Conference title game. Quarterback Brett Favre completed 19 passes in 29 attempts for 292 yards; two of his throws went for touchdowns. Packer running back Dorsey Levens gained 88 yards on only ten carries and also caught five passes for 117 yards and a touchdown. Final score: Green Bay 30, Carolina 13.

The New England Patriots, the Pittsburgh Steelers, and the Denver Broncos led their divisions in the American Conference in 1996; wild-card berths went to the Buffalo Bills, the Indianapolis Colts, and the Jacksonville Jaguars.

Jacksonville upended Buffalo, 30–27, in the first round of the playoffs, while Pittsburgh ousted Indianapolis by 42–14.

The Jaguars continued their winning ways in round two, defeating the favored Broncos by 30–27. In the meantime, the Patriots were hammering the Steelers, 28–3.

In the American Conference title game, New England's defense forced several Jacksonville turnovers, and the Patriots emerged with a 20–6 victory. Cornerback Otis Smith put the game away late in the fourth quarter by picking up a Jaguar fumble and returning it 47 yards for a touchdown.

Thus the Packers opposed the Patriots in Super Bowl XXXI, played on January 26, 1997, in the Louisiana Superdome in New Orleans, Louisiana. The Packers opened the scoring early, cashing in on a 54-yard touchdown pass from quarterback Brett Favre to wide receiver Andre Rison. The game was barely three and a half minutes old. And less than three minutes later, Green Bay scored again, this time on a 37-yard field goal by Chris Jacke.

Undaunted, New England responded by taking a 14–10 lead in the first quarter, as Patriot quarterback Drew Bledsoe connected on two touchdown passes. But the second quarter belonged entirely to Green Bay. Favre combined with receiver Antonio Freeman on an 81-yard score, the longest play from scrimmage in Super Bowl history. Jacke kicked another field goal. And Favre himself found the end zone on a 2-yard run. At halftime, the Packers led, 27–14.

The Patriots pulled to within 27–21 in the third quarter. But on the ensuing kickoff, Green Bay kick returner Desmond Howard fielded the ball on his own 1-yard line and blasted 99 yards for a score. It was a Super Bowl record for a kickoff return, and in fact a record for all-time NFL post-season play. Howard also set a Super Bowl mark with a total of 90 yards on punt returns, and his combined 244 yards on all runbacks tied another record.

The Green Bay defense, meanwhile, intercepted four of Bledsoe's passes, and Packer defensive lineman Reggie White set still another record with three sacks. The final score was 35–21, Green Bay. Desmond Howard became the first special-teams member ever named the most valuable player (MVP) of a Super Bowl.

THE 1997 REGULAR SEASON

Green Bay finished first in its division once again in 1997. The other National Conference division titlists were San Francisco and the New York Giants; the wild-card teams were Minnesota, the Detroit Lions, and the Tampa Bay Buccaneers.

Pittsburgh, New England, and the Kansas City Chiefs led their divisions in the American Conference; wild-card berths went to Denver, Jacksonville, and the Miami Dolphins.

THE CANADIAN FOOTBALL LEAGUE

The Toronto Argonauts won their second consecutive CFL championship, defeating the Saskatchewan Roughriders, 47–23, in the Grey Cup game, played in Edmonton, Alberta, on November 16, 1997. Toronto quarterback Doug Flutie was named Grey Cup MVP; he passed for three touchdowns and ran for another. Argonaut Adrion Smith ran back the opening kick of the second half 95 yards for a score; it was the longest kickoff return in the 85-year history of the CFL championship game.

In 1997, Barry Sanders of the Detroit Lions became only the third player in NFL history to rush for more than 2,000 yards in a single season, totaling 2,053.

During the regular season, Toronto had a 15–3 record, and Flutie led the league in passing with 430 completions in 673 attempts for 5,505 yards and 47 touchdowns.

COLLEGE FOOTBALL

Michigan, with an 11–0 record, rated number one in college football at the end of the regular season, whipped Washington State (10–1) in the Rose Bowl. Number-two Nebraska (12–0) defeated third-ranked Tennessee (11–1) in the Orange Bowl; UCLA (9–2) topped Texas A&M (9–3) in the Cotton Bowl; Florida State (10–1) overcame Ohio State (10–2) in the Sugar Bowl; and Florida (9–2) pummeled Penn State (9–2) in the Citrus Bowl.

Michigan cornerback Charles Woodson won the Heisman Trophy; he was the first defensive player in history to be accorded the honor.

University of Michigan cornerback Charles Woodson won the 1997 Heisman Trophy as the best college player.

COLLEGE FOOTBALL

Conference	Winner
Atlantic Coast	Florida State
Big Ten	Michigan
Big Twelve	Nebraska
Big West	Nevada, Utah State (tied)
Pacific-10	Washington State
Southeastern	Tennessee
Western Athletic	Colorado State

Citrus Bowl: Florida 21, Penn State 6
Cotton Bowl: UCLA 29, Texas A&M 23
Fiesta Bowl: Kansas State 35, Syracuse 18
Gator Bowl: North Carolina 42, Virginia Tech 3
Orange Bowl: Nebraska 42, Tennessee 17
Rose Bowl: Michigan 21, Washington State 16
Sugar Bowl: Florida State 31, Ohio State 14

Heisman Trophy: Charles Woodson, Michigan

1997 NFL FINAL STANDINGS

AMERICAN CONFERENCE

Eastern Division

	W	L	T	Pct.	PF	PA
New England	10	6	0	.625	369	289
Miami	9	7	0	.563	339	327
N. Y. Jets	9	7	0	.563	348	287
Buffalo	6	10	0	.375	255	367
Indianapolis	3	13	0	.188	313	401

Central Division

	W	L	T	Pct.	PF	PA
Pittsburgh	11	5	0	.688	372	307
Jacksonville	11	5	0	.688	394	318
Tennessee	8	8	0	.500	333	310
Cincinnati	7	9	0	.438	355	405
Baltimore	6	9	1	.406	326	345

Western Division

	W	L	T	Pct.	PF	PA
Kansas City	13	3	0	.813	375	232
Denver	12	4	0	.750	472	287
Seattle	8	8	0	.500	365	362
Oakland	4	12	0	.250	324	419
San Diego	4	12	0	.250	266	425

NATIONAL CONFERENCE

Eastern Division

	W	L	T	Pct.	PF	PA
N. Y. Giants	10	5	1	.656	307	265
Washington	8	7	1	.531	327	289
Philadelphia	6	9	1	.406	317	372
Dallas	6	10	0	.375	304	314
Arizona	4	12	0	.250	283	379

Central Division

	W	L	T	Pct.	PF	PA
Green Bay	13	3	0	.813	422	282
Tampa Bay	10	6	0	.625	299	263
Detroit	9	7	0	.563	379	306
Minnesota	9	7	0	.563	354	359
Chicago	4	12	0	.250	263	421

Western Division

	W	L	T	Pct.	PF	PA
San Francisco	13	3	0	.813	375	265
Carolina	7	9	0	.438	265	314
Atlanta	7	9	0	.438	320	361
New Orleans	6	10	0	.375	237	327
St. Louis	5	11	0	.313	299	359

GOLF

PROFESSIONAL		AMATEUR	
	Individual		**Individual**
Masters	Tiger Woods	**U.S. Amateur**	Matthew Kuchar
U.S. Open	Ernie Els	**U.S. Women's Amateur**	Silvia Cavalleri
Canadian Open	Steve Jones	**British Amateur**	Craig Watson
British Open	Justin Leonard	**British Ladies Amateur**	Alison Rose
PGA	Davis Love III	**Canadian Amateur**	Dave Goehring
World Series of Golf	Greg Norman	**Canadian Ladies Amateur**	Anna-Jane Eathorne
U.S. Women's Open	Alison Nicholas		
Ladies PGA	Chris Johnson		**Team**
		Walker Cup	United States
	Team		
Ryder Cup	Europe		

TIGER MASTERS THE MASTERS

Less than eight months after he turned professional, 21-year-old Tiger Woods made golf history at the 1997 Masters tournament. He shot an 18 under par 270, the lowest score in tournament history. He won by a 12-stroke margin, the widest in Masters history—or in the history of any other major U.S. tournament. Woods was the youngest person ever to win the Masters. And he was the first person of color to win a major U.S. tournament. Here, 1996 Masters champ Nick Faldo helps Woods on with the green jacket, symbol of a Masters victory.

Buffalo Sabres goalie Dominik Hasek scored a rare double in 1997. He won the Hart Trophy as the NHL's most valuable player and the Vezina Trophy as the league's best goalie.

HOCKEY

In 1997, hockey fans in Detroit celebrated the Red Wings' first Stanley Cup since 1955. Leaving no doubt about their desire to end a 42-year famine, the Red Wings devoured the Philadelphia Flyers in four straight games in the National Hockey League (NHL) playoff finals, playing superb defense.

Detroit coach Scotty Bowman won his seventh Stanley Cup as a coach—he amassed five with the Montreal Canadiens in the 1970s and a sixth with the Pittsburgh Penguins in 1992. He was the first to lead three different teams to NHL titles. (Bowman retired in 1997.)

The Red Wings finished the regular season second in the Central Division, with a record of 38 victories, 26 losses, and 18 ties (94 points). Philadelphia was second in the Atlantic Division (103 points), behind the New Jersey Devils (104 points). Leading the Central Division were the Dallas Stars (104 points). The Buffalo Sabres topped the Northeast Division (92 points), and the Colorado Avalanche scored 107 points, best in the league, to head the Pacific Division.

In the first round of the playoffs, Detroit defeated the St. Louis Blues, four games to two. They then swept the Anaheim Mighty Ducks in four games in round two. And in the Western Conference finals, the Red Wings eliminated Colorado, the defending Stanley Cup champs, four games to two.

Philadelphia advanced through the playoffs by beating Pittsburgh in five games in round one and Buffalo in five games in round two. Remarkably consistent, the Flyers again needed just five games to dispatch the New York Rangers in the Eastern Conference finals.

Games 1 and 2 of the Stanley Cup finals were contested at the Core States Center in Philadelphia. In Game 1, Detroit scored twice in the first period on a short-handed breakaway by Kirk Maltby and another breakaway by Joey Kocur; Philadelphia responded with one first-period goal. Sergei Fedorov gave the Wings their third score in the second period, and the Flyers also had one more. But Detroit captain Steve Yzerman found the

NHL FINAL STANDINGS

EASTERN CONFERENCE

Atlantic Division

	W	L	T	Pts.
New Jersey	45	23	14	104
Philadelphia	45	24	13	103
Florida	35	28	19	89
N.Y. Rangers	38	34	10	86
Washington	33	40	9	75
Tampa Bay	32	40	10	74
N.Y. Islanders	29	41	12	70

Northeast Division

	W	L	T	Pts.
Buffalo	40	30	12	92
Pittsburgh	38	36	8	84
Ottawa	31	36	15	77
Montreal	31	36	15	77
Hartford	32	39	11	75
Boston	26	47	9	61

WESTERN CONFERENCE

Central Division

	W	L	T	Pts.
Dallas	48	26	8	104
Detroit	38	26	18	94
Phoenix	38	37	7	83
St. Louis	36	35	11	83
Chicago	34	35	13	81
Toronto	30	44	8	68

Pacific Division

	W	L	T	Pts.
Colorado	49	24	9	107
Anaheim	36	33	13	85
Edmonton	36	37	9	81
Vancouver	35	40	7	77
Calgary	32	41	9	73
Los Angeles	28	43	11	67
San Jose	27	47	8	62

Stanley Cup: Detroit Red Wings

OUTSTANDING PLAYERS

Hart Trophy (most valuable player)	Dominik Hasek, Buffalo
Ross Trophy (scorer)	Mario Lemieux, Pittsburgh
Vezina Trophy (goalie)	Dominik Hasek, Buffalo
Norris Trophy (defenseman)	Brian Leetch, N.Y. Rangers
Selke Trophy (defensive forward)	Mike Peca, Buffalo
Calder Trophy (rookie)	Bryan Berard, N.Y. Islanders
Lady Byng Trophy (sportsmanship)	Paul Kariya, Anaheim
Conn Smythe Trophy (Stanley Cup play)	Mike Vernon, Detroit

Philadelphia net early in the third period for a 4–2 Wings' lead, and that was how the game ended.

Game 2 was another 4–2 victory for Detroit. They took a 2–0 lead in the first period on goals by Yzerman and Brendan Shanahan. Philadelphia's Rod Brind'Amour tied the game with a pair of scores. Undaunted by the Flyers' rally, the Red Wings put the game away with goals by Maltby in period two and Shanahan in period three. Up two games to none, Detroit now headed to its home ice in the Joe Louis Arena in the Motor City.

Philadelphia's John LeClair scored first in Game 3, but then the roof fell in on the Flyers. Yzerman, Fedorov, and Martin LaPointe notched first-period goals for Detroit. Fedorov cashed in again in period two, and Shanahan also scored; and LaPointe got his second goal of the game in period three. Final score: 6–1. As he had all through the playoffs, Red Wing goalie Mike Vernon played brilliantly.

In Game 4, Detroit's Niklas Lidstrom scored first, near the end of period one. Darren McCarty put the Wings up 2–0 in period two. The Flyers broke up the shutout when their star center Eric Lindros notched his first goal of the finals with just fifteen seconds left in the game. It didn't matter. The 2–1 winning margin gave the Red Wings a four-game sweep and the Stanley Cup.

Detroit goalie Mike Vernon received the Conn Smythe trophy as the most valuable player (MVP) of the playoffs; he compiled a 16–4 won-lost record throughout all the Stanley Cup rounds, permitting an average of only 1.79 goals per game.

For the regular season, Dominik Hasek of Buffalo won the Hart Trophy as the National Hockey League's MVP. He also won the Vezina Trophy as the league's best goalie. Hasek thus became the first player to win both awards since the great Jacques Plante of the Montreal Canadiens won them in 1962.

Mario Lemieux of Pittsburgh won the Ross Trophy as the leading scorer during the regular season, with 50 goals and 72 assists for 122 points. Lemieux retired after the playoffs ended, and he was inducted into the Hockey Hall of Fame in November.

Tara Lipinski: Princess of the Ice

In 1997, 14-year-old figure-skater Tara Lipinski skated, jumped, and twirled her way to the top. In February, she won the U.S. women's figure-skating championship. In March she triumphed at the world championships. Lipinski's skating was almost flawless. And at each championship she landed seven perfect triple jumps—including a triple-loop, triple-loop combination. She was the first American female to do this difficult jump in competition. After the world championships, Lipinski said: "By the end of the program I knew I had skated my best, and I was so happy with myself." Lipinski's performances made the 4-foot 8-inch, 75-pound skater from Sugar Land, Texas, the youngest ever U.S. and world champion. In both contests, she edged out defending champion Michelle Kwan. Kwan's "not my rival; she's an idol of mine," Lipinski insisted. But both will be among those competing for the gold at the 1998 Winter Olympic Games, in Nagano, Japan.

ICE SKATING

FIGURE SKATING

World Championships

Men	Elvis Stojko, Canada
Women	Tara Lipinski, U.S.
Pairs	Mandy Woetzel/Ingo Steuer, Germany
Dance	Oksana Gritschuk/Yevgeny Platov, Russia

United States Championships

Men	Todd Eldredge
Women	Tara Lipinski
Pairs	Kyoko Ina/Jason Dungjen
Dance	Elizabeth Punsalan/Jerod Swallow

SPEED SKATING

World Championships

Men	Ids Postma, Netherlands
Women	Gunda Niemann, Germany

SKIING

WORLD CUP CHAMPIONSHIPS

Men	Luc Alphand, France
Women	Pernilla Wiberg, Sweden

U.S. ALPINE CHAMPIONSHIPS

Men

Downhill	Tommy Moe
Slalom	Martin Tichy, Czech Republic
Giant Slalom	Sacha Gros
Super Giant Slalom	Tommy Moe
Combined	Chris Puckett

Women

Downhill	Hilary Lindh
Slalom	Kristina Koznick
Giant Slalom	Carrie Sheinberg
Super Giant Slalom	Hilary Lindh
Combined	Carrie Sheinberg

TRACK AND FIELD

"Fastest Man in the World"

A race between Canadian sprinter Donovan Bailey and U.S. sprinter Michael Johnson was the focus of much attention in 1997.

Each runner had won two gold medals at the 1996 Summer Olympic Games. One of Bailey's medals was for running the 100-meter dash in a world record 9.84 seconds. And one of Johnson's was for streaking through the 200-meter run in a world record 19.32 seconds.

Traditionally, the person who wins the 100 is given the unofficial title of Fastest Man in the World—in this case, Bailey. But because of Johnson's spectacular speed in the 200, people began clamoring for a race between the two athletes to decide who should get the title. The two agreed, and a distance of 150 meters—halfway between their respective specialties—was chosen.

The race was held June 1, 1997, at the SkyDome in Toronto, Canada. Some 30,000 spectators were there. At the crack of the starter's gun, they were out of the blocks, but near the halfway mark, it seemed clear that Bailey would win. Suddenly, Johnson pulled up with a limp—a strained muscle, he said—and never finished the race. Bailey won in 14.99 seconds.

Each sprinter got $500,000 for showing up, and Bailey got another $1 million for winning—a lot of money for what many people felt was a nonrace.

Pete Sampras won his fourth Wimbledon crown in 1997. The victory was his tenth Grand Slam singles title.

TENNIS

One player dominated tennis in 1997—Martina Hingis of Switzerland. The teenager won three Grand Slam singles titles, was runner-up in the fourth, and reached the women's number-one ranking. Among the men, Pete Sampras of the United States captured two Grand Slam events and established himself as one of the best players of all time. But he was shut out of the finals in the French and U.S. championships, and by the end of the year his grip on the men's top spot may have loosened slightly.

Sampras began 1997 in commanding fashion. In the finals of the **Australian Open** in January, he downed Carlos Moya of Spain in straight sets, 6–2, 6–3, 6–3. Playing in Melbourne's overwhelming summer heat, Sampras controlled the match from the first serve. The victory was his ninth Grand Slam title and his second Australian crown.

Hingis was just as overpowering in the women's finals. Dashing around the court with speed and grace, she outmatched Mary Pierce of France by 6–2, 6–2. Hingis thus became, at 16 years, 4 months, the youngest woman to win a Grand Slam event in this century. The previous youngest was Monica Seles, who was just two months older when she took the 1990 French Open.

In the 1997 **French Open,** played in Paris in June, the top-seeded Hingis made the finals, but she lost to ninth-seeded Iva Majoli of Croatia, 6–4, 6–2. Majoli, 19, was the lowest seed ever to take the French Open women's title, and the first Croatian to win a Grand Slam championship.

The men's French Open produced a surprise. Unseeded Gustavo Kuerten of Brazil

TOURNAMENT TENNIS

	Australian Open	French Open	Wimbledon	U.S. Open
Men's Singles	Pete Sampras, U.S.	Gustavo Kuerten, Brazil	Pete Sampras, U.S.	Patrick Rafter, Australia
Women's Singles	Martina Hingis, Switzerland	Iva Majoli, Croatia	Martina Hingis, Switzerland	Martina Hingis, Switzerland
Men's Doubles	Todd Woodbridge, Australia/ Mark Woodforde, Australia	Yevgeny Kafelnikov, Russia/ Daniel Vacek, Czech Republic	Todd Woodbridge, Australia/ Mark Woodforde, Australia	Yevgeny Kafelnikov, Russia/ Daniel Vacek, Czech Republic
Women's Doubles	Martina Hingis, Switzerland/ Natasha Zvereva, Belarus	Gigi Fernandez, U.S./ Natasha Zvereva, Belarus	Gigi Fernandez, U.S./ Natasha Zvereva, Belarus	Lindsay Davenport, U.S./ Jana Novotna, Czech Republic

Davis Cup Winner: Sweden

Martina Hingis: Number One

In March 1997, at the age of 16 years, 6 months, Martina Hingis became the youngest woman to earn tennis's number-one ranking. She replaced Steffi Graf of Germany, who had stood atop the women's game since June 1993.

It seems likely that Martina will dominate tennis just as Graf and Monica Seles did in previous years. Although she isn't as hard a hitter as either of them, her shot selection and placement are superb. And she can wear her opponents down by keeping them off balance and constantly on the run.

The teenage champ suffered a small setback in April. Injured when thrown from a horse—she loves to ride—Martina underwent knee surgery that same month. But she came back strong at the French Open just two months later. She beat Seles in the semifinals, and lost only to Iva Majoli in the finals. It was the only Grand Slam loss that Martina experienced in 1997.

Born in the former Czechoslovakia, Martina Hingis is a citizen of Switzerland. She was

named for another Czech-born tennis star, Martina Navratilova, who is now retired. Besides tennis and riding horses, Martina Hingis enjoys rollerblading—just like a lot of other teenagers.

swept 16th-seeded Sergei Bruguera of Spain in the finals, 6–3, 6–4, 6–2. Possessed of a powerful serve and forehand, 20-year-old Kuerten became the first Brazilian man to win a Grand Slam singles title. (Sampras was eliminated in the third round.)

In July, the center of the tennis world shifted to **Wimbledon,** in England. Sampras rebounded from his loss at the French Open to win his fourth Wimbledon. Top-seeded, he made quick work of the finals, defeating Cedric Pioline of France in 94 minutes, and winning in straight sets, 6–4, 6–2, 6–4. The victory was Sampras's tenth Grand Slam singles title.

Hingis, too, came back from her defeat at Paris to win at Wimbledon. Seeded first, she outlasted third-seeded Jana Novotna of the Czech Republic in the finals, 2–6, 6–3, 6–3. Novotna played aggressively in winning the first set, but a strained stomach muscle slowed her down thereafter.

Clearly on a roll, Hingis mowed down opponent after opponent at the **U.S. Open,** played in New York City in September. She didn't lose a single set in the whole tournament. In the finals, she faced another rising star, Venus Williams, a 17-year-old African American. Although a fine player, Williams couldn't raise a serious challenge against Hingis, who took the match by scores of 6–0, 6–4.

Sampras had won the U.S. Open men's crown in 1995 and 1996, but in 1997 he was eliminated in the fourth round by Petr Korda of the Czech Republic. Ultimately, the finals pitted 13th-seeded Patrick Rafter, from Australia, against Britain's Greg Rusedski. Rusedski wowed the crowd at Arthur Ashe Stadium with some supersonic serves—one reaching 143 miles per hour (230 kilometers per hour). But Rafter wasn't intimidated. Playing aggressively, though gracefully, and unafraid to take risks, the 24-year-old Rafter upended his rival in four sets, 6–3, 6–2, 4–6, 7–5. He was the first Australian to win the U.S. Open since John Newcombe in 1973.

Christophe Auguin of France *(center)* crosses the finish line in the 26,500-mile (42,600-kilometer) Vendée Globe round-the-world yacht race. Auguin completed the race in a record 105 days and 20½ hours.

SPORTS BRIEFS

A number of fascinating sports stories received special attention during 1997. Two grueling races were held—the round-the-world Vendée Globe yacht race, and the Iditarod Trail Sled Dog Race across the snowy wastes of Alaska. Two outstanding African-American sports stars were honored in special ways. Tennis great Arthur Ashe had a new stadium at the National Tennis Center in Flushing Meadows-Corona Park, New York, named after him. And at the start of the 1997 major-league baseball season, Jackie Robinson was honored for having broken professional baseball's color barrier fifty years earlier. Other sports stories included the debut of the Women's National Basketball Association and the defeat of the world's best chess player by a computer named Deep Blue.

THE MOST DANGEROUS RACE

On February 17, 1997, Frenchman Christophe Auguin sailed his 60-foot (18-meter) racing yacht *Geodis* into Les Sables d'Olonne, a resort on the Bay of Biscay in western France. Thousands of people cheered him, for he had just won the 26,500-mile (42,600-kilometer) Vendée Globe round-the-world yacht race. But he not only won it, he set a new world record for nonstop solo circumnavigation of the world in a yacht. Auguin finished the race in 105 days and 20½ hours, bettering the 109-day record set in 1989. And because it was a solo race, he was alone for each and every one of those days and hours. A sailor who touches land—for any reason—is disqualified.

With about a dozen yachts competing against him, Auguin had begun the race in France, in November 1996. He sailed down the Atlantic coast of Africa, and then eastward south of Australia and New Zealand. He then made his way around the southern tip of South America and back into the Atlantic Ocean. The southern part of the journey was so far south that icebergs, calved by Antarctica's great ice shelves, often littered the route. The temperature was frigid. Winds howled at 70 miles (113 kilometers) per hour. And towering waves smashed against the yachts. One of Auguin's competitors, Canadian Gerry Roufs, disappeared in the Antarctic Ocean. Three others were rescued at sea after their yachts capsized. One of them, Tony Bullimore of Great Britain, was trapped inside his overturned yacht for four days before an Australian Navy frigate rescued him.

When Auguin finally sailed into the harbor at Les Sables d'Olonne to claim his $73,000 in prize money, his nearest competitors were still 2,000 miles (3,200 kilometers) behind him. Auguin had previously won two other round-the-world yacht races, but when asked about the Vendée Globe, he said "This is the toughest race I have ever taken part in." "Would you do it again?" Auguin was asked. His reply: "One time was enough!"

THE LAST GREAT RACE

In early March 1997, 53 mushers—sled-dog racers—gathered in Anchorage, in southern Alaska. They were there for the running of the 25th Iditarod Trail Sled Dog Race, an annual event that has become known as "The Last Great Race." Among the competitors were 80-year-old Joe Redington, who founded the race in 1973; defending champion Jeff King; and Swiss-born Martin Buser, a two-time winner in thirteen tries.

Through snow and ice and frigid temperatures, the mushers and their dogs made their way more than 1,100 miles (1,770 kilometers) northwest to Nome, a city on the Bering Sea just 150 miles (240 kilometers) south of the Arctic Circle. The first to cross the finish line on Nome's Front Street was Martin Buser. He chalked up his third win in a time of 9 days, 8½ hours, far short of the 9-day, 2-hour record set in 1995 by Doug Swingley. Swingley finished second in the 1997 race, and Jeff King finished third. After accepting the $50,000 first-prize money and a new truck, Buser gave credit for the victory to his huskies, calling them "a bunch of really talented athletes." Five dogs—none of them Buser's—died during the race, and animal welfare activists charged that the Iditarod is too hard on the dogs.

ARTHUR ASHE STADIUM

In 1997, the National Tennis Center in Flushing Meadows-Corona Park, New York, was given a $250 million facelift. The reno-

Glow Bowling

Music blares from loudspeakers. Colorful laser beams dart through the air. Artificial fog swirls about. Are you at a rock 'n' roll concert or a disco? No, you're at a bowling alley! And you're enjoying the biggest fad ever to come down a bowling lane—glow bowling. At some bowling establishments, glow bowling is called cosmic bowling or xtreme bowling. But whatever name is used, the bowling lanes, the balls, the pins, the shoes all glow in fluorescent, neonlike colors. Why not join in, and go with the glow!

vation and expansion was completed in time for the August start of the 1997 U.S. Open tennis championship. The centerpiece of the facility's new look was Arthur Ashe Stadium, which replaced Louis Armstrong Stadium as the center-court stadium. With seats for 23,000 fans, it may be the world's biggest public tennis facility. It rises higher than nearby Shea Stadium, home of baseball's New York Mets. In fact, it's so high that tennis fans in the topmost rows can view Manhattan's stunning skyline during lulls in the tennis matches.

The new stadium was named after the late Arthur Ashe, an African American who made valuable contributions to the sport of tennis, and who also championed many humanitarian causes. Born on July 10, 1943, in Richmond, Virginia, Ashe began playing tennis when he was 7 years old. He reached the national junior semifinals in 1958 and won U.S. indoor titles in 1960 and 1961. As the fifth-ranked junior in the country, he won a scholarship to UCLA in 1962. In 1968, when he was 25 years old, Ashe won the U.S. Open, making him the first African American to win a tennis Grand Slam event. He went on to win the Australian Open in 1970 and Wimbledon in 1975 and to serve on the U.S. Davis Cup team for many years. He won a total of 33 titles during his career, and was inducted into the International Tennis Hall of Fame in 1985.

During and after his tennis career, Ashe was known for his fight for social justice. He fought against racial prejudice. He protested South Africa's policy of apartheid, or racial separation. And he taught tennis to inner-city children. Even after he contracted the virus that causes AIDS in 1988, Ashe continued his humanitarian work. In 1992, he helped raise $5 million for the establishment of a foundation to combat AIDS. Arthur Ashe died in February 1993. Four and a half years later, Arthur Ashe Stadium, a fitting and lasting tribute to an outstanding human being, was dedicated in New York City.

PROFESSIONAL WOMEN HOOPSTERS

It had to happen! It had to happen because the U.S. women's basketball team won Olympic gold at Atlanta in 1996. . . .because in 1995 the Connecticut Huskies, led by the flamboyant Rebecca Lobo to a record of 35–0, became only the second team in NCAA women's tournament history to finish a season undefeated. . . .and because young girls, as well as grown women, found role models they could relate to in team sports. What happened? The debut of two women's professional basketball leagues.

The American Basketball League (ABL) opened its 40-game season in October 1996. The teams were the Richmond Rage, Columbus Quest, Atlanta Glory, and New England Blizzard in the Eastern Conference;

Cynthia Cooper (left) battles Teresa Weatherspoon for control of the ball in the WNBA championship game. In 1997, two new women's pro basketball leagues proved immensely popular among fans.

A Tribute for Jackie Robinson

On April 15, 1947, Jackie Robinson joined the Brooklyn Dodgers as a rookie second baseman. In so doing, he became the first African American player in modern major-league baseball—thus paving the way for the integration of America's national pastime. Acting baseball commissioner Bud Selig called Robinson's feat "the most powerful and important event that ever took place in baseball history." On April 15, 1997, exactly 50 years later, Robinson was honored at New York City's Shea Stadium, where the New York Mets were to play Robinson's former team, the Dodgers.

President Bill Clinton spoke to the crowd of 50,000 baseball fans at Shea Stadium. Robinson's widow Rachel and his daughter Sharon were also there, along with such baseball greats as Sandy Koufax and Reggie Jackson. Larry Doby was there too. Doby was the second African American to enter major league baseball and the first to join the American League.

Before the Shea Stadium celebration, New York Governor George Pataki said, "It didn't take a great baseball player to tear down that barrier of segregation, it took a great man." But Jackie Robinson was both a great baseball player *and* a great man. During his rookie year, he batted .297, scored 125 runs, and led the National League in stolen bases with 29. The Dodgers won the pennant that year, and Robinson was named Rookie of the Year. In 1949, he was named the National League's most valuable player. And during his ten years with the Dodgers (1947–56), he led the team to six National League pennants and the 1955 World Series championship. His lifetime batting average was .311. In 1962, Robinson became the first African American to be elected to the Baseball Hall of Fame.

There are no statistics to show that Jackie Robinson was a great man, only actions. Until 1947, baseball, like other aspects of life in America, was segregated. African Americans played in the Negro Leagues. Many of these players were as good as or better than the white players in the major leagues. But the color of their skin kept them out of the major leagues. When Branch Rickey, the Brooklyn Dodgers' general manager, signed Robinson to a contract, he knew Robinson would be harassed by fans and players alike. "Do you want a ballplayer who's afraid to fight back?" Robinson asked Rickey. Rickey responded: "I want a player with guts enough *not* to fight back!" And that's exactly what Robinson did. He was taunted with racial remarks. He received hate mail and death threats. Fans threw garbage at him. Pitchers threw bean balls. Runners tried to spike him. Through it all, Robinson remained calm. It took time to end the racism, but within twelve years African Americans were playing on every major league team.

Child-Made Soccer Balls

In many countries, it's a common sight to see young children playing soccer at school or in town soccer leagues. But in Pakistan, tens of thousands of children under the age of 14 don't even go to school. That's because they and their families live in such poverty that they are forced to work. These children don't play soccer. But many of them stitch soccer balls together—and they are forced to do this for $1.20 a day, and the day is more than ten hours long.

In 1997, sporting goods manufacturers such as Nike, Reebok, Adidas, and Puma and groups that were concerned about the rights of children joined forces to stop the use of child labor in the manufacture of soccer balls. They will provide money for the inspection of factories where the balls are made, to make sure children aren't involved in the labor. They will also provide money to help educate these children. Most of their efforts will be concentrated in Pakistan, where 75 percent of all hand-stitched soccer balls are made. But attention has now been focused on other countries, where child labor is used to make sneakers and other sporting goods, as well as all types of clothing.

and Portland Power, Colorado Xplosion, San Jose Lasers, and Seattle Reign in the Western Conference. The championship series, held in March 1997, pitted the Columbus Quest against the Richmond Rage. Columbus, which had the regular season's best record, 31–9, defeated Richmond 3 games to 2. The team was led by Nikki McCray, who was named the ABL's most valuable player. Later in the year, McCray left the ABL for the WNBA.

For the ABL's 1997–98 season, which began in October 1997, the Richmond Rage moved to Philadelphia, becoming the Philadelphia Rage. Also, a fifth team, the Long Beach Stingrays, was added to the Western Conference.

The Women's National Basketball Association (WNBA), which is wholly owned and run by the National Basketball Association (NBA), started its 28-game season in June 1997. The Eastern Conference teams were the Charlotte Sting, Cleveland Rockers, Houston Comets, and New York Liberty. The Western Conference teams were the Los Angeles Sparks, Phoenix Mercury, Sacramento Monarchs, and Utah Starzz. The August championship, which featured a four-team, single-game elimination format, saw the Houston Comets defeat New York Liberty 65–51. The star of that game was Cynthia Cooper, who was also named the WNBA's most valuable player.

For its 1998 season, which begins in June 1998, the WNBA hopes to add two teams, in Detroit and Washington, D.C. In addition, each team will play 30 games, instead of 28, and the championship will be decided by Eastern Conference-Western Conference playoffs.

Blue, an International Business Machines (IBM) computer. The score was 3½ to 2½. This was the first time that a machine beat any chess champion in a traditional match. The first time that Kasparov and Deep Blue played, in February 1996, Kasparov defeated the machine 4 games to 2.

As a result of the 1996 loss, IBM made a number of improvements in the computer. It doubled the speed at which Deep Blue could calculate moves, allowing the computer to examine 200 million chessboard positions a second. And it hired former

World chess champion Garry Kasparov of Russia ponders his next move in this match against Deep Blue, an IBM computer. Kasparov lost the six-game match—the first time a machine ever beat a chess champ.

The success of the two leagues in their inaugural seasons was clear—enthusiastic fans crammed the stadiums and watched on television. WNBA attendance averaged more than 9,000 a game. And the WNBA championship game drew a substantial TV audience, even though it was up against the U.S. Tennis Open and college football.

DEEP BLUE GIVES KASPAROV THE BLUES

In May 1997, Garry Kasparov, Russian chess grandmaster and world champion, was defeated in a six-game chess match by Deep

U.S. chess champion Joel Benjamin to help program the computer to better understand chess strategy. With these improvements, Deep Blue was ready for the rematch with Kasparov.

The match lasted nine days. Kasparov won game 1 and Deep Blue game 2. Games 3, 4, and 5 ended in draws. In game 6, however, Kasparov was forced to concede defeat after 19 moves. Deep Blue walked away with $700,000. Kasparov won $400,000. But he retained his world championship title, which he has held since 1985.

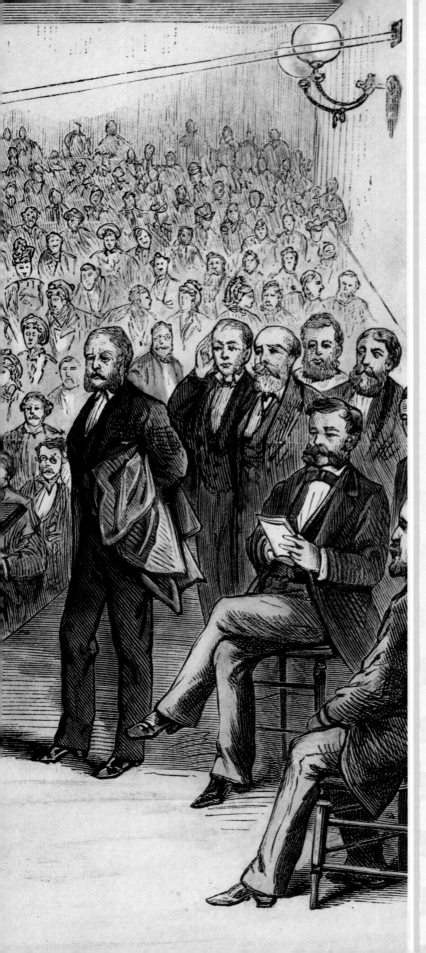

LIVING HISTORY

On March 15, 1877, the people who crowded into this hall in Salem, Massachusetts, saw—and heard—something that truly amazed them. Alexander Graham Bell used his new invention, the telephone, to speak and sing to his assistant, who was 15 miles (24 kilometers) away in Boston. In 1997, the world marked the 150th anniversary of Bell's birth and the birth of another great inventor, Thomas Alva Edison. Edison developed the phonograph, the first useful electric lightbulb, and many other devices. Bell and Edison doubtless knew that their work was important. But even they couldn't have predicted how greatly their inventions would change people's everyday lives.

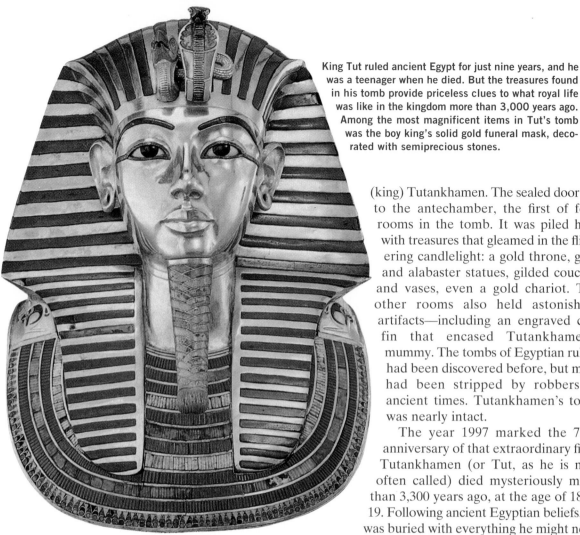

King Tut ruled ancient Egypt for just nine years, and he was a teenager when he died. But the treasures found in his tomb provide priceless clues to what royal life was like in the kingdom more than 3,000 years ago. Among the most magnificent items in Tut's tomb was the boy king's solid gold funeral mask, decorated with semiprecious stones.

TUTANKHAMEN: THE BOY KING

On November 26, 1922, while the hot sun baked the Egyptian desert outside, an English archeologist named Howard Carter bored a small hole in a sealed door at the end of an underground passageway. Anxious colleagues watched as he thrust a lighted candle into the opening and peered in.

"Can you see anything?" Lord Carnarvon, the British nobleman who had financed Carter's expedition, nervously asked.

"Yes," Carter replied excitedly, "wonderful things."

Wonderful things indeed! Carter had found the tomb of the ancient Egyptian pharaoh (king) Tutankhamen. The sealed door led to the antechamber, the first of four rooms in the tomb. It was piled high with treasures that gleamed in the flickering candlelight: a gold throne, gold and alabaster statues, gilded couches and vases, even a gold chariot. The other rooms also held astonishing artifacts—including an engraved coffin that encased Tutankhamen's mummy. The tombs of Egyptian rulers had been discovered before, but most had been stripped by robbers in ancient times. Tutankhamen's tomb was nearly intact.

The year 1997 marked the 75th anniversary of that extraordinary find. Tutankhamen (or Tut, as he is now often called) died mysteriously more than 3,300 years ago, at the age of 18 or 19. Following ancient Egyptian beliefs, he was buried with everything he might need or want in the afterlife—food, weapons, clothing, jewelry, religious objects, musical instruments, furniture. His tomb thus contained not only a rich treasure, but priceless clues to Tutankhamen's life in ancient Egypt.

THE BOY KING

Three thousand years ago, the culturally and politically advanced civilization of ancient Egypt was flourishing. The powerful Egyptian kingdom in northeastern Africa stretched along the Nile River for 600 miles (1,000 kilometers). It also controlled Nubia, in what is today Sudan, as well as the lands along the eastern Mediterranean. When Tut came to the throne, the Egyptian civilization, one of the world's first, had already existed for 1,500 years. And the pyramids at Giza, which housed the tombs of past Egyptian kings, had been standing for 1,000 years.

Much about Tutankhamen's life and death remains a mystery. We know he was only 9 or 10 years old when he came to the throne, probably around 1350 B.C. In his magnificent gold funeral mask and other portraits, he appears as a handsome, slender youth, with a face described as refined and cultured.

Scholars aren't sure who his parents were. But Tut was a close relative, perhaps even a younger brother, of the pharaoh Akhenaton. Soon after Akhenaton came to the throne in 1367 B.C., he broke with tradition by forbidding the worship of all gods except Aton, represented by the sun disk. And he moved Egypt's capital from Thebes to a new city farther down the Nile. Akhenaton's belief in just one god was remarkable for the time, but his decree upset Egyptians who were used to worshipping many gods. And it infuriated the priests because it closed their temples and lessened their power and position in the kingdom.

After Akhenaton's death, there was a period of turmoil and confusion. Then Tutankhamen took the throne. Within a few years, the old religion was restored, and the capital returned to Thebes. This was done in Tut's name; but since Tut was still so young, it's doubtful that he had much to do with the decision. Powerful advisers ran the kingdom. Among them were Ay, who became pharaoh after Tut, and the military leader Horemheb, who followed Ay on the throne.

Tut was just a boy when he married Ankhesenamen, a daughter of Akhenaton and Queen Nefertiti. Paintings and sculptures show that the young king and queen were a handsome couple. No doubt crowds gathered to greet them when they visited the cities of their realm, traveling up and down the Nile in a procession of elegant barges.

Following the fashions of the day, the king and queen wore black wigs and dressed in finely pleated linen clothes, accented with colorful jeweled belts and neck collars. The king had many elaborate articles for ceremonial wear—and court life was filled with ceremony. But there was music and entertainment, too, and paintings show that the young king apparently enjoyed fishing and duck hunting in the marshes along the Nile.

Tutankhamen's reign lasted just nine years. Then he died—but no one knows why or how. His mummy shows no sign of disease, although such signs would probably have disappeared over time. There are signs of injury, however, including damage to his skull. Tut may have been killed in an accident—a fall from his chariot, perhaps. Or maybe, as some people have suggested, Tut was murdered. Both Ay and Horemheb have been suspected. Perhaps one of these advisers realized that, as Tut grew older, he

Tut's ornate throne was carved of wood and covered in gold. The backrest shows the young king and his equally young queen.

187

The paintings in ancient Egyptian tombs tell us a great deal about daily life 3,000 years ago. We know, for example, that most Egyptians were poor farmers. Above: A peasant plows his field while his wife follows, planting seeds. Right: Workers harvest grapes.

would take control of the country himself. Both advisers were close enough to the king to kill him or arrange his death. And each in turn succeeded him. When Horemheb became pharaoh, he seems to have launched a campaign to wipe out the young king's memory, erasing his name and image from monuments.

We may never know the true story of Tut's death. But we do know a great deal about the Egypt he ruled.

TUT'S KINGDOM

The Nile was the heart of Egyptian life. Its yearly flooding helped create a band of lush green farmland in the North African desert, and it carried people and goods throughout the kingdom. Most Egyptians were poor farmers. They raised cattle, goats, ducks, and geese, and they grew such crops as wheat for bread, barley for beer, and grapes, dates, and palms for wine.

Members of Egypt's middle class—merchants, manufacturers, and scribes (people skilled in Egyptian picture writing, or hieroglyphics) generally lived in towns and cities. So, too, did craftspeople and artists, some of whom painted scenes of everyday life on the walls of the tombs built for the kings.

Egyptian royalty and the upper classes, including nobles, government officials, senior army officers, doctors, and high-ranking priests, controlled huge estates. And the king controlled everything. He owned all the land and was considered a god himself, as well as the high priest of the many gods worshipped by the Egyptian people.

The homes of wealthy Egyptians were filled with elegant furniture, and flowers decorated every room. At their frequently held banquets, Egyptians dressed in their most festive attire. Guests were given gifts of jewelry and perfume. And musicians entertained them with performances on the harp, flute, lyre, lute, and tambourine. The sumptuous meals included roast goose, duck, or ox meat. Sweets and fresh or dried fruits were served for dessert, and a variety of wines was offered. Because ancient Egyptians so enjoyed their present life—which averaged only 30 years—they wanted to ensure that their afterlife would be as good. They pictured this afterlife as an eternal period of blessings, bountiful harvests, and sports and games. The deceased, they believed, maintained the prestige of rank reached on Earth. They also believed that "you *can* take it with

Left: An artisan decorates a vase. The ancient Egyptians were extraordinary craftspeople. Above: A musician entertains guests on the harp, one of several instruments that were enjoyed in ancient times.

189

Treasures of the Tomb

When Howard Carter and Lord Carnarvon discovered the tomb of Tutankhamen in 1922, they unlocked the door to a vast treasure chest of ancient Egyptian objects. There were more than 5,000 works of art and luxury items from Egypt's golden age—everything a king might need to make the afterlife pleasant.

Furniture included several ornate thrones, beds, and a gilded couch in the form of two lionesses—tails curving up at one end, and heads at the other. A child's chair, perhaps made for Tut as a boy, was carved from ebony and inlaid with ivory and gold.

There were fine clothes, cosmetic jars filled with precious oils, wine jars, games, and toys. Even the simplest everyday items were richly carved and decorated with religious symbols and scenes from the king's life. Four chariots were also placed in the tomb. They were so large that they had to be taken apart to pass through the narrow entrance.

For protection, and perhaps for hunting in the afterlife, there were bows and arrows, swords, shields, and daggers. Figures of gods and goddesses were also placed in the tomb to

A carved alabaster cosmetic jar

you"—that is, that they could take their possessions into the next life. And because of this belief, rich and powerful people built large tombs and filled them with everything they might want in the afterlife.

Most important of all for the afterlife, the body of a person who had died had to be preserved. This was done by drying out the body, embalming it, and wrapping it in linen—a process called mummification. This enabled Egyptian mummies—such as Tutankhamen's—to survive for centuries.

TUT'S TOMB

Like most Egyptian royalty, Tut was buried in an area along the Nile River that is known as the Valley of the Kings. Over the centuries, many great tombs dotted the landscape of this royal burial ground.

In the 19th century, archeologists began digging in the valley, looking for tombs. Some 30 royal burial chambers were unearthed, but most had been looted long ago and contained little of value to the diggers. By the early 20th century, most archeologists had concluded that there was nothing left to find in the valley. As for Tut, they weren't sure that he had ever even lived.

But one archeologist disagreed. Howard Carter was certain that the tomb of Tutankhamen existed. With financial backing from Lord Carnarvon, he searched for it. After years of frustration and false leads, however, Carnarvon was ready to call it quits. Carter persuaded his patron to let him try for one more season.

Carter had staked out an area between several known tombs as the most likely site protect the king. One of the most elegant was a golden statue of the goddess Selket. Selket's emblem, a scorpion, is perched atop her head—Egyptians believed she had magical powers that could cure the scorpion's sting.

One of the most magnificent items in the tomb was Tutankhamen's funeral mask, which covered the head and shoulders of the boy king's mummy. It was fashioned from solid gold and richly decorated with many semiprecious stones.

A golden statue of the goddess Selket

And hidden among the layers of the mummy's bindings were more than 140 amulets and pieces of jewelry—a dazzling array of gold, gems, and enamel. One notable item was a gold pendant gleaming with semiprecious stones. Its centerpiece was a scarab, a beetle that symbolized the rebirth that Egyptians believed would follow the king's death.

A necklace with a scarab centerpiece

of Tut's resting place. He had excavated all of it except one small section, where workers at the dig had their huts. Just as he was ready to move on, he decided to give the area one more shot. He ordered the huts torn down. The very next day—November 3, 1922—workers discovered stone steps cut into the rock. Clearing away the rubble, Carter and his men found that the stairway led to an outer door bearing the royal seals.

Carter telegraphed Carnarvon in England, telling him to come at once. With Carnarvon at his side, he opened the first door. It led to a rubble-filled passageway, at the end of which was a second sealed door. Behind that door lay the "wonderful things" that would soon astound the world.

In the weeks after they opened the tomb, Carter and his party explored its four rooms—the antechamber, the burial chamber, the annex, and the treasury. Each room was filled with priceless artifacts. The burial chamber yielded the greatest treasure: a large sarcophagus that was carved from a single block of quartzite. In the sarcophagus were three coffins, one inside the other. The innermost coffin, which was made of solid gold, held Tut's mummy. It also held something that touched Carter deeply: A small wreath of flowers had been placed on the mummy, perhaps by Tut's grieving teenage queen.

"Amid all that regal splendor," Carter later wrote, "there was nothing so beautiful as those few withered flowers, still retaining their tinge of color. They told us what a short period of time three thousand years really was—but yesterday and the morrow."

Hot off the printing press: Each of the new U.S. $100 bills on this sheet is filled with special hard-to-duplicate security features. The newly designed bills are part of an ongoing battle to foil counterfeiters.

BOGUS BILLS

Is that crisp new $100 bill real, or is it a clever fake? The amount of phony, or counterfeit, money has increased enormously in recent years. That problem led the United States to introduce new $100 bills in 1996, and new $50 bills in 1997—with special security features that make them very hard to copy. The new bills represented the first major redesign of U.S. paper money in nearly 70 years. The changes were the latest strategy in the fight against counterfeiters. Counterfeit currency is a problem as old as paper money itself—and that's very old indeed.

SALT TO SILVER TO PAPER

Imagine a world without money. How could you get the things you need? If you couldn't make them yourself, you'd have to barter—that is, trade something for them. For example, maybe a tailor would agree to make you a pair of jeans if you cleaned up the tailor shop every day for a week. If the tailor didn't want anything you could offer in trade, you'd be out of luck.

That's how business was done for thousands of years. As towns and cities grew, though, people developed better ways. They agreed to use certain goods as a means of exchange—a kind of money. Often, these goods were items everyone needed, like salt and grain. A farmer could trade baskets of grain for a blanket, and the blanket weaver could then trade that grain for a goat.

Still, baskets of grain and blocks of salt were bulky and cumbersome, especially for merchants who traveled far to trade. Moreover, items like grain could spoil. About 5,000 years ago, in what is today the Middle

East, Sumerian merchants began to use silver bars in exchange for goods. The idea of metal money caught on. Official coins, with guaranteed weights and values, were used in China as early as 1000 B.C., and by the Lydians, in Asia Minor, by 640 B.C.

The Chinese invented both paper and the printing press, so it isn't surprising that they were the first to use paper money. Unlike a gold or silver coin, paper money had no value of its own. People accepted it because the government guaranteed its value. Paper money was used in China perhaps as early as A.D. 900. It wasn't widely used in Europe until the 1600s.

In the American colonies, people used European money at first. They also used shell beads called wampum in trade with Indians. And goods that were in demand—such as nails or gunpowder—sometimes served as money. Massachusetts was the first colony to mint its own coins. In 1764, Britain forbade the colonies to print their own paper money, and that became a sore point with Americans.

After independence in 1776, all the colonies issued their own money. The Continental Congress issued paper bills that many people considered worthless. That gave rise to the expression "not worth a continental." With so many different kinds of money, trade was very confusing. A single money system was finally established in 1790.

MAKING IT, FAKING IT

From the time that countries began to make paper money, counterfeiters have been trying to fake it. Most counterfeiters have been criminals who hope to get rich by fooling others with phony bills. But sometimes countries at war have counterfeited their enemies' money, hoping to undermine con-

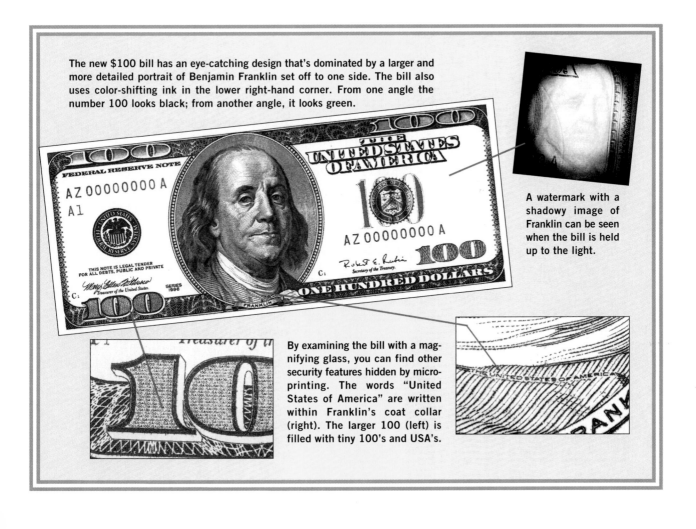

The new $100 bill has an eye-catching design that's dominated by a larger and more detailed portrait of Benjamin Franklin set off to one side. The bill also uses color-shifting ink in the lower right-hand corner. From one angle the number 100 looks black; from another angle, it looks green.

A watermark with a shadowy image of Franklin can be seen when the bill is held up to the light.

By examining the bill with a magnifying glass, you can find other security features hidden by microprinting. The words "United States of America" are written within Franklin's coat collar (right). The larger 100 (left) is filled with tiny 100's and USA's.

Dollar Coins

Check your pockets for coins. You may find nickels, dimes, and quarters—but chances are you won't find dollars. In years to come, however, that may change. The next new dollar may be a coin instead of a bill.

Dollar coins haven't been widely used since the early 20th century, when silver dollars circulated. By the 1940s, paper bills had largely replaced them. From 1971 to 1978, the U.S. Mint issued $1 coins honoring President Dwight D. Eisenhower (right), but people preferred paper. The Mint tried again in 1979 with a $1 coin showing Susan B. Anthony (below), a 19th-century women's rights advocate. The coin flopped, and production stopped in 1981.

Now some government officials think the time is right to try again. They have proposed a new gold-colored $1 coin. The coins would cost about eight cents each to produce, compared to about four cents each for paper bills. But coins last 30 years, while a bill is worn out in less than a year and a half. Thus the government might save millions of dollars by switching to coins.

But that will only happen if people accept a $1 coin, and many people aren't excited by the idea. Coins are bulky and heavy, and loose change slides around. But a dollar bill folds up neatly in a pocket or a wallet.

fidence in the currency. The British issued counterfeit continentals during the Revolutionary War. During World War II, Nazi Germany produced $630 million worth of fake British currency, hoping to force the British economy to collapse.

Counterfeiting was a major problem in the United States in the 1800s. During the Civil War, as much as a third of all the paper money in circulation was fake. The federal government set up the Secret Service after the war to put a stop to counterfeiting. And the Treasury Department, which issues U.S. currency, took steps to make bills harder to copy.

U.S. paper money is produced at the Bureau of Engraving and Printing in Washington, D.C. The bureau uses a special paper, made from cotton and linen fibers. This paper has a unique feel, and it contains tiny red and blue flecks that are hard to duplicate. The designs of the bills are engraved on steel plates by master artisans. They are printed with special ink through a process called intaglio, which results in sharp, precise images. Up to 32 bills are printed at once, on big sheets of paper. They are identical, except that each carries its own serial number. The printed bills are checked, cut apart, starched and pressed, and bundled for distribution.

Until recent times, it was very difficult for counterfeiters to make good copies of U.S. bills. That didn't stop them from trying. But without the skills, equipment, or ink and paper used to make true currency, most counterfeit bills looked blurry and dark. Some attempts were really crude—like drawing extra zeros on a $10 bill, to turn it into a $100. Still, in poor light or when people didn't look closely at a bill, even poor fakes might pass.

Counterfeiting became a lot easier in the 1980s as high-quality color copiers became widespread. Almost anyone with access to one of these machines could produce a reasonable fake, just by putting a real bill in the copier machine and pushing a few buttons. It was so easy that people who didn't mean to commit a crime were tempted to try it. These so-called

Just a few strokes of a pen turned this $10 bill into a $100 bill. Although crude, even a poor fake could pass as genuine in situations where it wasn't examined closely. (Did *you* notice the difference in the numbers and the words?)

casual counterfeiters became a major problem for Treasury officials.

Beginning in 1990, the United States added two anti-counterfeiting features to $20, $50, and $100 bills. One was a security thread—a thin polyester strip embedded in the bill, carrying the letters "USA" and the denomination of the bill. The thread could be seen only when the bill was held up to the light, so it couldn't be photocopied. The second was microprinting, tiny letters so small that they could barely be read with a magnifying glass—and would be blurry in copies.

But it didn't take counterfeiters long to come up with fake security threads. And copiers continued to improve, producing sharper and sharper images. After the U.S. government seized almost $165 million in bogus bills in 1993, officials realized that more security features were needed.

THE NEW $100'S

The first redesigned bills rolled off the presses in 1996—$80 billion in $100 bills. The Treasury Department is releasing the new bills gradually, by replacing old, worn-out bills as they are turned in. In addition to security threads and more microprinting, the new bills have a new look. Benjamin Franklin still appears on the $100 bill, but his portrait is larger and more detailed. That makes it even harder to copy. It's also placed to one side, making room for a watermark—a ghostly image of Franklin pressed into the paper rather than printed on it. The watermark can be seen only when the bill is held up to the light.

Color-shifting ink is another security feature. From one angle, the number 100 in the lower right-hand corner of the bill looks black. From another, it looks green. And parts of the design are formed of fine, concentric lines, a pattern that's very hard to reproduce. On a copier, the fine lines blend into a wavy pattern called a moiré.

The $100 bill was chosen for the first redesign because it's the most widely used unit of U.S. currency, especially abroad. In fact, most of the first new $100's released went overseas, where much business, legal and illegal, is transacted using the bills. In countries where the value of local currency is uncertain, people also sometimes hoard $100's. And foreign counterfeiters had learned to make sophisticated copies of the old bills.

Will the new bills be counterfeit-proof? Perhaps not. But it will probably take counterfeiters quite a while to figure out how to duplicate the range of security features that these bills include.

IT'S A RECORD!

Polar explorer Borge Ousland of Norway (above) set a new world record in 1997. On January 19, he completed a solo trek across Antarctica, becoming the first person to cross the continent alone and unaided by dogs, supply drops, or motorized vehicles. Ousland hiked, skied, and parasailed his way across some 1,700 miles (2,735 kilometers), from the Weddell Sea to Scott Base on the Pacific Coast. It was the longest polar trek ever. At the end, the explorer was exhausted—but happy to have achieved what he called the most important goal of his life. "It's a great relief to have fulfilled a dream with something that's never been done before," he said.

Ousland's feat was extraordinary. But his wasn't the only world record set during the year. In fact, records of one sort or another are being set, and broken, all the time. People are fascinated by records and record holders—by whatever or whoever is biggest, smallest, fastest, slowest, oldest, first, or best in any field. Records fill entire books, such as the famous *Guinness Book of World Records.* It's human nature to want to break records. As soon as someone runs a mile in record time, someone else will be out there trying to do it faster.

In the pages that follow, you'll find eleven more record holders. They represent a wide range of categories—animal, vegetable, and even mineral. While none of them set out to break a record, they all became champions in their own way.

Top Draw: The Hope diamond is the most popular museum object in the world. Each year about five million people see this glittering gem at the National Museum of Natural History in Washington, D.C. It's now the centerpiece of the museum's mineral exhibit, which opened in 1997. The diamond holds another record, too: At 45 carats, it's the world's largest blue diamond. The tint is caused by an impurity in the stone. Supposedly, a curse will strike anyone who handles the gem. There's no evidence for the curse—but people love a good story.

Award Winner: What movie holds the record for winning the most Academy Awards? *Ben-Hur,* a 1959 epic that walked away with eleven Oscars, including Best Picture and Best Director (William Wyler). The movie, which had a running time of about three-and-a-half hours, was based on an 1880 novel by Lew Wallace. Set in Jerusalem and Rome at the time of Christ, the film's most famous scene is a thrilling chariot race in which the hero, the Jewish prince Judah Ben-Hur (right, played by Charlton Heston), defeats his arch rival, the Roman commander Messala (Stephen Boyd). Heston won an Academy Award as best actor for the role.

Best Seller: There's no mystery about the identity of the world's top-selling fiction author. More than two billion copies of books by British mystery writer Agatha Christie (1890–1976) have been sold worldwide. Christie wrote a total of 78 mysteries, mostly set in genteel British society. They featured clever plots and colorful detectives—among them the Belgian Hercule Poirot, who puzzles out crimes by using his "little gray cells," and Jane Marple, an elderly, gossipy woman from a small English village. It was a formula that worked, as Christie's book sales clearly showed. The only book to have outsold Christie is the Bible.

Baseball's Best: What are these players so excited about? They're on major league baseball's winningest team—the New York Yankees. In the 76 years from 1921 to 1997, the Yankees won a total of 34 league championships and 23 World Series. Their best years were from 1947 to 1964. In those eighteen years, the team won 15 pennants and 10 World Series, including five in a row from 1949 to 1953.

Oldest: The bristlecone pine isn't the biggest tree or the prettiest tree. It holds the record as the longest-living tree. Some bristlecone pines are almost 5,000 years old, making them the oldest living things on Earth. The trees grow on high mountain slopes in the western United States. Conditions there are harsh, with cold winter temperatures, hot summer sun, strong winds, and frequent droughts. The bristlecone pines grow very slowly—in 100 years, the trunk of a bristlecone may grow only an inch thicker. Their twisted shapes and many bare branches are evidence of their struggle to stay alive. But these trees are tough—bristlecone pines can survive even if all but a few of their branches and roots die.

Most Valuable: The *Mona Lisa,* painted by Leonardo da Vinci around 1503, is considered the most valuable painting in the world. The ranking is based on an estimate made in 1962, when the *Mona Lisa* traveled from its home at the Louvre, in Paris, to New York City, for a three-month exhibit. Insurance appraisers then valued the painting at $100 million. No painting has ever sold for such an amount. But the *Mona Lisa* might—if it was ever for sale. The painting is famous for the mysterious smile of the subject, thought to be the wife of a merchant in Florence, Italy. Leonardo portrayed her in softly glowing light and deep shadows, against a wild landscape. Even in his own day, the painting was recognized as a masterpiece. Leonardo took it to France in 1517. He died there two years later, and the painting became part of the French royal collection. Since then it has become one of the most famous artworks of all time.

Long-Reigning: Queen Victoria ruled Great Britain for almost 64 years, from 1837 until her death in 1901. That made her the longest-reigning British monarch—and the longest-reigning queen of any land. Victoria came to the throne when she was 18 years old, after the death of her uncle King William IV, who had no children. In Great Britain's parliamentary system, her role as queen was mainly a symbolic one. But Victoria helped unify the country during the years when the British Empire reached the height of its worldwide power. Her sense of duty, moral values, and model conduct won the respect and devotion of her subjects. And her taste in art, music, and fashion set the tone for the time period that today bears her name—the Victorian Era.

Longer-Reigning: Queen Victoria didn't break the record set by Louis XIV of France. The longest-reigning king in modern history, he ruled for 72 years, from 1643 until his death in 1715. However, for the first years of his reign, he was king in name only. Louis was just 4 years old when he came to the throne, and ministers ran the country. But once he took up the reins of government, he proved to be a powerful ruler—probably the strongest in French history. Louis extended his control over the nobles, ruling as an absolute monarch. He chose the sun as his emblem, and he became known as the Sun King. His court at Versailles was famous for extravagance. In his day, France became the strongest nation in Europe, and a center for art and literature. But Louis left behind a legacy of war and debt.

King of Hits: Since Elvis Presley burst onto the rock music scene in 1956, more than a billion copies of his records have been sold. That makes Presley, who died in 1977, the most successful solo recording artist ever. With more than 170 hit singles and 80 top-selling albums, he also ranks among the most productive. Early in his career, Presley helped shape rock 'n' roll with songs such as "All Shook Up," "Heartbreak Hotel," and "Hound Dog." He was the top teen idol of the 1950s—although parents were shocked by his long hair and the way he swiveled his hips on stage. Later, he made films and developed a glitzy Las Vegas nightclub act. Elvis's millions of fans were stunned by his death. Their devotion outlived him. In 1997, the 20th anniversary of his death, fans flocked to Memphis, Tennessee, to pay tribute to the rock star's memory and visit his former home, Graceland. And a new four-CD collection of Presley's songs was released. Elvis may be gone, but his music—and record sales—live on.

Slowest: The three-toed sloth holds a strange place in the record books—it's the slowest mammal in the world. The sleepy sloth, which lives in the tropical rain forests of South America, spends most of its life hanging from tree branches, nibbling leaves. On the rare times that it comes down to the ground, it crawls along at an average speed of just 6 to 8 feet (2 to 2.5 meters) a minute, or under a tenth of a mile (.16 kilometer) in an hour. Sloths aren't exactly speed demons up in the trees, either, although they can climb about twice as fast as they crawl. No wonder that "sloth" is a synonym for laziness. But if three-toed sloths are lazy, it's for good reason. Their leafy diet provides very little energy, so they use as little energy as possible. Sloths conserve energy not only by moving slowly, but also by sleeping a lot—as much as 20 hours a day.

Fastest: The cheetah is the world's fastest land mammal. On the African plains where they live, cheetahs in pursuit of prey have been clocked at speeds up to 70 miles (113 kilometers) an hour. That's two-and-a-half times the speed of the fastest human sprinter—and about 700 times the speed of a three-toed sloth. A cheetah can't keep up that pace for long, however. If it doesn't catch its prey in a quick dash, it has to pull up and rest. When it comes to long-distance running, the pronghorn antelope is the champ. It can cruise along at 60 miles (97 kilometers) an hour for about 9 miles (14 kilometers).

From the mid-1600s through the 1700s, pirates menaced the Caribbean and the Atlantic, seizing any ship that came within their grasp. During the golden age of piracy, the most notorious pirate of all was Blackbeard.

PORTRAIT OF A PIRATE

His name alone made sailors' blood run cold—Blackbeard, the most ruthless pirate ever to sail the high seas. For a few years in the early 1700s, Blackbeard terrorized the Caribbean and the Carolina coast. Then his luck turned. In June 1718, his flagship, *Queen Anne's Revenge,* ran aground on a sand bar and sank off North Carolina. Blackbeard survived, but just a few months later the pirate was cornered and killed by British soldiers.

For almost 280 years, the rotting hulk of the *Queen Anne's Revenge* lay under the murky coastal waters, its location known only to passing fish. Then, in March 1997, a team of marine archeologists announced that they had found, off Beaufort, North Carolina, a wreck they were sure was that of Blackbeard's ship.

It was an exciting discovery. The archeologists didn't expect to find chests of pirate gold aboard—Blackbeard and his crew would have had time to get valuables off the ship before it went down. But the searchers did hope to find treasure of another sort: information. There are scores of tales and legends about pirates, but little is known about their real lives.

GOLDEN AGE OF PIRACY

A Spanish galleon, carrying a cargo of silver, is bound for home when a strange ship approaches. Is it friend or foe? The galleon's lookout can't tell. The ship sails closer, and then suddenly a flag rises to the top of her mast—a black flag, bearing a skull and crossbones. Pirates!

There have been pirates as long as people have been traveling in ships, and there are still pirates in some parts of the world. But the pirates most people in North America think of preyed on ships in the Caribbean and the

Atlantic from the mid-1600s through the 1700s. At the start of that golden age of piracy, Spain controlled an empire in the Americas. Ships crossed the Caribbean and the Atlantic, carrying the riches of the New World back to Spain. Soon, English, French, and other European sailors settled in the Caribbean area and began to loot the Spanish ships. These sailors were called buccaneers.

In those days, nations that were at war often licensed private ships to attack enemy vessels. The people who served on these ships were known as privateers. And while buccaneers had no formal licenses, their actions were often supported by their governments. However, both privateers and buccaneers often crossed the line into piracy, seizing any ship that came within their grasp.

A number of pirates were former navy sailors or deserters who "jumped ship" to escape harsh conditions. Some had lost their jobs on land and turned to crime. Piracy seemed to offer easy money and wild living, and it was easier to

Blackbeard (*above*) was said to be one of the cruelest pirates ever to brandish a cutlass. Like other pirates, he devised his own flag (*below*)—a dreaded sight to sailors.

escape capture at sea than on land. Pirates faced harsh punishment, usually hanging. But only a few of them were ever caught.

In books and movies, pirates are usually portrayed as blood-thirsty villains or swashbuckling romantic heroes. But historians say that neither picture is correct. New evidence from the ocean floor is helping to change some of the ideas people have long held about pirates. Much of the evidence comes from the wreck of the *Whydah*, a pirate ship that sank in 1717 off Cape Cod and was discovered in 1984.

Pirates seldom, if ever, buried treasure or made their victims "walk the plank." Piracy was certainly violent, but it wasn't as murderous as people have come to believe. Some pirates were fierce criminals who tortured and killed their victims. But most wanted to capture valuable ships, not sink them. Prisoners might be set ashore or invited to join the pirate crew. When a pirate was known for mercy, ships were more likely to surrender without a fight.

Still, those who didn't give up when they saw the "Jolly Roger"—the black pirate flag—had to be prepared to fight.

Pirates had a strict society, with its own rules and quite a bit of democracy. On many ships, the crew elected the captain. Crews signed on for a share of the loot, and shares were measured out meticulously. But piracy didn't always pay well. Instead of piles of gold doubloons, the booty might be nothing more than a cargo of cotton, or some supplies for the ship.

A replica of Blackbeard's flagship, *Queen Anne's Revenge.*

Pirates were considered criminals in their day, but some became legends. For example, Henry Morgan's adventures were so celebrated that he was knighted and made lieutenant governor of Jamaica. Fame didn't help William Kidd, though, who was captured and hanged in 1701. Then there was Bartholomew Roberts, who was known for his plumed hats and strict rules—he frowned on drinking, gambling, and swearing. John Avery, called Long Ben, stole a fortune on the seas but died without a doubloon. And, of course, there was Blackbeard.

THE NOTORIOUS BLACKBEARD

By all accounts, Blackbeard was one of the cruelest pirates ever to wave a pistol. Actually, Blackbeard carried six pistols, draped across his chest. In battle, he stuck lighted cannon wicks under the brim of his hat, so that his head was wreathed in smoke. He boasted of torturing his prisoners, kept his crew on their toes by firing randomly at them, and was said to drink a mixture of rum and gunpowder.

Blackbeard's real name was Edward Teach. He was nicknamed for his long black beard, which he sometimes wore in braids. Teach was born in England, perhaps in Bristol, but his early life is a mystery. He was a privateer in the Caribbean in the early 1700s, when Britain was at war with France and Spain. After the war ended in 1713, he turned to piracy. Although his first known raid was made in 1716, historians think he was probably seizing ships long before that.

Among his prizes was a French merchant ship that he turned into his flagship, outfitting it with 40 cannons and renaming it *Queen Anne's Revenge.* A fleet of smaller vessels was also under his command. With these ships, Blackbeard terrorized the Caribbean and the coasts of Virginia and the Carolinas, attacking towns as well as ships. He based his ships in North Carolina and kept them safe by sharing his spoils with that colony's governor.

After the *Queen Anne's Revenge* sank in 1718, Blackbeard turned his attention to the North Carolina coast. He demanded supplies from planters and tolls from passing ships. Since their governor wouldn't help them, North Carolinians turned to Virginia's governor. He sent British troops, who caught up with the pirate on Ocracoke Island on November 22, 1718. There, Blackbeard was killed in hand-to-hand fighting.

Infamous ladies of the high seas—Anne Bonny and Mary Read.

Ladies of the High Seas

In the early 1700s, a time when women were supposed to be delicate and sensitive, two of the most feared pirates to sail Caribbean waters in the early 1700s were women.

Anne Bonny was the daughter of a wealthy Carolina planter, who hoped his daughter would marry well. But Anne was rebellious. She met and married a young sailor, and her father was so angry that he ordered her to leave home. Anne and her husband went to the Bahamas, and he left her there. But before long she met and fell in love with Calico Jack, an infamous pirate. When Calico Jack returned to sea, Anne went with him. She took to piracy right away, wielding pistols and a cutlass as they boarded and plundered ship after ship.

On one of those ships was a young sailor who joined the pirate crew. Imagine everyone's surprise when this sailor turned out to be a woman! Mary Read had grown up in England. She had worked as a sailor and fought in the army, always disguised as a man. She and Anne Bonny soon became good friends, pillaging and plundering side by side.

The pirates' crime spree ended in October, 1720, when they were captured by the British. Calico Jack was hanged, and Mary Read died in prison. Anne Bonny was imprisoned, too, but no one knows what finally happened to her.

SUNKEN TREASURE

The discovery of the *Queen Anne's Revenge* came after a ten-year-long search. Archeologists consulted old documents, including reports by witnesses of the ship's sinking, to narrow down the location. Then they combed the water off Beaufort with an underwater metal detector.

In November 1996, they found what they were looking for—the ship's 40 metal cannons gave its location away. Divers quickly confirmed the find: The ship was sitting under just 20 feet (6 meters) of water. "If you could have seen through that dirty water, it was right there," one of the searchers said.

The search team brought up still more artifacts that pointed to the identity of the ship—a ship's bell dated 1709, the brass barrel of a blunderbuss, a cannon ball. The searchers hope that, as the sea gives up more items from the ship, they'll be able to learn the truth behind the legend of Blackbeard.

From a display of empty soda cans at the Children's Garbage Museum to a portrait titled "Pablo Presley" at the Museum of Bad Art—almost anything that can be collected has a museum dedicated to it somewhere.

MUSEUMS— FROM A TO Z!

You might expect to see a model of a dinosaur in a museum. But a 1-ton dinosaur made of trash? That's Trashosaurus, a featured attraction at the Children's Garbage Museum and Education Center of Southwest Connecticut. This museum is devoted entirely to things that people throw away.

Strange? Not at all. The Children's Garbage Museum is one of hundreds of specialty museums scattered throughout North America and the rest of the world—and it's far from the oddest. Just about anything that can be collected, from bad art to shoes, is on display somewhere. Some of these museums began as personal col-

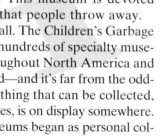

lections. Others were founded by companies or associations. Either way, whatever your hobby or interest may be, chances are that there's a museum devoted to it.

ART TOO BAD TO IGNORE

Good art winds up in museums. Bad art winds up in garage sales. But a museum in Dedham, Massachusetts, is different. The Museum of Bad Art, or MOBA, began when Scott Wilson, an antiques dealer, pulled a painting from a trash pile, planning to salvage the frame. Something about the work—perhaps its incredible ugliness—caught the fancy of Wilson and his friends. They began to search for other dreadful paint-

If you love comic books, visit the Words & Pictures Museum. You'll find original drawings of many of your favorite heroes, including the Teenage Mutant Ninja Turtles.

ings. Today visitors to the MOBA gallery in the Dedham Community Theater can see plenty of "art too bad to be ignored"—such as a portrait of Mary Todd Lincoln fashioned from layers of plastic lace.

ALL ABOUT AUTOMOBILES

The Henry Ford Museum & Greenfield Village, in Dearborn, Michigan, boasts a fabulous collection of classic cars. Along with a 1923 Stutz Bearcat, a 1930 Bugatti Royale, and other treasures, there are displays that show how the automobile has changed American life. You can see reproductions of a 1920s gas station, a 1940s roadside diner, and a 1960s motel room. Other sections of the museum feature displays of all sorts of early machinery and inventions. And there are reproductions of homes, shops, a sawmill, and a working farm of the 1800s.

CARTOONS AND COMIC BOOKS

If you're a fan of cartoons and comic books, then you're in luck—you can visit a number of specialty museums. The Cartoon Art Museum in San Francisco specializes in the "funnies," which are newspaper comic strips. The Words & Pictures Museum in Northampton, Massachusetts, focuses on comic books. Its collection includes 12,000 original pictures, presenting such comic book heroes as Batman, Captain America, and the Teenage Mutant Ninja Turtles as well as many lesser known characters.

The International Museum of Cartoon Art in Boca Raton, Florida, has the world's largest collection of cartoon art and related items. More than 1,000 artists are represented in the collection, which traces the history of cartooning from woodcuts done in the 1800s to the animated cartoons of today. Original car-

All Aboard the Artrain

If you can't travel to visit a museum, maybe a museum will travel to visit you. That's the idea behind Artrain, a museum in a train. Artrain was started in 1971 in Michigan. Since then it has traveled to more than 500 towns and opened its doors to 2.5 million visitors. It has carried thirteen different exhibitions. The latest, an exhibition of works from the Smithsonian Institution, is on a three-year national tour. Thirty prints by leading artists are displayed in three of the train's cars. The fourth car holds a studio where artists demonstrate techniques (above, an artist carves a model of a stingray). A caboose serves as an office for the traveling staff.

Artrain doesn't have a locomotive. It hitches rides on other trains, relying on railway companies to move around from one town to the next. The train's stops are planned carefully, with special events and school visits in mind. Local volunteers work with the train staff to help make each stop a success. When Artrain pulls into a town, kids and adults line up to see the treasures inside.

toons, funnies, comic books, filmstrips, and models of famous cartoon characters are on display. Visitors can learn how comic books are made, buy books on cartooning, and even purchase original works by famous cartoonists.

CELEBRITIES

Are you starstruck? Seek out the dozens of pint-sized museums devoted to movie stars, singers, and other celebrities.

● Actor Jimmy Stewart is honored at a museum in Indiana, Pennsylvania, his hometown. Tucked away on the third floor of the town library, it displays artifacts that trace his career and family history.

● At the Lucy–Desi Museum in Jamestown, New York, fans of Lucille Ball can see gowns and even wigs worn by the famous television comedian.

● The Roy Rogers–Dale Evans Museum in Victorville, California, recalls television's early days, when this cowboy-cowgirl duo starred in a Western series. Among the displays is Roy Rogers' horse Trigger, which was stuffed and mounted after the horse's death in 1965.

● The collection at the Debbie Reynolds Hollywood Movie Museum in Las Vegas, Nevada, was assembled by Reynolds herself. While it includes items from her acting and singing career, it mostly honors Hollywood's golden era. On display are such items as a pair of Fred Astaire's dance shoes and an elaborate headdress worn by Elizabeth Taylor in the movie *Cleopatra*.

THE CIRCUS

The Circus World Museum preserves the excitement of the traveling shows that once brought clowns, daredevil and aerial acts, exotic animals, and other wonders to small towns and cities across America. It's located in Baraboo, Wisconsin, on a site that was once the winter headquarters of the Ringling Brothers Circus. Here, a steam calliope fills the air with music as visitors tour an old-time circus Midway, a wild-animal menagerie, and a replica of P. T. Barnum's famous 19th-century sideshow. The museum has the world's largest collection of circus wagons. You can learn how clowns put on makeup and ride an antique carousel. Best of all, the museum has its own circus. Under a red, white, and blue Big Top, aerialists and acrobats defy gravity, elephants show off their training, and clowns delight everyone.

GARBAGE

The Children's Garbage Museum, in Stratford, Connecticut, is located next to a recycling plant. A glassed-in walkway lets museum visitors view the plant's operations. In the museum itself, hands-on exhibits and activities encourage kids to learn how garbage can be used to produce energy, how aluminum and plastic are recycled, how worms turn trash into new soil, and more. The "Trash Bash" is a game in which kids, wearing hard hats and goggles, stand in booths to answer questions about recycling. If they give a wrong answer, clean "trash" rains down from above.

ICE THE OLD-FASHIONED WAY

When you want a glass of cold juice, you go to the refrigerator and get it. But 75 years ago, keeping food fresh and cold wasn't so easy. The Ice House Museum, in Cedar Falls, Iowa, shows how it was done in the old days. In winter, workers sawed huge blocks of ice from rivers and ponds. Horses dragged the blocks to ice houses, where they were stored. Then, all year, icemen cut smaller blocks from the big ones, loaded them into horse-drawn wagons, and went door to door, delivering ice. Placed in the family icebox, a block would keep food cold for days as it slowly melted.

Roller skates of all kinds—from stilt skates to hoof skates for horses—can be found at the National Museum of Roller Skating.

Then it was time for the iceman to call again. The museum, located in a former icehouse, has displays that show the tools, wagons, and other equipment that the icemen used.

ROLLER SKATES

In-line skates are only the latest twist in roller skating—a sport that goes back, believe it or not, to the 1760s. That's when a British inventor named Joseph Merlin made a grand entrance into a party on roller skates—and crashed into a mirror. Skating's history is traced at the National Museum of Roller Skating, in Lincoln, Nebraska. On display are skating costumes, medals and trophies, photographs and posters, films and videotapes, and all sorts of publications about skating. And, of course, there are roller skates— among them stilt skates, motorized skates, combination ice and roller skates (with interchangeable blades and wheels), and even hoof skates for horses.

SHOES BY THE THOUSAND

Sandals from ancient Egypt. . .Napoleon Bonaparte's socks. . .moon boots worn by astronauts. . .rock star Elton John's shiny platform shoes. That's just a sampling of the more than 10,000 items in the collection of the Bata Shoe Museum in Toronto, Canada. Devoted entirely to footwear, this museum began with the personal collection of Sonja Bata, a shoe manufacturer. It opened to the public in 1996, in a building that looks a little like. . .well, a shoe box. Inside you can see everything from Inuit boots, to slippers worn by Queen Victoria in 1840, to Elvis Presley's patent-leather loafers. There are tiny silk slippers, worn by Chinese women whose feet were bound, and shoes with metal spikes used by French peasants to crush chestnuts. The museum's motto is *Per Saecula Gradatim*— Latin for "one step at a time."

SURF'S UP!

The surf's always up at the Surfing Museum in Santa Cruz, California. Located in a small brick lighthouse overlooking the Pacific Ocean, this museum is dedicated to the early days of California's most famous sport. Its collection includes classic wooden surfboards from the 1950s and 1960s, old photos, and a wetsuit mangled by a shark. (The surfer who wore the suit survived the attack.) The museum is staffed by veteran surfers, some of whom have been searching for the "perfect wave" for more than 50 years.

AND ZILLIONS MORE...

Special museums range from the famous to the obscure. Each year, for example, thousands of people visit the National Baseball Hall of Fame and Museum, in Cooperstown, New York, and the Rock and Roll Hall of Fame in Cleveland, Ohio. Far fewer visitors make it to the Banana Museum, in Altadena, California. Those who do can see 15,000 banana-related items— including glass, sequined, and stuffed

The Bramble Boot, a fanciful leather sculpture, is one of the many unusual samples of footwear that can be seen during a visit to the Bata Shoe Museum.

More Than Museums

Did you ever wonder how jelly beans are made? You can find out all about these and many other products on factory tours. Most of these tours are free, but the companies that offer them usually want people to make arrangements in advance.

Board Games: The Milton Bradley factory in East Longmeadow, Massachusetts, produces Scrabble, Monopoly, and other famous games, as well as jigsaw puzzles. You can watch as workers and machines turn out as many as 1,800 games in an hour.

Chocolate: At the Hershey's Chocolate World Visitors Centers—one in Hershey, Pennsylvania, and another in Oakdale, California—you can see how chocolate is made and enjoy a sample after your tour.

Crayons: Watch how molten wax and pigment are turned into crayons at the Crayola factory in Easton, Pennsylvania. Two million crayons come off this factory's production line each day.

Ice Cream: You'll get to sample the flavor of the day at the Ben & Jerry's factory in Waterbury, Vermont, which offers tours and information about ice-cream making.

Jelly Beans: See jelly beans being made at the Herman Goelitz Candy Company in Fairfield, California. Don't miss the jelly-bean-mosaic portrait of President Ronald Reagan (above), who was a big fan of the candy.

Teddy Bears: The Vermont Teddy Bear Company of Shelburne, Vermont, takes visitors through workshops where stuffed bears are sewn by hand. You may even get a chance to help, by brushing a new bear's fur.

bananas; a petrified banana, found in the back of a closet; and little leather coats to keep bananas warm in winter.

You can also visit the Frog Fantasies Museum, in Eureka Springs, Arkansas; the Tooth Fairy Museum, in Deerfield, Illinois; the Lunch Box Pop Art Museum, in Columbus, Georgia; the Barbie Hall of Fame, in Palo Alto, California; the Burlingame PEZ Museum, in Burlingame, California; the Museum of Questionable Medical Devices, in Minneapolis, Minnesota; the Dog Museum, in St. Louis, Missouri; the Antique Sewing Machine Museum, in Arlington, Texas; and the Madison Museum of Bathroom Tissue, in Wisconsin.

Tourists who wander off the beaten path in Europe can visit some odd museums, too. There's the Cumberland Pencil Museum in Keswick, England. Another British museum, in Maidstone, displays a collection of dog collars. The Museum of Sugar Art in Cordes, France, is filled with flowers and other decorative creations, all made of sugar by master chefs. Basel, Switzerland, has the Cat Museum. Austria's special museums feature beekeeping, chimney sweeps, salt mining, wood carving, witchcraft, and other exotic subjects. The Spargelmuseum, in Schrobehausen, Germany, is completely devoted to white asparagus—how that vegetable is grown and eaten, its history and supposed medicinal uses, and its appearance in art, decoration, and literature.

So whenever you're traveling with family and friends, keep a lookout for these fascinatingly odd museums. Who knows what you'll discover!

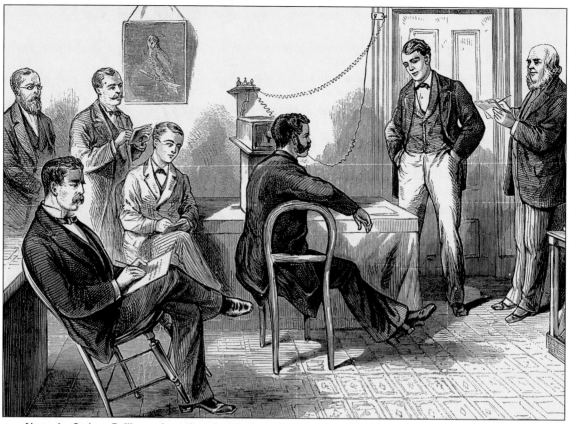

Alexander Graham Bell's new invention, the telephone, is demonstrated in 1877 Boston. The 150th anniversary of the birth of this great inventor—and of another great inventor, Thomas Alva Edison—was celebrated in 1997.

TWO GREAT INVENTORS: MAKING LIFE BETTER

You come home after school and pop your favorite recording into the CD player. The phone rings—it's a friend who missed tonight's social-studies assignment. You switch on a light, grab your assignment pad, and tell your friend what's due. Then you chat and make plans to see a movie on the weekend.

Recorded music, telephones, electric lights, movies—they're so much a part of life that people take them for granted. Yet none of them existed 150 years ago. We have them thanks to the work of two remarkable inventors, Alexander Graham Bell and Thomas Alva Edison. By an odd coincidence, they were born less than a month apart: Edison on February 11, 1847, and Bell on March 3 of that year. Thus 1997 was the occasion for a double birthday celebration—the 150th anniversary of the birth of both inventors.

Bell and Edison didn't work together. But they shared many interests, and sometimes their projects overlapped. And both men were tireless workers who never stopped looking for ways to make life better.

A TEACHER OF THE DEAF

While the world knows Alexander Graham Bell as the inventor of the telephone, he always described himself as a "teacher of the deaf." It was his interest in speech and hearing that started him on the path to invention.

Bell was born in Edinburgh, Scotland. His father and grandfather were well-known speech teachers. His mother, a portrait painter and musician, taught her three sons at home while they were young. When Bell was 13, after a few years of formal schooling, he spent a year with his grandfather. That year convinced him to become a speech teacher, too. Bell was especially fascinated by the mechanics of speech and sound. He even made a working model of the human speech organs, using rubber, cotton, and a bellows.

In 1867, Bell joined his father's teaching practice in London. Besides lecturing at various schools, he taught speech to the deaf, using a technique his father had developed. He might have spent his life in England. But both his brothers died of tuberculosis, and his own health began to fail. In 1870, his worried father moved the family to Canada.

After a year in the Ontario countryside, Bell recovered his health. He moved to Boston, Massachusetts, and resumed teaching. He also began to investigate the relationship between sound and electricity. The parents of two of his students funded this work. One of those students was Mabel Hubbard, a young woman who had lost her hearing following a childhood illness. She and Bell fell in love and eventually married.

The telegraph was the only method of fast long-distance communication at the time, and it was still new. Bell was fascinated with the device and found a way to improve it. He developed a harmonic telegraph, which could send several messages over the same wire at the same time. In the process, he grew convinced that the vibrations of sound could be converted into electricity—so that speech, rather than telegraph code, could travel over wires. He began to alter his telegraph with the help of his assistant, Thomas A. Watson.

On March 10, 1876, Bell was working on the latest version of his device at the Boston boarding house that served as his lab. Watson was in another room, with a receiver wired to Bell's transmitter. Suddenly Bell spilled some acid. He called out, "Mr. Watson, come here. I want you!" Watson heard the words clearly on his receiver. Both men forgot about the acid in their excitement—the invention worked!

Bell's telephone was acclaimed as a marvel. He and Watson traveled widely to demonstrate it, cheerily calling "Ahoy" (the telephone greeting Bell preferred) over the wires. By August 1877, some 700 customers had

Phone Talk

Alexander Graham Bell would probably be astounded—and delighted—by today's telephones. Here are three of the latest advances.

● Wireless cellular phone service allows people to talk on the phone just about anywhere. It's already common. A new version—called PCS, or personal communications service—uses digital signals for better clarity. The digital phones can also function as pagers and answering machines.

● The latest wireless merges a computer with a cellular telephone. With one handheld unit (shown above), you can surf the Internet, send e-mail and faxes, and chat with friends.

● Forgot a friend's phone number? No problem. Just say the name, and your phone will make the connection. Voice dialing is available in just a few areas now, but more will have it soon. You program the phone by dialing an access code, speaking a name, and dialing the appropriate phone number. A computer at the other end takes in the information. Thereafter, just wait for the beep, speak the name—and the computer puts you through.

telephones. Long-distance lines linked New York and Boston in 1884, and after that telephone networks spread across North America and around the world.

Meanwhile, Bell became a U.S. citizen and settled in Washington, D.C. There and at his summer home in Nova Scotia, Canada, he continued to work on inventions. Bell found ways to transmit speech over short distances on a beam of light and to distill drinking water from water vapor. He developed a cooling system for the study of his Washington home and an electrical device that could locate bullets in the body. He developed wax phonograph cylinders, which provided better sound than early metal cylinders.

Bell was also interested in flight, and he experimented with kites that could lift people. But none of his later inventions had the impact of the telephone. After he died in 1922, North America's phones were silent for an hour in his honor.

Thomas Edison with the phonograph he invented in 1877. People were amazed when they heard his voice on the machine, reciting the rhyme "Mary Had a Little Lamb."

THE WIZARD OF MENLO PARK

The phonograph, the first practical lightbulb, and the motion-picture camera are Thomas Alva Edison's most famous inventions. But he worked on many others—everything from electrical storage batteries to waxed paper and talking dolls. His creativity and business savvy were legendary. But Edison always denied that he was a genius. "What people choose to call genius is simply hard work," he said.

Edison's achievements are all the more remarkable because he was largely self-taught. He was born in Milan, Ohio, and grew up there and in Port Huron, Michigan. Full of pranks and questions, he had a difficult time at school and he quit at a young age. He continued his studies at home, helped by his mother, and eagerly read everything that came his way. He especially liked science, and he set up a chemistry lab in the basement of his home.

At 12, Edison got a job selling newspapers, candy, and sandwiches on trains that ran between Port Huron and Detroit. Eventually he edited and printed his own small newspaper and sold it to passengers. He moved his chemistry lab into a baggage car, and he used layovers in Detroit for trips to the public library there.

One day, when Edison was 15, he snatched the 3-year-old son of a station agent out of the path of a moving boxcar. The station agent offered to teach him to operate the telegraph as a reward. Edison mastered the art of receiving coded messages despite the fact that he was losing his hearing, a problem that worsened as he grew older. In 1863, he went to work as a telegraph operator. His skills allowed him to find jobs in several midwestern cities and then in Boston.

Edison tinkered with telegraph equipment, but his first patented invention was a device to record legislative votes. No one wanted it. From then on, Edison decided, he would

Recordings: From Tinny to Terrific

The first phonograph "record" produced by Thomas Edison was a sheet of tinfoil wound around a metal cylinder. A needle, or stylus, traveled over patterns on the foil, and its movement created vibrations that produced sounds. But the sounds were scratchy and "tinny," and it wasn't long before people found ways to make better recordings. First came wax cylinders. Then came steel plates, which could be used to stamp out thousands of shellac discs. Vinyl replaced shellac. Electronic amplifiers and stereo speakers replaced the huge horns on old-fashioned phonographs. Magnetic tape recordings came on the scene.

In the 1980s, the digital compact disc (CD) changed the recording industry. Unlike records, which are played with a stylus, or tapes, which are played with magnetic heads, compact discs are played by a beam of laser light, producing crisp, clear sound.

Now a new disc format promises even better sound quality and multi-channel "surround sound." Because the new discs can carry video and text as well as sound, they are called DVDs—digital versatile discs. DVD video and computer discs are already on the market, and DVD audio disks are expected to be available before the year 2000. What would Edison think?

work only on inventions that would sell. He did better with his next effort—an improved stock ticker. After he moved to New York City in 1869, he made several improvements to the telegraph and devised one that could handle four messages at once.

In 1876, Edison opened a new laboratory in Menlo Park, New Jersey. There he and his staff improved existing products and came up with new devices. One of the first was a new telephone transmitter, with better range and clarity than Bell's model. Another was the phonograph—Edison's most original invention. When people heard this machine reproduce his voice in 1877, they were amazed. He became known as the Wizard of Menlo Park.

But it was Edison's lightbulb that had the greatest impact on the world. He didn't invent the first bulb, but he was the first to combine a long-lasting bulb with fixtures, wiring, and an electrical source—a complete lighting system. In 1882, he opened the first commercial electrical station, serving about 85 customers in New York City.

Edison's first wife, Mary Stilwell, died in 1884. In 1886 he married Mina Miller, and the next year he moved his staff to a larger "invention factory" in West Orange, New Jersey. A steady stream of inventions flowed from this lab: a dictating machine, a motion-picture camera and the kinetoscope, which showed moving pictures, and countless other devices. In all, Edison obtained 1,093 patents. And when he died, in 1931, he left behind millions of documents detailing his ideas—notebooks, sketches, and descriptions of inventions that worked and many that didn't. Historians are still pouring over them, marveling at his creativity.

SPOTLIGHT ON YOUTH

WWW.COOLSITES

What's the biggest soap bubble ever blown? What did an ancient Egyptian pharaoh dream about the sphinx? What's the latest album by your favorite music group? What's the most active volcano in the world? Find the answers on the Internet's World Wide Web—one of the coolest places to be. The Web is a huge community in cyberspace filled with thousands of "sites" that contain tons of information. If your computer is connected to an on-line service, you can "visit" the four fun Web sites shown here. Each site has an address that begins with the letters http. Type in the address, and in seconds you'll be at the site.

Blowin' Bubbles
http://bubbles.org

Join Professor Bubbles in his rainbow-colored Bubblesphere and learn why bubbles have color, why they are always round, and why they pop. See some really big bubbles, including giant ones that can completely enclose the professor.

The site also has many great activities, including several you could turn into science projects. Learn the formula for the ultimate bubble solution, and how to make your own bubble tools from coat hangers, tin cans, even your hands. Play Tic Tac Bubble. And make sure to check out Professor Bubbles' Busy Box Bubble Blower!

Touring Ancient Egypt
http://www.memphis.edu/egypt/main.html

Hook up to this Web site and you'll find yourself on an archeological adventure to the past—to the days of sphinxes and pharaohs. Click onto the "Color Tour of Egypt," and visit awesome places such as Luxor, where a long avenue of sphinxes leads to a gigantic temple. Lots of color pictures illustrate the text.

This site also shows various artifacts found in and around tombs and temples. You can see the mummy of Iret-iruw, who lived some 2,300 years ago. In 1987, this mummy spent a day in a modern hospital, having a CAT scan and being examined by medical specialists. Check out the site to learn what the specialists discovered.

Popcorn Power
http://www.popcorn.org

Popcorn lovers who are looking for new taste treats should check out The Popcorn Institute's site. There you'll find all the directions you'll need to whip up apple popcorn brittle, yogurt popcorn, and lots of other goodies. There are directions for popcorn crafts, too, including holiday popcorn balls, popcorn pompoms, crazy daisies, and even a popcorn carousel.

In the Encyclopedia Popcornica you'll discover how popcorn pops, the best way to store popcorn, and how popcorn poppers have evolved through the years. After you've checked out all the interesting things on this site, put your new knowledge to work and go on a scavenger hunt—where you may even win some free popcorn!

VolcanoWorld
http://volcano.und.edu

Volcanoes are erupting all around the world. You can see where all the action is at VolcanoWorld. For example, read about the debris that catapulted out of Soufriere Hills on the tiny West Indian island of Montserrat during 1997, destroying homes and coating a once-beautiful landscape with a thick layer of gray ash.

Are there volcanoes—active, dormant, or dead—in your neighborhood? The site describes all the known volcanoes around the globe. It also lets you explore volcanoes on Mars, Venus, and the moon. For live action, check out the video clips, where you'll find images of fiery eruptions and flowing lava.

There's also a list of questions that people ask volcanologists (scientists who study volcanoes). If you have a question, submit it and a volcanologist will reply.

People who can design, program, build, or sell computer systems are especially in great demand. So are people with skills in fields that depend on computers, such as word processing and computer-aided design.

Computers are changing the way people live and work, and the computer field itself is rapidly changing. It's likely that in coming years, many more new jobs will be created in this field. What are these jobs? Which of them might be suitable for you? Here's a sampling of the many occupations available in the computer field. Each has its own training and educational requirements—and its own demands and rewards.

CREATING COMPUTERS

Computers and peripherals—display screens, printers, disk drives, modems, keyboards, trackballs—are called hardware. The engineers who design and develop these parts of a computer system are called **hardware engineers.**

Often, many computer engineers are involved in the design of a new computer. Each makes contributions in his or her specialty. For example, the main part of a computer—its "brain"—consists of small processing units called chips, which contain thousands of tiny electrical circuits. **Electrical engineers** decide how many circuits to put on a chip and how they are to be connected. They design different chips for different types of computers, and they design the printed circuit boards that hold the chips. **Chemical and metallurgical engineers** develop the materials used in chips and circuit boards. **Mechanical engineers** design the housing for the computer. **Manufacturing engineers** oversee the production process.

If you're interested in developing new computers, you need a good background in science

CAREERS IN COMPUTERS

We're living in the Age of Computers. Computers are everywhere—in millions of homes, in schools, and in every type of workplace. Banking, farming, retailing, moviemaking, manufacturing, publishing: Name a business, and you're sure to find people there working with computers. In many offices, almost every desk has a computer terminal.

The rapid spread of computers into all parts of society has led to an equally rapid growth in the number of computer-related jobs. In fact, these days, some knowledge of computers is important in almost every career.

and math. Computer engineers usually have college and graduate school degrees in one or more branches of engineering. They continue to study after they begin working, to keep up with the many changes that are taking place in computer technology.

Many kinds of **hardware technicians** assist computer engineers in creating new products. **Electrical technicians** inspect and test the electronic parts and wiring that go into the computers. **Chemical technicians** etch the printed circuit boards. **Drafters** prepare drawings and blueprints that will be used by the people who manufacture the computers.

Technicians have usually attended vocational or technical schools. They may also receive on-the-job training. The amount of education or training they need varies with the type of work they do.

DEVELOPING SOFTWARE

Programmers write the instructions, or programs, that tell a computer what to do. Computer programs are called software, and so programmers are often called **software engineers.**

There are two types of programmers. **Operating systems programmers** develop software that tells the computer how to operate itself and its peripheral equipment. **Applications programmers** write software that tells the computer how to perform specific tasks, such as keeping track of financial data.

Many applications programmers specialize in certain kinds of software or in software for specific fields. Scientific programmers develop programs in aerospace, engineering, and other technical fields. Business and commercial programmers write programs to help with billing, record-keeping, sales projections, and other

business tasks. Game programmers develop game software. Educational programmers develop programs that are used to teach important skills. Some software engineers specialize in multimedia programs, developing programs with sound, pictures, and even video clips for CD-ROM disks. Others focus on computer security. They design software that prevents unauthorized people from getting into computers. As more and more pri-

Hardware engineers design the mechanical parts of a computer system. These engineers are using a computer to aid in the design of an electronic chip—a small computer processsing unit that contains thousands of tiny electrical circuits.

vate information—tax records, health records, school records—is stored in computers, computer security has become a growing field.

Programmers are often part of a development team. For instance, creating a multimedia educational program may involve several programmers—each working on a different part of the program—as well as teachers, artists, and even musicians.

Programming requires clear, logical thinking, as well as creativity. It also requires a great

223

Software engineers, like these programmers who create video computer games, write the instructions that tell a computer what to do. Programming requires clear, logical thinking, as well as creativity and patience.

deal of patience, because programs must be tested and revised over and over again until they are free of errors.

Some programmers are self-taught and begin working while still in high school. Most programmers, however, have college degrees in computer science, engineering, or math.

SYSTEMS ANALYSTS

Pretend that you own a chain of sporting-goods stores, and you've decided to computerize your operation. You want the computers to keep track of inventory, handle billing and employee records, and write checks. What kind of computers do you need? What kinds of programs?

A business that uses computers needs someone to plan, organize, and evaluate how the computers can best be used. Such a person is called a **systems analyst.** Systems analysts are problem solvers. They look at a business's needs and develop plans to meet those needs with computers. Sometimes they develop plans for expanding an existing computer system.

After the business managers approve the plans for a computer system, the analysts supervise installation of the equipment. When

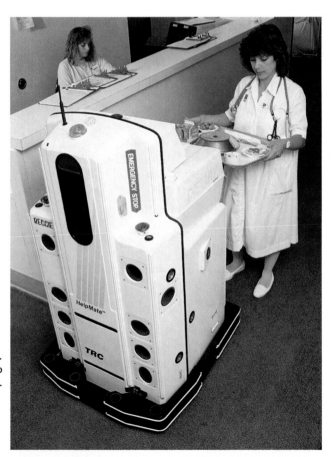

Computers are the brains in all robots made today. HelpMate, a hospital service robot, is programmed to handle chores like delivering medications and meals.

the system is operating, the analysts continually evaluate it. If they feel improvements can be made (which often happens as new products come on the market), they design updates.

Some systems analysts work for companies that have large computer systems or want to install such systems. Others work for consulting firms that develop systems under contract. Sometimes systems analysts also design software. Maybe your sporting-goods business needs a special inventory program—one very different from anything being sold in computer stores. A systems analyst can create the specifications for this program. These specifications are then given to a programmer, who creates the needed software.

To become a systems analyst, you need a college degree and experience as a programmer. Many systems analysts also have specialized training in the industries in which they work, such as banking or insurance.

COMPUTER OPERATORS

Computer operators enter information into computers and run the programs. With personal computers and desktop terminals, computer operation has become part of many jobs. For example, the bookkeeper for your sporting-goods company would use a computer to produce a payroll report. Store managers would use computers to track inventory. But some jobs call for special expertise in computer operations. These jobs include word processing and computer-assisted design. In addition, companies with large, centralized computer systems hire operators to run and monitor those systems. The operators sometimes work in shifts, around the clock, making sure that everything is functioning correctly. They keep log books in which they indicate what programs were run and what problems occurred. If the computer screen, or monitor, shows that an error has been made, the operators locate the problem. They may try to solve the problem, or they may stop the program until a service technician can fix the system.

Not long ago, businesses with large computer systems needed dozens or even hundreds of operators. Nowadays much of the

On Line After School

Looking for an after-school job? You could bag groceries at the supermarket, or flip burgers at the local fast-food restaurant, or baby-sit. But if computers are your thing, you have other options. Many teens are finding that they can turn their interest in computers into cash—because they have skills that companies need.

Software makers, computer manufacturers, network services, mail-order companies, and many other employers are discovering that kids today often have impressive computer skills. They've grown up with computers. They understand how computers work and how they're put together. They may have learned programming at an early age, writing simple games or scheduling programs. They know computer languages, the codes used to write programs.

What sort of work is available part-time? Some teens have found work repairing computers. Others are hired to do programming or to work "on-line," maintaining network computer bulletin boards. Some earn money by writing and selling their own games and other programs. The hottest new job is designing Web sites for companies that want to be on the Internet.

These jobs are good stepping stones to a career in computers. You'll earn valuable experience as well as extra money.

Bill Gates: Computer King

When Bill Gates was 19, he dropped out of Harvard University to go into business with a high-school friend, writing programs for microcomputers. The first of these desktop computers had just come on the market, and no one knew if they would succeed. Gates, however, was certain that the machines would start a revolution. And he was right—spectacularly right. The company he co-founded, Microsoft, dominates the personal computer software industry today. It made him a billionaire at age 31, the youngest person ever to earn that much money. In 1997, at 41, Gates was the richest person in the world, worth almost $24 billion.

People who meet Gates are often struck by his intelligence, his humor, and his knowledge, especially in the fields of science and history. Even as a boy, he was brilliant, intense, and competitive. The son of a lawyer and a teacher, Gates was born on October 28, 1955, in Seattle, Washington. His first contact with computers came in 1967, when his school set up a training terminal. He was hooked at once. By the time he was in high school, he was earning money writing computer programs. Still, he didn't think computers would be his life. He enrolled at Harvard as a prelaw major. But when his friend Paul Allen showed him an article describing the first commercial microcomputer, everything changed.

Microsoft, which Gates and Allen founded in 1975, grew quickly. The company's first big break came in 1980, when it was selected to write the operating system for IBM's new personal computer. That system, MS-DOS, became the standard for PC's. Microsoft went on to develop a wide range of PC software products, including programs for word processing and financial management. In 1985, it introduced its Windows software, which uses graphics in place of typed commands. In the 1990s, it introduced the Microsoft Network and Internet software. By spotting new trends and marketing products aggressively, Microsoft grew into a multibillion-dollar corporation.

All this time, Gates worked tirelessly, seven days a week and fifteen hours a day. Today he still puts in long hours, but he takes most Sundays off. He dresses casually, in slacks and running shoes, even at work. In 1997 he and his wife, Melinda, and their year-old daughter were planning to move into a new $40-million home, built into a bluff on a lake near Seattle, with its own library, movie theater, and indoor pool.

Gates may be enjoying being the world's richest man, but those who know him are sure of one thing: When new trends appear in the computer industry, Bill Gates and Microsoft are sure to be leading the way.

work has been automated, and operations staffs are usually small. A supervising operator or operations manager is in charge. This person hires employees, sets their schedules, and helps them solve problems. The supervisor also schedules how the computers will be used and makes sure that the computers are kept in good condition.

Most computer operators attend two-year community colleges or technical schools. After gaining experience and proving themselves on the job, they may become supervising operators. Supervisors often have more education, to help in solving technical problems.

INFORMATION, PLEASE

Storing, sorting, and retrieving information are among a computer's most important jobs. Vast amounts of related information can be stored in computer files, forming a collection of facts and figures called a database. When you want to find a specific piece of information, the computer quickly sorts through the files and finds the data you need.

Government agencies and large corporations that track large amounts of information have database management systems. A **database administrator** helps organize the system and keeps it up to date. These administrators make certain that there are backup copies of all data, in case of emergencies. They may also make improvements in the system, to make it easier for people to get the data they need.

Database administrators need college degrees. They also need experience in programming and systems analysis, as well as an understanding of the business or industry in which they are working.

People who enter the information into databases are called **data entry operators.** The kind of data they work with depends on where they work—for example, customer orders for a sporting-goods store or patient records for a hospital. Data entry operators usually have high-school diplomas and good typing skills, and they are well organized.

NETWORKING

Networks are creating the next wave in the computer revolution, and they are also cre-

ating new jobs. Many companies today have installed internal computer networks, so that their employees can share information and send messages to each other through electronic mail (e-mail). Some of these systems are very complicated, and a **network administrator** is hired to make sure they run smoothly.

Computers can also communicate over phone lines with outside networks and information services. That has created jobs for **telecommunications experts,** who design and maintain the switching and other equipment that makes "on-line" communication possible.

The Internet, a vast collection of computer networks that reaches around the world, is creating some especially exciting job opportunities. Businesses, schools, and organizations of all

People can network all over the world with computers. At this "cybercafe," customers can surf the Internet while enjoying a cup of coffee and dessert.

kinds—even individuals—can be contacted directly on the part of the Internet called the World Wide Web. They have set up sites, or home pages, that include text, graphics, and even animation. **Web-site designers** are in great demand today. Programming skills, creativity, and an understanding of how the Internet works are the requirements for this career. Many individuals, including many teens, are finding work in this new, wide-open field.

With computers being used for more and more aspects of business, many companies have set up information systems departments to ensure that they make the best use of their equipment. **Information systems managers** coordinate the work of computer operators, systems analysts, database managers, and network and telecommunications experts. This job varies from company to company. It requires extensive experience working with computer systems and networks, familiarity with the latest developments in technology, understanding of the industry you work in, and the ability to work with others and understand their computer needs.

SERVICE TECHNICIANS

Service technicians, also known as field engineers and service engineers, keep computer systems running smoothly. They install new equipment, maintain it, and make repairs. Some service technicians work for a specific manufacturer and handle only that manufacturer's computers. Others work for companies that sell computers made by a number of different manufacturers.

Like many others in the computer field, technicians are problem solvers. They have to be able to determine what's wrong with a machine and how it can best be fixed. To do this, technicians must understand basic electronics and be able to use oscilloscopes and other types of testing equipment. They must be familiar with the technical manuals and maintenance procedures for the equipment they service.

Some technicians begin working after high school as apprentices to qualified technicians. Most, however, attend vocational or technical schools that offer courses in this field. They continue to take courses after graduation because new computer equipment is always being introduced.

COMPUTER ARTISTS

Many traditional fields have expanded as a result of computers. One of the most exciting is the field of computer art. **Graphic designers** use graphics software to design advertisements, book and magazine pages, television commercials, even animated sequences in a movie. **Digital illustrators** specialize in creating electronic art, including scientific illustrations, cartoons, and maps. Some computer illustrations are so finely "drawn" that they resemble paintings or photographs. **Technical drafters** use computers to produce engineering blueprints and similar plans.

Most computer artists have studied at schools of art or design. Like other artists,

Today, all kinds of design work can be produced on the computer. Left: Graphic designers create designs for book and magazine pages, advertisements, television commercials, and even animated movies. Below: This picture is an example of artwork that was created entirely on a computer. Digital illustrators can create images that are so technically perfect they look like hand-rendered art or photographs.

they have an excellent sense of color and design and a talent for drawing. They may also have programming experience and an understanding of computer technology. Technical drafters generally have technical school training in drafting, as well as a good grounding in math and an understanding of engineering drawings.

OTHER CAREERS

There are many other careers in the computer field, some requiring more technical knowledge than others. **Technical writers** develop the manuals that tell people how to use computers and software. Besides a knowledge of computers, they need strong language skills, so they can present the instructions clearly and logically.

A **sales representative** may work for a manufacturer, selling that company's computers or software directly to businesses; or for a store, selling computers and software to the public. Computer salespeople often have college degrees in business or economics, rather than in computer science. They must be able to get along well with people.

Training specialists teach other people how to use computers and programs. Many computer and software manufacturers employ training specialists to teach their customers how to get the most out of their machines and programs.

Large organizations may hire **computer librarians** to organize, catalog, and maintain disks, tapes, instruction books, and other materials related to computers. The librarian also maintains libraries of programs on computer. Knowledge of programming and library science are needed.

Even if you aren't planning a career in computers, you should become familiar with these machines. Millions of people—mechanics, authors, secretaries, chemists, insurance agents—use them in their jobs. Knowing how to use a computer can help you along the road to success no matter what career you choose.

Fleece the Lamb, Nuts the Squirrel, Snort the Bull, Snip the Siamese Cat, Spike the Rhinoceros—adorable little **Beanie Babies** were the "gotta-have-it" toys of 1997. Beanie fans couldn't get enough of the plush bean-bag animals. Ty Toys, the company that makes the toys, introduced the first nine animals in 1994. Kids and even adults loved them—they were cute and cuddly, and their bodies, filled with plastic pellets rather than real beans, could be posed. Since then a critter craze has swept the United States and Canada. About 100 more "species" have been created, and some Beanie lovers hope to put together a complete collection. But in 1997, Beanie Babies were in short supply in many areas. Kids and their parents waited in long lines to get them, and often new shipments sold out within hours. "This is the hottest product that has ever appeared in retailing, period," said one store owner. Demand was greatest for some of the early designs that are no longer being made. Collectors were reported to be paying thousands of dollars for "retired" Beanies such as Patti the Platypus and Peanut the Elephant—toys that originally sold for about $5!

David Levitt of Seminole, Florida, won't let good food go to waste. In 1993, when he was 11, he designed a county-wide program to deliver unused school cafeteria food to the poor. The program's success earned him special recognition at a 1996 White House ceremony. In 1997, the 15-year-old high-school sophomore was urging Florida to set up a similar program statewide.

Fasten your seat belt and get ready for **GameWorks,** a high-tech video arcade with state-of-the art virtual reality. The first GameWorks opened in Seattle, Washington, in March 1997. Its creators, who include movie producer Steven Spielberg, plan to open about 100 more worldwide. Besides racing virtual cars and zapping aliens on giant video screens—for more than $1 a play—patrons can use computers to surf the Internet.

Rebecca Sealfon of New York City jumped for joy as she spelled out "euonym" (a word meaning "an apt name") to win the 1997 National Spelling Bee. Rebecca was the first winner to be schooled at home, and she may have been the most enthusiastic winner ever. She bested 244 other contestants at the May finals in Washington, D.C., to take home a $5,000 cash award, a laptop computer, and other prizes. Rebecca, 13, credited studying and luck for her victory. But she had showed early talent as a speller. At age 2, she could spell "elephant" backwards!

Adam Ezra Cohen, 17, of New York City, won the 1997 Westinghouse Science Talent Search, the most prestigious high-school science contest in the United States. His entry was an "electrochemical paintbrush"—an amazing device that can print 50 words in a space no wider than a human hair. It was one of about 100 inventions that Adam had developed.

Who would ever have guessed that kids would enjoy being nagged? Electronic **"cyberpets"**—Tamagotchi, Giga Pets, and Nano Pals— were a hot fad in 1997. These toys bombarded their owners with beeps, signaling their demands: "Feed me!" "Clean me!" "Pet me!" If you care for the "pet" by pressing the right buttons to meet its needs, the electronic display shows it thriving. If you neglect it, it— oops—dies or flies back to its home planet. But there's no need to grieve. All you have to do is press the reset button, and the little creature hatches on screen once again. The original cyberpet, Tamagotchi, was developed in Japan, where it became a huge craze. Its name, roughly translated, means "watch cute egg." Millions were sold in North America when the toys hit the market early in 1997. Some cyberpet owners became so involved with their little electronic buddies that schools began to ban the toys—kids were interrupting tests and lessons to answer their pets' beeps and feed and care for them. But even school officials noted that cyberpets were a great way for kids to learn about the responsibilities involved in caring for a real pet.

For **Chelsea Clinton,** 1997 was a banner year. On June 6, the 17-year-old daughter of President Bill Clinton and Hillary Clinton graduated from high school (above). President Clinton addressed Chelsea and her classmates at the Sidwell Friends School in Washington, D.C., at the ceremony. Then, in the fall, Chelsea went off to college at Stanford University, near San Francisco, California. It was a big change. Since moving into the White House with her parents in 1993, Chelsea had tried to keep out of the limelight and lead as normal a life as possible. It wasn't easy—she was surrounded by Secret Service agents wherever she went. But, for the most part, she succeeded.

During 1997, Chelsea began to appear in public a bit more, celebrating her 17th birthday in New York City with her parents in March and traveling to Africa with her mother. Meanwhile, with excellent marks in high school, she had her choice of top colleges. She considered Yale University, where her parents first met, before picking Stanford. Chelsea was one of 1,650 entering freshmen at that school, where just one of every ten applicants was accepted. She was said to be planning a pre-med major, and it was likely that she'd continue to study dance, as she had during high school.

The President and First Lady accompanied their daughter to California—along with an entourage of Secret Service agents, reporters, and photographers. That made Chelsea's arrival on campus (below) a media event. But once the school term began, she was just another student, or nearly so. True, her dorm room had bulletproof glass windows; but it was still a dorm room. She walked to classes and ate meals at the school dining hall. And while her Secret Service escorts were still with her, they wore casual clothes, to blend in.

By outsmarting the makers of the Scholastic Aptitude Tests (SATs), **Colin Rizzio,** of Peterborough, New Hampshire, became an overnight celebrity in 1997. Colleges and universities rely on SAT scores when they select students. So, like thousands of other high-school students, Colin took the SATs in the fall of his senior year. But he was the only one to notice an ambiguous algebra question. The question seemed simple: It asked students to compare two values. But Rizzio realized that the answer would depend on whether a key variable was a positive or negative number. After the test was over, he checked with a math teacher at his school. Then he sent an e-mail message to the Educational Testing Service (ETS), publishers of the test, questioning the question. Three months later, the testing service acknowledged that he was right. It was the first time in fifteen years that ETS had admitted that an SAT question was flawed. And as a result, as many as 45,000 students saw their SAT scores rise 10 to 30 points. That hardly mattered to Colin. A math whiz and a member of his school's math team, he had aced the test, scoring 750 out of a possible 800 points. But by besting the test makers, he made news. Reporters came knocking on his door, and he was flown to New York City to appear on the television show *Good Morning America.*

Want to be a great chef? Just "mix things together until they make a recipe," says **Justin Miller** of Baden, Pennsylvania. Justin, 7, published his first cookbook in 1997 and has been on television 40 times, whipping up cookies with the likes of David Letterman and Rosie O'Donnell. But he has to stand on a milk crate to reach the stove.

The tiny rover that explored the Martian surface in 1997 was named by **Valerie Ambroise,** 15, of Bridgeport, Connecticut. Valerie suggested the name Sojourner after studying about Sojourner Truth, the former slave who crusaded for equal rights in the 1800s. Her entry was chosen from 3,500 others in a 1995 essay contest. (Valerie is shown here with Vice President Al Gore and a model of the Sojourner rover.)

237

In March 1997—only two months after his 14th birthday—**Etienne Bacrot** of France became the youngest chess grandmaster ever. Etienne started playing the complex game at age 4. "I just sat down, looked, and understood," he said. He scored his first win in official competition at age 7. To achieve the title of grandmaster, he defeated two adult grandmasters in tournament play. Etienne is determined to get to the top of the chess world. He has a professional chess coach, and he practices the game for two hours every day. But he still has time to play Ping-Pong and video games with his friends.

Han-Na Chang of Valley Cottage, New York, is a rising star in the world of classical music. Han-Na, who turned 14 in 1997, began playing the cello at age 6 in her native South Korea. Her family moved to the United States so that she could study at the famous Julliard School in New York City. She has a grueling schedule, with school, homework, and five hours of practice a day. The work has paid off: Han-Na has played with some of the world's top orchestras, and in 1994 she won the prestigious Rostropovich International Cello Competition. When she isn't playing concerts or practicing, she enjoys reading, seeing movies, and hanging out with friends.

A starring role on Nickelodeon's television series *The Secret Life of Alex Mack* helped make 16-year-old **Larisa Oleynik** one of 1997's most talked-about TV actresses. Alex is a girl who, thanks to a chemical spill, has strange and special powers. Larisa, who lives in northern California, started acting at 8 and landed the part at age 12. Off-camera, she's perfectly normal.

Melissa Joan Hart had a chance to demonstrate special powers, too— as the star of ABC's *Sabrina, the Teenage Witch.* The show, a hit with kids and teens, was based on a 1996 movie that in turn was based on a comic-book character. Television fans already knew Melissa as the star of another series, *Clarissa Explains It All.*

Columns of comical clowns, their true identities hidden beneath their enormous masks, join in Carnival festivities in the little European country of Liechtenstein. Since ancient times, people all around the world have created wonderful masks for ceremonies, performances, celebrations, and special events. Funny, frightening, or fabulously beautiful, masks allow wearers to pretend to be whatever they choose. And onlookers can share the fun, by believing in the magic of masks.

Beautiful, comical, or frightening—a mask lets you be whatever you want. That's why people around the world create masks like these, for celebrations and for other special times.

THE MAGIC OF MASKS

Have you ever put on a mask for Halloween? Then you know what fun it is to become, for just a short time, a monster or a superhero. More than a costume alone, a mask lets you change your identity. With your face hidden, you can pretend to be whatever the mask represents.

That probably explains why masks have been used by people in societies all over the world, from ancient times right up to the present. Some masks are strictly for protection—hospital masks, for example, and the masks worn by baseball catchers and hockey goalies. Some are for concealment, like the masks robbers wear to keep people from identifying them. But the most wonderful masks are those created for special events—for ceremonies, performances, and special celebrations. They are works of art that set the imagination free, for wearers and watchers alike.

CEREMONIAL MASKS

From Africa to America to the South Pacific, masks have played important roles in religious and other ceremonies. Most of these ceremonies developed in ancient times, as ways to bring people together for important events. They include coming-of-age rituals, initiation rites, marriages and funerals, and ceremonies that mark the changing seasons. In some places, these traditional ceremonies are still observed. In others, they are only remembered.

In Africa, beautifully carved masks have been an important part of rituals and ceremonies for centuries. Tribal cultures have different styles, rituals, and mask designs. The masks represent ancestors, animals, and spirits. Some masks were worn by warriors to frighten enemies. Today tribal traditions are dying out in Africa, and these masks are becoming rare.

Many Native American groups also used masks in ceremonies. Centuries ago, the Yupik people of southern Alaska marked the approach of spring with masked dances. Their masks, carved of driftwood and decorated with feathers and fur, represented forces of nature, such as the wind; mythical beings; and animals such as loons, foxes, seals, and fish. These were magical masks— dancers who put them on seemed to become the beings the masks represented. Through the ceremonies, the Yupiks asked for the help of the spirit world in the year to come. When they were done, the dancers traditionally burned or buried the masks, or left them in the wilderness.

The Yupik ceremonies mostly died out in the early 1900s. However, some of the masks survived in private collections. Two hundred of the finest were gathered in an exhibit, sponsored by the Smithsonian Institution, that was on view in New York City and Washington, D.C., in 1997.

While Yupik ceremonies are seldom performed today, Native Americans along the Pacific coast of Canada are reviving traditions that make use of colorful wooden masks. The masks are carved of alder, birch, or cedar, painted with elaborate designs, and finished with shredded bark, eagle's down, and other natural materials. Each tribe in this region—Tlingit, Haida, Kwakiutl, and others—has its own distinctive style of mask making, and its own ceremonies and stories to go with the masks.

Many of the masks represent the spirits of animals, such as bears, eagles, hawks, and frogs. These animals are the symbols of various clans, or extended families. The masks often combine human and animal features in marvelous ways. This makes sense because in Native American beliefs, spirits can take animal or human form. Only certain people may rightfully wear these masks, though. Families own the rights to specific masks and dances, which have been passed down through generations.

The masks were traditionally used at a ceremonial gathering called a potlatch. Families prepared for years before inviting guests to a potlatch. Dances went on for days in a communal house. The performances were filled with special effects, such as mysterious voices and spirits that seemed to descend from the sky. Then, at the end of the potlatch, the host gave lavish gifts to all the guests. Sometimes families were ruined by the expense. In 1884, the Canadian government banned the pot-

This fierce-looking ceremonial mask was used by the Dan people of Ivory Coast, in West Africa. The mask maker used shells and braided hair in the design.

through mouth openings that, in many cases, were shaped like trumpets, to project their voices into the open-air theaters. The masks had another advantage: Since people in the audience had no idea what the actors looked like, one actor could play several roles. In fact, it took just three leading players—but perhaps 30 or 40 masks—to perform most plays. All the actors were men, even those in women's roles.

A traditional form of Japanese drama still makes use of masks. In Japanese No plays, as in ancient Greece, all the characters are played by male actors who wear masks and elaborate costumes. The mask

latch. But the ban was lifted in 1951, and today artists are re-creating ancient masks and creating new interpretations of the ancient designs.

DRAMA AND DANCE

Many types of theater can trace their origins to religious ceremonies. It's not surprising, then, that masks have been important on the stage.

When plays were performed in ancient Greece, all the actors wore masks, from the leading players down to the members of the chorus. The masks were mostly made of linen, cork, and other light materials, and none have survived to the present day. But paintings and sculptures from ancient Greece show what they looked like.

Each Greek mask carried an expression that showed the basic traits of the character it represented. The masks were big, so the audience could see the features clearly. Actors peered through peepholes in the masks' huge, white-painted eyes. They spoke

This elaborate and brilliantly painted Kwakiutl sun mask is a fine example of the beautiful carved wood masks made by Indians of the Pacific Northwest.

All the actors in Japanese No theater wear masks. The expression of this wooden No mask clearly shows the comical nature of the character it represents.

Masks take leading roles in performances elsewhere in Asia, too. For example, in Yangju, a Korean town, street performers wear masks to act out folk tales and comical stories. The performances are usually given on major holidays, and everyone turns out to watch them. Masked dance dramas that mix ceremony and theater are performed in Indonesia, Tibet, Sri Lanka, and other countries. Many of these performances present myths and religious tales.

Mexico has one of the richest traditions of masked dance dramas. Some of these dances can be traced back to ancient times, to rituals of the Maya and other Indians. Others are based on stories from the Bible or historical events—the Spanish conquest of Mexico, for example, and Mexico's fight for independence. Many towns and villages have their own special dances, performed in the town's central plaza during festivals and religious holidays.

The Mexican masks are made of wood, leather, papier-mâché, and other materials, designs, like the No plays themselves, are hundreds of years old. Many of the masks are expressionless. The actors who wear them show emotions through subtle gestures, such as the flutter of a fan. Other masks show the nature of the characters, who include gods and demons as well as people. There are nearly 300 different masks for the No plays. Actors choose the masks they wear carefully and treat them with great respect. Traditionally, an actor greets a mask ceremonially before putting it on. It's as if these masks, like those used in ancient ceremonies, have a bit of magic in them.

Mexican mask-making traditions go back to ancient times. The Huichole Indians of Central Mexico used hundreds of beads to create this intricate design.

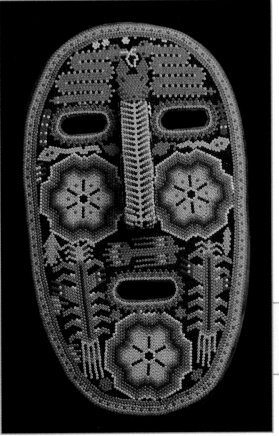

brightly painted. They portray men and women, saints and devils, and animals, depending on the story that's being acted out. The jaguar, or tigre, is an especially popular character. In a dance drama that has many

ration for Easter. Carnival feasts began as a way to use up meat and other foods that would spoil during Lent.

Masquerade balls and costumed parades are part of Carnival celebrations everywhere.

Shimmering gold and silver masks create an air of elegance and mystery for two Carnival-goers in Venice, Italy. Venice is famous for its Carnival, but it is only one of many cities that celebrate this event. Masked balls and parades are always part of the merrymaking.

variations, a tigre threatens farmers, who choose a marksman to hunt down the beast. Mexico's dance dramas are a living tradition—new dances, and new masks, are always being created.

CARNIVAL!

Mexicans also don masks during Carnival, a period of feasting and merrymaking just before Lent in the Christian calendar. Traditionally, Christians fast and give up luxuries during the forty days of Lent, in prepa-

No one knows how this tradition began. Perhaps early merrymakers didn't want to be seen eating, drinking, and dancing, so they put on masks. Today Carnival wouldn't be the same without masks. And wherever Carnival is celebrated, mask making is an art form.

Carnival began in Europe. It's still celebrated there, in cities from Munich, Germany, to Venice, Italy. In Nice, on the French Riviera, masked revelers pelt each other with eggs, flour, and confetti. The celebration in Nice also features a famous parade of huge papier-mâché caricature masks, called "big heads." In parts of Switzerland, people put on scary animal masks. That tradition dates back to ancient times, when people thought these frightening masks could drive away the spirits of winter.

When Europeans came to America, they brought Carnival with them. The Carnival in Rio de Janeiro, Brazil, is world-famous. Carnival is also an exciting time in Trinidad, in the Caribbean. Many people there join Carnival bands, called "mas bands" (for masquerade). They spend all year getting ready for the event, choosing a theme and designing and making their costumes. During Carnival, they parade and dance in the streets, playing calypso music. Some mas bands have hundreds of members—dancers, singers, and musicians who play on steel drums and other instruments.

In New Orleans, Louisiana, Shrove Tuesday is Mardi Gras—French for "Fat Tuesday," because of the way people indulge on this day. It's the last day of Carnival, and the time for one of the world's most famous Carnival celebrations. Thousands of visitors arrive in New Orleans each year for Mardi Gras. And people in New Orleans prepare all year for the event.

Many people in New Orleans belong to Carnival clubs, or krewes, which are something like the Trinidad mas bands. Each krewe chooses a theme and selects a king and queen to lead its festivities. For months, the krewes plan and make their elegant costumes and elaborate parade floats. In the

A glittering court jester joins the fun at Mardi Gras in New Orleans, Louisiana. For one riotous day, the jester's identity is hidden by a smiling mask.

weeks before Mardi Gras, they sponsor dances, balls, and costumed parades. The biggest parade of all is on Mardi Gras itself.

People don't have to join a krewe to share in the fun of Mardi Gras. Anyone can put on a costume and a mask and join in. Clowns, pirates, kings and queens, cartoon characters, caricatures of famous people, birds and beasts, dragons—they're all dancing in the streets. For this one day, the revelers are free to be whatever wild and fanciful being they choose to be, thanks to the magic of masks.

ACADEMY
AWARDS

CATEGORY	WINNER
Motion Picture	*The English Patient*
Actor	Geoffrey Rush (*Shine*)
Actress	Frances McDormand (*Fargo*)
Supporting Actor	Cuba Gooding, Jr. (*Jerry Maguire*)
Supporting Actress	Juliette Binoche (*The English Patient*)
Director	Anthony Minghella (*The English Patient*)
Cinematography	John Seale (*The English Patient*)
Song	"You Must Love Me" (*Evita*)
Foreign-Language Film	*Kolya* (Czech Republic)
Documentary Feature	*When We Were Kings*
Documentary Short	*Breathing Lessons: The Life and Work of Mark O'Brien*

1997

Geoffrey Rush (best actor) in *Shine.*

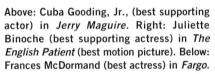

Above: Cuba Gooding, Jr., (best supporting actor) in *Jerry Maguire*. Right: Juliette Binoche (best supporting actress) in *The English Patient* (best motion picture). Below: Frances McDormand (best actress) in *Fargo*.

SAY, WHA?

Two friends meet on the street. Here's what they say:

"Yo, wuss up?"

"I'm buggin'—studying 24/7."

"Chill, B. Stop o-in'. Want to see that new film? I hear it's phat."

"Cool. Gotta check with my rents, though. Hook me up with your digits."

And here's a translation:

"Hi, how are you?"

"I'm really busy—studying all the time."

"Relax, friend. Stop overdoing it. Want to see that new film? I hear it's excellent."

"Great. I need to ask my parents, though. Give me your phone number."

If the slang these friends are using is hard for some people to understand—well, that's one reason they're using it. Slang is informal language, with words that are made up, cut short, or used in unusual ways. Young people are the greatest users and inventors of slang expressions. What's the appeal?

Slang is fun, punchy, and colorful. It lets you express yourself in new, creative, sometimes startling ways. Most of all, slang is a way to show that you belong to a select group. Those who are "in" understand your talk, but outsiders don't. That's why teenagers invent so much slang—they love to use words their parents don't understand.

SLANG OLD AND NEW

People have probably been using slang as long as they have been using language, and every language has its own slang words and phrases. Slang doesn't follow any rules, but it does take some common forms. It may include brand-new words along with old words given a new spin—"bad" used to mean really good, for instance. It cuts words short, as in "dis," for dismiss, or "rents" for parents. It makes comparisons and plays on characteristics—legs become "stems"; money becomes "beans." It blends words, rhymes them, and plays with their sounds for catchy effects, as in "take a chill pill" for "calm down."

New slang words and expressions are constantly popping up. Most disappear just as quickly. As soon as a slang term is used widely—widely enough to appear in this article, for example—it's likely to fall out of fashion. But some slang words hang on and become part of regular speech. "Motel," "hairdo," and "skyscraper" are examples of words that began as slang terms. That's one of the ways that language grows and changes.

Slang isn't considered proper in formal writing. But many famous writers have used it. It might surprise you to learn that the English playwright William Shakespeare was a great inventor of slang. Shakespeare's plays are filled with expressions such as "beat it" and "not so hot," which are part of informal speech today.

Not long after Shakespeare's time, you might have heard an Englishman who had a bad meal complain about the "lousy grub."

Slang Around America

24/7: All the time (24 hours a day, 7 days a week)
Ag: Aggravated
Bad: Good
Chill: Relax
Chillin': Hanging out
Da bomb: The best
Digits: Phone number
Fresh: Trendy
Get to steppin': Go away
Hook me up with: May I have
Last-year: Outdated ("That's so last-year")
On lock down: Grounded
Outtie: Leaving ("I'm outtie")
Peeps: Family (from "people")
Phat: Very good
Raise up out of my face: Leave me alone
Rollin': Hanging out
Sweet: Good
Take the clue bus: Figure it out
Yo!: Hi

"Beat it!"

"Lousy" and "grub" are two slang words that were used in the 1600s, fell out of favor for many years, and then popped up again in recent times. But most slang expressions from those days have disappeared for good. You won't hear your friends using Shakespearean insults like "capon" (chicken) or exclamations like "a pox on your throat!"

"Cool! Dig that crazy cat."

AMERICAN SLANG

English settlers in North America spoke British English, and used British slang, for many years. But by the time of the Revolutionary War, Americans were developing their own ways of speaking. It wasn't long before they began to invent their own slang.

The Western frontier was especially rich with new expressions. Frontier folk were just as famous for their outrageous "tall talk" as for their unlikely tall tales. A bad snowstorm became a "helliferocious blizzard." The final or ultimate anything—answer, joke, punch—was the "sockdolager." Dishonest traders "hornswoggled" their unfortunate customers.

Back in the East, people frowned on these wild frontier expressions. "The use of slang is at once a sign and a cause of mental atrophy," essayist Oliver Wendell Holmes stated flatly in the 1850s. However, that didn't stop slang from catching on. And in the 20th century, attitudes toward slang changed. Even grammarians admitted that slang had a place in informal speaking and writing. Writers began to use slang as a way to add color to their work. The poet Carl Sandburg called slang "language which takes off its coat, spits on its hands, and goes to work."

In the 1920s and 1930s, newspaper columnists, sports writers, cartoonists, songwriters, and comedians helped popularize new slang. Anything great was "the cat's pajamas," "the bee's knees," or just "the end." Fine clothes were "glad-rags." A policeman was a "flatfoot," and a fireman was a "smoke-eater." If you wanted someone to go away, you said "skiddoo," or "twenty-three skiddoo."

Slang remained a way for people to set themselves apart from the rest of society, to show that they were "in" or "with it." In the 1950s, "Beatniks" met at coffee houses to listen to jazz and poetry, and they developed their own lingo. Anything great was "cool" or "crazy" or "real gone." Anything that wasn't cool was "square." Guys were "cats," and girls were "chicks." If you liked or appreciated something, you were said to "dig it"—as in "dig that crazy cat!"

In the 1960s, "hippies" invented new slang. If something was wonderful, it was "groovy" or "outasight" or "far out." If it wasn't, it was a "bummer." If you were tense, you were "uptight," and you needed to "get your head together." "Peace" was the all-purpose greeting. If you were right, you were "right on!"

"That's awesome, totally rad!"

Slang Around the World

AUSTRALIA:
Babes, buds: Female friends
Bonza, choice, sick, mad, unreal, zesty: Good
Crumblies, olds: Parents
Festy, sad, seedy: Bad
Mates, dudes: Male friends
Mingle: Hang out

BRITAIN:
Ace, mega, top: Good
Angon: Wait a minute
Bodge: Mess up
Folding: Money
Givuss: May I have
Pants: Nonsense

CHINA:
Bang ("baang"): Cool
Beng zhao ("behng jow"): Relax; don't worry
Ge mer ("guh mer"): Man
Jie mer ("jee-yuh mer"): Woman
Jue le ("juway luh"): Excellent
War ("wah-ar"): Hang out

FRANCE:
Goleri ("go-lay-REE"): Relaxed
Mec ("meck"): Young man
Meuf ("mef"): Young woman
Mortel ("more-TELL"), fatal ("fah-TALL"): Excellent
Pourra ("poo-RAH"): Bad
Space ("spaiss"): Hip; the latest

KENYA:
Aristo ("ar-ris-toe"): Clever, educated
Charlie ("CHA-lee"): Young man; boy
Diambo ("di-AM-bo"): Bad; trouble
Kulo sana (coo-loh sah-nah): The best
Plati ("pla-tee"): Outdated
Poa (Poh-AH"): Relaxed

RUSSIA:
Drugan ("droo-GAHN"): Male friend; buddy
Khrenovo ("hren-OH-vuh"): Bad
Klyovo (CLO-vuh), kruto (CREW-tuh): Great.
Kuchkovat'sya ("kooch-koh-VAHT-syah"): Hang out
Otpad ("aht-PAHD"): The best
Rasslabsya (rahss-SLOB-syah"): Relax

By the early 1980s, young people were using new slang. It originated with teens in the San Fernando Valley, near Los Angeles, California. In "Valley" speak, something great was "tubular," "awesome," or "totally rad." The opposite was "grody to the max." If you were upset, you were "aggro." You needed to rest, or "max-relax." "Hey, dude," was a typical greeting. To tell someone to be quiet, you'd say, "Bag yer face."

Today's slang includes some words from the past, like "cool" and "dude." But there are lots of new words. New slang comes from many sources—city streets, the entertainment world, schools and colleges, even professional "jargon" from the military and dozens of other occupations.

Movies, television, and radio help new slang spread quickly. And in most cases, that means slang expressions go in and out of style faster than ever. But the odds are that some of today's slang—maybe even a word *you* invent—will live on, helping the language grow.

Twenty years after they first blasted their way onto movie screens, Han Solo and Chewbacca were back to thrill fans in 1997. Chewie (the Wookiee on the left) and Han (played by Harrison Ford) were two of the memorable characters in **Star Wars,** the epic science-fiction movie created by George Lucas in 1977. This film and its sequels, *The Empire Strikes Back* and *The Return of the Jedi,* tell of a heroic struggle to defeat an evil empire in a distant galaxy. The movies ushered in a new era of dazzling special effects, and they were huge hits. But Lucas wasn't satisfied with the films. As computers made fantastic new special effects possible, he decided to revise them.

Thus, the films returned to movie theaters in early 1997, with cleaned-up soundtracks, restored colors, and, most of all, souped-up special effects. New alien creatures, even entire new scenes, were created, and audiences loved them. When the films finished their run, fans had still more to look forward to. In October, the Smithsonian Institution in Washington, D.C., opened an exhibit based on the films. And George Lucas was at work on a new project—creating three all-new Star Wars films.

Gourmet cook, decorator, author, style-setter, television star, business tycoon, brand name. With millions of fans and boundless energy, **Martha Stewart** is all that and more. In 1997, she was busier than ever, adding a line of retail products to a business empire that includes her own magazine and TV show.

In April 1997, the **Museum of African American History** moved into a new $38-million building in Detroit, Michigan. Its expanded exhibitions—which included everything from African masks to the space suit worn by astronaut Mae Jemison—made the museum the largest one devoted to African-American experiences. Among the exhibits is a re-creation of the hold of an 18th-century slave ship (below). Other displays focus on such major chapters in African-American history as the Underground Railroad and the civil-rights movement.

Making the jump from television to movies, **Jennifer Aniston** appeared in her first starring film role in 1997. In *Picture Perfect,* the 28-year-old actress played an advertising executive who "invents" a fiancé to further her career. Aniston, whose parents were both actors, grew up in New York City. She's best known for her role as Rachel on the hit television series *Friends,* which continued in 1997.

One of 1997's most surprising TV stars was **Sister Wendy Beckett,** 67, a British nun. Her series *Sister Wendy's Story of Painting,* a hit in Britain, was shown in the United States on public television. It took viewers on an enthusiastic whirlwind tour of great art, from cave paintings to Renaissance masterpieces to modern works.

High-definition television (HDTV) came a step closer in 1997. When it finally arrives, this new system will produce wide-screen television pictures more than four times as sharp as today's pictures, accompanied by six-channel "surround sound." The U.S. government has been working for years with the television industry to develop HDTV. It's a major change in the way TV signals are sent and received.

In conventional TV, pictures and sound are converted into electronic analog waves for broadcasting. HDTV uses digital signals. Pictures and sound are converted into a digital code, made up of 0's and 1's—the same code used by computers. The receiver decodes the information and displays the pictures and sound. Because the new HDTV sets will process digital code, it will be easy to equip them to play digital video disks and function like computers. One day, you may be able to watch movies, play video games, and surf the Internet—all on your TV set.

That's a few years away, but it's coming. In 1997, the government granted an extra channel to each of the nation's 1,600 television

HDTV

CONVENTIONAL TV

stations. Beginning late in 1998, broadcasters are to start using one channel for conventional programming, and the other for HDTV. Digital HDTV will arrive in big cities first, and only people who have digital HDTV sets will be able to receive the signals. Those sets are expected to be expensive at first, costing $2,500 or more. But prices will probably drop quickly as manufacturers compete for sales. If all goes as planned, analog signals will go off the air in 2006, leaving only HDTV.

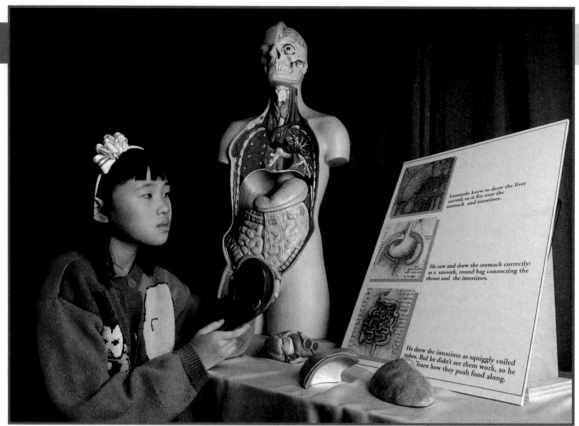

Leonardo da Vinci was one of the greatest artists of all time. But he was much more. Leonardo, who lived from 1452 to 1519, was also an architect, an engineer, a scientist, and an inventor whose ideas were well ahead of his time. Leonardo's wide-ranging interests reflected the revival of science and culture that occurred during the Renaissance period. But his talent and intellect were unique.

From March to September 1997, the many sides of Leonardo's genius were the focus of a major exhibition at the Museum of Science in Boston, Massachusetts. The show, **"Leonardo da Vinci: Scientist, Inventor, Artist,"** used hands-on displays to help visitors understand and appreciate the master's work. For example, in the display shown above, visitors could compare lifelike models of the human torso to sketches made by Leonardo. Then they could make their own sketches of the models, using their observation skills just as he had done 500 years earlier.

Several hands-on exhibits allowed visitors to experience other aspects of Leonardo's creativity. At one, visitors could create an arched bridge. In the show's Art Studio section, they could draw—and explore light, shadow, and perspective. They could practice writing backward—as Leonardo did—with the help of a mirror. They could drop scale models of parachutes designed by Leonardo. Models of a paddleboat, a helicopter, and other devices were also on exhibit. Leonardo sketched these machines in detail but, like many of his inventions, never actually built them.

The show also featured a multi-media presentation about Leonardo and many artworks by the master. But art wasn't the main focus of this show. Its purpose was to give people insight into the mind of a genius.

Recognize this character? It's **Superman!** One of our best-known comic-book superheroes was given a brand-new look—and new superpowers—in 1997. No more blue tights and red cape. The new Superman was a sort of cyberman, an energy-based being who emitted bolts of electricity. Instead of flying like a bird or a plane, he zapped off to battle evil like a bolt of lightning. The change was part of a long-running storyline, in which the Man of Steel lost his powers and struggled to regain them. But some fans missed the old, familiar Superman. Was the new look a permanent change? DC Comics, the company that publishes the comic book, wouldn't say.

Die-hard fans helped keep *Party of Five* on the air in 1997. A series about five orphan siblings who rely on each other to handle everything from romantic crushes to alcoholism, PO5 first aired in 1994. It won several awards—but small audiences. However, the show developed a loyal following. Hearing that the Fox network planned to cancel it in 1997, they wrote millions of letters—and kept the show going.

Scientist Ellie Arroway (Jodie Foster) picks up a radio signal from aliens in the sci-fi film *Contact*.

MOVIE TIME!

Batman returned. Aliens made contact. Skyjackers went after the president of the United States. And an ancient Greek hero sprang to life—with a very "Nineties" attitude. Those were just a few of the imaginative ideas that came to the movie screen in 1997. While many of the year's films weren't exactly true to life, they ranked high as entertainment.

ALIENS AND MORE

Some of the year's most dazzling special effects appeared in the science-fiction fantasy *Contact*. It starred Jodie Foster as Ellie Arroway, a brilliant scientist who searches for signs of life in space—and finds them. Radio signals from the star system Vega turn out to be coded messages from aliens. The Vegan communications contain instructions for building a spacecraft that can reach their system, and after some twists and turns in the plot Ellie gets to go on the mission. The movie, based on a novel by astronomer Carl Sagan, has an underlying theme about the conflict between religious faith and rational science. But for many moviegoers, first-rate special effects and camera work were the real draws. The filmmakers even managed to bring President Bill Clinton into the action by slipping in footage from actual news conferences.

Special effects also starred in *The Lost World: Jurassic Park,* a sequel to the 1993 hit *Jurassic Park*. In the first film, prehistoric dinosaurs were brought to life in a disastrous attempt to build a theme park. Supposedly, all those dangerous reptiles died at the end of the movie. But at the start of the sequel, survivors turn up on a Caribbean island. Jeff Goldblum once again played Dr. Ian Malcolm, a concerned scientist who tries to save the world—and himself—from the monsters. But greedy hunters snag a Tyrannosaurus Rex and transport it to San Diego, California. Of course, it gets loose and rampages through backyards. The film wasn't quite as successful as the first, which broke box-office records, but it packed plenty of thrills and scares.

A birthday wish is the basis for the story of *Liar Liar.* This film featured the popular comedian Jim Carrey as Fletcher Reede, a slippery lawyer for whom lying is a way of life. His son Max (Justin Cooper) wishes that his father be forced to speak the truth for 24 hours, and the wish comes true. Fletcher goes through comic agonies as true words pop out of his mouth in place of glib fibs—no matter how hard he tries to lie.

Deception played a part in the plot of *My Best Friend's Wedding,* which scored as one of the year's most popular romantic comedies. Julia Roberts starred as Julianne, a restaurant critic who realizes she's in love with an old college friend (Dermot Mulroney) who is about to marry another woman (Cameron Diaz). She sets out to sabotage the wedding with all sorts of schemes and sneaky tricks, and she won't give up—even when her plots backfire on her.

Roberts also starred in *Conspiracy Theory,* a very different kind of movie. It was a suspenseful thriller about a Justice Department lawyer (Roberts) who's pestered by a nutty New York City cab driver (Mel Gibson). He sees sinister plots everywhere and wants her to investigate them. She dismisses him as a crank—until one of his conspiracy theories turns out to be true.

Men in Black: Aliens Among Us!

What if aliens from outer space are here on Earth, walking around among us—and we don't know it? That idea was the premise for *Men in Black,* a science-fiction spoof that was one of 1997's big hits. The film starred Tommy Lee Jones and Will Smith as a pair of straight-lipped, black-suited secret agents. Their

mission: to keep tabs on hundreds of extraterrestrials who are on Earth. Most of the aliens are disguised in human bodies and blend in peacefully, but there are a few bad guys. Worst of all is Edgar (Vincent D'Onofrio), who is bent on ruling the world.

In their alien forms, Edgar and other extraterrestrials are portrayed by computerized models, created by special-effects experts. Before Edgar adopts his disguise, for example, he looks like a giant roach. An alien infant is a little bundle of tentacles. Then there's a group of small sluglike aliens that make themselves at home in the agents' office, drinking coffee and offering advice all day. Special effects like these helped account for the film's $80 million cost—but they also helped make it a hit.

Cliff-hanging suspense drew audiences to another 1997 thriller, *Air Force One.* Early in this film, terrorists masquerading as reporters get on board the official plane carrying U.S. President James Marshall (Harrison Ford). Tension-filled moments follow as they hijack the plane, and officials on the ground try to mount a rescue operation. On board, the president tries to outsmart the terrorists, fighting for his life and the lives of his wife and daughter, who are also on board.

DOGS AND SUPERHEROES

When it came to films for young people, 1997 might have gone down as the "year of the dogs." Dogs were the stars in a number of popular movies, upstaging human actors at every turn.

A beagle named Frannie played the title role in *Shiloh,* based on a book by Phyllis Reynolds Naylor. In the story, set in West Virginia, Shiloh runs away from an abusive owner. Marty Preston, an 11-year-old boy played by Blake Heron, takes the dog in—and learns important lessons about honesty, compromise, and the meaning of ownership.

The film with the most dogs was *101 Dalmatians,* which opened late in 1996. This movie was a live-action remake of a classic Walt Disney animated feature. It starred Glenn Close as the evil Cruella DeVil, a clothing designer who wants to make a fur coat from Dalmatian puppies. But the real stars were the canines—99 puppies, 2 adult Dalmatians, and an Airedale who hopped on his hind legs.

Shine: A Tale of Personal Triumph

A gentle story about an Australian pianist turned out to be one of the most highly praised films of 1997. *Shine* was based on the life of David Helfgott, who was a brilliant pianist as a child. (In the movie, he was played as a teen by Noah Taylor, shown here, and as an adult by Geoffrey Rush.) As a young man, pressured by his father to succeed, Helfgott suffered a breakdown that ended his career before it really began. Years later, he gradually recovered and once again began to play concerts.

The film detailed the relentless pressure that contributed to Helfgott's emotional problems, as well as the slow steps in his recovery. It brought awards to Rush, a veteran Australian stage actor who had little film experience. And it gave a boost to the career of the real David Helfgott, who played to sold-out crowds on a North American concert tour. While music critics weren't enthusiastic about his skill, audiences applauded the way he had overcome his painful past to return to the stage.

The Disney animated film *Hercules* put a "Nineties" twist on the story of an ancient Greek hero.

New feature-length cartoons from the Disney studios have been big hits in recent years. The 1997 release was *Hercules,* a happily updated story about the "Superman" hero of ancient Greek mythology. In the film, Herc (Tate Donovan) is the son of the supreme gods of Mount Olympus, Zeus and Hera. Kidnapped as an infant and raised among people, he gains fame by beheading monsters and performing other amazing feats of strength and bravery. He's the superstar of his day, with endorsement contracts, an agent (Danny DeVito), and a glamorous girlfriend (Susan Egan). And when Hades (the god of the underworld, played by James Woods) tries to oust Zeus from Olympus, Herc saves the day.

A Saturday morning cartoon series was the inspiration for the live-action feature film *George of the Jungle.* Brendan Fraser starred as a man who, like Tarzan, was raised by apes in the jungle. Unlike Tarzan, George isn't very coordinated—when he swings from vines, he usually hits trees. The action in this comedy moves from the jungle to San Francisco, where George swings from cables on the Golden Gate Bridge and, of course, wins the love of the heroine (Leslie Mann).

The comic-book superhero Batman was back on the screen in 1997. *Batman and Robin* was the fourth in a series of feature films about the caped crusaders, this one starring George Clooney as Batman and Chris O'Donnell as his sidekick. In the movie, the dynamic duo face off against the evil Mr. Freeze (Arnold Schwarzenegger) and Poison Ivy (Uma Thurman). The good guys win, as always—but not without plenty of action, special effects, and tongue-in-cheek puns.

Peri Gilpin, David Hyde Pierce, Kelsey Grammer, Jane Leeves, and John Mahoney in *Frasier* (best comedy series).

EMMY

Awards

CATEGORY	WINNER
Comedy Series	*Frasier*
Actor—comedy series	John Lithgow (*3rd Rock from the Sun*)
Actress—comedy series	Helen Hunt (*Mad About You*)
Supporting Actor—comedy series	Michael Richards (*Seinfeld*)
Supporting Actress—comedy series	Kristen Johnson (*3rd Rock from the Sun*)
Drama Series	*Law and Order*
Actor—drama series	Dennis Franz (*NYPD Blue*)
Actress—drama series	Gillian Anderson (*The X-Files*)
Supporting Actor—drama series	Hector Elizondo (*Chicago Hope*)
Supporting Actress—drama series	Kim Delaney (*NYPD Blue*)
Miniseries	*Prime Suspect 5: Errors of Judgment*
Variety, Music, or Comedy Series	*Tracey Takes On...*

1997

Above: John Lithgow (best actor, comedy series), Kristen Johnson (best supporting actress, comedy series), French Stewart, Jane Curtin, and Joseph Gordon-Levitt in *3rd Rock from the Sun.* Right: Benjamin Bratt, Jerry Orbach, Carey Lowell, and Sam Waterston in *Law and Order* (best drama series). Below: David Duchovny and Gillian Anderson (best actress, drama series) in *The X-Files.*

Two of 1997's top artists: Folk singer Jewel (above) had a best-selling album, *Pieces of You,* and also won an MTV Video Music Award. The rock group the Wallflowers (right), led by Jakob Dylan, had a string of hit singles and music videos.

THE MUSIC SCENE

In 1997 the electronic dance music known as techno, or electronica, was heavily promoted as the next big trend by the music industry and the media. But as the year progressed, music lovers seemed more taken with tuneful pop ballads, spunky hip-hop stylings, "retro" novelty songs—and plain old-fashioned rock 'n' roll.

WHAT'S NEW?

One of the most popular rock acts of the year was the Wallflowers. Their album *Bringing Down the Horse,* released in 1996, remained on the album charts for much of 1997 and yielded a string of popular singles and videos. The band's leader, Jakob Dylan, is the son of folk-rock legend Bob Dylan. But the Wallflowers underplayed this famous connection, relying instead on solid musicianship and songwriting—as well as Jakob's video-friendly good looks.

Another of the year's top artists, Jewel, also saw her 1996 debut album gain momentum as *Pieces of You* rose to number four on the album charts. And its hit single, "You Were Meant for Me," won the Alaskan-born singer an MTV Video Music Award for best female video.

Other young bands with hit songs included Third Eye Blind ("Semi-Charmed Life"), the Verve Pipe ("The Freshmen"), Matchbox 20 ("Push"), the Cardigans ("Lovefool"), Sugar Ray ("Fly"), and Tonic ("If You Could Only See"). The lively sound of Ska continued to make its way into the mainstream, with hits by Sublime ("The Wrong Way"), the Mighty Mighty Bosstones ("Knock on Wood"), and Reel Big Fish ("Sell Out").

A number of bands issued eagerly awaited follow-ups to earlier hit albums. The Foo Fighters, led by former Nirvana drummer Dave Grohl, carried the banner for alternative rock with *The Colour and the Shape.* Fans of punk rock snapped up the Offspring's *Ixnay on the Hombre* and Green Day's *Nimrod.* Live released its third album, *Secret Samadhi.* And British group Oasis, led by brothers Liam and Noel Gallagher, continued to evoke the sounds of the Beatles and other classic British rock bands on its third album, *Be Here Now.*

Underscoring the year's variety were several unusual tunes that received widespread airplay. "How Bizarre," from New Zealand group OMC, featured rapped verses and a trumpet refrain reminiscent of the Tijuana

SPOTLIGHT ON. . .
Hanson

With their bouncy pop sound and blond good looks, the three young brothers who make up Hanson seemed destined to become the year's top teen idols. Their album *Middle of Nowhere* landed at the top of the charts and included the hit singles "MMMBop" and "Where's the Love?"

Despite their youth, the Hansons—Zachary, 11, Taylor, 14, and Isaac, 16—have been making music for some time. Born and brought up in Tulsa, Oklahoma, the boys were singing together at an early age. Inspired by their father's collection of rock oldies, they began to write songs and then taught themselves to play instruments—Zac picked up drums, while Taylor learned piano and Isaac guitar. Soon they were playing at neighborhood parties, state fairs, and even in the parking lot of a Tulsa bar (they were too young to be allowed inside). By the time they were signed by a major record label, the boys were veteran performers and had produced and sold two homemade CDs.

Family plays a major role in the Hansons' lives and careers. They and their three other siblings were raised as evangelical Christians and were schooled at home by their mom. Their parents support their musical goals and help with business decisions. These strong family ties will surely help the boys keep their newfound fame in perspective. "It can go as fast as it can come," says Isaac. "But," Taylor adds, "for now, it's great fun."

The Spice Girls, a quintet from Great Britain, were one of the year's top pop acts.

Brass. British band Smashmouth's tongue-in-cheek "Walking on the Sun" could have come straight off a '60s movie soundtrack. And Chumbawamba's rousing "Tubthumping" sounded exactly as its name indicated.

A song that seemed out of step with the current music scene nevertheless became a smash hit. Christian musician Bob Carlisle's "Butterfly Kisses," a tribute to his daughter on her 16th birthday, unexpectedly climbed to the top of the pop charts.

Several of rock's evergreens were heard from during the year. The Rolling Stones were touring in support of *Bridges to Babylon*—their latest milestone in a career that began with the release of their first single an astounding 34 years earlier. Another legend, former Beatle Paul McCartney, released *Flaming Pie*, his first album in four years. John Fogerty, leader of long-ago band Creedence Clearwater Revival, had a highly praised album, *Blue Moon Swamp*, his first effort in eleven years. Bob Dylan released his 41st album, *Time Out of Mind*. And one of the top bands of the '70s, Fleetwood Mac, appeared to be headed for a comeback with *The Dance*, a mix of their old standards and new music.

KIDS ROCK!

For a time in 1997, it seemed that teenagers were taking over the music scene. In addition to the pop sounds of Hanson, several other young musicians could be heard performing in a wide range of musical styles. Jonny Lang, already a top-notch blues singer and guitarist at 16, scored with a gold album, *Lie to Me,* and a summer tour with blues great B. B. King. Another 16-year-old, Ben Kweller, was leader of an up-and-coming rock band, Radish. Australian grunge rockers Silverchair, a trio of 17-year-olds, followed up their monster 1995 debut, *Frogstomp*, with a new effort, *Freak Show*. And Fiona Apple, whose worldly songs and sultry singing style seemed older than her 19 years, had a very popular debut album, *Tidal*. She also won an MTV Video Music Award as best new artist for her video "Sleep to Dream."

Another top pop act, the Spice Girls, although not teens themselves, seemed tailor-made to appeal to young fans. The British quintet's debut album, *Spice*, took the music world by storm in 1997. The group offered catchy dance tunes, a distinct look and personality for each girl (complete with nicknames like "Sporty Spice" and "Baby Spice"), and a feminist rallying cry ("Girl Power!"). The combination proved unbeatable: Two Spice Girls singles, "Wannabe" and "Say You'll Be There," hit the top of the charts. The group released a second album, *Spice Work,* in November.

SOUL, R&B, AND HIP-HOP

A number of soulful ballads recorded in 1996 remained on the charts in '97. Among them were "Un-Break My Heart," by Toni

Braxton; "All By Myself," by Celine Dion; "Don't Let Go (Love)," by En Vogue; "I Believe I Can Fly," by R. Kelly; and "Nobody," by Keith Sweat. Dion, who won two Grammy Awards, also released a new album, *The Reason,* which included a duet with Barbra Streisand ("Tell Him"). R&B vocal group Boyz II Men ventured into the worlds of techno and hip-hip on their third album, *Evolution.* Another vocal group, Backstreet Boys, had a hit single, "Quit Playing Games (with My Heart)," from their self-titled debut album.

Hip-hop artists continued to be highly visible both on the charts and in music videos. One of the year's biggest successes was producer and rapper Sean "Puffy" Combs, known as Puff Daddy. In addition to producing songs for nearly every big hip-hop act, he himself had a number-one album, *No Way Out,* and a hit single, "I'll Be Missing You." The single was based on the old Police hit "Every Breath You Take."

Several other artists were adding rapped verses over remixes of familiar hits. Notably, Janet Jackson blended portions of Joni Mitchell's classic "Big Yellow Taxi" with vocal stylings by rapper Q-tip and her own singing on "Got 'Til It's Gone," the first single from her latest release, *The Velvet Rope.*

The mingling of hip-hop with the sounds of soul and R&B continued. The leader in this trend was producer-singer Kenneth "Babyface" Edmonds. In 1997 he produced a movie, *Soul Food,* and its soundtrack, and also continued to work with a number of hot artists. Babyface produced two songs on singer Mary J. Blige's platinum-selling album, *Share My World.* Other singers who, like Blige, combined soul with hip-hop on new albums were Mariah Carey (*Butterfly*) and Swedish singer Robyn (*Robyn Is Here*). Actor and rapper Will Smith scored on two fronts, starring in

WHAT IS. . .Techno?

The pop music world in 1997 was abuzz with talk about techno, a hot new sound that uses synthesizers, drum machines, and sampled snippets of prerecorded music to create mesmerizing dance music. With its repetitive rhythms and impersonal, machine-generated feeling, techno truly sounds like the music of the next century.

Techno, also known as electronica, isn't really new. It's been popular on the club scene for several years, especially in Europe, where British groups the Chemical

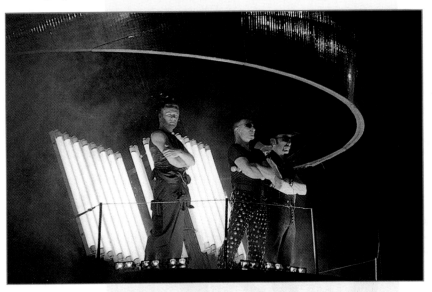

Brothers and the Prodigy have had big hits. And rap and hip-hop artists have used similar electronic techniques for years. But as alternative rock and other top musical styles of the '90s began to grow stale, the music industry was banking on techno to provide a fresh sound.

However, techno wasn't catching on quite as much as expected, although the Prodigy's album, *The Fat of the Land,* debuted at number one on the U.S. album charts. And several major rock acts, including U2 (shown above), Smashing Pumpkins, and David Bowie, were weaving elements of the music into their latest work. So music fans could expect to hear more of this futuristic sound in the very near future.

the motion picture *Men in Black* and recording the title cut on the film's hit soundtrack. Hip-hop artists Snoop Doggy Dogg and A Tribe Called Quest were also featured on the soundtrack. Wyclef Jean, one of the three members of top hip-hop group the Fugees, released *Wyclef Jean Presents the Carnival,* a creative mixture of hip-hop, Creole, and Afro-Cuban sounds.

Other hip-hop highlights included a long-awaited second album from the popular Wu-Tang Clan, top-selling efforts from Bone Thugs-N-Harmony and Blackstreet, and strong debuts by two young woman rappers, Missy Elliott and Foxy Brown.

Canadian singer Celine Dion won two Grammys for her 25-million-selling album, *Falling Into You.*

1997 Grammy Awards

Record of the Year	"Change the World"	Eric Clapton, artist
Album of the Year	*Falling Into You*	Celine Dion, artist
Song of the Year	"Change the World"	Gordon Kennedy, Wayne Kirkpatrick, Tommy Sims, songwriters
New Artist of the Year		LeAnn Rimes
Pop Vocal Performance—female	"Un-Break My Heart"	Toni Braxton, artist
Pop Vocal Performance—male	"Change the World"	Eric Clapton, artist
Pop Vocal Performance—group	"Free as a Bird"	Beatles, artists
Rock Vocal Performance—female	"If It Makes You Happy"	Sheryl Crow, artist
Rock Vocal Performance—male	"Where It's At"	Beck, artist
Rock Vocal Performance—group	"So Much to Say"	Dave Matthews Band, artists
Country Vocal Performance—female	"Blue"	LeAnn Rimes, artist
Country Vocal Performance—male	"Worlds Apart"	Vince Gill, artist
Country Vocal Performance—group	"My Maria"	Brooks and Dunn, artists
Rhythm and Blues Vocal Performance—female	"You're Makin' Me High"	Toni Braxton, artist
Rhythm and Blues Vocal Performance—male	"Your Secret Love"	Luther Vandross, artist
Rhythm and Blues Vocal Performance—group	"Killing Me Softly With His Song"	Fugees, artists
Music Video Performance	"Free as a Bird"	Beatles, artists
Alternative Music Performance	*Odelay*	Beck, artist
Score for a Motion Picture	*Independence Day*	David Arnold, composer
Musical Show Album	*Riverdance*	Bill Whelan, producer
Classical Album	*Corigliano: Of Rage and Remembrance (Symphony No. 1, etc.)*	Leonard Slatkin, conductor

As usual, many performers toured during the summer to promote their music. More and more, traveling music festivals were becoming staples of the summer tour scene. These all-day, multiband events were a good bargain for concert-goers and allowed lesser-known bands to benefit from the star power of top acts.

By far the most talked-about festival was the Lilith Fair, headlined exclusively by women artists. It was organized by Canadian singer Sarah McLachlan in response to the male-dominated lineups of many of the most popular festivals. In addition to McLachlan (who also had a successful album, *Surfacing*), the Lilith Fair included a rotating cast of performers, among them Jewel, Sheryl Crow, the Cardigans, Paula Cole, Tracy Chapman, Fiona Apple, and Cassandra Wilson.

The summer's other major tours included H.O.R.D.E., headlined by Beck and veteran rocker Neil Young; hip-hop celebration Smokin' Grooves; the ska-oriented Warped Tour; and of course the original '90s rockfest, Lollapalooza.

Rapper and actor Will Smith was doubly successful, starring in the motion picture *Men in Black* and recording its popular title song.

MUSIC NOTES

Movie soundtracks continued to be popular in 1997, often serving as convenient samplers of the current music scene. In addition to *Men in Black*, the year's other top soundtrack albums included *Spawn*, which showcased hard rockers Metallica and Henry Rollins along with techno wizards D. J. Spooky and Goldie; *My Best Friend's Wedding*, which featured reinterpretations of Burt Bacharach songs by Ani DiFranco and others; and *Batman and Robin*, with songs by chart-toppers Smashing Pumpkins, Jewel, and R. Kelly.

The tragic death of England's Princess Diana in August prompted Elton John to revise his song "Candle in the Wind" in her honor. He performed the new version at Diana's funeral service and later recorded it for use as a fundraiser for Diana's favorite charities. The recording quickly broke all sales records. By October, the song had sold more than 35 million copies, surpassing Bing Crosby's "White Christmas," to become the best-selling single of all time. All profits were slated for a memorial fund established in Diana's name.

The ranks of the Rock-and-Roll Hall of Fame were increased in May, when the twelfth annual awards were held in Cleveland, Ohio. Inducted were Motown stars the Jackson Five; pioneering funk-rock band Parliament-Funkadelic; harmony-singing brothers the Bee Gees; folky rock musicians Joni Mitchell, Buffalo Springfield, and Crosby, Stills, and Nash; and "blue-eyed soul" group the Rascals. The late bluegrass musician Bill Monroe and gospel singer Mahalia Jackson were honored as early influences on rock. Ohio-based record executive Sid Nathan was inducted in the nonperformer category.

IT'S ANIME!

Travel forward in time to the year 2029. Through amazing new technology, people can plug their *minds* directly into the Internet. But an electronic villain is on the loose— a rogue computer program that roams the worldwide electronic network, manipulating people's minds. Who can stop it? Only Major Motoko Kusanagi. Part human, part robot, she's a detective with superpowers.

That's the situation that sets the stage for the science-fiction film *Ghost in the Shell*. Chances are this movie didn't come to your neighborhood multiplex. It was shown in relatively few theaters when it was released in 1996. But it's become a top-selling video, one of the most popular examples of the cartoon films called *anime* (pronounced AH-nee-may).

Anime is Japanese animation, and it's taking the world by storm. Cartoons are very popular in Japan, among adults as well as kids. And Japanese *anime* has long been popular in other Asian countries, such as South Korea and Vietnam. Until recently, *anime* had few fans in Western countries. Now that's changing, as young people especially are discovering these cartoons.

FROM ASTRO BOY TO SAILOR MOON

Anime started in Japan in the 1960s. The first big animated television hit was *Tetsuwan Atom,* which featured a popular comic-book character. American viewers got to know this show as *Astro Boy.* A few other Japanese cartoons made it to America in the years that followed: *Speed Racer, Star Blazers,* and *Robotech.* These shows were popular in Japan, but they drew only a limited number of American fans. Because they were produced on very low budgets, they were choppier and less smooth than American cartoons. Sometimes the Japanese scripts were poorly translated into English.

Anime began to draw a larger audience in the 1980s, through video sales and rentals. One of the most popular films was *Akira,* a dark science-fiction tale. And some of the biggest fans turned out to be college students. They discovered an important difference between Japanese and American cartoons: While American cartoons are mostly made for children, *anime* isn't just for kids.

In Japan, animated films draw audiences of all ages, and they account for as much as half of box-office revenues each year. It's not unusual to see grown-ups reading *manga* (Japanese comic books). In fact, many Japanese comic books and animated films are meant for adults. *Anime* for adults often features complicated plots, and sometimes violence. Many films don't have happy endings.

Still, a lot of *anime* is created for children or for people of all ages. One of the most pop-

My Neighbor Totoro is a charming *anime* video about two children who discover a world populated by magical beasts.

ular *anime* TV shows is *Sailor Moon*. This show was brought to U.S. and Canadian television in 1995, along with two other popular shows, *Dragon Ball Z* and *Teknoman*. *Sailor Moon*'s heroine is a 14-year-old girl who changes into a super-heroine to fight evil. The show developed a devoted group of fans in the United States and Canada, ranging in age from preschoolers to adults in their 30s. They liked *Sailor Moon*'s curious mixture of romance and adventure.

A GROWING POPULARITY

As word of *anime* has spread, the video market for *anime* has grown. Many video shops—and even music stores and comic-book stores—now carry a wide range of *anime* titles, including children's, family, action, and horror films. One of the most enchanting current *anime* videos is *My Neighbor Totoro,* about two children who discover a world filled with magical creatures. New releases like this one are snapped up by fans, who keep in touch through clubs and Internet news groups.

And *anime* fans had something special to look forward to in 1998. *Princess Mononoke,* a full-length animated feature set in ancient Japan, was slated to be released in North America. The film broke box-office records in Japan.

The technical quality of Japanese animated films has improved a great deal since the early days. Also, new films are likely to be dubbed into English, rather than carrying English-language subtitles. And Japanese filmmakers are working with U.S. companies to bring more *anime* to America. Fans just can't wait!

The adventures of a teenage superheroine are the basis of *Sailor Moon,* a popular *anime* TV show in the United States and Canada.

FUN TO READ

Young Bennett Gibbons has everything a little cow could want. Well, almost everything—Bennett has no playmates because there are no other little cows in the neighborhood. So when a pig family moves in next door, he's thrilled that their son Webster is just his age, and the two become best friends. But Bennett's parents don't approve. After all, pigs roll in the mud and go "oink"—things a well-bred cow would never do. Can friendship cross social—not to mention species—lines? The answer is in Tim Egan's delightful picture book Metropolitan Cow.

The Goose-Girl at the Well

There was once a very old woman who lived with her flock of geese in a little house far off in the mountains. Surrounding her house was a large forest, and every morning the old woman took her crutch and hobbled into it and collected grass and all the wild fruit she could reach for her geese. The old woman was quite active, more so than anyone would have thought considering her age, and she carried everything home on her back. Anyone would have thought that the heavy load would have weighed her to the ground, but she always brought it safely home.

If anyone happened to meet her along the way, she would greet him quite courteously. "Good day, dear countryman. It is a fine day. Ah, you wonder how I can drag grass about. But everyone must carry his burden on his back."

Nevertheless, people did not like to meet her, and they often chose a roundabout way because some thought she was a witch.

One morning a handsome young man was walking through the forest. The sun shone brightly, the birds sang, a cool breeze crept through the leaves, and he was full of joy and gladness. Suddenly he saw the old woman kneeling on the ground cutting grass with a sickle. She had already thrust a whole load into her sack, and near it stood two baskets that were filled to the top with wild apples and pears.

"But good little woman," said he, "how can you carry all that?"

"I must carry it, dear sir," answered she. "Rich folk's children have no need to do such things, but with the peasant folk, the saying goes, 'Don't look behind you; you will only see how crooked your back is!'"

She then said to him, "Will you help me? You have a straight back and young legs. It would be nothing to you. Besides, my house is not very far from here."

The young man took pity on the old woman. "My father is certainly no peasant," replied he, "but a rich Count. But so that you may see that it is not only peasants who can carry things, I will take your bundle."

"If you will try it," said she, "I shall be very glad. You will certainly have to walk for an hour, but what will that mean to you? Only you must carry the apples and pears as well."

It now seemed to the young man that it was going to be a little harder work than he had thought. But the old woman would not let him off, and she packed the bundle on his back, and hung the two baskets on his arm.

"See, it is quite light," said she.

"No, it is not light," answered the Count, and made a sorry face. "The bundle is as heavy as if it were full of cobblestones, and the apples and pears are as heavy as lead! I can scarcely breathe."

276

He had a mind to put everything down again, but the old woman would not allow it. "Just look," said she mockingly, "the young gentleman will not carry what I, an old woman, have so often dragged along. You are ready with your fine words, but when it comes to actually working, you want to take to your heels."

So the young man followed her, and as long as he walked on level ground it was still bearable. But when they came to the mountain, and he had to climb, it was beyond his strength. The drops of perspiration stood on his forehead and ran, hot and cold, down his back.

"Old woman," said he, "I can go no farther. I want to rest a little."

"Not here," she answered. "When we have arrived at our journey's end, you can rest."

"Old woman, you are shameless!" said the Count, and he tried to throw off the bundle. But he labored in vain; it stuck as fast to his back as if it grew there. He turned and twisted, but he could not get rid of it.

The old woman laughed at him and sprang about on her crutch quite delightedly. "Don't get angry, dear sir," said she. "You are growing as red in the face as a turkey-cock! Carry your bundle patiently and I will give you a good reward when we get home."

What could he do? He was obliged to submit to his fate and crawl along patiently behind the old woman. She seemed to grow more and more nimble, and his burden still heavier. Then, all at once, she sprang up and jumped onto the bundle and seated herself on top of it; and however withered she might be, she was yet heavier than the stoutest country lass. Groaning continually, the young man climbed the mountain and at last reached the old woman's house just as he was about to drop.

When the geese saw the old woman, they flapped their wings, stretched out their necks, and ran to meet her, cackling all the while. Behind the flock walked, stick in hand, a girl, strong and big, but very ugly. "Good mother," said the goose-girl to the old woman, "has anything happened to you? You have stayed away for such a very long time."

"By no means, my dear daughter," answered she. "I have met with nothing bad, but on the contrary, with this kind gentleman, who has carried my burden for me. Only think, he even took me on his back when I was tired! The trip has not seemed long to us; we have been merry and have been making jokes with each other all the time."

At last the old woman slid down and took the bundle off the young man's back and the baskets from his arm. She then looked at him quite kindly, and said, "Now seat yourself on this bench and rest. You have earned your wages, and you shall find that they are generous." Then she said to the goose-girl, "Go into the house, my dear daughter. It is not becoming for you to be alone with a young gentleman. He might fall in love with you."

The Count did not know whether to laugh or cry. "Such a sweetheart as that," thought he, "could not ever touch my heart."

In the meantime, the old woman stroked and fondled her geese as if they were her children, and then went into the house with her daughter. The youth lay down on the bench, which was under a wild apple tree. The air was warm and mild. "It is quite delightful here," thought he, "but I am so tired that I cannot keep my eyes open. I will sleep a little."

When he was rested a bit, the old woman came and shook him until he awoke. "Sit up," said she, "you cannot stay here. I have certainly treated you hardly; still, it has not cost you your life. Of money and land you have no need. Here is something else for you." Thereupon she thrust into his hand a little book, which had been cut out of a single emerald. "Take great care of it," said she, "for it will bring you good fortune."

The young man sprang up and thanked the old woman for her present, and he set off without even once looking back at her.

"Go into the house, my dear daughter. It is not becoming for you to be alone with a young gentleman. He might fall in love with you."

The Count wandered for three days in the wilderness before he could find his way out. He then reached a large town, and as no one knew him, he was led into the royal palace where the King and Queen were sitting on their thrones. The Count fell on one knee, drew the emerald book out of his pocket, and laid it at the Queen's feet. She bade him rise and hand her the little book.

The Queen took the precious book from the young man, opened it up—and immediately began to weep bitterly. "Of what use to me are the splendors with which I am surrounded," she cried. "Every morning I awake in pain and sorrow. I had three daughters, the youngest of whom was beautiful to behold. She was white as snow, with cheeks as rosy as apple blossoms. Her hair was as radiant as sunbeams. And when she cried, not tears fell from her eyes but pearls."

The Queen continued her story. It seemed that when the youngest daughter was fifteen years old, the King had summoned all three sisters to come before him. He said: "My daughters, I know not when my last day may arrive. I will today decide what each shall receive at my death. You all love me, but the one of you who loves me best shall fare the best."

Each daughter said that she loved him best.

"Can you not express to me," said the King, "how much you do love me, and thus I shall see what you mean?"

The eldest spoke. "I love my father as dearly as the sweetest sugar."

The second said, "I love my father as dearly as my prettiest dress."

But the youngest was silent. Then the father said, "And you, my dearest child, how much do you love me?"

"Very much, Father, but I can think of nothing to compare my love with," she answered.

But her father insisted that she should name something. So she said at last, "The best food does not please me without salt; therefore, I love my father as dearly as salt."

When the King heard that, he fell into a passion and said, "If you love me like salt, then your love shall be repaid with salt." And he divided his kingdom between the two older daughters, but had a sack of salt bound on the back of the youngest and ordered two servants to lead her into the wild forest.

"We all begged and prayed for her," said the Queen, "but the King's anger was not to be appeased. How she cried when she had to leave us! The whole road was strewn with the pearls that flowed from her eyes. The King soon afterward realized how foolish he had been and repented of his unwarranted harshness. He had the whole forest searched for the poor child, but no one could find her. I can't bear to think that wild beasts may have devoured her. Many a time I console myself with the hope that she is still alive and may have hidden herself in a cave, or has found shelter with compassionate people. So imagine my surprise when I opened your emerald book and saw inside a pearl of exactly the same kind as those that used to fall from my daughter's eyes. You must tell me how you came by that pearl!"

The Count told her that he had received it from the old woman in the forest, who had appeared very strange to him and must surely be a witch; but that he had neither seen nor heard anything of the Queen's beautiful child. The King and Queen, however, resolved to seek out the old woman. They thought that where the pearl had been, they would learn news of their daughter.

The old woman was sitting in that lonely place at her spinning wheel, spinning. It was already dusk, and a log that was burning on the hearth gave a scanty light. All at once there was a noise outside. The geese were coming home from the pasture and uttering their hoarse cries. Soon afterward the daughter also entered. She sat down beside the old woman and worked at her own spinning wheel, twisting the threads as nimbly as a young girl. Thus they both sat for two hours and exchanged never a word. At last something rustled at the window, and two fiery eyes peered in. It was an old night owl, which cried, "Uhu!" three times. The old woman looked up and said "Now, my little daughter, it is time for you to go out and do your work."

The daughter rose and went out, and where did she go? Over the meadows, onward into the valley. Soon she came to a well, with three old oak trees standing beside it. The moon had risen, large and round over the mountain, and it was so light that one could have found a needle. The daughter removed a skin that covered her face and, bending down to the well, she began to wash herself. When she had finished, she dipped the skin into the water and laid it out in the moonlight to dry.

But how the maiden was changed! When the gray mask came off, her golden hair broke forth like sunbeams and spread about her like a mantle. Her eyes shone as brightly as the stars in heaven, and her cheeks bloomed a soft red, like apple blossoms.

The fair maiden, however, was sad. She sat down and wept bitter tears. And the pearls flowed out of her eyes and rolled through her long hair to the ground. There she sat and would have remained sitting a long time if there had not been a rustling and crackling in the boughs of a nearby tree. She sprang up like a doe that has been overtaken by the shot of the hunter. Just then the moon was obscured by a dark cloud, and in that instant the maiden slipped on the gray skin and vanished.

She ran back home, trembling like a leaf. The old woman was standing on the threshold and the girl was about to relate what had befallen her, but the old woman laughed kindly and said, "I already know all." She led her into the house and lighted a new log. She did not, however, sit down to her spinning again, but fetched a broom and began to sweep. "All must be clean and sweet," she said to the girl.

"But, Mother," said the maiden, "why do you begin work at so late an hour? What do you expect?"

"Do you know then what time it is?" asked the old woman.

"Not yet midnight," answered the maiden.

"Do you not remember," continued the old woman, "that it is three years today since you came to me? Your time is up; we can no longer remain together."

The girl was terrified and cried, "Alas! dear Mother, will you cast me off? Where shall I go? I have no friends and no home to which I can go. I have always done as you bade me, and you have always been satisfied with me. Do not send me away."

"Do not say a word more," said the old woman. "Go to your chamber, take the skin off your face, put on the silken gown that you wore when first you came to me, and then wait until I call you."

The King and Queen, meanwhile, had journeyed forth with the Count in order to seek out the old woman in the wilderness. The Count had accidentally strayed away from them and lost his way. He continued forward until darkness came and then climbed a tree, intending to pass the night there. When the moon lit up the surrounding country, he perceived a figure coming down the mountain. She had not a stick in her hand, but he could tell that it was the goose-girl.

She sat down and wept bitter tears. And the pearls flowed out of her eyes and rolled through her long hair to the ground.

"Oho," cried he, "there she comes, and if I can just get hold of one of the witches, the other shall not be far away!" But how astonished he was when she went to the well, took off the skin, and washed herself, and her golden hair fell down about her and she was more beautiful than anyone he had ever seen in the whole world. He hardly dared to breathe. He stretched his head as far forward through the leaves as he dared and stared at her, when the bough suddenly cracked. And at that very moment the maiden slipped into the skin, sprang away like a doe and, as the moon was covered by a cloud, disappeared from his eyes. Hardly had she disappeared before the Count descended from the tree and hastened after her with nimble steps.

He had not been gone long before he saw, in the moonlight, two figures coming over the meadow. It was the King and Queen, who had seen from a distance the light shining in the old woman's little house and were going to it. The Count told them what wonderful things he had seen by the well, and they did not doubt that it had been their lost daughter. They walked onward full of joy and soon came to the little house. The geese were sitting all around it with their heads thrust under their wings sleeping.

The King and Queen looked through the window and saw the old woman sitting there quietly spinning, nodding her head and never looking around. The room was perfectly clean, as if the little mist men, who carry no dust on their feet, lived there. Their daughter, however, they did not see. They gazed at all this for a long time, and at last took heart and knocked softly at the window. The old woman appeared to have been expecting them; she rose and called out quite kindly, "Come in. I know you already."

When they had entered the room, the old woman said, "You might have spared yourself the long walk if you had not three years ago unjustly driven away your child, who is so good and lovable. No harm has come to her. For three years she has tended the geese, and with them she has learned no evil but has preserved her purity of heart. You, however, have been sufficiently punished by the misery in which you have lived." Then she called in a kindly voice, "Come out, my little daughter."

Thereupon the door of the maiden's chamber opened, and the Princess stepped out in her silken garments, with her golden hair and her shining eyes, and it was as if an angel from heaven had entered. She went up to her father and mother and fell on their necks and kissed them. There was no help for it—they all had to weep for joy. The young Count stood near them, and when the Princess saw him she blushed as red as a moss rose and she did not even know why.

The King said, "My dear child, I have given away my kingdom. What shall you have upon my death?"

"She needs nothing," said the old woman. "I give her all the tears that she has wept on your account; they are precious pearls, finer than those that are found in the sea and worth more than your whole kingdom. And I leave her my little house as payment for her services."

When the old woman uttered those words, she disappeared from their sight. The walls rattled a little, and when the King and Queen looked around, the little house had changed into a splendid palace, with a royal table filled with food and servants running hither and thither.

The story goes still further, but my grandmother, who related it to me, had partly lost her memory and had forgotten the rest. I shall always believe that the beautiful Princess married the handsome Count, and that they remained together in the palace and lived there in all happiness. Whether the snow-white geese were in fact young maidens whom the old woman had taken under her protection, and whether they now received their human form again and stayed as handmaids of the young Princess, I do not exactly know, but I suspect it.

But this much is certain: The old woman was not a witch. She was a wise woman who meant only good. Very likely it was she who, at the Princess's birth, gave her the gift of weeping pearls instead of tears. That does not happen nowadays, or else the poor would soon become rich.

I shall always believe that the beautiful Princess married the handsome Count, and that they remained together in the palace and lived there in all happiness.

POETRY

BEASTS AND BIRDS

The dog will come when he is called,
  the cat will walk away;
The monkey's cheek is very bald,
  The goat is fond of play.
The parrot is a prate-apace,
  Yet knows not what she says;
The noble horse will win the race,
  Or draw you in a chaise.

The pig is not a feeder nice,
  The squirrel loves a nut,
The wolf would eat you in a trice,
  The buzzard's eyes are shut.
The lark sings high up in the air,
  The linnet in the tree;
The swan he has a bosom fair,
  And who so proud as he?

ADELAIDE O'KEEFE (1776–1855)

AUTUMN COVE

At Autumn Cove, so many white monkeys,
bounding, leaping up like snowflakes in flight!
They coax and pull their young ones down from the branches
to drink and frolic with the water-borne moon.

LI PO (8TH CENTURY)

A NUT TREE

I had a little nut tree,
  Nothing would it bear,
But a silver nutmeg,
  And a golden pear.
The King of Spain's daughter
  Came to visit me,
And all was because of
  My little nut tree.
I skipped over water
  I danced over sea,
And all the birds in the air
  Could not catch me.

ANONYMOUS

FLINT

An emerald is as green as grass,
    A ruby red as blood;
A sapphire shines as blue as heaven;
    A flint lies in the mud.

A diamond is a brilliant stone,
    To catch the world's desire;
An opal holds a fiery spark;
    But a flint holds fire.

CHRISTINA ROSSETTI (1830–1894)

SNOWDROP

Many, many welcomes,
February fair-maid,
Ever as of old time,
Solitary firstling,
Coming in the cold time,
Prophet of the gay time,
Prophet of the May time,
Prophet of the roses,
Many, many welcomes,
February fair-maid.

ALFRED, LORD TENNYSON (1809–1892)

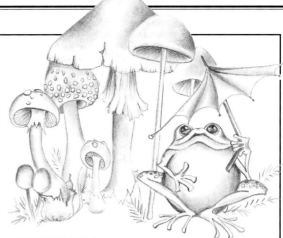

TOADSTOOLS

I found a ring of toadstools,
    Yellow, pink and white,
But not a single toad or frog
    Was anywhere in sight.

Perhaps the toads sit on them
    And so keep their feet dry;
But I should think that toads would find
    The footstools rather high.

Maybe when playing leapfrog
    The toads jump up and stop,
Or Mother Frog helps baby
    To climb upon the top.

But when it's misty weather
    Or rain falls from the sky,
The stools make fine umbrellas
    To keep toads nice and dry.

RUPERT SARGENT HOLLAND (1878–1952)

OVER HILL, OVER DALE

Over hill, over dale,
Thorough bush, thorough brier,
Over park, over pale,
Thorough flood, thorough fire!
I do wander everywhere,
Swifter than the moon's sphere;
And I serve the fairy queen,
To dew her orbs upon the green;
The cowslips tall her pensioners be;
In their gold coats spots you see;
Those be rubies, fairy favours,
In those freckles live their savours;
I must go seek some dewdrops here,
And hang a pearl in every cowslip's ear.

WILLIAM SHAKESPEARE (1564–1616)

JOHN CABOT'S PERILOUS VOYAGE

On a summer day in 1497, an Italian explorer named John Cabot, sailing under the English flag, reached the coast of North America. Cabot, whose real name was Giovanni Caboto, may well have been the first European to set foot on the North American continent since the Viking explorer Leif Ericson and his seafaring Norsemen had landed there 500 years earlier. (Although Christopher Columbus reached the islands of the Caribbean, he never set foot on the mainland of North or South America.) The year 1997 marked the 500th anniversary of Cabot's discovery, which became the basis of Britain's claim to North America.

Born in Genoa, Italy, probably in 1451, Cabot's family later moved to Venice. There, young Cabot began a career as a merchant. On one of his trading voyages, Cabot visited Mecca,

June 24, 1497: Italian explorer John Cabot sights land off the coast of Newfoundland, in what is now Canada.

in what is now Saudi Arabia. Mecca was then a great center of trade, where products from Europe and Asia were bought and sold.

But the overland journey to obtain spices, silk, and other precious goods from Cathay (China) and other Eastern lands was long and slow. Like his fellow Italian explorer Christopher Columbus, John Cabot believed that the Earth was a globe and that Asia could be reached more directly from Europe by sailing west across the Atlantic Ocean. After failing to persuade the rulers of both Spain and Portugal to back an ocean voyage to Cathay, Cabot went to England. There he obtained the backing of a group of merchants and of England's King Henry VII.

Cabot sailed from the English port city of Bristol late in May, 1497, with a crew of eighteen on a small ship named the Matthew. On June 24, he landed somewhere on the coast of North America—probably near Newfoundland or Cape Breton Island in what is now Canada. Cabot was sure that he had reached the northeast coast of Asia, and he quickly sailed back to England to report his find.

Encouraged by the news, Henry VII gave Cabot a small fleet and sent him on another voyage in 1498. This voyage is shrouded in mystery. It's believed that Cabot first sailed back to Newfoundland and then south as far as Chesapeake Bay before storms wrecked most of his ships. Cabot probably perished during one of the storms as there is no trace of him after this voyage.

The following fictionalized account of the first Cabot voyage was inspired by actual events. The story is seen mainly through the eyes of John Cabot's fifteen-year-old son Sebastian, who is believed to have accompanied his father on that memorable first voyage.

The rain fell in solid sheets, drenching the sailors on the tiny ship *Matthew* as it lurched about on the storm-tossed sea. Looking skyward as he clung for dear life to a taut line of rigging, young Sebastian Cabot watched dark gray clouds swirl overhead. The storm had come up on them suddenly, and now the three-masted sailing ship plunged and reared up like a frightened horse.

Sebastian's stomach rolled with each movement of the raging North Atlantic. He watched as the rising waves tossed the *Matthew* about as if it had no more weight than a piece of cork. Not far from his perch on the ship's sterncastle, or rear deck, Sebastian could see his father John Cabot, the ship's master, wrapped in his cloak and hood. And he could hear the older Cabot shouting orders to the crew.

"Come on lads, into the rigging with you," John Cabot cried out, "Trim the topsails on mizzen and mainmasts. Be quick about it." The words came out sharp and clear, despite the captain's distinctly Italian accent.

Sebastian inched closer to his father, holding on to whatever ship's fixtures were bolted down.

"Father, do you think we can outrun the storm?" the youngster called out, a slight tremor of fear in his voice.

The ship's captain looked at his son, his long beard flapping in the wind like the sails overhead, his dark eyes flashing. He grabbed Sebastian by the collar of his short jacket and replied with a hearty laugh, "Outrun it? Why my boy, we'll be lucky if this devil's own wind doesn't scoop us up and hurl us all the way to the palace of the Great Khan of Cathay!"

Then he added with a wink, "This storm is but God's will—a heavenly hand to speed us on our way to the spices and jewels of Asia."

He gripped his son around the shoulder with his left hand, while holding on to a hatch top with his right to keep his balance on the swaying deck. Through the open hatch Sebastian could see the helmsman on the deck below struggling with the tiller that controlled the ship's rudder.

"Ahoy, mate," John Cabot cried out to the helmsman. "Hold your tiller steady as you are. I'll guide you."

With a strained look on his face, the helmsman cocked his head toward the open hatch above him and shouted, "Aye captain, but I'm having a bad time of it in these heavy seas. An extra pair of hands would be useful."

Cabot turned to his son. "Well then, youngster, go below and give the mate a hand. And while you're down there kick some life into those young swabbies and tell them to man the pumps. We're taking on too much water."

Then he gave his son a friendly shove. "Do a proper job of it and I'll see you get an extra ration of salt horse and hardtack," he said with a hearty laugh.

At the mention of the standard ship's fare of pickled beef and pork and hard biscuit, Sebastian felt a queasy sensation in his stomach. After a month of this diet, he could barely face another slab of briny beef and tooth-cracking biscuit.

Gingerly making his way down to the lower deck, Sebastian ordered several ship's boys to help the older able-bodied seamen work the pumps. Then he made his way to the helmsman.

"Give a hand here, boy," the helmsman instructed him. "We have to tack to port to keep the wind from knocking us over."

For the next hour, Sebastian and the helmsman worked the tiller as great waves lashed at the *Matthew* and seawater poured through the open hatch above. It came down on them in drenching cascades every few moments, until both of them were soaked to the skin.

Sebastian wondered whether the small ship, barely 60 feet long, could survive the buffeting of wind and waves. True, the *Matthew* was a sturdy ship, made of solid oak and well caulked with tar. But would it be able to stand up in such heavy weather? Or would they all end up floundering in the raging sea, dragged under by the white-capped waves—or worse, devoured by sharks. He shuddered at the thought.

To keep his mind off such dark thoughts, Sebastian allowed his mind to wander back to when he lived comfortably with his family in the English port city of Bristol, with its narrow cobbled streets and jolly taverns. There he had heard ruddy-faced sailors pause between frothy mugs of beer to tell tall tales of sea monsters and exotic lands. Some had spoken of venturing to the lands in the northwest where there were limitless schools of fish and vast forests that could provide timber for thousands of ships. It was along the route charted by the Bristol seamen that the *Matthew* now traveled in its search for the wealth of Asia.

Sebastian also remembered the gay pageantry that surrounded the departure of the *Matthew* from its Bristol berth. He recalled how his father had spoken glowingly of finding a route to China across the northern seas that would be shorter than the one his fellow Italian Christopher Columbus had charted in the southern latitudes.

The great throng of people gathered on the dock had cheered John Cabot and his crew as they readied their ship to sail out of port. Banners were hoisted and a herald trumpeter played a fanfare. Then an official of King Henry VII read from a proclamation stating that John Cabot was authorized "to seek, find and discover islands, countries and regions which before this time have been unknown to Christians."

Such fine-sounding words, Sebastian had thought at the time. Later, when they were at sea, his father had explained that they could lay claim to any land they came upon—as long as it wasn't occupied by people from other European countries. Even better, his father told him, the Cabots would be entitled to four-fifths of all the wealth that resulted from trade between England and any new lands they found. The other one-fifth would go to the English king as his fee for allowing them to sail under his banner. And, of course, the English merchants who backed the voyage—and who provided the ship—would also have to get a share of the profits.

When Sebastian pointed out that the King of England was getting a pretty hefty fee considering that he was risking neither money nor a ship, his father had shrugged and remarked, "Henry is a smart fellow. That's why he's the king."

Sebastian recalled how wonderful those early days at sea had been. Everything was new and exciting as he learned about life on board a ship. And learn he did, performing every chore from hoisting sail to making sure that the ship's timepiece, a glass with sand, was turned over every half hour. Oh yes, Sebastian thought, those early days had been fun. But after a month at sea, those same chores had become just a lot of hard work.

The youngster was abruptly snapped out of his dreamy state by the sound of the helmsman's voice bellowing in his ear.

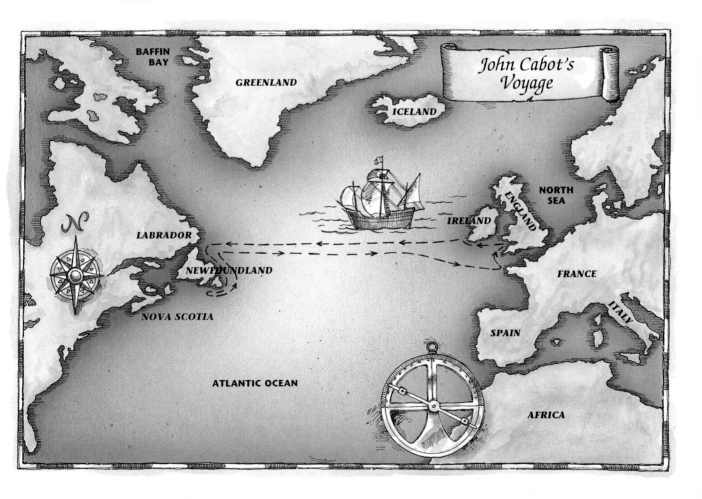

"Don't fall asleep at the tiller, boy," he shouted, adding a playful slap on the cheek. "I think we've seen the worst of the storm. The sea is not near as angry as it was."

Sure enough, Sebastian could feel the ocean beneath them calming down. The waves smacking into the ship's creaking timbers were less ferocious. The wind had become more of a whistle than a shriek. Released from his duty at the tiller, Sebastian scampered up the gangway to the main deck. Overhead, the mass of dirty gray clouds had parted to reveal a radiant black sky alive with sparkling stars.

Sebastian was soon joined by his father. Pointing skyward, John Cabot observed, "Those stars will lead us straight to Cathay. Soon we'll see the sun's rays bouncing off golden-domed palaces. We'll smell the delicious spices of the Orient and be able to drape ourselves in fine silk clothing."

He turned to his son and his weathered face broke into a smile. "Now go get some sleep, my boy. And dream sweet dreams of hauling baskets of rubies and emeralds on board the *Matthew* to take back to Bristol."

Sebastian made his way along the slippery deck of the gently pitching and rolling ship to a point near the mainmast where spare sail and ship's tools were stored. There he found a section of reasonably dry canvas that he could use as a blanket. Removing his wet jacket and cap, he crawled under the canvas, stretched out and stared up at the twinkling stars. Like the other sailors on board the *Matthew,* Sebastian slept wherever he could. Only the captain of the ship had a sleeping cabin in the sterncastle.

Just as he was dozing off, Sebastian felt a rough tap on his shoulder. He looked up to see one of the crew, an old-timer named Will, staring down at him, his eyes narrowed and his mouth curled in a sneer.

"Here, lad, I hope your dad ain't leading us to our doom," he said angrily. "Some of the crew ain't at all happy about how this voyage is going."

Sebastian propped himself on one elbow and responded sharply. "My father is as good a captain as ever sailed a ship. He just brought us through a storm safely didn't he?"

Will picked at his chipped and yellowed teeth. "No matter that—the fact is we've been at sea more than 30 days. By my reckoning we should have made the coast of Asia by now."

"Oh, stop your grumbling, Will," Sebastian snapped back, "You always see the dark side of things. Now leave me be."

With a few muttered curses, Will moved off into the darkness. Sebastian rolled over and allowed his tired body to sink into a deep sleep.

In the morning, he awoke with a start to the shrill sound of the bosun's whistle calling the morning watch to their stations. Dawn found clear skies and a brightly shining sun.

After a breakfast of dried peas, hard biscuit, and cider—which Sebastian preferred to the grimy water in the ship's barrels—the youngster sought out his father. John Cabot was on the sterncastle taking a sighting with his brass astrolabe—a mariner's instrument for determining latitude, the distance north and south of the equator measured in degrees.

Sebastian watched his father carefully point the astrolabe toward the sun, then take a reading from the degree markers etched into the rim of the circular instrument. John had told his son during the voyage that these readings weren't very exact, since the ship could never be kept on an absolutely straight course.

The older Cabot preferred a method of navigation called "dead reckoning." This was a simpler procedure in which the ship's master set his course by his compass. Then he kept track of the number of miles the ship sailed from its starting point in a given period of time. Sebastian had often helped his father determine the ship's speed. He would run to the high forecastle at the bow, or front, of the ship. Leaning out over the bowsprit, he would wait for his father's signal and then drop a small piece of wood into the ocean. By calculating how long it took for the wood chip to travel from bow to stern, they could make a rough estimate of the *Matthew's* speed.

As soon as his father had finished making his calculations with the astrolabe, Sebastian joined him and Hugh Elliott, a Bristol merchant who was on board to represent his city's commercial interests.

Sebastian reported the previous night's conversation with Will to the two men. John Cabot seemed undisturbed. "Pay no mind to Will, son," Cabot assured the youngster. "He's a chronic grumbler."

Hugh Elliott swept a hand through his wavy blond hair and commented, "Nonetheless, Master Cabot, it may be well to take precautions against a mutiny. Perhaps we should arm the loyal members of the crew."

At this suggestion, Sebastian's eyes lit up. "I'll run down and grab a sword from the rack, Father," he exclaimed gleefully.

The older Cabot shook his head from side to side. "That won't be necessary, Sebastiano," he said, calling his son by his Italian name. "These are good fellows. And they all know that the penalty for mutiny is to be hanged from a yardarm. Mark my words, at first sight of land they'll all be happy as pigs at a trough."

Cabot reached out with both arms to embrace his son and the Bristol merchant. "Now let's all see to our duties. I'm confident that my calculations are right and that in a few days we will see the shores of Cathay."

For the next few days, the *Matthew* plodded on, its lookouts searching for some sign of land. By now even Sebastian was beginning to feel a sense of desperation. Although the seas were calm and the weather fair, most of the crew members went about their duties with gloom clouding their sun-bronzed faces.

And then, on the 23rd day of June—33 days after leaving Bristol—Sebastian spotted something that made his heart leap. Cupping his hands over his eyes to shade them from the sun's glare, he peered intently at an object floating in the water. What was it—a piece of wood, a tree branch? Yes, that's what it was, a branch from a large tree.

"Father, look," Sebastian shouted excitedly, pointing at the leafy branch as it swept by them, rising and falling with the white-capped waves.

"By God," exclaimed the older Cabot, his eyes wide with joy. "See that, lads," he shouted to the crew. "A sure sign of land."

Cheers went up from the crew, and during the next few hours, the weary seafarers saw more signs of the nearness of land. Seagulls and other coastal birds appeared overhead, squawking a greeting. More twigs and tree branches floated past them. Soon they could smell the faint aroma of pine and other trees.

Nightfall descended and a heavy fog rolled over ship and sea, engulfing them in a gray haze. John Cabot ordered his son to climb up to the crow's nest atop the mainmast, where a solitary lookout was perched. "Two sets of eyes are better than one, my boy. And you're a sharp-eyed lad."

So into the rigging he went. Climbing slowly, gripping each crossline of rigging carefully, Sebastian made his way aloft. His body tense, his palms sweaty, the youngster could barely bring himself to look down. When he did, it made him dizzy, so he kept his eyes fixed on the lookout's perch above.

Struggling up the rigging of a swaying ship was the teenager's least favorite activity. This is work for a monkey, he thought to himself as he struggled to reach the lookout's platform. As he neared it, he felt a helping hand grip him by the arm and haul him up the last few feet. Finally, Sebastian was safely in. A smiling Italian seaman named Antonio, who also served as the ship's barber, greeted him.

"Nice to have some company on this lonely watch," the older man said. "Now catch your breath and then look sharply off to port while I look to starboard. There's a good deal of ice in these waters."

"Ice!" blurted a startled Sebastian. "You mean icebergs. But it's summer."

"Aye, icebergs, lad," Antonio replied. "Summer or no, they're all over these waters."

Good grief, thought Sebastian. If this little tub hits an iceberg, we'll split apart. We'll all be food for the fish.

The fog was starting to lift, but a gauzy haze still surrounded the ship. And then, all at once, looming up out of the mist like a great white mountain, a large ice floe appeared off the ship's port (left) side. A startled Sebastian tried to shout a warning, but the words stuck in his throat. Frantically, he tugged at Antonio's sleeve. "Ice . . . to port," he stammered.

A wide-eyed Antonio shouted below. "Ahoy, helmsman, ice to port—steer to starboard."

As the iceberg came nearer, it seemed to a terrified Sebastian that the two masses—ship and iceberg—must collide. He hid his hands in his face and braced himself for the crunching impact he was certain would come.

All at once, the ship swerved sharply to starboard with a great creaking of timbers. Just in time, the helmsman had worked the tiller so that the *Matthew* veered out of the path of the huge iceberg.

"It's all right, Sebastian," the lookout reassured him, patting him on the head. "We're out of harm's way—but only by a hair. That's the closest shave I've seen—and I've been a barber for fifteen years."

For the next few hours, the helmsman steered the *Matthew* cautiously through the ice floes. Sebastian remained aloft in the crow's nest as the first rays of light appeared in the East and darkness faded. Dawn came and the mist melted away.

At 5 A.M. on the morning of June 24, 1497, Sebastian and his lookout companion saw the dim outline of land on the horizon. Almost simultaneously the two sang out "Land Ho!"

Below them on the ship's main deck, barefoot sailors scampered into the rigging to catch a glimpse of the gray-green land mass that was just visible in the distance. The seamen shouted happily and threw their caps in the air.

Sebastian made his way down the rigging to join his father on the sterncastle. As he reached the deck, Will the grumbler grabbed him in a joyful bear hug, grinning widely and flashing a mouthful of cracked and yellow teeth.

"I always knew your father would bring us through," Will cackled. "God bless him, I never lost faith in him for a minute."

That's not the way I remember it, Sebastian thought, as he broke away from Will and rushed to be by his father's side. "You've done it, Father! We've made it," he roared as father and son embraced.

Soon they were joined by Hugh Elliott, the Bristol merchant. "My compliments, Master Cabot—you have brought us safely through."

As the sun rose in the sky, they were able to see a second land mass some miles to the north, which they made out to be an island. Since this was St. John the Baptist Day, Cabot decided to name the island St. John's.

But as they drew closer to the rocky mainland, a question remained. Where could they land? There was too much ice in the area, and the rugged coastline spreading out before them seemed bleak and forbidding.

"Too many reefs and shoals," Cabot remarked, and then he ordered the helmsmen to steer south. As they cruised along the heavily forested land mass, Cabot ordered the crew to lower sail and ready the anchor. Approaching a likely harbor, Cabot called to the leadsman in the bow to cast off the dipsy lead—a weighted line for taking a measurement of the sea's depth. "By the mark, eighty!" shouted

the leadsman—meaning that there were eighty fathoms of water, about 240 feet, beneath the ship.

That was more than enough for the *Matthew,* and Cabot ordered the helmsman to steer into the cove. Soon the little ship was gently swaying at anchor.

"Strange that there are no other ships about," the older Cabot mused. "No welcoming procession from the Khan. Surely we must have been observed."

"We may have arrived at some remote corner of Cathay," remarked Hugh Elliott. "Perhaps unknown even to the people of this region."

"You may be right," said Cabot. "Well, we'll soon find out. But first, let's get cleaned up. We don't want the Great Khan to think we're a bunch of savages."

The ship's master put on a fine velvet doublet and a clean shirt and hose. Then he ordered Antonio the barber to cut his hair and trim his long beard. When the barbering was done, Cabot ordered the ship's longboat lowered. A dozen of them, including Sebastian, piled in and rowed to shore.

Once on land, Cabot formed them into a procession. At the head marched a ship's boy carrying a cross. Behind came the two Cabots, Hugh Elliott and eight seamen. As a precaution, the sailors were armed with pikes, crossbows and swords.

They advanced inland, through dense woodlands. Cabot called a halt in a small clearing. Then he had two flags unfurled, one bearing the cross of St. George of England and another with the lion of St. Mark—the symbol of the Italian city of Venice. A prayer was said as the cross was planted and John Cabot announced in a loud voice, "I claim this new found land in the name of King Henry of England." Only a few birds chirped in response.

When the ceremony was over, the little group explored the immediate area. Following a narrow trail they came upon what appeared to be a campsite. There they found fishing nets. Sebastian picked up a painted stick and a needle that might have been used to make the nets and gave them to his father. But there were no people to be seen.

Looking around at the gloomy forest, Sebastian felt a slight shudder of fear. The place was spooky; mosquitoes swarmed around them. What were those shadows in the trees? Perhaps they were being watched even at that moment by hostile natives waiting for a chance to pounce on them.

Apparently, his father had similar feelings. Gathering his small band, he ordered them to return to where they had beached their longboat. Soon they were back on board the *Matthew*.

Hoisting anchor, Cabot directed the *Matthew* to sail southward. For the next few weeks, the small band of seafarers coasted the length of the new found land, hoping to find settlements or some other sign of life. Several times they saw shadowy figures moving through the thick forests that crowned the rugged cliffs lining the shore. But there was no sure way of knowing whether these were humans or animals.

By sailing close to the land, they were able to see what appeared to be cultivated fields that might be on the outskirts of villages. Because he had so few men and weapons, Cabot decided to make no further landings. But what they did find were waters teeming with fish. They were there for the taking—cod, haddock, and many other types. Sebastian and his fellow crewmen spent many pleasant hours casting nets and baskets weighted with stones, then hauling them up overflowing with squirming fish. Here were the fisheries the Bristol men had long been searching for.

Finally, after three weeks of prowling the coast, the *Matthew* returned to its original landing point. There, one day in late July, Cabot stood on the sterncastle deck with his son and Hugh Elliott and pondered the situation.

Stroking his beard, his dark eyes focused on a distant chain of mountains, Cabot remarked, "I'm sure we have reached the northeastern corner of Cathay, though I am mystified at not having found port cities—or any people to greet us. It troubles me."

Hugh Elliott tried to cheer up the ship's master. "Don't be so glum, Master Cabot. Perhaps what we have explored is merely a remote outlying island. But be of good cheer for what we have found. These wonderful fishing grounds—and great forests with trees enough to build thousands of ships. My Bristol friends will be most pleased."

"Yes, Father," Sebastian chimed in. "And next time we'll come back with more ships and make even more wonderful discoveries."

John Cabot's face broke into a big smile, and he placed an arm around his son's shoulder. "Yes, Sebastian, of course. This is only the beginning. Tomorrow we sail for England to tell everyone of these new lands."

The three of them stood together watching the sun, now a dazzling red ball, slowly descend beyond the western horizon of the mysterious land they had discovered.

EPILOGUE

The *Matthew* returned to Bristol on August 6, and Cabot went immediately to London to report his findings to King Henry, giving him a colorful account of the voyage. The nets and the needle they had found were displayed as evidence, and Cabot described the woodlands and fisheries along the coast.

Pleased by the report, King Henry gave John Cabot a cash reward and promised that he would give support for another voyage. Word of Cabot's discoveries spread quickly throughout London and the explorer became an instant celebrity. "He is called the Great Admiral," a foreign observer recorded, "and vast honor is paid to him and he goes dressed in silk, and these English run after him like mad."

The following year, in May 1498, Cabot sailed again from Bristol. Now he was the admiral of a fleet of five ships. This voyage ended in disaster, and no more was heard from John Cabot. However, his son Sebastian carried on in his father's footsteps, making his own voyages to North and South America in search of a shortcut to Asia. Unable to find such a sea lane, Sebastian later became the head of an English company that opened up trade between England and Russia.

Although the Cabots failed in their efforts to find a direct sea route to Asia, their voyages played an important role in opening up the New World to exploration and settlement by Europeans. So it might be fairly said that John Cabot hadn't failed after all; he had actually succeeded beyond his wildest dreams. When he came ashore on that June morning in the year 1497, he laid the foundation for the future English-speaking countries of North America—Canada and the United States.

HENRY I. KURTZ
Author, *John and Sebastian Cabot*

LOOKING AT BOOKS

From a medieval Jewish folktale to a thoroughly modern story about a boy caught up in a video game, books kept kids turning pages in 1997. Picture books, fantasy, fiction based on real-life problems, science, history, biography—there was something for everyone on bookstore and library shelves.

AWARD-WINNING BOOKS

David Wisniewski's *Golem* is based on a story that's been told for generations. This supernatural tale is set in the Czechoslovakian city of Prague, some 400 years ago. There, the story goes, a rabbi named Judah Loew prays for a way to protect the Jews from violence and hatred. The answer comes to him in a vision: the Golem, a giant made of clay and given life by mystical spells. Rabbi Loew creates the Golem—and then struggles to

control it. Wisniewski's version of this folktale brings the monster to life in intricate papercut illustrations. It won the 1997 Randolph Caldecott Medal, awarded to the best American picture book for children.

To compete in the Academic Bowl, you'd expect to study hard. But the four sixth-graders who are picked for the Academic Bowl team in E. L. Konigsburg's novel *The View from Saturday* learn more from each other than from their books. Even their teacher, who is confined to a wheelchair after an accident, gains new understanding as the team works toward the state championship. This book won the 1997 John Newbery Medal as the most distinguished work of American literature for young people. It was the second Newbery for Konigsburg, who won in 1968 for *From the Mixed-Up Files of Mrs. Basil E. Frankweiler*.

In Canada, the Governor General's award for illustration in an English-language chil-

dren's book went to Eric Beddows for *The Rooster's Gift*. In this story by Pam Conrad, a rooster believes he makes the sun rise by crowing at dawn. But one day he doesn't crow—and the sun comes up anyway. What, he wonders, is his gift? Beddows' detailed illustrations capture the folksy charm of the barnyard.

The Governor General's award for English-language text went to Paul Yee, for *Ghost Train*. This bittersweet story is set in California in the 1800s, when Chinese workers were building railroads in the West. Choon-yi, the 14-year-old daughter of one worker,

A book from Japan won the 1997 Batchelder Award, given to the best foreign children's book translated for publication in the United States. *The Friends,* written by Kazumi Yumoto and translated by Cathy Hirano, is about three sixth-graders who spy on an elderly neighbor. They expect him to die at any minute; instead, he becomes their friend.

PICTURE BOOKS

Drawings in misty shades of gray set the tone for *Night Driving*. In this story by John Coy, a father and son drive all night to reach

The Seasons Sewn: A Year in Patchwork (inset—Dolley Madison Star)

follows her father to America—only to find that he's been killed in a rock slide. But her father appears to her in a dream and asks her to paint a picture of "the train that runs on the road I built." Choon-yi's painting is the ghost train of the title, filled with the souls of workers who died building the railroad.

a mountain campground. They swap stories, play word games, and drink coffee to stay awake. Peter McCarty's illustrations add warmth by portraying cars, gas stations, and roadside restaurants of the 1940s.

In *The Seasons Sewn: A Year in Patch-work,* Ann Whitford Paul shows how traditional quilt patterns offer windows on America's early days. For example, the Dolley Madison Star recalls the wife of President James Madison. It was Dolley Madison who started the tradition of the White House egg roll at Easter. About two dozen other designs, each paired with a scene from the past, are portrayed in Michael McCurdy's scratchboard illustrations.

Alphabet books are always popular with young children, but David Pelletier's inventive book *The Graphic Alphabet* is clever enough to appeal to anyone. In this book, the letters portray the meanings of the words they represent. "A" stands for avalanche, and bits of the letter are sliding down its sloping sides. "B" is formed from a series of dots that bounce across the page. So it goes through "Y" (a gaping yawn) and "Z" (zigzag).

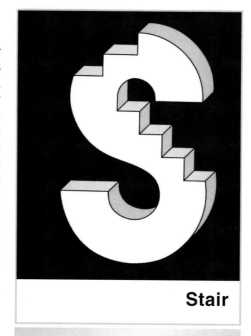

Stair

The Graphic Alphabet

Words and pictures practically pop off the page in *Power and Glory,* a picture book that has all the energy of the video game it's about. When a boy gets a new video game for his birthday, he immediately sits down to play it. The book follows his efforts to fend off video monsters—and interruptions from his family—and get to Level 2. Emily Rodda wrote the story. Geoff Kelly created the colorful illustrations, which point up comical similarities between the monsters in the game and the family members who interrupt it.

FOR MIDDLE AND OLDER READERS

At one time or another, most kids worry about being different. But Moql, the main character in Eloise McGraw's *The Moorchild,* really *is* different. She's half fairy and half human, and she doesn't fit in either world. The fairies switch Moql for a human infant, and she grows up as a changeling in a medieval village. Her memories of the fairy world, her new ties to the human world, and her struggle to find her proper place are the threads woven through this story.

Ruth White's *Belle Prater's Boy,* a novel for young adults, is built around a mystery: What happened to young Gypsy Leemaster's aunt, Belle Prater? She walked out of her house one day and was never seen again. But the heart of this story is the friendship that develops between Gypsy and Woodrow, Belle

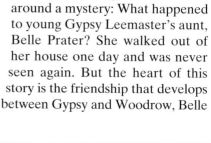

Power and Glory

The Rooster's Gift

Prater's son, who comes to live with her grandparents in Coal Station, Virginia.

Older readers who love fantasy reached for *The Golden Compass* by Philip Pullman. The first volume in a planned trilogy, it's set in a mythical world where people are paired with animals. When mysterious forces threaten this partnership, a young girl named Lyra sets out to stop them.

Beverley Naidoo's *No Turning Back* is set in the very real—and very rough—world of modern South Africa. Jabu, the hero, is a young runaway in Johannesburg. Along with other *malunde*—street kids—he lives hand to mouth, begging and doing odd jobs. His story is told against a backdrop of political turmoil, as black leaders finally come to power in this racially divided country.

Recent nonfiction books cover a wide range. In *Growing Up in Coal Country,* Susan Campbell Bartoletti uses first-hand accounts and photographs to show the harsh life led by children in Pennsylvania coal mining towns in the 1890s. *The Bone Detectives: How Foren-sic Anthropologists Solve Crimes and Uncover Mysteries of the Dead,* by Donna M. Jackson, explains how scientists help solve crimes with no more evidence than a skeleton.

Andrea D. Pinkney's lively biography *Bill Pickett: Rodeo-Ridin' Cowboy* tells the story of a famous African-American cowboy. Scratchboard pictures by Brian Pinkney illustrate the book. In a different mood, Russell Freedman chronicles the life of a great Native American leader in *The Life and Death of Crazy Horse.* Drawings by Amos Bad Heart Bull, a Sioux historian, add to this story.

Starry Messenger, a book depicting the life of the famous scientist, mathematician, astronomer, and philosopher Galileo Galilei, ranks as one of the most creative biographies of recent years. Using drawings, maps, time-lines, and samples of Galileo's writings, Peter Sis tells the story of a scientist as famous for his courage as for his discoveries. These books show that nonfiction can be every bit as exciting as fiction, and just as much fun to read.

301

After winning the Masters, Tiger Woods delivers his trademark victory gesture. Just 21 years old, he made golf history and became a sports superstar.

and he turned to deliver his trademark victory gesture—a sharp right uppercut. The crowd exploded with cheers.

Woods, 21, had just become the youngest person ever to win the Masters. And he set records doing it: His final score of 270 strokes for four rounds was the lowest in the history of the tournament, and his margin of victory—12 strokes—was the widest not only in the Masters but in any major American tournament. There was more: Woods, who is of mixed African and Thai heritage, was the first person of color to don the coveted green blazer that's awarded to the Masters champion each year.

Tiger Woods's Masters win made him the sports superstar of 1997. Other professional golfers described him as "phenomenal" and "the type of player that comes along once in a thousand years." His amazing talent was breathing new life into golf and drawing fans and players, especially young players, to the game. How did this young star accomplish so much, so soon? Tiger Woods wasn't born with a golf club in his hands. But he was learning how to hold one before his first birthday.

READ ALL ABOUT... TIGER WOODS

A solid wall of spectators packed the sloping lawns around the 18th green at Augusta National Golf Club on April 13, 1997. It was the final day of the Masters, one of professional golf's most demanding and prestigious tournaments, and all eyes were on the young golfer standing on the green—Tiger Woods. Tiger was one stroke away from making history, and he was perfectly focused on the job at hand. As his final putt dropped into the cup, a thousand-watt smile spread across his face,

A GOLF PRODIGY

In the 1960s, Tiger's dad, Earl Woods, served in Vietnam as a member of the Green Berets, the elite U.S. Army commandos. He was stationed in Thailand when he met Kultida Punsawad, a secretary at an army office there. Earl and Tida married and returned to the United States. On December 30, 1975, in Cypress, California, their only child was born. They named him Eldrick, but they called him by another name—Tiger, after a South Vietnamese army buddy who had fought side by side with Earl.

About this time, Earl left the army for a job in private industry. He also began to pursue a

Tiger's amazing talent was apparent—he was already collecting golf trophies—when he was 4 years old!

new hobby—golf. It wasn't long before Tiger showed an interest. When Earl hit practice balls into a net in the garage of the family's one-story home, he set up Tiger's high chair so that his son could watch. Pretty soon, Tiger was mimicking his dad's swing. When the boy was 11 months old, Earl cut down one of his clubs and gave it to him.

Some young people are prodigies—they show amazing talent in a certain field at a remarkably early age. There are chess prodigies, music prodigies, and math prodigies. Tiger turned out to be a golf prodigy. At age 2, he was featured on television, putting with comedian Bob Hope. Often, he'd call his father at work to ask if they could practice later in the day. He began to train with a professional at age 4, but his father remained his coach, too. They developed a close relationship.

Earl never pressured Tiger to practice. He made up games and contests to make sure that golf would be fun for the boy. But as Tiger grew older, Earl began to put his son through what he called the "Woods finishing school." He'd try to distract Tiger in the middle of a swing, dropping golf clubs and making noise, or tease and intimidate him with words. The goal was to teach him to stay focused on his game no matter what. Earl knew that Tiger would need that concentration to succeed in competition.

And Tiger did succeed in competition, right from the start. He won his first junior world title at age 8, in the 10-and-under division. By age 14, he had picked up five more junior world titles, along with many local championships. He enjoyed other sports, including basketball, but they took second place as he focused more and more on golf. In 1990, he played in a pro-junior event in Fort Worth, Texas, and outscored 18 of the 21 professionals. The next year, he won the U.S. Junior Amateur championship. He won that title again in 1992 and 1993. No one had ever won the junior championship three times before.

In 1994, Tiger graduated from high school—and from the junior division. That summer he faced his biggest competitive challenge yet: the U.S. Amateur championship. Playing against golfers who were much more experienced, he won the event, becoming the youngest amateur champion ever.

Tiger attended Stanford University on a golf scholarship, planning to major in economics. When he wasn't in class or studying, he was usually on the golf course, or hitting balls at the school's driving range. He defended his amateur title successfully in 1995 and 1996, winning the championship an unprecedented three times in a row. He also won the 1996 National Collegiate Athletic Association championship.

Between school terms, he had a chance to play as an amateur in some of the most famous tournaments in the world, including the Scottish Open and the British Open. Playing alongside top professionals helped

303

Tiger Woods is very close to both his parents. He considers his mother, Kultida (left), and his father, Earl (below), to be his biggest fans. And he credits much of his success to their support and encouragement. From the beginning, Earl often played golf with Tiger, and made sure that golf was fun for him. Poor health has kept Earl from attending many of his son's tournaments, but Kultida has been there at every hole. Speaking of his son, Earl has said: "The first priority was to raise a good person. Golf was a bonus."

him fine-tune his game. In fact, he finished tied for 22nd in the British Open in 1996—better than many of the pros.

ON THE PRO TOUR

That finish helped Tiger make a tough decision. In August 1996, he announced that he was leaving school and joining the ranks of professional golfers. Now he would be competing head to head with the best players in the world, vying for hundreds of thousands of dollars in prize money. He promised his parents that he would complete college at some point. But he felt that he was ready to take on the Professional Golfers Association (PGA) tour, and they supported his decision.

Tiger's amateur career had made him a star in the golf world, and his decision to turn pro made news. It also brought offers from companies that were eager to be associated with this rising young player. His good looks, winning smile, and confident, easy manner made him a natural choice to represent products. Before he played his first tournament as a pro, he had signed endorsement contracts that were said to be worth about $60 million.

Clearly, people expected a lot from Tiger. Could he live up to their expectations? The answer came a little over a month after he turned pro, when he won the Las Vegas Invitational. The victory occurred in a sudden-death playoff against Davis Love 3d, a top veteran player, and it qualified him to play in the Masters. In case anyone thought that win was a fluke, Tiger went on to capture two more tournaments before heading for Augusta, Georgia, in April 1997.

Just playing in the Masters is the dream of many golfers. For Tiger, the tournament had special significance. Traditionally, golf has been a game for the wealthy, played at expensive country clubs. And for years, blacks and other minorities were excluded from those clubs. They were more likely to learn the game as caddies—carrying clubs for members—than as players. Thus there have been few black touring golf pros. None was invited to the Masters until 1975, when Lee Elder qualified to play. Augusta National, the home of the event, didn't have a black member until 1990. When Tiger previously played there, as an amateur, he had received racist hate mail.

That history put a lot of pressure on Tiger—but it didn't seem to bother him. The night before his final round, he relaxed by playing video games and Ping-Pong. Then he got up the next morning and set records. Of his Masters victory, Tiger said, "I'm the first, but I wasn't the pioneer." Lee Elder and other black professional golfers had paved the way, he said. "If it wasn't for them, I might not have had a chance to play."

Tiger's caddie, Mike Cowan, and his coach, Bruce Harmon, also came in for thanks. The biggest thanks went to his father. Earl Woods had been ill with heart trouble and had undergone surgery not long before the Masters. But he made it to the course to see his son finish the tournament, and give him an enormous hug.

Winning the Masters clinched Tiger's superstar status. Wherever he played, mobs of spectators gathered. Sports writers wondered if he'd be the first to win all four tournaments in golf's Grand Slam—the Masters, the U.S. Open, the British Open, and the PGA Championship. "It can be done," Tiger said.

But it wasn't to happen in 1997. Tiger was exhausted by business meetings, photo

A golf whiz kid himself, Tiger set up a foundation to encourage other kids—especially minority kids—to take up the sport. Here he helps a youngster with his swing.

shoots, and personal appearances. He had no time to relax and hang out—to watch cartoons, ride a bike on the beach, or do other things he enjoyed. And his golf game suffered as a result. He finished 19th in the U.S. Open in June. Although he bounced back to win other tournaments later in the year, the rest of the Grand Slam events eluded him.

But this was just year one of Tiger Woods's professional career. He had already become the top-ranked golfer in the world, and the biggest money earner. And he was determined to stay on track. "I'm not going to be what some other people in my position have become: a prisoner of their fame," he said. He was also determined to build up the sport of golf. He established a foundation aimed at introducing golf to young people, especially in cities. He was active in another foundation that promoted golf among minorities. With a champion like Tiger Woods to look up to, kids everywhere may be picking up golf clubs.

Around the turn of the century, a journalist named Lyman Frank Baum set out to write a "modern" fairy tale. It would be, he said, a story with the "wonderment and joy" of traditional tales, but without the "heartache and nightmares." Baum's book became one of the most popular children's classics of all time: The Wonderful Wizard of Oz.

The story tells of a girl from Kansas named Dorothy, who, with her dog Toto, is transported by a cyclone to the fantasy land of Oz. (Baum is said to have taken the name from one of his file drawers, which was labeled O-Z.) Dorothy sets off down a yellow brick road to find the Wizard of Oz, who she is told has the power to send her home. She is soon joined by three new friends—the Scarecrow, the Tin Woodman, and the Cowardly Lion—who also believe that the wizard can grant their wishes. Along the way, they share many adventures.

The Wonderful Wizard of Oz was a best-seller from the day it appeared in May, 1900. L. Frank Baum wrote thirteen other Oz books, but the first is still best known. Just as famous as the book is the 1939 film The Wizard of Oz, with music by Harold Arlen. It starred Judy Garland as Dorothy, Ray Bolger as the Scarecrow, Jack Haley as the Tin Man, and Bert Lahr as the Lion.

Here's an excerpt from the book, telling how Dorothy meets her friends.

The Wizard of Oz

She bade her friends good-bye, and again started along the road of yellow brick. When she had gone several miles she thought she would stop to rest, and so climbed to the top of the fence beside the road and sat down. There was a great cornfield beyond the fence, and not far away she saw a Scarecrow, placed high on a pole to keep the birds from the ripe corn.

Dorothy leaned her chin upon her hand and gazed thoughtfully at the Scarecrow. Its head was a small sack stuffed with straw, with eyes, nose, and mouth painted on it to represent a face. An old, pointed blue hat was perched on his head, and the rest of the figure was a blue suit of clothes, worn and faded, which had also been stuffed with straw. On the feet were some old boots, such as every man wore in this country, and the figure was raised above the stalks of corn by means of the pole stuck up its back.

While Dorothy was looking earnestly into the queer, painted face of the Scarecrow, she was surprised to see one of the eyes slowly wink at her. She thought she must have been mistaken at first, for none of the scarecrows in Kansas ever wink; but presently the figure nodded its head to her in a friendly way. Then she climbed down from the fence and walked up to it, while Toto ran around the pole and barked.

"Good day," said the Scarecrow, in a rather husky voice.

"Did you speak?" asked the girl, in wonder.

"Certainly," answered the Scarecrow. "How do you do?"

"I'm pretty well, thank you," replied Dorothy politely. "How do *you* do?"

"I'm not feeling well," said the Scarecrow, with a smile, "for it is very tedious being perched up here night and day."

"Can't you get down?" asked Dorothy.

"No, for this pole is stuck up my back. If you will please take away the pole I shall be greatly obliged to you."

Dorothy reached up both arms and lifted the figure off the pole, for—being stuffed with straw—it was quite light.

"Thank you very much," said the Scarecrow, when he had been set down on the ground. "I feel like a new man."

Dorothy was puzzled at this, for it sounded queer to hear a stuffed man speak, and to see him bow and walk along beside her.

"Who are you?" asked the Scarecrow when he had stretched himself and yawned. "And where are you going?"

"My name is Dorothy," said the girl, "and I am going to the Emerald City, to ask the Great Oz to send me back to Kansas."

"Where is the Emerald City?" he inquired. "And who is Oz?"

"Why, don't you know?" she returned, in surprise.

"No, indeed. I don't know anything. You see, I am stuffed, so I have no brains at all," he answered sadly.

"Oh," said Dorothy, "I'm awfully sorry for you."

"Do you think," he asked, "if I go to the Emerald City with you, that Oz would give me some brains?"

"I cannot tell," she returned, "but you may come with me, if you like. If Oz will not give you any brains you will be no worse off than you are now."

"That is true," said the Scarecrow. "You see," he continued confidentially, "I don't mind my legs and arms and body being stuffed, because I cannot get hurt. If anyone treads on my toes or sticks a pin into me, it doesn't matter, for I can't feel it. But I do not want people to call me a fool, and if my head stays stuffed with straw instead of with brains, as yours is, how am I ever to know anything?"

"I understand how you feel," said the little girl, who was truly sorry for him. "If you will come with me I'll ask Oz to do all he can for you."

"Thank you," he answered gratefully.

They walked back to the road. Dorothy helped him over the fence, and they started along the path of yellow brick for the Emerald City.

Toto did not like this addition to the party at first. He smelled around the stuffed man as if he suspected there might be a nest of rats in the straw, and he often growled in an unfriendly way.

"Don't mind Toto," said Dorothy to her new friend. "He never bites."

"Oh, I'm not afraid," replied the Scarecrow. "He can't hurt the straw. Do let me carry that basket for you. I shall not mind it, for I can't get tired. I'll tell you a secret," he continued, as he walked along. "There is only one thing in the world I am afraid of."

"What is that?" asked Dorothy. "The farmer who made you?"

"No," answered the Scarecrow. "It's a lighted match."

After a few hours the road began to be rough, and the walking grew so difficult that the Scarecrow often stumbled over the yellow bricks, which were here very uneven. Sometimes, they were broken

or missing altogether, leaving holes that Toto jumped across and Dorothy walked around. As for the Scarecrow, having no brains, he walked straight ahead, and so stepped into the holes and fell at full length on the hard bricks. It never hurt him, however, and Dorothy would pick him up and set him upon his feet again, while he joined her in laughing merrily at his own mishap.

The farms were not nearly so well cared for here. There were fewer houses and fewer fruit trees, and the farther they went the more dismal and lonesome the country became.

At noon they sat down by the roadside, near a little brook, and Dorothy opened her basket and got out some bread. She offered a piece to the Scarecrow, but he refused.

"I am never hungry," he said, "and it is a lucky thing I am not, for my mouth is only painted. If I should cut a hole in it so I could eat, the straw I am stuffed with would come out, and that would spoil the shape of my head."

Dorothy saw at once that this was true, so she only nodded and went on eating her bread.

"Tell me something about yourself and the country you came from," said the Scarecrow, when she had finished her dinner. So she told him about Kansas, and how gray everything was there, and how the cyclone had carried her to this queer Land of Oz.

The Scarecrow listened carefully, and said, "I cannot understand why you should wish to leave this beautiful country and go back to the dry, gray place you call Kansas."

"That is because you have no brains," answered the girl.

"No matter how dreary and gray our homes are, we people of flesh and blood would

rather live there than in any other country, be it ever so beautiful. There is no place like home."

Toward evening they came to a great forest, where the trees grew so big and close together that their branches met over the road of yellow brick. It was almost dark under the trees, for the branches shut out the daylight; but the travelers did not stop, and went on into the forest.

"If this road goes in, it must come out," said the Scarecrow, "and as the Emerald City is at the other end of the road, we must go wherever it leads us."

"Anyone would know that," said Dorothy.

"Certainly; that is why I know it," returned the Scarecrow. "If it required brains to figure it out, I never should have said it."

After an hour or so the light faded away, and they found themselves stumbling along in the darkness. Dorothy could not see at all, but Toto could, for some dogs see very well in the dark; and the Scarecrow declared he could see as well as by day. So she took hold of his arm and managed to get along fairly well.

"If you see any house, or any place where we can pass the night," she said, "you must tell me; for it is very uncomfortable walking in the dark."

Soon after the Scarecrow stopped.

"I see a little cottage at the right of us," he said, "built of logs and branches. Shall we go there?"

"Yes, indeed," answered the child. "I am all tired out."

So the Scarecrow led her through the trees until they reached the cottage, and Dorothy entered and found a bed of dried leaves in one corner. She lay down, and with Toto beside her soon fell into a sound sleep. The Scarecrow, who was never tired, stood up in another corner and waited patiently until morning came.

When Dorothy awoke the sun was shining through the trees and Toto had long been out chasing birds. There was the Scarecrow, still standing patiently in his corner, waiting for her.

"We must go and search for water," she said to him.

"Why do you want water?" he asked.

"To wash my face clean after the dust of the road, and to drink, so the dry bread will not stick in my throat."

"It must be inconvenient to be made of flesh," said the Scarecrow thoughtfully, "for you must sleep and eat and drink. However, you have brains, and it is worth a lot of bother to be able to think properly."

They left the cottage and walked through the trees until they found a little spring of clear water, where Dorothy drank and bathed and ate her breakfast. She saw there was not much bread left in the basket, and the girl was thankful the Scarecrow did not have to eat anything.

When she had finished her meal, and was about to go back to the road of yellow brick, she was startled to hear a deep groan nearby.

"What was that?" she asked timidly.

"I cannot imagine," replied the Scarecrow. "But we can go and see."

Just then another groan reached their ears, and the sound seemed to come from behind them. They turned and walked through the forest a few steps, when Dorothy discovered something shining in a ray of sunshine that fell between the trees. She ran to the place and then stopped short, with a cry of surprise.

One of the big trees had been partly chopped through, and standing beside it, with an uplifted ax in his hands, was a man made entirely of tin. His head and arms and legs were jointed upon his body, but he stood perfectly motionless, as if he could not stir at all.

Dorothy looked at him in amazement, and so did the Scarecrow, while Toto barked sharply and made a snap at the tin legs, which hurt his teeth.

"Did you groan?" asked Dorothy.

"Yes," answered the tin man, "I did. I've been groaning for more than a year, and no one has ever come to help me."

"What can I do for you?" she inquired softly. For she was moved by the sad voice in which the man spoke.

"Get an oilcan and oil my joints," he answered. "They are rusted so badly that I cannot move them at all. If I am well oiled I shall soon be all right. You will find an oilcan in my cottage."

Dorothy at once ran back to the cottage and found the oilcan, and then she returned and asked anxiously, "Where are your joints?"

"Oil my neck, first," replied the Tin Woodman. So she oiled it, and as it was quite badly rusted the Scarecrow took hold of the tin head and moved it gently from side to side until it worked freely, and then the man could turn it himself.

"Now oil the joints in my arms," he said. And Dorothy oiled them and the Scarecrow bent them carefully until they were quite free from rust and as good as new.

The Tin Woodman gave a sigh of satisfaction and lowered his ax, which he leaned against the tree.

"This is a great comfort," he said. "I have been holding that ax in the air ever since I rusted, and I'm glad to be able to put it down at last. Now, if you will oil the joints of my legs, I shall be all right once more."

So they oiled his legs until he could move them freely; and he thanked them again and again for his release. For he seemed a very polite creature, and very grateful.

"I might have stood there always if you had not come along," he said; "so you have certainly saved my life. How did you happen to be here?"

"We are on our way to the Emerald City to see the Great Oz," she answered, "and we stopped at your cottage to pass the night."

"Why do you wish to see Oz?" he asked.

"I want him to send me back to Kansas. And the Scarecrow wants him to put a few brains into his head." she replied.

The Tin Woodman appeared to think deeply for a moment. Then he said: "Do you suppose Oz could give me a heart?"

"Why, I guess so," Dorothy answered. "It would be as easy as to give the Scarecrow brains."

"True," the Tin Woodman returned. "So, if you will allow me to join your party, I will also ask Oz to help me."

"Come along," said the Scarecrow heartily, and Dorothy added that she would be pleased to have his company. So the Tin Woodman shouldered his ax and they all passed through the forest until they came to the road that was paved with yellow brick.

The Tin Woodman had asked Dorothy to put the oilcan in her basket. "For," he said, "if I should get caught in the rain, and rust again, I would need the oilcan badly."

It was a bit of good luck to have their new comrade join the party, for soon after they had begun their journey again they came to a place where the trees and branches grew so thick over the road that the travelers could not pass. But the Tin Woodman set to work with his ax and chopped so well that soon he cleared a passage for the entire party.

Dorothy was thinking so earnestly as they walked along that she did not notice when the Scarecrow stumbled into a hole and rolled over to the side of the road. Indeed, he was obliged to call to her to help him up again.

"Why didn't you walk around the hole?" asked the Tin Woodman.

"I don't know enough," replied the Scarecrow cheerfully. "My head is stuffed with straw, you know, and that is why I am going to Oz to ask him for some brains."

"Oh, I see," said the Tin Woodman. "But, after all, brains are not the best things in the world."

"Have you any?" inquired the Scarecrow.

"No, my head is quite empty," answered the Woodman. "But once I had brains, and a heart also. So, having tried them both, I should much rather have a heart."

"All the same," said the Scarecrow, "I shall ask for brains instead of a heart; for a fool would not know what to do with a heart if he had one."

"I shall take the heart," returned the Tin Woodman; "for brains do not make one happy, and happiness is the best thing in the world."

Dorothy did not say anything, for she was puzzled to know which of her two friends was right, and she decided if she could only get back to Kansas and Aunt Em it did not matter so much whether the Woodman had no brains and the Scarecrow no heart.

What worried her most was that the bread was nearly gone and another meal for herself and Toto would empty the basket. To be sure, neither the Woodman nor the Scarecrow ever ate anything, but she was not made of tin or straw, and could not live unless she was fed.

All this time Dorothy and her companions had been walking through the thick woods. The road was still paved with yellow bricks, but these were much covered by dried branches and dead leaves from the trees, and the walking was not at all good.

There were few birds in this part of the forest, for birds love the open country where there is plenty of sunshine. But now and then there came a deep growl from some wild animal hidden among the trees. These sounds made the little girl's heart beat fast, for she did not know what made them: but Toto knew, and he walked close to Dorothy's side, and did not even bark in return.

"How long will it be," the child asked of the Tin Woodman, "before we are out of the forest?"

"I cannot tell," was the answer, "for I have never been to the Emerald City. But my father was there once, when I was a boy, and he said it was a long journey through a dangerous country, although nearer to the city where Oz dwells the country is beautiful. But I am not afraid so long as I have my oilcan, and nothing can hurt the Scarecrow, while you bear upon your forehead the mark of the Good Witch's kiss, and that will protect you from harm."

Just as he spoke there came from the forest a terrible roar, and the next moment a great Lion bounded into the road. With one blow of his paw he sent the Scarecrow spinning over and over to the edge of the road, and then he struck at the Tin Woodman with his sharp claws. But, to the Lion's surprise, he could make no impression on the tin, although the Woodman fell over in the road and lay still.

Little Toto ran barking toward the Lion, and the great beast had opened his mouth to bite the dog, when Dorothy, fearing Toto would be killed, rushed forward and slapped the Lion upon his nose as hard as she could, while she cried out: "Don't you dare to

bite Toto! You ought to be ashamed of yourself, a big beast like you, to bite a poor little dog."

"I didn't bite him," said the Lion, as he rubbed his nose with his paw where Dorothy had hit him.

"No, but you tried to," she retorted. "You are nothing but a big coward."

"I know it," said the Lion, hanging his head in shame. "I've always known it. But how can I help it?"

"I don't know, I'm sure. To think of your striking a stuffed man, like the poor Scarecrow."

"Is he stuffed?" asked the Lion in surprise, as he watched her pick up the Scarecrow and set him upon his feet, while she patted him into shape again.

"Of course he's stuffed," replied Dorothy, who was still angry.

"That's why he fell so easily," remarked the Lion. "It astonished me to see him whirl about so. Is the other one stuffed also?"

"No," said Dorothy, "he's made of tin." And she helped the Woodman up again.

"That's why he nearly blunted my claws," said the Lion. "When they scratched against the tin it made a cold shiver run down my back. What is that little animal you are so tender of?"

"He is my dog, Toto," answered Dorothy.

"Is he made of tin, or stuffed?" asked the Lion.

"Neither. He's a-a-a meat dog," said the girl.

"Oh! He's a curious animal and seems remarkably small, now that I look at him. No one would think of biting such a little thing except a coward like me," continued the Lion sadly.

"What makes you a coward?" asked Dorothy, looking at the great beast in wonder, for he was as big as a small horse.

"It's a mystery," replied the Lion. "I suppose I was born that way. All the other animals in the forest naturally expect me to be brave, for the Lion is everywhere thought to be the King of Beasts. I learned that if I roared very loudly every living thing was frightened and got out of my way. Whenever I've met a man I've been awfully scared. But I just roared at him, and he has always run away as fast as he could go. If the elephants and the tigers and the bears had ever tried to fight me, I should have run myself—I'm such a coward; but just as soon as they hear me roar they all try to get away from me, and of course I let them go."

"But that isn't right. The King of Beasts shouldn't be a coward," said the Scarecrow.

"I know it," returned the Lion, wiping a tear from his eye with the tip of his paw. "It is my great sorrow, and makes my life very unhappy. But whenever there is danger, my heart begins to beat fast."

"Perhaps you have heart disease," said the Tin Woodman.

"It may be," said the Lion.

"If you have," continued the Tin Woodman, "you ought to be glad, for it proves you have a heart. For my part, I have no heart, so I cannot have heart disease."

"Perhaps," said the Lion thoughtfully, "if I had no heart I should not be a coward."

"Have you brains?" asked the Scarecrow.

"I suppose so. I've never looked to see," replied the Lion.

"I am going to the Great Oz to ask him to give me some," remarked the Scarecrow, "for my head is stuffed with straw."

"And I am going to ask him to give me a heart," said the Woodman.

"And I am going to ask him to send Toto and me back to Kansas," added Dorothy.

"Do you think Oz could give me courage?" asked the Lion.

"Just as easily as he could give me brains," said the Scarecrow.

"Or give me a heart," said the Tin Woodman.

"Or send me back to Kansas," said Dorothy.

"Then, if you don't mind, I'll go with you," said the Lion, "for my life is simply unbearable without a bit of courage."

"You will be very welcome," answered Dorothy, "for you will help to keep away the other wild beasts. It seems to me they must be more cowardly than you are if they allow you to scare them so easily."

"They really are," said the Lion, "but that doesn't make me any braver, and as long as I know myself to be a coward I shall be unhappy."

So once more the little company set off upon the journey, the Lion walking with stately strides at Dorothy's side. Toto did not approve of this new comrade at first, for he could not forget how nearly he had been crushed between the Lion's great jaws. But after a time he became more at ease, and presently Toto and the Cowardly Lion had grown to be good friends.

THE NEW BOOK OF KNOWLEDGE
1998

The following articles are from the 1998 edition of
The New Book of Knowledge. They are included
here to help you keep your encyclopedia up to date.

SOUTH AMERICA

South America ranks fourth in area and fifth in population among the world's continents. One of the two continents of the Western Hemisphere, it is linked to North America by the Isthmus of Panama. South America is bounded by various bodies of water: the Caribbean Sea on the north, the Atlantic Ocean on the northeast and east, the Pacific Ocean on the west, and on the south, the Drake Passage, a strait connecting the two oceans.

On the map, South America looks roughly like an inverted triangle, with its broadest landmass in the north and tapering almost to a point in the south. At its widest, it measures about 3,200 miles (5,150 kilometers) from east to west. It extends some 4,600 miles (7,400 kilometers) from north to south.

South America has some of the most impressive geographical features of any continent. The Andes, which run its entire length, are the world's longest mountain chain; Aconcagua, in the Argentinean Andes, is the highest mountain in the Western Hemisphere. The Amazon, which empties into the Atlantic Ocean, is the world's largest river in volume of water flow, and its enormous drainage basin is covered by the world's most extensive area of rain forests. Angel Falls on the Churun River in Venezuela is the highest waterfall in the world, while Chile's Atacama Desert, where it has not rained for centuries, is considered the driest region on Earth.

South America is home to twelve independent countries, of which Brazil is by far the largest and most populous. Suriname is the smallest, both in area and population. South America also includes two nonindependent territories: French Guiana, an overseas department of France; and the Falkland Islands, a British crown colony.

The people are chiefly of Indian, Spanish, and Portuguese descent. But there are also significant numbers of South Americans of other European, African, and Asian origin as well as many of mixed ancestry. The Indians, the original inhabitants, were supplanted by the Spanish and Portuguese, who, beginning in the early 1500s, explored, conquered, and then colonized the region. Together with later settlers and immigrants, the three groups constitute the present-day population of the continent.

South America makes up most of the larger cultural region known as Latin America, which also includes Mexico, Central

America, and many of the islands of the Caribbean Sea. These three regions, although geographically part of North America, share a common heritage and historical experience with South America.

Some of the many aspects of South America:
Opposite page: A Peruvian funerary mask; a gaucho herding sheep on the Pampa, Argentina's most fertile region. *Above:* A Brazilian worker sifting coffee beans. *Left:* A vineyard in the Elqui River valley in north central Chile, which produces grapes for the nation's popular wines. *Below left:* The snow-covered Andes, one of the world's longest and highest mountain systems, tower above a crystal-clear lake in southern Argentina.
Below: A trail made by the Inca Indians high in the Peruvian Andes.

▶ THE LAND

South America can be divided into three main geographical regions: the Andes in the west; the Eastern Highlands in the east, which include the Brazilian and Guiana highlands; and a vast lowland in the interior that also contains a distinctive upland area, the Patagonian plateau, in the southeastern part of the continent.

Geographical Regions

The Andes occupy the entire western strip of South America. This mountain system stretches from Venezuela in the north to Tierra del Fuego at the continent's southern tip. The Andes are not one continuous mountain chain of geologically related rocks but, rather, a series of ranges with varied landforms. They reach their highest point at Argentina's Aconcagua, the highest mountain peak in the Western Hemisphere, which rises to 22,834 feet (6,960 meters).

The Andes drop abruptly toward the Pacific Ocean, leaving a very narrow coastal plain. Scattered throughout the mountains are valleys of various sizes, where most of the population is concentrated. Except for southern Chile, where numerous inlets make the coastline a maze of channels and islands, the Pacific coast is largely unindented. Historically, the Andes have tended to hinder transportation and communication between east and west, making the economic development and unity of the continent more difficult.

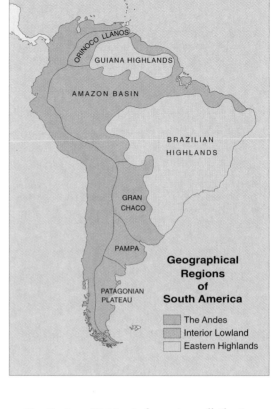

Geographical Regions of South America

- The Andes
- Interior Lowland
- Eastern Highlands

The Eastern Highlands have two distinct sections—the Brazilian Highlands and the Guiana Highlands.

The eroded, or worn-down, mountains of the Brazilian Highlands are the oldest part of the South American continent. Consisting mainly of gently rolling hills, with a few imposing plateaus, they extend southward from the Amazon River basin through a large area of Brazil, Uruguay, and parts of Paraguay and Bolivia. The highest elevation is in the Pico da Bandeira in eastern Brazil. At the Brazilian coastline (except in the northeast), the highlands break off abruptly into a series of steep cliffs called the Great Escarpment. The region has excellent farming and grazing land as well as a wealth of mineral resources.

The Guiana Highlands are a mixture of rounded hills, low mountains, plateaus, and narrow valleys. They stretch across the southeastern half of Venezuela into southern Guyana, Suriname, French Guiana, and

Venezuela. The region is known to have a variety of mineral deposits, but its natural resources are still largely undeveloped.

The Interior Lowland lies between the Andes and the Eastern Highlands. Within this great expanse are the Orinoco Llanos, the Amazon Basin, the Gran Chaco, the Pampa, and the Patagonian plateau.

The Orinoco Llanos is an area of rolling, grassy plains ("llanos" means "plains") situated in Colombia and Venezuela and watered by the Orinoco River.

Most of the Amazon Basin, the vast area drained by the Amazon River, is covered by dense rain forests. A narrow strip of this region extends eastward to the Atlantic, separating the Guiana and Brazilian highlands.

The Gran Chaco is a wild, sparsely settled plain consisting of scrub vegetation and grasses occupying parts of Bolivia, Paraguay, and northern Argentina. South of the Gran Chaco is the Pampa, or grasslands, of Uruguay and Argentina. This is one of the

Above: Glaciers such as this one abound in Argentina's south Patagonian Andes, a cold and remote region near the Chilean border.

Opposite page: A plateau between the peaks of the Andes of north central Ecuador provides rich agricultural land.

Right: The Atacama Desert in Chile is one of the driest places on earth, but it is rich in sodium nitrate and other minerals.

northeastern Brazil. Mount Roraima, on the border between Venezuela and Guyana, is the highest point. The land is covered by dense forests, with occasional small areas of savanna, or tropical grassland. Magnificent waterfalls tumble from the plateaus, among them Angel Falls, situated on the headwaters of the Caroní River in southeastern

most productive of the continent's agricultural regions.

The Patagonian plateau is situated south of the Pampa. Stretching from the Colorado River to the southern tip of the continent, it faces the eastern edge of the Andes. It consists mainly of high plateaus rising steeply from the Atlantic Ocean and cut by deep

COUNTRIES OF SOUTH AMERICA

COUNTRY	CAPITAL
Argentina	Buenos Aires
Bolivia	La Paz (administrative)
	Sucre (legal)
Brazil	Brasília
Chile	Santiago
Colombia	Bogotá
Ecuador	Quito
Guyana	Georgetown
Paraguay	Asunción
Peru	Lima
Suriname	Paramaribo
Uruguay	Montevideo
Venezuela	Caracas

NONINDEPENDENT TERRITORIES OF SOUTH AMERICA

TERRITORY	STATUS
Falkland Islands (Islas Malvinas)	British dependency; claimed by Argentina
French Guiana	Overseas department of France

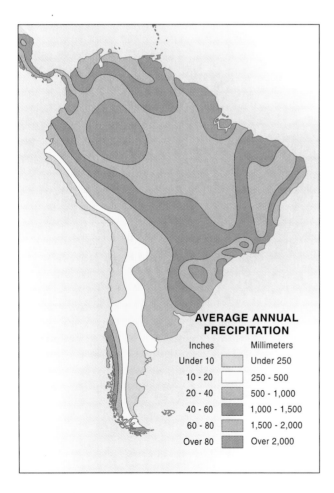

AVERAGE ANNUAL PRECIPITATION

Inches	Millimeters
Under 10	Under 250
10 - 20	250 - 500
20 - 40	500 - 1,000
40 - 60	1,000 - 1,500
60 - 80	1,500 - 2,000
Over 80	Over 2,000

INDEX TO SOUTH AMERICA PHYSICAL MAP

South America

	A	90°W
	B	80°W
	C	70°W
	D	60°W
	E	50°W
	F	40°W
	G	

North America

CARIBBEAN SEA

NORTH ATLANTIC OCEAN

20°N

10°N — 1 — 10°N

La Columna ▲ **VENEZUELA**

MALPELO ISLAND *(Col.)*

Angel Falls

Mt. Roraima ▲ **GUYANA**

SURINAME **FRENCH GUIANA** *(Fr.)*

COLOMBIA

LLANOS

GUIANA HIGHLANDS

ORINOCO

Orinoco R.

Magdalena R.

2 — Equator — Rio Negro — Amazon R. — MARAJÓ ISLAND — Equator — 2 — 0°

0° — Japurá R.

ECUADOR

Chimborazo ▲

GALÁPAGOS ISLANDS *(Ecu.)*

AGUJA POINT

CAPE SÃO ROQUE

A M A Z O N

B A S I N

Amazon R.

Marañón R.

Juruá R.

Purus R.

Madeira R.

Tapajós R.

Xingu R.

Parnaíba R.

CAATINGAS

Ucayali R.

3 — Huascarán ▲ — **BRAZIL** — 3 — 10°S

P E R U

Paulo Afonso Falls

São Francisco R.

Tocantins R.

Lake Titicaca

Illampu ▲

BRAZILIAN HIGHLANDS

PACIFIC OCEAN

4 — **B O L I V I A** — MATO GROSSO — 4 — 20°W

Lake Poopó

Três Marias Res.

ATACAMA DESERT

Paraguay R.

CHACO

Pico da Bandeira ▲

Furnas Res.

Tropic of Capricorn — 20°S

5 — Tropic of Capricorn — 5

SAN FÉLIX ISLAND *(Chile)*

SAN AMBROSIO ISLAND *(Chile)*

GRAN

Pilcomayo R.

PARAGUAY

Paraná R.

CAMPOS

Iguazú Falls

Río Salado

SOUTH ATLANTIC OCEAN

CHILE

Uruguay R.

6 — Aconcagua ▲ — 30°S — 6

JUAN FERNÁNDEZ ISLANDS *(Chile)*

Paraná R.

URUGUAY

ARGENTINA

Río de la Plata

A N D E S

PAMPA

Río Colorado

	Tropical Rain Forest
	Coniferous/Evergreen Forest
	Deciduous Forest
	Chaparral
	Grassland
	Desert and Semidesert
	Alpine Tundra
	Ice Sheet

7 — CHILOÉ ISLAND — Chubut R. — VALDÉS PENINSULA — 40°S — 7

North

TAITAO PENINSULA

Cerro San Valentín ▲

PATAGONIAN PLATEAU

8 — Strait of Magellan — FALKLAND ISLANDS *(Brit.)* — 8

TIERRA DEL FUEGO

CAPE HORN

SOUTH GEORGIA *(Brit.)*

0 500 1000 mi
0 500 1000 km

Azimuthal Equal-area Projection

	A	B	C	D	E	F	G
110°W	100°W	90°W	80°W	70°W	60°W	50°W	40°W	30°W	20°W	10°W

canyons. An arid, cool, and windswept region, with only limited vegetation, it is subject to frequent storms the year round. It makes up approximately one-quarter of Argentina's total land area.

Rivers and Lakes

The interior lowland is drained by three great river systems, the largest of which is the Amazon. Second in importance is the Río de la Plata. The third main river system is the Orinoco.

The Amazon. The Amazon is exceeded in length only by the Nile in Africa. It carries more water than any other river in the world, draining an area nearly as large as Australia. Originating high in the Peruvian Andes and fed by hundreds of tributary rivers in six countries, it crosses the widest part of South America before emptying into the Atlantic off northeastern Brazil.

Río de la Plata. The Río de la Plata is formed by the Paraná and its principal tributaries, the Paraguay and Uruguay rivers. It is South America's most important inland waterway. The Paraná rises in the highlands of

With a total drop of 3,212 feet (979 meters), Angel Falls in Venezuela is the world's highest waterfall.

southeastern Brazil and flows in a generally southerly direction along the eastern border of Paraguay. It then crosses into Argentina, where the Uruguay joins it to form the Río de la Plata estuary on the Atlantic between Uruguay and Argentina.

The Orinoco. From its headwaters in the Guiana Highlands, the Orinoco River flows northeastward through Venezuela to the Atlantic Ocean. More than half of the Orinoco is navigable by fairly large ships. A small stream called the Casiquiare links the Orinoco to the Amazon by way of the Río Negro.

Other Major Waterways. The Magdalena is the principal river of Colombia and its chief artery of trade. Together with its main tributary, the Cauca, it flows northward through Colombia's Andean ranges to the Caribbean Sea.

The São Francisco is the main waterway leading to the interior of eastern Brazil. It rises in the Brazilian Highlands and flows in a northeasterly direction, parallel to the coast, before turning abruptly on its journey east to the Atlantic Ocean. Navigation along its route is interrupted by the Paulo Afonso Falls.

A village floating on reeds on Lake Titicaca. Situated in the Andes on the Bolivia-Peru border, Titicaca is South America's largest lake and the world's highest navigable body of water.

Lakes. South America has relatively few lakes. The largest, Lake Maracaibo, is situated on the continent's northern coast, in western Venezuela. The Maracaibo basin is one of the major oil-producing regions. Lake Titicaca, which forms part of the border between Peru and Bolivia, in the Andean region, is the world's highest navigable body of water. Nearby is the much smaller Lake Poopó, about half Titicaca's size. Lagoa dos Patos, in southern Brazil, is actually an arm of the Atlantic Ocean. A low peninsula separates it from the open sea.

Islands

Aside from Tierra del Fuego in the far south and along the heavily indented southern coast of Chile, South America has few significant islands. Some of the more important ones are described below.

The Juan Fernández Islands, lying off the central Chilean coast, are of interest chiefly because of their association with the story of Robinson Crusoe. A Scottish seaman,

Alexander Selkirk, shipwrecked there in the early 1700s, became the model for the fictional Crusoe. The main island is now called Robinson Crusoe. (Chile also governs Easter Island, far out in the South Pacific, but it is not considered a part of the continent.)

The Galápagos Islands, situated about 600 miles (965 kilometers) off the coast of Ecuador, are famous for their distinctive animal life, which includes the giant Galápagos tortoise. The Caribbean island of Margarita is an integral part of Venezuela. The Falkland Islands in the South Atlantic, although under British rule, were long claimed by Argentina, which calls them Islas Malvinas. The Falklands were the site of a brief war between Britain and Argentina in 1982.

Climate

South America has varied types of climate. These are influenced by such factors as elevation, distance from the equator, winds and currents, and nearness to the surrounding oceans and seas.

South America does not have the extremes of temperature found in North America. Its great northern bulge lies on or near the equator, giving this large area of the continent a tropical climate, except in the higher elevations of the Andes. The Amazon Basin, Guiana Highlands, much of the Brazilian Highlands, and some coastal areas are hot and humid the year round, with heavy rainfall and temperatures averaging about 80°F (27°C).

Much of the narrower, southern half of the continent has more distinct winter and summer seasons, although winters are generally mild. Since the region is south of the equator, the seasons are reversed, with winter falling between June and August and summer between December and February. A Mediterranean type of climate is found in central Chile and parts of Argentina, which benefit from the moderating influences of the surrounding oceans.

An aerial view of the lower Amazon River floodplain. The Amazon, the second longest river in the world after the Nile, is South America's most important river.

Because of their great height, the Andes act as a climatic barrier, blocking the passage of moisture-laden winds from the east and contributing to the semi-arid and desert conditions of the Peruvian coast and northern Chile. The coldest regions of South America are in Tierra del Fuego and the Andes, where temperatures can fall below 32°F (0°C). Some of the highest temperatures occur in the Gran Chaco, with readings well above 100°F (38°C) common in summer.

Except for the arid regions, rainfall is generally plentiful or adequate throughout most of the continent. Some tropical areas have separate wet and dry seasons. Snow falls mainly in the higher Andes, where many of the peaks are permanently snow covered.

Natural Resources

South America's considerable natural resources include areas of good soil, abundant deposits of many minerals, and a great diversity of plant and animal life.

Soils. The continent has two main types of fertile soils. One is alluvial, or soil deposited by rivers, found in the floodplains of the rivers. The other is the grassland soil found in the Pampa of Argentina and similar areas of Uruguay. Soils of the desert areas can also be made to produce crops if irrigated. The least fertile are mountain soils, which are too thin and stony, and soils of the tropical forests, whose nutrients have been washed away by the heavy rainfall.

Vegetation. More than 40 percent of South America is forested. Most of this consists of tropical rain forest, or selva, occupying the Amazon Basin, parts of the Guiana and Brazilian highlands, and the Pacific coast of Colombia. Among the numerous varieties of trees found here are mahogany, rosewood, Brazil nut, wild rubber, palm, and cacao. Plants and tropical flowers, including many kinds of orchids and giant water lilies, grow in profusion. Tropical thorn trees and other scrub vegetation cover much of the Gran Chaco. Small areas of evergreen forest are found in southern Brazil and central Chile.

The extraordinary diversity of the Amazonian selva is now threatened by deforesta-

The llama (*top*) and the vicuña (*right*), both relatives of the camel, are used as beasts of burden in many areas of South America, especially in the Andean region. The red howler monkey (*above*) inhabits the Orinoco River basin of Venezuela. Orchids (*above right*) grow in profusion in the rain forests of northern South America.

tion. This is due to a number of factors, including increased road building, logging, and the growth of new settlements.

About 30 percent of the continent consists of grasslands. The tropical grassy plains, or savanna, that cover parts of Venezuela and Colombia and much of the Brazilian Highlands are most suitable for grazing cattle. The temperate grasslands of the Pampa of Uruguay and eastern Argentina are utilized

The jaguar (*above*), a threatened species, inhabits the forests and grasslands of South America. The anaconda (*right*), a water snake that can grow to a length of 25 feet (7.6 meters), has just made a meal of a caiman, a small alligator-like reptile.

for farming as well as cattle raising.

Animal Life. South America's wild animal life is as varied as the continent itself. The larger mammals include great cats such as the jaguar and mountain lion and the smaller ocelot. The sure-footed llama, alpaca, guanaco, and vicuña—all relatives of the camel—have traditionally been used as pack animals in the high Andes and are also prized for their fine wool.

Other distinctive forms of wildlife are the capybara, the world's largest rodent, which may exceed 100 pounds (45 kilograms) in weight; the piglike peccary; the vampire bat; the howler monkey; the giant armadillo; and the anaconda, a water snake that can reach a length of 25 feet (7.6 meters).

South America is also home to many unusual species of fish. These include the voracious piranha, which feeds in schools that can devour large prey in minutes; the electric eel; and the air-breathing lungfish.

South America is thought to have more species of birds than any other continent. The rain forests are home to tiny, jewel-like hummingbirds and various kinds of vividly colored parrots, macaws, and large-beaked toucans. Larger birds include the rhea, a kind of ostrich, which inhabits the savannas; the harpy eagle, which is large enough to prey on monkeys; and the Andean condor, the largest of its kind, with a wingspan of some 10 feet (3 meters).

Minerals. South America has abundant deposits of many kinds of minerals, although these resources are not distributed evenly across the continent. The regions richest in mineral production are in the Eastern Highlands, parts of the Andes, and northwestern Venezuela.

The faces of South America reflect its people's Indian, African, and European ancestry. *Clockwise from top left:* A young gaucho, or cowboy, on Argentina's Pampa; schoolgirls on a park bench; girls in costume for the pre-Lent Carnival in Rio de Janeiro, Brazil; young people in the traditional dress of their ancestors, the Incas, who had a powerful empire long before the arrival of Europeans; an Amazonian Indian from north central Brazil.

suitable for extensive human settlement because they are very densely forested, extremely mountainous, or too barren for cultivation. Like its mineral resources, the continent's population tends to be very unevenly distributed.

Distribution and Growth

The great majority of the people live along the fringes of the continent, often on the

Brazil is the world's second largest producer of iron ore, after China, and Chile ranks as one of the world's two leading copper-mining countries (the United States is the other). Bolivia is among the world leaders in tin production. Venezuela has South America's largest petroleum deposits and is a major oil exporter. Colombia has the continent's only sizable coal deposits. It produces much of its gold and is one of the world's chief sources of emeralds. Brazil is also a major producer of bauxite (aluminum ore) and manganese. Peru exports significant amounts of lead, zinc, and silver, while Chile has, in addition to copper, large deposits of sulfur and nitrates.

▶ **THE PEOPLE**

South America covers about 12 percent of the world's land surface but contains less than 6 percent of its people. Many areas of the continent are not

Left: Young Colombian girls enjoy a rainy day. *Above:* Brazilians turn out by the thousands to cheer on their favorite soccer team at Rio de Janeiro's Marracana Stadium. Soccer is South America's favorite sport.

coastal areas or within a relatively short distance from them. Much of the interior is sparsely inhabited. The most heavily populated region stretches along the Atlantic coast from Belém, near the mouth of the Amazon in Brazil, to Buenos Aires, on the Río de la Plata in Argentina. A second, smaller area of high population density extends from Bogotá, in Colombia, to the Pacific coast between Ecuador and central Peru. Population distribution has been strongly affected by growing urbanization, or the movement of people from the countryside to the cities.

Above: In Venezuela, a carnival spirit accompanies the celebration of the annual Feast of Corpus Christi, a Roman Catholic holiday. *Right: Christ the Redeemer*, a huge statue, overlooks Rio de Janeiro, Brazil.

South America's population is increasing rapidly, due to improved living conditions and a traditionally high birthrate. Its average population growth, about 1.8 percent a year, is second only to that of Africa. Growth rates for individual countries can vary widely, however, ranging from about 2.8 percent in Paraguay to less than 1 percent in Uruguay. More than one-third of the population is under 15 years of age.

Ethnicity

Most of South America's Indian population is concentrated in two distinct regions, the high Andes (particularly in such countries as Bolivia, Peru, and Ecuador) and the tropical rain forests. Argentina, central Chile, Uruguay, and southern Brazil have populations of predominantly European ancestry.

Blacks were originally brought to the continent as slaves during the early colonial period; their descendants now live chiefly in parts of Brazil and in northern coastal areas. South Americans of Asian origin include East Indians, who make up more than half the population of Guyana; Chinese, found mainly on the Pacific coast; and Japanese, who have settled largely in Brazil and Peru. There are also scattered communities of Syrians and Lebanese.

People of mixed race make up more than half of South America's population. The largest single ethnic group consists of mestizos (a Spanish term), who are of Indian and European ancestry. They are found in many parts of the continent but primarily in Venezuela, the Andean countries, and Paraguay.

Language and Religion

Spanish and Portuguese are the continent's dominant languages. Portuguese is the official language of Brazil, and Spanish that of most of the other countries. Numerous Indian languages are also spoken, and many Andean Indians know no Spanish, speaking only Quechua or Aymara. Bolivia, more than half of whose people are Indians, has made

Like other South American capitals, Buenos Aires has many beautiful public squares. Overlooking this square is the Palace of the National Congress, the seat of Argentina's two-chamber legislature.

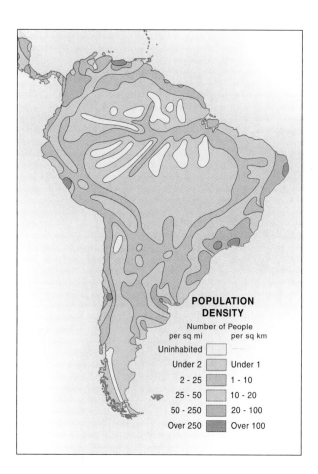

POPULATION DENSITY

Number of People

per sq mi	per sq km
Uninhabited	
Under 2	Under 1
2 - 25	1 - 10
25 - 50	10 - 20
50 - 250	20 - 100
Over 250	Over 100

INDEX TO SOUTH AMERICA POLITICAL MAP

★ Capital City

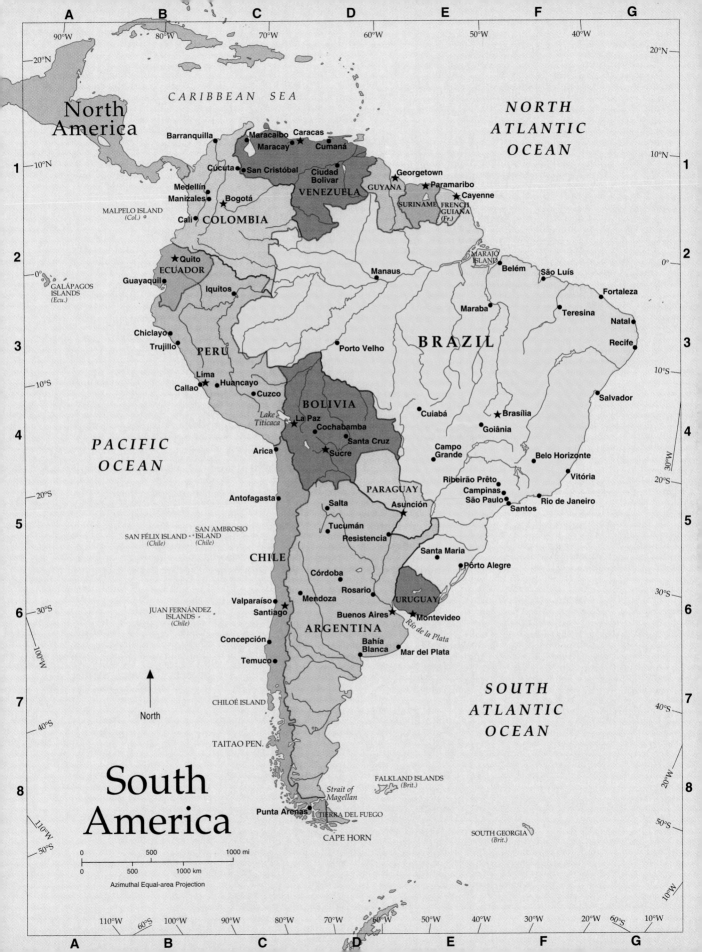

Quechua and Aymara official languages, along with Spanish. Aymara is one of the two official languages of Peru. In Paraguay the Guaraní Indian language is used by so many people that it is considered an official language.

Guyana, Suriname, and French Guiana differ from the rest of South America in that their official languages are English, Dutch, and French, respectively. Other languages spoken—including German, Italian, Polish, Hindi and other East Indian languages, Chinese, and Japanese—reflect the varied national origins of many South Americans.

Roman Catholicism was brought to South America by the Spanish and Portuguese and remains the religion of the great majority of the people. In some areas, particularly the central Andean highlands, the Indians combine Roman Catholicism with elements of their earlier, traditional religions. Some African religious practices and beliefs are followed in parts of Brazil, including the *macumba* ceremonies and other voodoo rites.

Protestantism came to South America with small groups of European Protestant immigrants and missionaries from the United States, but its influence is relatively slight. Argentina has the continent's largest Jewish community. Most South Americans of Chinese ancestry are Buddhists, and those of East Indian descent are either Hindus or Muslims.

Education

All South American countries provide free public education. In addition, there are numerous private schools, many of them church sponsored. Education levels vary widely, however, from country to country and between rural areas and the cities. The literacy rate, or percentage of people able to read and write, ranges from a high of more than 96 percent in Guyana to about 78 percent in Bolivia.

There are numerous universities, in addition to colleges and techni-

The increasing movement of rural people to such South American cities as São Paulo, Brazil (*above*), has been accompanied by the growth of slums, such as these (*left*) in Rio de Janeiro, Brazil.

cal schools. Some universities date from the first century of the colonial era. The oldest, the National University of San Marcos in Lima, Peru, was founded in 1551.

▶ CITIES

The rapid growth of South America's cities began in the second half of the 1900s, as increasing numbers of people arrived from the rural areas attracted by the possibility of a better life. Today, about 75 percent of the population is concentrated in and around the metropolitan areas of the major cities. Uruguay, Argentina, and Chile have the largest urban populations, while Guyana, Suriname, and Bolivia have the smallest. The inability of the cities to absorb all the newcomers, however, has resulted in severe overcrowding, the growth of slums and shantytowns, and problems of unemployment or underemployment.

South America's largest urban centers are São Paulo, Rio de Janeiro, Buenos Aires, Lima, Bogotá, and Santiago.

São Paulo, Brazil's most populous city and the center of its industry, is the largest city in South America and its fastest growing metropolitan area. Rio de Janeiro, Brazil's second largest city and chief port, is famed for its magnificent site on one of the world's most scenic harbors. Buenos Aires, Argentina's capital and chief port, is a cosmopolitan city reflecting its varied European heritage. Lima, Peru's capital and leading city, was founded in 1535 by Francisco Pizarro, conqueror of the Inca Indian empire. Bogotá, capital and chief city of Colombia, lies high in the Andes, more than 8,600 feet (2,600 meters) above sea level. Santiago, Chile's capital and commercial center, is situated in the heart of the country's wine-producing region.

▶ THE ECONOMY

Agriculture has long been the mainstay of South America's economy. Industrialization

toes, which can be grown in the harsh environment of the Andes. Major commercial crops include coffee, bananas, sugarcane, wheat, and cacao (or cocoa beans). Brazil is the world's leading exporter of coffee, followed by Colombia. Brazil and Ecuador are the continent's major exporters of bananas, and Brazil is also a world leader in the production of sugarcane and cacao. Argentina's Pampa and other regions produce enormous

The rain forests of the Amazon Basin are a source of valuable hardwoods. But the destruction of these forests through logging and other human activities poses a serious threat to the environment.

quantities of wheat, sorghum, and other grains, as well as flax, citrus fruits, potatoes, tea, and grapes.

Brazil and Argentina are the continent's major cattle-raising countries, particularly beef cattle. Argentina leads in sheep raising and wool production, with Uruguay second in importance.

Manufacturing

Manufacturing is concentrated mainly in and around the major cities. Brazil, Ar-

was relatively slow in developing, since, historically, the continent was viewed chiefly as a source of agricultural commodities and raw materials, particularly its minerals. Manufacturing has been steadily increasing in importance, however. Fishing and the processing of forest products are also significant economic activities in certain areas.

Agriculture

Only about one-third of South America's farmable land is currently under cultivation. Small areas of intensively farmed land are often separated by vast expanses of unused land. While commercial crops are usually grown on large estates or plantations, the bulk of the continent's agriculture consists of subsistence farming, that is, the cultivation of basic food crops, most frequently on small plots of land.

Corn, a staple of the diet for much of South America, is the most widely grown food crop. Rice is also cultivated, as are pota-

Corn, shown here being dried at a Bolivian farming settlement, is South America's most widely grown food crop and a staple of the diet for most South Americans.

gentina, and Chile are the most highly industrialized of the South American nations. Brazil, the continent's industrial giant, produces a variety of manufactured goods, including textiles, steel, processed foods, motor vehicles, aircraft, chemicals, and electronic equipment. Argentina's major industries are based chiefly on meatpacking and the manufacture of wool textiles and leather goods. Chile produces wood and wood products (including paper), transportation equipment and machinery, processed fish, and wines. Venezuela's economic development has centered around its large petroleum industry.

Mining, Fishing, and Forestry

Gold, silver, and gems were first mined by the Indians, and it was this evidence of the continent's great mineral wealth that attracted early European explorers and colonizers.

Manufacturing, including food and beverage processing, is increasingly important to the economies of South America. Chilean wines (*left*), Colombian steel (*right*), and Brazilian automobiles (*below*) are among the continent's products.

Fish are important both as a source of food and as an export. Peru and Chile have the continent's largest commercial fishing industries. Peru ranks as one of the world's leading fishing nations, its most valuable catches being anchovies and pilchards (sardines). Much of the catch is processed as fish meal, used in animal feed.

South America has few of the softwood forests necessary for the production of lumber. But the tropical rain forests are a source of valuable hardwoods, chiefly mahogany and rosewood, which are used to make fine furniture. Other important forest products include rubber, nuts, tannin (used in tanning leather), palm oil, waxes, and chicle (the base for chewing gum). Brazil is the leading exporter of forest products.

Trade

Although South America now exports increasing quantities of manufactured goods to foreign countries—particularly clothing and shoes—agricultural products and minerals are still its chief exports. The most important are petroleum, coffee, iron ore, soybeans, copper, beef, corn, bananas, and cacao. Manufactured goods, including machinery and transportation equipment, are among the major imports.

The United States and Western Europe are the continent's major trading partners. Efforts to increase trade among the South American countries led to the formation of the Latin American Free Trade Association (LAFTA) in 1960 and its successor, the Latin American Integration Association (LAIA), in 1980. Composed of ten South American nations (Suriname and Guyana have not joined) and Mexico, the association sought to gradually reduce tariffs, or import taxes, among the member countries and, eventually, to eliminate all trade barriers among them.

Transportation

Historically, transportation across the continent has been hampered by natural land barriers. Population centers developed chiefly along the coastal areas because of the difficulty in penetrating much of the interior. In the past, only the navigable waterways made it at all possible to reach many inland areas. Today, there are networks of roads and railways, with the most extensive transportation systems found in Brazil, Argentina, and Chile. Most South American countries have national airlines, and air service often provides the only access to some sites, particularly in the rugged Andes.

The Spaniard Francisco Pizarro meets with Atahualpa, leader of the Incas of Peru, in 1532. Pizarro, who later lured Atahualpa into an ambush and had him executed, completed the conquest of the Inca Empire in 1533.

▶ HISTORY

The first people in South America, the ancestors of the Indians, probably came from the continent of North America by way of Central America, whose narrow shape made it a natural land bridge. The early peoples engaged in hunting, food gathering, and primitive forms of agriculture.

Indian Civilization

A number of Indian civilizations existed in the region before the arrival of the Europeans. At the time of the Spanish conquest, the most highly developed was that of the Incas, who lived in the Andean highlands of what are now Peru and Bolivia. They had an elaborate system of roads and farmed their hilly land by terracing it and using a system of irrigation. The Incas ruled a vast empire stretching from southern Colombia to northern Chile and Argentina and unified it under one government and one language, Quechua, still spoken by their descendants.

Discovery and Conquest

The first-known European to reach South America was Christopher Columbus, who landed at the mouth of the Orinoco River on his third voyage of discovery, in 1498. Columbus's explorations established Spain's claims in the Western Hemisphere. Portuguese claims to Brazil were bolstered by Pedro Álvares Cabral's expedition to its coast in 1500. A year later the navigator and mapmaker Amerigo Vespucci (for whom the Americas were named) confirmed that South America was a distinct continent, not a part of Asia as was previously thought.

Exploration was followed by rapid conquest and colonization. The first permanent Spanish settlement on the continent, San Sebastián, was established in present-day Colombia by Alonzo de Ojeda in 1510. Spanish adventurers known as conquistadores, who were drawn to the region by the

The rich cultural heritage of early Indian civilizations can be seen in artifacts such as this stone figure from the San Agustín National Archaeological Park in Colombia.

lure of gold and silver, quickly overcame the native peoples. Although relatively few in number, the Europeans were better armed and equipped. In addition, the Indian rulers were often weakened by civil war.

In the 1530s, Peru, the heart of the Inca Empire, fell to a force of less than 200 men led by the conquistador Francisco Pizarro. Pizarro established a new capital, Lima, which became the center of Spain's South American empire.

Spanish colonial rule saw the introduction of Spanish culture. This palace in Lima, Peru, reflects Spain's Moorish architectural style.

Colonial Rule

The chief colonial official was the viceroy, who served as the monarch's personal representative. Eventually, Spanish South America was divided into three viceroyalties: Peru in the west (first established in 1544), New Granada in the north (founded in 1717), and La Plata in the south (founded 1776). Portugal's colony of Brazil was divided into northern and southern states in 1750 but was then reunited in 1775, with Rio de Janeiro as its capital.

Roman Catholic priests had arrived with the first colonists, to convert the Indians to Christianity. In addition to its religious activities, the church operated schools and hospitals, and it remained a powerful force both during and after the colonial era.

The production of minerals, chiefly gold and silver, was the main economic activity in the Spanish colonies. One-fifth of the wealth produced went to the monarch as the "royal fifth." Agriculture was based on Indian practices and improved upon by the Europeans, who introduced new crops and the large-scale cultivation of livestock. Indians worked in the mines and as farm laborers, often under harsh conditions.

Brazil's economy was at first based largely on agriculture. Sugarcane was the main commercial crop, produced by Indians and then by black slaves. Gold and diamonds were later discovered in the interior.

Revolution

Stirrings of discontent with colonial rule began in the late 1700s and increased in the early 1800s. The movements for independence in South America (similar movements arose in Mexico and Central America) were led chiefly by *criollos*, people of pure Spanish ancestry who had been born in the colonies. Well educated and often quite wealthy, the *criollos* resented the monopoly on high political office held by officials sent from Spain. Some were also influenced by the ideals of liberty represented by the recent American and French revolutions. The invasion of Spain by Napoleon I in 1807 and the overthrow of

IMPORTANT DATES

A.D. 300?–1000?	The Tiahuanaco, Mochica (early Chimu), and Nazca cultures flourished in Peru and Bolivia.
1100?–1525?	Inca Empire expanded to embrace lands and peoples extending from southern Colombia to northern Chile and Argentina.
1498	Christopher Columbus landed at the mouth of the Orinoco River on his third voyage of discovery.
1500	The Portuguese navigator Pedro Álvares Cabral reached the coast of Brazil.
1510	Alonzo de Ojeda founded the first permanent Spanish settlement at San Sebastián (in present-day Colombia).
1532–33	A Spanish force under Francisco Pizarro conquered Peru, center of the Inca Empire.
1544	Viceroyalty of Peru established.
1551	National University of San Marcos, first university in South America, founded in Lima, Peru.
1810	Independence movements against Spanish rule began in what are now Argentina, Colombia, and Venezuela.
1824	Final defeat of the Spanish armies in South America.
1830	Ten of the twelve present-day South American nations came into existence.
1865–70	War of the Triple Alliance pitted Paraguay against Argentina, Brazil, and Uruguay.
1879–84	Chile fought Bolivia and Peru in the War of the Pacific.
1890	The first meeting of the International Conference of American States was held, marking the beginning of the Pan American Union.
1932–35	Paraguay fought Bolivia in the Chaco War.
1933	The United States adopted the Good Neighbor Policy in its dealings with Latin America.
1948	Organization of American States (OAS) was chartered.
1960	Latin American Free Trade Association (LAFTA) was founded.
1966	Guyana (formerly British Guiana) became an independent nation.
1975	Suriname (formerly Dutch Guiana) became an independent nation.
1980	LAFTA was succeeded by the Latin American Integration Association (LAIA).
1982	Falkland Islands were invaded by Argentina but were recaptured by Britain after a brief war.
1994	The countries of the Western Hemisphere, meeting in the United States, agreed to create a free trade zone in the Americas.

the monarchy gave them their opportunity to revolt.

The leaders in the struggle for independence—including such figures as Simón Bolívar, José de San Martín, and Bernardo O'Higgins—suffered early defeats against Spanish troops before victory was finally achieved, in 1824. Only Brazil had no major war of liberation, winning independence from Portugal peacefully in 1822. By 1830, ten of the twelve present-day South American nations had come into being. Guyana (formerly British Guiana) gained independence in 1966, and Suriname (the former Dutch Guiana) did so in 1975.

Problems of Independence

The years following independence were difficult ones.

Unlike Brazil, which was a monarchy until 1889 and relatively stable, the new Spanish-speaking republics were frequently torn by political conflict. Typically, this pitted conservatives against liberals. The conservatives, who consisted mainly of the large landowners, favored a strong central government. The liberals, who were mainly from the cities, sought a more decentralized form of government and a reduction in the power and influence of the church. Unstable governments led to the rise of military rulers.

Relations among the South American countries themselves were often strained by

Simón Bolívar, "the Liberator," freed Venezuela, Colombia, Ecuador, Peru, and Bolivia from Spanish rule in the 1820s.

336

Argentina's President Juan Perón (1946-55, 1973-74) was one of the many South American leaders brought to power by military coups in the 1900s.

territorial and other disputes, which led to several long and bloody wars. Paraguay lost more than half its population in the War of the Triple Alliance (1865–70) against Argentina, Brazil, and Uruguay. Chile fought Bolivia and Peru in the War of the Pacific (1879–84). Paraguay again went to war, against Bolivia, in the Chaco War (1932–35).

The Modern Era

South America's economic development was spurred during the second half of the 1800s by the growth of overseas markets for its minerals and agricultural products. Immigration, chiefly from southern Europe, also increased. The outbreak of World War I in 1914 made the continent's raw materials even more important. Although the worldwide Great Depression of the 1930s brought on an economic crisis, conditions improved during the years of World War II (1939–45).

The postwar period was marked by the beginnings of industrialization, rapid urbanization, and increasing demands for economic and political reforms. With most South American countries dependent on exports of one or two basic commodities, a drop in world prices often caused the economy to falter. The resulting discontent led to the growth of revolutionary political movements. During the 1950s and 1960s, ineffective governments were often overthrown by the military. A pattern of military regimes alternating with civilian rule lasted until the early 1990s, when democratically elected governments were restored throughout the continent.

The Future

South America has a promising future but a number of problems to overcome. In con-trast to the early years of independence, the nations of the continent realize that cooperation is vital to all their interests, and many have banded together in regional pacts. In addition to the Latin American Integration Association, these include the Organization of American States (OAS), the Amazon Treaty of Co-Operation, and the Andean Common Market.

The continent's continuing problems include the rapidly growing population; poverty within the Indian, rural, and unemployed urban populations; and a shortage of teachers and educational facilities in many areas. Furthermore, there is a stag-

Peru's President Alberto Fujimori was popular for his fight against terrorism, the bane of several South American nations in the latter part of the 1900s.

gering burden of foreign debt owed by many countries of the region, which has forced their governments to adopt austerity measures that limit efforts at social and economic development.

KEMPTON E. WEBB
Columbia University
Author, *Latin America*

337

HUMAN BEINGS

Human beings are like no other creatures on Earth. Although we are mammals (animals with warm blood that feed their young with mother's milk), we live differently from all other mammals. We have elaborate language, in both spoken and written forms. Our language helps us conceive and communicate complex ideas. We have developed specialized tools that allow us to build complicated structures and machines. We plant crops and raise animals to feed ourselves. We have the ability to change our immediate environment, making it suitable for human habitation. And we can treat or cure many of the diseases that ail us.

The human brain, the most complex and highly developed of all brains, allows

A shared culture, or way of life, bonds human beings in the present, connects them to the past, and helps them imagine the future.

human beings to do these unique things. In fact, the scientific name for humans is *Homo sapiens*, which means "wise person."

The scientific grouping for human beings is in the order Primates, which includes apes, monkeys, and prosimians (such as lemurs and tarsiers). Our closest living relatives are chimpanzees and gorillas, although we are not directly descended from them.

The earliest human beings lived in Africa at least 2.5 million years ago. They had apelike faces, but they stood upright and had more humanlike teeth. They evolved, or changed over time, into the modern form that we know today.

▶ FEATURES OF HUMAN BEINGS

Several important features make us very different from other primates. We have a large brain relative to our body size. (An adult male gorilla weighing 500 pounds, or 225 kilograms, has a brain only about one-third as large as ours.) A spine that curves, especially in the lower back, places the human body's center of gravity directly above the

hips. This makes possible our upright posture and the ability to walk on two feet. This is called **bipedalism**. (Chimpanzees and gorillas can do this, but they prefer to move on all fours.) We are capable of speech and of using language. We have a unique dental structure (small canine teeth, but large rear teeth). Human hands are well proportioned for making and using tools. And we are able to modify our environment and to share knowledge as well as a cultural heritage.

Physical Traits. As a species, human beings exhibit a variety of body builds and skin pigmentations (coloring). Average male heights range from 5 feet 1 inch (155 centimeters) for some of the world's shortest male populations to 5 feet 11 inches (180 centimeters) for some of the world's tallest. Average female heights range from 4 feet 9 inches (145 centimeters) for some of the shortest female populations to 5 feet 6 inches (168 centimeters) for some of the tallest. Average weights for male populations range from 89 pounds (40 kilograms) to 170 pounds (77 kilograms), and average weights for female populations

338

range from 82 pounds (37 kilograms) to 158 pounds (71 kilograms).

Human skin color is also varied, ranging from pale pink to almost black. Hair color ranges from shades of blond or red to brown or black.

Human traits such as body build, skin pigmentation, and lung capacity have evolved to help people living in different parts of the world cope with heat, light, and oxygen levels in their environments. For example, the heavy pigmentation of dark-skinned people who live in the tropics provides protection from strong ultraviolet radiation from the sun, which can cause cancer.

Diet. The human body needs three main types of nutrients to survive: carbohydrates, proteins, and fats. These come from foods in our diet such as fruits and vegetables, grains, seeds, meat, eggs, and dairy products. Minerals and vitamins, which we need in small amounts, are also found in these foods.

Body Systems. Major organ systems in the human body include the respiratory system (lungs), nervous system (brain and spinal cord), circulatory system (heart and blood vessels), digestive system (stomach, liver, and intestines), and urinary system (kidneys and bladder). The skeletal and muscular systems support the body and allow it to move. The endocrine system produces hormones that act as chemical messengers in the body. The reproductive system allows us to produce offspring.

Life Cycle. Human beings are the slowest developing and longest lived of all primates. Each of the stages of the human life cycle is long. For example, humans have the longest gestation period (the time that a fetus develops in the mother's womb) among primates. We also become sexually mature and begin reproducing later than other primates, and we live longer.

Childhood is our most important period of development, as this is when we learn our social skills. Although the brain grows rapidly early in life, the body's growth slows during this time.

Human beings develop more slowly and live longer than any other primate. Parents play an important role in guiding their children's physical and social development.

After about a decade there is a noticeable growth spurt, marking adolescence and sexual maturity.

▶ HUMAN BEINGS IN GROUPS

An important, but not unique, feature of human beings is that they are social creatures. That is, they live together in groups. Most people feel a connection and sense of belonging to other individuals in their group. For example, family members often live together in the same household, raising children together and sharing resources such as food, money, and shelter.

People also share bonds of language and what is known as **culture**. Culture is a group's entire way of life. It includes many aspects of human activity, such as religious beliefs, laws, styles of clothing and jewelry, cooking practices, artistic expression (such as painting, sculpture, dance, and music), and recreation.

Culture distinguishes different groups of human beings around the world. For example, a teenager in India would eat different foods and wear different clothing than a teenager in South America. He or she would proba-

Compared with their primate relatives, human beings possess the greatest intelligence, the most elaborate language, and the most complex culture.

Religion is unique to human beings. This Muslim child learns the traditions of his religious culture, passed down from generation to generation, through observation and practice.

bly listen to different music and worship in a different way.

Is culture unique to human beings? Chimpanzees, which acquire information through social learning, have a simple culture. They make and use tools, share food, and cooperate in group activities, such as hunting. Like humans, they learn through observation, and they pass along from generation to generation their social traditions, such as special ways to crack open hard nuts using stones as hammers.

However, human culture is far more intricate and complex. People are unique not only in their speech and language skills, but in the ways in which they think about beliefs, emotions, and motives. We are keenly aware of ourselves and our thoughts. Human beings also have the capacity to imagine, to understand the past and think about the future, and to contemplate such things as our place in the

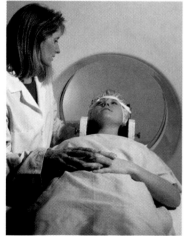

Only human beings can conceive of and create complicated devices like this computerized X-ray machine. Such tools help fulfill another uniquely human capability—treating and curing diseases.

universe. No single human being could ever invent or even fully experience his or her society's cultural traditions. A complex, changing culture distinguishes human beings from other animals.

Cultural changes and differences have been important sources of social richness and also of complex problems and conflicts. Throughout human history, wars have been fought not only over resources but also over religious differences and different ideas of laws and fair government.

▶ **HUMAN BEINGS AND THEIR ENVIRONMENT**

People today live in virtually every terrestrial (land) habitat on Earth, from equatorial rain forests to the driest deserts to arctic tundra. Our survival in these environments depends on our adaptability and our capacity, through teaching, to pass along knowledge from generation to generation.

Even in prehistoric times, early humans learned from each other how to control fire, build shelters, and make clothing. Later, they learned to grow crops and raise animals for food. The ability to share knowledge has contributed to the remarkable expansion of the human race around the world.

However, the success of human beings has produced some negative side effects. Our population growth and ability to change the environment around us has endangered or driven to extinction many plant and animal species. We have also overused or depleted many natural resources, and we have polluted the environment. People are trying to learn how to save endangered species and how best to replenish, recycle, and protect valuable natural resources. The survival of future generations of human beings depends on it.

LAURIE GODFREY
Department of Anthropology
University of Massachusetts

FAIRIES

"Fairy" is a general name for a variety of supernatural beings that appear in the legends of many of the world's peoples. They are said to inhabit a world, called Faerie, that exists alongside ours. Virtually all the world's folklore includes tales of these small, mischievous beings. The best-known stories are from the British Isles and Scandinavia; the fairies of these traditions are the focus of this article.

▶ KINDS OF FAIRIES

Fairies come in many different forms, ranging in appearance from the large, hairy *fenodyree* to the diminutive brownies and leprechauns. According to legend, there are two main kinds of fairies: solitary fairies, who live alone, and trooping fairies, who live in groups. While all fairies are said to resemble humans, it is the trooping fairies who are most humanlike in their appearance and way of life.

Brownies and Pixies. In English folklore, these creatures are usually described as small bearded men dressed in brown. They are helpful to farming people, often doing their chores, and may have a special relationship with one person on the farm. Some stories tell of people who dare to play tricks on brownies. This was not commonly done, however, because the brownie would then turn into a **boggart**, a creature that, if not quite evil, is very mischievous and certain to get its revenge. Or the boggart might simply leave the farm, taking the luck and prosperity of the family with it.

Leprechauns. Ireland's leprechaun is the fairy shoemaker. He is most often pictured as a small man in clothes and cap of bright green and red. The leprechaun typically has a treasure, which humans try to obtain by capturing him and forcing him to reveal its location. But the leprechaun usually has a way of foiling these attempts and keeping his riches.

Pooka (Puca). The pooka is a mischievous creature featured in the folklore of England, Ireland, and Wales. It likes to mislead travelers and play practical jokes. In its more demonic form, the pooka can appear as a horse that takes riders on wild rides, sometimes carrying them into a lake or river and drowning them. The most famous pooka is Robin Goodfellow, or Puck, a character in the play *A Midsummer Night's Dream*, by William Shakespeare. *Harvey*, a modern play and film, features a pooka in the form of a giant invisible rabbit.

Banshee. The banshee, from the Irish *bean sidhe* ("woman of the fairies") is a creature whose wail-

Shakespeare's comedy *A Midsummer Night's Dream* features fairy characters. Bottom, a human victim of fairy mischief, has his head changed into a donkey's.

In Irish folklore, the leprechaun is the fairy shoemaker. A wily creature, he usually foils human attempts to discover the location of his treasure.

Arabic tales such as those in the *Arabian Nights* tell of genies, powerful and often frightening spirits who, like fairies, may use their magic to help humans.

Genies. The genie, or, more correctly, jinn, of Arabic and Islamic folklore is a spirit much like the solitary fairies of Europe. Like them, genies are magically powerful and can be of great help to humans. In folktales a genie often appears as a magical helper for the hero, as in the story of Aladdin and the lamp. A genie may take the form of an animal—mistreating animals is therefore discouraged. Like European fairies, genies will sometimes take a human baby and leave one of their own in its place. It is possible for a human man to marry a female genie. But the man must keep his wife's true identity a secret, and their children will always belong to the mother.

Elves. The elves of Germany and Scandinavia are the most humanlike dwellers in Faerie. They resemble people in size and appearance, although they are usually far more beautiful. They are ruled by kings, go on hunts, and have wars. They are known for their music and dancing. In ancient Scandinavia, elves were sometimes divided into two kinds: light and dark (or white

ing cry foretells a death. In Ireland, banshees are associated with a particular family. When family members hear the banshee's wail, they know that a relative is about to die.

Fenodyree. The *fenodyree* is a kind of brownie from the Isle of Man in the Irish Sea. A friendly creature, the *fenodyree* is large, hairy, and very strong. According to one common story, it was cast out of Faerie for falling in love with a human girl. Like brownies, *fenodyrees* are helpful to farmhands and maidens and expect a portion of food and drink as a reward. If this is forgotten, a farmer might find his cattle untended or even that one has fallen and died. The *fenodyree* has a demonic form, called the *glashtin*, that is similar to the demonic form of the pooka.

and black). The light elves are creatures of the sky and forest and are friendly to humans. The dark elves are smaller than light elves and live underground. They sometimes cause harm to humans. Like the pixies and brownies of British tradition, the dark elves like clean places and often reward especially tidy servants.

Tuatha de Danann. The *Tuatha de Danann* ("people of Dana," an ancient Irish goddess) are the ancestors of the fairy folk of modern Ireland. They possess great learning as well as magical powers. Many years ago, they fought a great war with humans over the control of Ireland. When they lost, they retreated into the hills and valleys and became a people of the twilight. Magical walls were built to hide them from the human world, so humans seldom come into contact with them.

▶ **FAIRY INTERACTIONS WITH HUMANS**

Although they live in parallel worlds, fairies and humans rarely cross paths. In olden days, encounters with the fairies were so feared that it was considered dangerous even to speak their name. For this reason fairies were referred to by many names other than their own, for example, the Good People, the Fair Folk, and the Good Neighbors.

Fairy Circles. In English and Irish folktales, fairies are often encountered when a human approaches or enters a fairy circle. These circles, places where the fairies dance and play music by night, are greatly feared by humans because of their connection to the fairies. To enter the fairy ring puts one in the power of the fairies. The consequences can be good but are more often bad.

In one Irish story a kindly hunchback hears a group of fairies singing "Sunday, Monday" over and over again in Irish. He

adds "And Tuesday!" to their song. The fairies are so pleased with his addition that they remove his hump, and he has good fortune ever after. But the same story also warns people of the dangers of angering the fairies. On learning of the hunchback's good fortune, one of his neighbors goes to the fairy circle, hears

In legend, fairy circles—where fairies dance and play music by night—are enchanted places rarely seen by humans. Those who do enter are in the fairies' power.

the fairies singing, and adds "And Wednesday" in such a tuneless way that the song is ruined. The fairies are so angry at him that they beat him badly, and he never has a day's luck afterward.

Changelings. The changeling is a fairy child who has been substituted for a human one.

The changeling is usually rather grumpy, eats enormous amounts of food, and never seems to grow. There are several ways of getting the fairies to come back and get the changeling. A threat will always bring the fairy mother back to get her child. In an Icelandic story, a mother begins to beat the changeling. The fairy mother immediately appears, complaining that it is unfair that she treats the human child so well while her own is treated so badly. The fairy mother takes her child back and returns the human baby.

Other tales tell of mothers who get rid of changelings by tricking them into revealing themselves. The mother might pretend to cook food in an eggshell. Astonished at this unusual activity, the fairy gives itself away, exclaiming that even though it has lived for a long time, it has never seen this done. Once it has revealed its identity, the changeling will leave and the human child will be returned to its mother.

Visits to Faerie. Humans occasionally visit Faerie, but it is always dangerous to do so. Time is different there than in the human world. People taken into a fairy dance, for example, may think they have been dancing for only a few hours, but when they return home they find that many days, weeks, or even years have passed.

Human visitors to Faerie should also beware of eating or drinking fairy food. Stories tell of people who have done so; they fall into a deep sleep and, on waking, return home to discover that so much time has passed, no one knows who they are. The story of Rip Van Winkle is an American version of this legend. In other stories, people who eat fairy food are trapped forever in Faerie; or they become ill, longing for a second taste of the tempting fare.

Encounters with fairies always hold an element of danger. Christina Rossetti's poem "Goblin Market" tells of the consequences of tasting fairy food.

▶ FAIRIES IN LITERATURE

Fairies have been part of British and Scandinavian literature from their beginnings. Creatures such as the fierce monster Grendel in the Old English poem *Beowulf*, for example, have many of the same characteristics as the demonic forms of fairies. Middle English romances often feature fairies, and there is a long tradition of fairies in English and Scandinavian ballads as well. Shakespeare's play *A Midsummer Night's Dream* is perhaps the most famous literary use of fairy lore. The play takes place on a midsummer's night, during which Puck and other fairies play many of their typical tricks on the human characters. Edmund Spenser, a contemporary of Shakespeare, also drew on English fairy lore for his *Faerie Queene*, a long allegorical poem set in Faerie.

J. M. Barrie's popular play *Peter Pan*, first performed in 1904 and later retold in books and films, features a fairy character. But it contains little traditional English fairy lore. The modern author who most successfully used fairy lore is J. R. R. Tolkien, in his books *The Hobbit*, *The Lord of the Rings*, and *The Silmarillion*. Like the *Tuatha de Danann*, the elves of *The Lord of the Rings* are pictured as a wise and powerful race in decline, slowly surrendering the world to humans. Tolkien also drew on Scandinavian and Celtic sources in creating his elves.

DAVID E. GAY
Folklore Institute, Indiana University

PSYCHOLOGY

Do you ever wonder what it means to be smart, to be mentally ill, or to love someone? Do you sometimes wish you could be more successful in school, or at least more interested in what school has to teach you? If you answered yes to any of these questions, you may be interested in psychology.

▶ WHAT IS PSYCHOLOGY?

Psychology is the study of the mind (the means by which people learn, think, and feel) and behavior (what people do). Scientists who study psychology are called **psychologists**. Psychologists generally focus on the individual person, either alone or in relation to other people and to the environment. Psychologists are not the only scientists who study people. Two other kinds of scientists who study people are sociologists and cul-

Psychology examines the mind and studies behavior to better understand such things as what we think and feel; how we learn and change; and why we act the way we do.

tural anthropologists. They study people in ways that are somewhat different from those of psychologists, however.

Sociologists study human relationships and how those relationships are affected by people working and living together. For example, sociologists might be interested in comparing the family lives of people who have jobs with the family lives of people who are unemployed. **Cultural anthropologists** seek insights into various cultures. For example, they might be interested in comparing the customs of people in Mexico City, Mexico, to the customs of people in Tokyo, Japan. What distinguishes psychologists from sociologists and anthropologists, then, is that psychologists focus on individuals, whether by themselves or in relation to the world. All three kinds of scientists have common goals, however.

▶ GOALS OF PSYCHOLOGISTS

In their work, psychologists generally have four goals: description, explanation, prediction, and modification (change) of behavior. Psychologists typically begin their work by describing behavior.

Description involves observing what, when, and how people think, feel, or act in various kinds of situations. To create accurate descriptions, psychologists must make observations and gather **data** (observable facts).

For example, psychologists might try to describe the kinds of behavior that distinguish children who succeed in school from those who do not. The data the psychologists would seek might then be the observed behavior of the children who are succeeding and of those who are not succeeding. The psychologist would be most interested in the kinds of behavior the successful students show that the unsuccessful ones do not show, as well as the behavior the unsuccessful students show that the successful students do not show. The psychologist would also be interested in explaining why the two groups of students show these different kinds of behavior.

Explanation concerns why people think, feel, or act as they do. To explain various data, psychologists propose **theories**, which are organized sets of general ideas or principles that explain a phenomenon. Theories give rise to possible **hypotheses**, which are specific ideas about how to interpret and explain the particular data that are observed.

For example, suppose psychologists observe that successful students pay more attention to their teachers in the classroom than do unsuccessful students. How might the psychologists explain the behavior they have described? One theory might be that the difference between students who pay attention and those who do not is interest in schoolwork. A hypothesis following from this theory would be that the successful students will describe themselves as more interested in schoolwork than will unsuccessful students.

There are also other theories that could explain the data. Here, as is usually the case in psychology, more than one theory can be used to explain data; the psychologist must go about figuring out which theory is correct. For example, it may be that the successful students pay more attention not because they are interested in what the teacher says, but because they want to get good grades in school. A hypothesis following from this theory would be that the successful students would tell a psychologist that grades matter a lot to them, while unsuccessful students would tell the psychologists that grades do not matter so much. If this hypothesis is correct, one could predict that the successful students are likely to want to get high grades in the future as well.

Psychologists generally try to describe, explain, predict, and modify (change) behavior. For example, to explain why some students do well in school, a psychologist might theorize that such students are more interested, pay closer attention, or want better grades than less successful students.

Prediction refers to educated guesses about what will happen in the future. Part of the job of a psychologist is to predict future behavior from past behavior.

For example, one task of psychologists is to try to predict future success in school. Of course, one basis for their predictions is past success: Students who get higher grades in their early school years tend to get higher grades in their later school years. But psychologists can also use other measures to predict future success in school. Often the goal of such prediction is to know when psychological techniques might be used to modify behavior in order to help people obtain greater future success than is currently predicted for them.

Modification refers to change. Psychologists help people modify, or change, their be-

Tests provide a way of measuring certain characteristics. Achievement tests are used to measure the skills and knowledge a person has acquired through education.

havior when that behavior results in unsatisfactory outcomes for those people.

For example, a psychologist might work with students to help them achieve higher grades in school or simply to help them pay more attention in class. Psychologists therefore not only assess people but also help them to change so that they can be happier and more successful in their lives. In order to help people change, however, psychologists use a variety of methods in order to figure out exactly what problems the people face.

▶ METHODS IN PSYCHOLOGICAL RESEARCH

As scientists, psychologists use a variety of methods to study behavior and the thoughts and feelings that lie behind it. They choose the methods that best fit the problem they wish to study. Five of the main methods they use are tests, surveys, case studies, naturalistic observation, and experiments.

A **test** is a procedure for measuring a characteristic at a particular time and in a particular place. Tests can measure many different kinds of characteristics.

For example, an **ability test** might measure how well you are able to do something, such as remembering people's names or faces. An **achievement test** might measure your knowledge of a school subject, such as mathematics or biology. Ability and achievement tests typically have "right" and "wrong" answers, or at least "better" and "worse" answers, but not all tests do. A **personality test** might measure what you are like as a person—for example, how much you like to be with other people versus how much you prefer to be alone. There are no right or wrong answers on personality tests, only answers that show a person to be one way or another.

Another method that assesses what people are like is a **survey**. This is a measure of beliefs or opinions. Surveys never have right or wrong answers—they only assess what people think or believe. For example, a psychologist might conduct a survey of people's preferences in political candidates, such as

conservative versus liberal candidates, or a survey looking at people's preferences in foods, for example, meat versus fish.

Surveys usually provide a relatively small amount of information about a lot of people. Sometimes, though, psychologists want more detailed information about fewer people. In such instances, a **case study** may be more appropriate. This involves very intensive investigation of just a few individuals, or even of only one individual. Usually, psychologists will investigate a few individuals very intensively in order to be able to draw general conclusions about how these individuals think or feel. Some sources of information psychologists might use as data include autobiographies (first-hand accounts of people's lives), notebooks, and products the people have created. If the people being studied are alive, their activities can also be observed. The psychologists may then apply the conclusions to other people as well. A potential problem with case studies is that because only a small number of individuals are studied, the conclusions may not always apply to other people.

Surveys gather information on people's beliefs or opinions through the use of questionnaires and interviews.

What is personality?

The word "personality" means the behavioral characteristics of a person. These characteristics include ways of perceiving, thinking, feeling, and acting. When people say that someone has "a lot of personality," they may mean that he or she does things in an outgoing, warm, or charming manner. One person does not actually have more personality than another, but different people do have different personality traits. These traits include shyness, sociability, generosity, hostility, aggressiveness, and a sense of humor.

Some psychologists describe people's behavior in terms of personality types. For example, the Swiss psychologist Carl Jung (1875–1961) defined **extroverts** as people whose interests are directed toward the world around them and toward other people and **introverts** as people who are directed toward their

When taking a Rorschach test, a person describes what he or she "sees" in a series of inkblots. These interpretations are used to assess various aspects of the individual's personality.

own thoughts and feelings. An extrovert might prefer to spend the day meeting new people, while an introvert might prefer to spend the day reading, writing, or listening to music. No one, however, is completely one personality type or the other.

For example, a psychologist interested in what qualities make a composer great might do an intensive case study of Wolfgang Amadeus Mozart, the great classical composer. In doing this case study, the psychologist's goal would be to figure out what it was about Mozart that enabled him to be such a wonderful composer. Another psychologist interested in leadership might study Winston Churchill, the great British prime minister, or perhaps Martin Luther King, Jr., the great American civil rights leader.

Another way to find out what makes a great composer or leader is through **naturalistic observation**. Also known as **field study**, this involves watching and listening to people and recording what they do as they go about their everyday, normal activities. A psychologist interested in leadership might decide to study what makes great leaders by actually observing them at work. For example, the psychologist might carefully observe the day-to-day activities of a general in the military or of a spiritual leader of a religion. The goal of the psychologist would be to understand what it is the leaders do, and how it is they feel and think, that

enables them to succeed as leaders. Such observations, though, are typically only of a small number of individuals; moreover, it is sometimes difficult for psychologists not to let their prior beliefs influence the conclusions they draw.

Another method, that of the **experiment**, remedies these problems. Strictly speaking, an experiment is an investigation in which the experimenter makes a careful and controlled study of cause and effect. For example, an experimenter may study a type of behavior under one set of conditions. The experimenter would then explore how a change in those conditions affects the behavior being studied. The experimenter is able to determine such cause-and-effect relationships by controlling **variables**, or characteristics that vary across people or situations. An experiment requires that the psychologist always be able to control certain variables.

For example, suppose the experimenter has a theory that success in school is a result of student interest. The experimenter hypothesizes that students will learn a lesson better if it is presented in an interesting way than if it is presented in a boring way. In order to study whether student interest causes greater or lesser success in learning, the experimenter needs to be able to control the variable of student interest. The variable that the experimenter controls is called the **independent variable**. How might the experimenter control the independent variable of student interest?

The experimenter might present exactly the same lesson in two different ways. Under one set of conditions, the lesson might be presented in a way that makes it very interesting to students (for example, by showing how the lesson is relevant to the students' lives). Under a second set of conditions, the exact same lesson content might be presented in a way that makes it very boring to students (perhaps by showing that the lesson has nothing at all to do with the students' lives). In both sets of conditions, students are tested at the end of the lesson on the material they learned. The test scores are referred to as the **dependent variable**, because their values depend on the values of the independent variable (in this case, student interest).

If the experimenter is correct, then students with interesting presentation of material should learn better than students with boring presentation of material. If the students in the first condition do learn better, the experimenter's hypothesis is confirmed: Levels of student interest (the independent variable) determine students' demonstrated levels of learning (the dependent variable).

Some investigations resemble experiments but are not truly experiments. One example is a **correlational study**, where levels of performance on one variable are related to levels of performance on another variable. No independent variable is controlled, however. For example, suppose a psychologist asks a large group of students how interested each of them is in school and creates a measure of

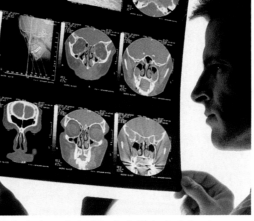

Biological psychologists study biological structures (such as the brain) and processes to understand why a person thinks, feels, and behaves in certain ways.

the students' interest. The experimenter is not varying student interest through an experimental manipulation but is simply recording levels of student interest in an existing course of study. The psychologist also finds out how well the students are doing in school. Suppose that the students who are more interested in school are also doing better in school. Can we conclude that being more interested in school led to better grades?

The answer is no. Why? In this correlational study the experimenter did not have control of the variable of student interest, as in the true experiment described earlier. In this study, it is possible that greater interest led to better grades—but there are also two other sensible interpretations of the data.

A second interpretation is that better grades led to greater interest—that receiving high grades resulted in students being more interested in their schoolwork. A third interpretation is that both interest and school grades were dependent on something else, such as the amount of time students spent on their work. It is possible that students willing to put more time into their schoolwork became more interested in this work and also received higher grades.

When the investigator does not have control of the variable being studied (in this case, student interest), the investigator cannot draw firm conclusions about what caused what. The extent to which an investigator can gain control depends in part upon the specific field of psychology in which he or she works, because in some fields it is easier to gain control than in others.

▶ FIELDS OF PSYCHOLOGY

Although psychology can be seen as a single science, it is often divided into various fields of specialization. Many psychologists

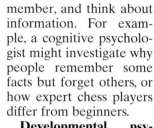

A clinical psychologist helps her patient deal with his fear of heights by working with him on the rooftop of a tall building. If not treated, fears like this can make it difficult for a person to function effectively in everyday life.

identify themselves as specializing in one (or more) of these fields. Six of the main fields are biological psychology, clinical psychology, cognitive psychology, developmental psychology, personality psychology, and social psychology. These fields represent only a small number of the many different possibilities for specialization.

Biological psychology (which is also called **psychobiology**) deals with the biological structures and processes that give rise to thoughts, feelings, and behavior. For example, a biological psychologist might study the parts of the brain that are involved in anger or in fear.

Clinical psychology deals with the understanding and treatment of abnormal behavior. For example, a clinical psychologist might investigate why some people are afraid of being in very high places, such as at the top of a high building looking down, even if the people are inside the building and thus safe from falling.

Cognitive psychology deals with how people perceive (that is, see and hear), learn, re-

member, and think about information. For example, a cognitive psychologist might investigate why people remember some facts but forget others, or how expert chess players differ from beginners.

Developmental psychology is the study of how people change, but also remain the same, over time. For example, a developmental psychologist might study how children's use of language changes as the children grow older.

Personality psychology focuses on the relatively permanent personal qualities that lead people to behave as they do. For example, a personality psychologist might study why some people are tense and nervous, even in apparently safe settings, while other people are relaxed and hardly ever feel or act nervous.

What personal characteristics and qualities enable some people to absorb the stress of waiting (*left*) while others boil over with anger and frustration (*above*)? Personality psychologists attempt to answer such questions.

Social psychologists are interested in the social conditions that lead to a particular behavior. For example, in what situations might someone be altruistic (kind, generous, and helpful to others)?

Social psychology is concerned with how people interact with each other, both as individuals and in groups. For example, a social psychologist might study why people are sometimes generous and helpful, while at other times they are not. The social psychologist focuses more on the situations that lead a given person to behave in a particular way, while the personality psychologist focuses more on people who behave in one way or another, regardless of situation.

Plato (427?–347 B.C.), a philosopher who lived in ancient Greece, believed that the mind resides in the brain. He also believed that much of what we know we are actually born knowing—but we are unaware that we know it. According to Plato, for example, you were born knowing much of the mathematics you learn in school. What schooling helps you do is to become aware of what you already know!

Aristotle (384–322 B.C.), a student of Plato, believed that the mind resides in the heart. Unlike Plato, Aristotle believed that most knowledge is acquired from the environment.

The roots of psychology can be traced back many centuries to several important philosophers (*counterclockwise from left*): René Descartes of France; Plato and his student Aristotle of ancient Greece; Immanuel Kant of Germany; and John Locke of England. The philosophers of ancient Greece were the first to propose ideas on how the mind works.

▶ **HISTORY OF PSYCHOLOGY**

The various fields of specialization within psychology have evolved over time, as has psychology as a whole. Just how has thinking in psychology evolved?

Origins in Philosophy

The history of psychological thinking has its origins some two thousand years ago in the work of ancient philosophers (and may go back even farther than that to times for which we do not have written records). Two of the most important philosophers of ancient times were Plato and Aristotle.

Structuralists focused on the mind's more immediate experiences. For example, a structuralist would want to know exactly what you see when you look at this picture—tall, multishaped objects rising into the air. The concept of a city would be of no interest.

For example, you are not born knowing mathematics—you learn it in school or at home.

Centuries later, René Descartes (1596–1650), a French philosopher, agreed with Plato that many of the ideas we have (such as about mathematics) are inborn. The English philosopher John Locke (1632–1704), in contrast, agreed with Aristotle that what we learn we learn from the environment. Immanuel Kant (1724–1804), a German philosopher, tried to bring together the two positions, arguing that some categories of knowledge are inborn, but other categories are learned from the environment.

Schools of Psychology

By the late 1800s, psychology had separated itself from philosophy. People had begun to realize that psychology had its own contribution to make toward our understanding of people, independent of the contribution of philosophy. Psychologists began to invent and then follow different **schools of thought**, or ways of thinking, about psychological phenomena.

The first of these schools was called **structuralism**. Its goal was to understand the structure (relations of elements) of the mind by discovering its basic components or contents. An early structuralist was Wilhelm Wundt (1832–1920), a German psychologist who believed that psychology should focus on immediate and direct experience. For example, suppose you look at a green, grassy lawn. To Wundt, the concepts of lawn and grass would be of no interest. Wundt would want to know

exactly what you see—your basic sensations—for example, narrow, pointed, vertical green objects sticking out of the ground.

Many psychologists came to believe that structuralism had little to do with how people really thought about things in their lives or in the world. For example, when you see a lawn, you think about the grass on it and how nice it looks, not about narrow, pointed, vertical green objects sticking out of the ground.

William James (1842–1910), an American philosopher and psychologist, helped found a school of thought called **functionalism**, which dealt with what people do and why they do it. For example, the functionalist might be concerned with why people plant and maintain lawns in the first place, rather than with exactly what people see when they look at a lawn.

An outgrowth of functionalism was a school of thought called **pragmatism**, whose followers believed that knowledge is important only to the extent that it is useful. For example, John Dewey (1859–1952), an American philosopher, educator, and psychologist, studied how psychology can be applied to improving education for children. Dewey suggested, for example, that children will learn best if they are genuinely interested in what they learn. He believed, therefore, that schools should make what they teach interesting to their students.

American psychologist Edwin Guthrie (1886–1959), like John Dewey, was interested in learning. Guthrie was a believer in **associationism**, which held that learning occurs when two observed events become associated in people's minds because the events occur closely together in time. For example, if every time you wear a certain hat people compliment you, eventually you will learn that wearing that hat leads to compliments—you have associated that particular hat with the compliments.

Not everyone agreed with Guthrie. Edward Lee Thorndike (1874–1949), an American psychologist, suggested that learning occurs not as a result of two things occurring closely together in time but, rather, as a result of reward. According to Thorndike, you learn to associate the hat with compliments not because the compliments occur right after you put on the hat but because you feel rewarded when you receive the compliments.

Some psychologists carried the basic ideas of associationism to an extreme. A school of thought that grew out of associationism, known as **behaviorism**, suggested that psychologists should focus only on observable behavior. Mental activities such as thinking or feeling were not viewed as relevant to psychology because they could not be observed.

Behaviorists were (and continue to be) very interested in how the environment could be controlled in order to produce certain kinds of behavior. For example, an early American behaviorist, John Watson (1878–1958), believed that he could take any baby and turn the baby into whatever he wanted—such as a lawyer, a doctor, or even a thief—just by controlling the child's environment throughout the child's development. Later, American psychologist B. F. Skinner (1904–90) proposed what he called the experimental analysis of behavior. He suggested that all of our learning and thinking could be understood in terms of how we respond to the rewards and punishments of the environment in which we live.

Today many psychologists interested in learning and thinking have rejected behaviorism in favor of **cognitivism**, which is the belief that much of human behavior can be understood in terms of how people think. Cognitivists such as American social scientist Herbert Simon (1916–   ) and English psychologist Donald Broadbent (1926–88) suggested that in some ways people function much like computers, processing one piece of information after another, more flexibly but not nearly as fast as does a computer. Other cognitivists, such as American psychologist David Rumelhart (1942–   ), have suggested that people process a lot of information all at once, rather than one piece after another.

At the same time that some psychologists have focused on the cognitive and rational side of the human mind, others have focused more on the emo-

(Continued on page 357)

CONTEMPORARY THEORY AND RESEARCH IN PSYCHOLOGY

At the beginning of this article, a number of questions were raised—exactly the types of questions that psychologists seek to answer. These questions provided just a sample of the whole range of questions psychologists consider. Let us return to those questions at the beginning of the article and look at some of the work psychologists are doing today to answer them.

What Does It Mean to Be Smart?

Intelligence is usually defined as the ability to adapt to the environment and to changes in it. But what, exactly, is intelligence, and how can it be measured?

At the beginning of the 1900s, French psychologist Alfred Binet (1857–1911) was asked to create a test of intelligence that would distinguish between those children who were unsuccessful in school because they were genuinely very low in intelligence and those children who were unsuccessful because they showed problems in their social behavior.

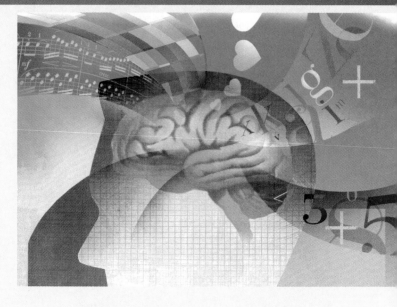

Above: Some psychologists believe that artistic and creative abilities (such as musical skills), along with practical abilities, are important to intelligence.

Right: Severe depression—marked by feelings of overwhelming sadness, helplessness, hopelessness, and a lack of enthusiasm—is an example of mental illness.

Binet and his collaborator, psychologist Theodore Simon (1873–1961), devised such a test, which measured children's word knowledge, their ability to perform basic arithmetical operations, and their ability to see similarities and differences between words and pictures. Binet and Simon's test came to be referred to as an **intelligence test**.

Theories of intelligence from the early 1900s, and from more recent times as well, emphasize the kinds of abilities Binet and Simon tested as central to intelligence. For example, Charles Spearman (1863–1945), an English psychologist, viewed the ability to see the relations (similarities and differences) between words and pictures as one important aspect of intelligence. American psychologist Louis Thurstone (1887–1955) believed that a wider range of abilities, including word knowledge, number skills, memory, and the ability to imagine objects rotating in one's head, was also important to intelligence.

Today psychologists are suggesting even wider ranges of abilities as important to

intelligence. For example, Howard Gardner (1943–   ), an American psychologist and neurologist, has suggested the importance of bodily movement abilities such as those shown by athletes or dancers and of musical abilities such as those shown by orchestra musicians as important to intelligence. Robert Sternberg (1949–   ), an American psychologist and educator, has suggested that creative abilities (the abilities involved in producing new and useful ideas) as well as practical abilities (the abilities involved in getting along with other people and in getting one's work done) are important to intelligence. Moreover, Sternberg and his colleagues have shown that when students are taught in school in a way that fits well with their abilities, they learn more than when they are taught in a way that does not fit well. Current work in psychology, therefore, is making progress in helping teachers solve the problem of how best to support children's learning in school settings.

What Does It Mean to Be Mentally Ill?

People who are mentally ill are unable to function effectively in their daily lives. In the past, there was little we could do for such people. Today, as psychologists come to understand mental illness more completely, they are better able to recognize and treat it.

An example of a mental illness is major depression. All of us are depressed from time to time. But people suffering from major depression are severely depressed much or even all of the time. They tend to think little of themselves, have trouble going to sleep or getting up in the morning, and expect things to go badly for them. Often, they lose interest in eating as well as in other activities that form important parts of almost everyone's daily schedule.

There are different theories of depression. These theories are not necessarily in conflict—depression may well have multiple causes. For example, some psychodynamic psychologists suggest that depression can start with our feeling as though we have lost the love of someone important to us, perhaps because the person died or perhaps because the person has simply ceased to love us. Some behaviorist psychologists believe that depressed people do not get enough rewards in their lives or get too many punishments. Cognitively oriented psychologists suggest that depressed people tend to think in distorted ways—for example, they exaggerate their faults and fail to recognize their strengths.

Can anything be done to help people who are depressed? **Psychotherapy**—interventions that use the principles of psychology to help people feel better—has been shown to be effective in aiding people with depression. For example, a psychotherapist might help people to overcome the sense of loss of love, or to find ways of producing more rewards in their lives, or to recognize their strengths as well as their failings. Moreover, drug therapy, especially when it is used in addition to psycho- therapy, has been found to be effective in treating people who are depressed. In short, psychotherapists today can help people over- come depression and other mental illnesses that once might have ruined years of these people's lives.

What Does It Mean to Love Someone?

Psychology helps us understand not only things that make people unhappy but also

things that make people happy. One such thing is love. Some recent work is providing us with a new understanding of what love is.

For example, Robert Sternberg has proposed that three major components of love are intimacy—how close we feel to someone, how well we communicate with the person, how comfortable we are with the person, and how much we trust the person; passion—how excited we feel about a person; and commitment—the extent to which we view our love for a person as something that will last forever. Different kinds of love arise from different combinations of these components.

Another theory of love suggests that there are three different ways of loving, in particular, and that which way we love will depend on experiences we have as infants. Psychologists Phillip Shaver (1944–) and Cynthia Hazan (1954–) have argued that some people, when they love, tend generally to feel happy and secure in the love they give and receive. Other people tend to be avoidant—they always seem to be trying to create distance, or a sense of separation, between themselves and the people they love. Still other people never feel as

though they receive enough love—they are always afraid the love they receive will not be enough, or even that they will lose the person they love.

According to Shaver and Hazan, these different patterns of loving start in infancy, when, according to Mary Ainsworth (1913–), a well-known American developmental psychologist, infants attach to their mothers in one of these three ways. In other words, Shaver and Hazan have evidence to suggest that the kind of relationship the infant forms with the mother will determine the kind of loving relationship the person later forms as an adult.

What Makes Students Interested in Schoolwork?

What should parents and teachers do if they would like to help children become interested in their schoolwork? There have been a variety of answers to this question. For example, behaviorally oriented psychologists who emphasize the role of reward might suggest the importance of grades or of various kinds of prizes to keep students interested and performing well. Or parents might give their children gifts to reward the children's good performance.

Research by psychologists, including Americans Mark Lepper (1944–) and Edward Deci (1942–), however, suggests that concrete rewards such as grades, prizes, and gifts may actually decrease children's interest in their schoolwork. The result of such rewards may be that children focus on their work not for its own sake but merely for the sake of the rewards. No one is suggesting that rewards never be used. But Lepper and Deci, like John Dewey many years before them, have realized that the best way to interest children in anything is to make it exciting.

Left: Sigmund Freud founded the school of psychoanalysis. He suggested that early childhood experiences have a great influence on how well adjusted and happy people are as adults.

Right: According to humanistic psychology, people can achieve personal excellence and reach their full potential if they set their minds to it.

tional and sometimes less rational side. For example, the **psychodynamic** school of thought, formulated by Sigmund Freud (1856–1939), an Austrian physician and the founder of psychoanalysis, suggested that very early childhood experiences, over which people have almost no control, contribute greatly to people's happiness and adjustment later in their lives. Freud suggested a series of stages children go through early in their development that later lead them either to be better or more poorly adjusted in their lives. Freud also suggested that much of the think-

SOME FIELDS OF PSYCHOLOGY

Academic psychologist—works in a college or university teaching and doing research.

Clinical psychologist—diagnoses and treats patients for psychological problems.

Consumer psychologist—helps determine consumer preferences in products and services.

Human-factors psychologist—works in organizations to design machines that are convenient and comfortable for people to use.

Industrial/organizational psychologist—works in business or industry to help in hiring and placement and in creating a good work environment.

Military psychologist—works in the armed forces to help in selection, placement, and counseling.

School psychologist—works in schools to help diagnose and correct students' problems.

ing we do is **unconscious**—below our level of awareness. He further believed that we use this unconscious thinking to defend ourselves against unwanted thoughts. Freud actually proposed a specific list of mechanisms we use to defend ourselves against such thoughts. For example, **repression** is a defense mechanism whereby we hold troubling thoughts at an unconscious level, preventing them from becoming conscious so that we will not be troubled by them.

Some psychologists believed that Freud placed too much emphasis on unconscious thinking and also the extent to which we lack control of our own lives. According to the **humanistic** school of psychology, represented by psychologists such as Americans Carl Rogers (1902–87) and Abraham Maslow (1908–70), most thinking is conscious, and people can take control of their lives and reach their full potential if only they set their minds to it.

All of these different schools of thought have led to the discipline of psychology as it exists today.

Robert J. Sternberg
IBM Professor of Psychology and Education
Yale University

HEART

The heart is a powerful living pump that performs an amazing task: It sustains life. It is the driving force of the **circulatory system**, the network of organs and vessels through which blood flows. From its place under the breastbone, this fist-sized structure drives blood to every cell in the body. Blood ebbs and flows with each beat of the heart, cleansing and nourishing cells. The heart beats unceasingly from about eight months before birth until the moment of death. If the blood flow to a part of the body were to stop—even for a matter of minutes—tissues could suffer damage and even die.

▶ PARTS OF THE HEART

Your heart is a strong hollow muscle about the size and shape of your fist. It is located near the center of the chest, between the lungs. While a newborn baby's heart weighs about ⅔ ounce (19 grams), an adult's heart weighs about 11 ounces (300 grams).

The heart is encased in a thin fluid-filled sac called the **pericardium**. The slippery fluid in the pericardium protects the heart from rubbing against the lungs and the chest wall as it beats. The muscular wall of the heart is made up of three layers: the **epicardium**, a soft, moist outer membrane; the **myocardium**, a thick, muscular middle layer; and the **endocardium**, a smooth inner membrane.

Inside the heart, there are four hollow spaces, or **chambers**. They are created by a thick wall called the **septum** and leaflike flaps called **valves** that open and close. The septum divides the heart into left and right halves, and the valves divide each half into upper and lower parts. The upper chambers, or **atria** (singular: atrium), serve as holding tanks for blood entering the heart. The lower chambers, or **ventricles**, receive blood from the atria and pump it out of the heart either to the lungs or to the rest of the body.

Heart

Lungs

The Structures of the Heart

With each beat, the heart pumps oxygen-rich blood through the circulatory system to every living tissue of the body. Located near the middle of the chest, this hollow, fist-sized muscle functions like two separate pumps. The right side of the heart sends oxygen-depleted blood to the lungs for a new oxygen supply. The left side then drives the reoxygenated blood to the rest of the body.

Exterior view of heart

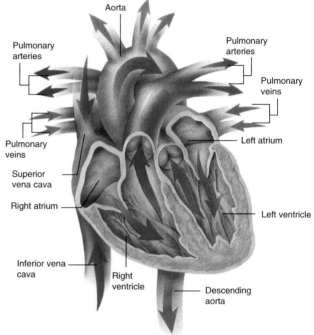

Aorta

Pulmonary arteries

Pulmonary arteries

Pulmonary veins

Pulmonary veins

Superior vena cava

Left atrium

Right atrium

Left ventricle

Inferior vena cava

Right ventricle

Descending aorta

The septum prevents the crossing of blood from one side of the heart to the other, while the **atrioventricular valves** guard the openings between the upper and lower chambers, making sure that blood flows through in only one direction. The **tricuspid valve**, which has three cusps, or flaps, controls the flow of blood from the right atrium to the right ventricle. The **mitral valve**, which has two cusps, controls the flow of blood from the left atrium to the left ventricle. **Semilunar valves**, named for their half-moon shape, also protect the openings that lead out of the heart into large blood vessels.

Veins are the vessels that carry blood from the lungs and the rest of the body to the heart. Blood from the lungs enters the left atrium through the **pulmonary veins**. Blood from the rest of the body enters the right atrium through the body's two largest veins: the **superior vena cava** and the **inferior vena cava**. The superior vena cava carries blood from the head and arms to the right atrium, while the inferior vena cava carries blood from the trunk and legs.

Arteries are the vessels that carry blood away from the heart. From the left ventricle, blood courses through the largest artery in the body, called the **aorta**. As the aorta branches and divides, it carries blood throughout the body. The **coronary arteries**, which branch off from the aorta, encircle the heart and provide it with a steady supply of oxygen and nutrients. Blood from the right ventricle travels through the **pulmonary artery** and its branches to the lungs.

Special cells in the heart form structures that produce and carry messages regulating the heartbeat. These structures include the **sinoatrial node (SA node)**, which is located in the wall of the right atrium near the opening of the superior vena cava, and the **atrioventricular node (AV node)**, which lies between the atria and the ventricles.

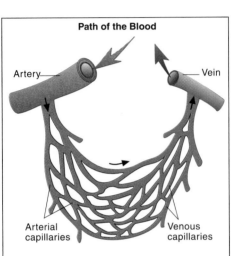

Path of the Blood

Artery

Vein

Arterial capillaries

Venous capillaries

Oxygen-rich blood travels from the heart through arteries to delicate networks of capillaries. Here, the important transfer of oxygen to, and waste from, cells takes place before the blood returns to the heart through the veins.

▶ **HOW THE HEART WORKS**

The heart beats in a rhythmic cycle of relaxation and contraction, without stopping, throughout a person's lifetime. With each cycle, the heart fills and empties, sending life-sustaining blood to all the cells of the body.

The Heart as a Pump

The heart, divided by the septum, is actually two separate pumps. The right atrium and ventricle form one pump, and the left atrium and ventricle form the other pump. The right pump receives blood from the body and sends it to the lungs for a fresh supply of oxygen. Deoxygenated, or used, blood is de-

livered to the right atrium by the venae cavae (plural of vena cava) and flows down into the right ventricle, which pumps it out through the pulmonary artery to the lungs. The left pump receives oxygenated blood from the lungs and pumps it out to the body. Oxygenated blood from the lungs flows into the left atrium through the pulmonary veins, then flows down into the left ventricle, which pumps it forcefully out into the aorta, whose many branches supply the body's cells.

Regulating the Heartbeat

In a 75-year lifetime, the heart beats more than 2.5 billion times, pumping a total of about 50 million gallons of blood. The heartbeat rate is controlled by the SA node, or **pacemaker**. It starts the electrical impulses that carry the messages for the heart to beat. Although the heartbeat is usually very regular, it changes throughout a person's lifetime. At birth, a baby's heart beats about 120 times a minute. The rate gradually slows down as the child grows and the heart gets bigger. The larger heart of the growing child can pump out more blood with each beat and thus does not need to beat as fast. Adults typically have a heartbeat rate of about 70 beats per minute.

The pacemaker sets its own rhythm, but it can be influenced by other internal or external factors. For example, hormones, such as adrenaline, can speed up the rate. Adrenaline is the "fight or flight" chemical secreted by the adrenal glands when fear, anger, and other strong emotions are felt. Some drugs like caffeine can quicken the heartbeat. So can heavy exercise. During heavy exercise, when the muscles need extra energy, the heartbeat rate may double. When you are sleeping or in a deeply restful state, which can occur during activities such as meditation, your heartbeat slows down. Some people, such as athletes, have slower heartbeats than the average person. Their hearts have been strengthened by exercise and can pump more blood with each beat.

The Stages of a Heartbeat

The relaxing phase of each heartbeat is called **diastole**. While the heart is relaxing, blood flows into the atria and trickles down through the open atrioventricular valves into the ventricles. Soon tiny bursts of electricity are sent out by the pacemaker and travel across the atria. Responding to the electrical messages, the muscles of the atria contract slightly. As they contract, more blood is forced into the ventricles until the ventricles are filled and the valves close, preventing blood from flowing back into the atria.

The electrical impulses continue across the atria to the AV node and are relayed through pathways that line the ventricles. The impulses excite the muscles of the ventricles to begin the contracting phase of each heartbeat, called **systole**. As the atrioventricular valves close, the semilunar valves pop open, and blood shoots out from the ventricles into the arteries.

While the ventricles are contracting, the atria begin to fill with blood. After each ventricular contraction, the heart muscle relaxes and the cycle starts over again. The whole cycle usually takes less than a second.

▶ DISORDERS OF THE HEART

The leading cause of death in the United States and other industrialized nations is **cardiovascular disease**—any disease that affects the heart and blood vessels. Disorders can result from a variety of causes and affect different parts of the heart.

Coronary Artery Disease

Coronary artery disease (CAD), in which the blood supply to the heart is reduced, typically begins with **atherosclerosis**, in which fatty deposits build up on the inner walls of arteries. These deposits, called **plaques**, gradually narrow the openings through the arteries. After a while, deposits of fibrous tissue and

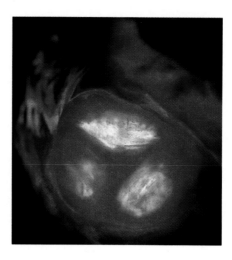

A heart valve's thin, leaflike flaps open and close with each heartbeat to control the flow of blood through the heart.

calcium salts among the plaques cause the normally smooth, elastic walls of the arteries to harden, thicken, and lose their elasticity. This condition is called **arteriosclerosis**, or hardening of the arteries.

When a coronary artery is partially blocked, the amount of blood that can reach the heart decreases. Sometimes, only enough blood reaches the heart to provide oxygen when the heart is at rest. With any exertion that causes the heart to beat faster, the demand for blood can be higher than the supply. When this happens, the oxygen-starved heart tissues burn with a pain known as **angina pectoris**, or, simply, angina. The pain usually disappears when the activity is stopped. Drugs are also used to increase the blood flow to the heart and thereby reduce the pain.

As plaques build, they can completely block an artery, or their roughened surface can attract blood platelets and a vessel-clogging blood clot may form. When this happens in one of the coronary arteries, the flow of blood to a part of the heart is blocked. Deprived of oxygen and nutrients for too long a time, heart cells die. This is called a **myocardial infarction**, or **heart attack**. Depending on

The gradual clogging of a coronary artery with fat can trigger a heart attack.

This is a typical young adult's coronary artery—clear of fatty deposits.

Over time, deposits stick to the artery's walls and reduce the blood flow to the heart.

Continued fat buildup may completely block the blood flow and cause a heart attack.

how much of the heart muscle is affected, the heart may work less efficiently or it may stop completely. **Cardiac arrest**, the complete stoppage of the heart, can lead to death.

The prompt use of clot-dissolving drugs may help restore the flow of blood to the heart and reduce the damage to the heart muscle. **Balloon angioplasty** is a surgical procedure used to widen the channel in a blocked coronary artery. In **bypass surgery**, a small portion of an artery or vein is used to form a new blood pathway to the heart muscle, bypassing the blocked artery.

Cardiomyopathy

Cardiomyopathy is a disorder of the heart muscle. It can develop from a variety of causes, including vitamin or mineral deficiency or alcohol abuse, or it can be hereditary. As the disease progresses, the muscle tissue may grow improperly, causing the left ventricle to enlarge or the septum between the ventricles to become thickened and extremely rigid. The effects of the disease weaken the heart and make it an inefficient pump. Some kinds of cardiomyopathy are treated with drugs to improve the heart's pumping ability. Others require surgery to remove abnormal muscle. In severe cases, a **heart transplant**, in which the diseased heart is replaced with a donor heart, may be necessary.

Heart Failure

Diseases of the heart can reduce the heart's pumping ability and lead to a condition known as heart failure. This can result from a variety of disorders, including coronary artery disease, mechanical problems such as valve defects, and diseases of the heart muscle.

As heart failure progresses, the body's efforts to counteract the disorder increase the workload of the heart, making it even harder for the heart to pump. When the heart is unable to pump enough blood to meet the body's needs, blood begins to pool in the ventricles or back up into the veins. The increased pressure in the veins causes fluid to leak out into the tissues (or in the lungs, if the left side of the heart is damaged). This condition is called **congestive heart failure**. It can be treated with drugs, such as **digitalis**, to widen blood vessels, increase fluid excretion, and strengthen heart contractions. If these treatments are not successful, the individual may undergo a heart transplant.

Arrhythmias

Coronary heart disease, as well as other heart disorders and drugs, may make the heart beat in an irregular pattern, called an **arrhythmia**. When the abnormal rhythm is faster than 100 beats a minute, it is called **tachycardia**. When it is slower than 60 beats a minute, it is called **bradycardia**. Some arrhythmias are harmless, but others can cause the heart to beat in such an ineffective manner that blood flow is altered and insufficient oxygen and nutrients reach the body's cells.

Bradycardia can occur when the pacemaker becomes weak or is damaged and its ability to

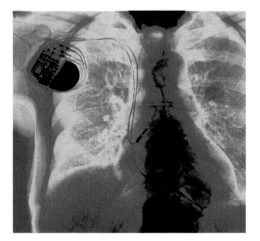

This X ray shows an artificial pacemaker implanted in a patient's chest. By generating regular electrical impulses, this device helps regulate the heartbeat rate.

Tachycardia occurs when the electrical signals produced in either the atria or ventricles cause a rapid heartbeat. Tachycardias can be the most dangerous arrhythmias, especially ventricular tachycardia. This may cause rapid, irregular contractions called **fibrillations**. When the heart muscle fibrillates, the heart quivers and is unable to pump blood effectively. Sudden death can result unless the fibrillation is stopped and a normal rhythm is restored. To prevent ventricular tachycardia, a device called a **defibrillator** can be inserted. It detects a racing heartbeat and delivers an electric shock that briefly stops the heart, allowing the SA node to restart the normal heart rhythm.

Inflammatory Diseases

Inflammatory diseases can affect any part of the heart and can arise from infectious disorders, such as bacterial or viral infections, as well as conditions such as arthritis.

When an inflammatory disease attacks the endocardium, it is called **endocarditis**. Rheumatic fever is one such disease. A common result of such infections is scarring of the heart's valves and blood vessel openings. Less blood can pass through the scarred and narrowed vessels, so that the heart has to work harder to pump enough blood for the body's needs. Damaged heart valves may fail to close completely, resulting in leakage of blood back into the ventricles while they are trying to pump it out. Defective valves can be replaced surgically with artificial valves made of metal and plastic or of animal or human tissue.

Pericarditis, the inflammation of the membrane that surrounds the heart, can also interfere with the heart's pumping action. During the inflammatory process, fluid may collect under the pericardium and squeeze the heart. As it becomes harder for the heart to pump, death may follow unless the fluid is drained to relieve the pressure.

The heart muscle becomes inflamed in **myocarditis**. Damage to the muscle tissue of the heart can severely affect its ability to work. In the most serious cases, the heart may not recover sufficiently and the individual may need a heart transplant.

generate regular electrical impulses fails. It can also occur when the pathway along which the electrical impulses travel is blocked. Drugs can help the heart maintain a regular rhythm. If drugs are not effective, a battery-operated device, called an artificial pacemaker, can be implanted in the chest to regulate the heartbeat rate.

EXAMINING THE HEART AT WORK

A healthy heart is essential to life. Basic techniques used to assess whether the heart is functioning properly include listening to the heartbeat and measuring the heartbeat rate, tracking electrical activity, and measuring blood pressure.

Listening to the Heartbeat. During each heartbeat, when the heart valves close properly, two distinct sounds, "lub-dub," are produced. These can be heard at the surface of the chest using a stethoscope, an instrument that magnifies sounds. As the heart contracts and the valves between the atria and the ventricles snap shut, the "lub" sound can be heard. After the heart relaxes, the valves between the ventricles and the aorta and pulmonary arteries close, producing the "dub" sound.

Measuring the Heartbeat Rate. The heartbeat rate can be measured at sites on the body, such as the inside of the wrist or the temple, where the arteries pass close to the surface of the skin. The ebb and flow of blood in the arteries can be felt as a vibration, or pulse, at these sites. The pulse rate, which is the same as the heartbeat rate, can then be counted to check for variations.

Tracking Electrical Activity. The electrical activity of the heart can be viewed using an instrument called an **electrocardiograph (EKG)**. An electrocardiograph can help detect abnormal heart rhythms, as well as damage to the heart. Electrodes, which are attached to various parts of the body, pick up the faint electrical currents generated by the heart. A record of the activity, called an **electrocardiogram**, is printed on paper as a series of wavy lines. This can be examined for indications of injury or abnormalities. Because

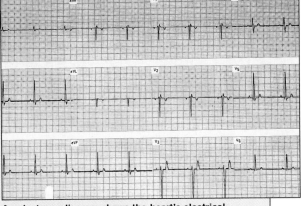

An electrocardiogram shows the heart's electrical activity (this one during exercise) and helps doctors diagnose problems.

some conditions are not revealed during an ordinary EKG, a stress EKG may be given. During a stress EKG, an electrocardiogram is recorded while the individual is exercising.

Measuring Blood Pressure. Blood pressure is determined by the amount of blood flowing through the circulatory system, the rate and strength of the heart's contractions, and the elasticity of the blood vessel walls. Exercise and emotions such as worry or excitement can raise blood pressure; depression and grief can cause it to fall.

Blood pressure is measured in millimeters of mercury using a device called a **sphygmomanometer**. Two pressures are typically measured: the pressure during systole and the pressure during diastole. The measurements are presented in the form of a fraction: systolic pressure over diastolic pressure, for example $^{120}/_{80}$. A young adult's systolic pressure averages 100 to 120 millimeters of mercury; the average diastolic pressure is 60 to 80. Blood pressure tends to increase with age, from a systolic pressure of about 40 at birth up to 160 at age 80.

Birth Defects

Some heart defects are **congenital**, that is, present at birth. Congenital heart defects can be inherited or the result of influences on the mother's body during pregnancy, such as infection by the rubella virus or poorly controlled diabetes.

The most common congenital heart defects are holes in the septum. These openings permit the oxygenated blood from the lungs and the deoxygenated blood from the body to mix. Too much blood is pumped to the lungs, and the heart has to work harder to get enough oxygen to body cells.

A child with a congenital heart defect may tire easily and have bluish skin because the blood sent to the body carries less than the normal amount of oxygen. Drugs may be used to treat some structural defects. However, most require surgery to correct them.

ALVIN SILVERSTEIN
VIRGINIA SILVERSTEIN
Coauthors, *The Circulatory System*

PURITANS

The Puritans were Protestant reformers who originated in England and later spread to the New England colonies. Because their goal was to "purify" religion and politics of all corruption, these Protestants were at first called Puritans by their enemies. Eventually they adopted the name for themselves as a badge of honor.

▶ THE PURITANS IN ENGLAND

The Puritan movement began as a part of the Protestant Reformation in England in the early 1500s, when King Henry VIII broke ties with the Pope and the Roman Catholic Church. Henry's daughter, Queen Elizabeth I, continued to move the country toward Protestantism. However, some reformers felt that Elizabeth was not extreme enough in her measures to rid the country of Catholic influences. These people came to be known as the Puritans.

Puritans in England became increasingly critical of Catholic influences on the Church of England, which brought them into conflict with the king.

The Puritans emphasized the importance of an individual's personal relationship to God and to the Bible. They wanted to eliminate all frivolity and decoration from the church, such as organ music, stained-glass windows, incense, and fancy religious robes—anything that drew attention away from one's inner spirituality. The Puritans also wished to improve the quality of the ministry. They encouraged ministers to write their own original and inspiring sermons, rather than simply quoting from *The Book of Common Prayer*.

Due to their criticism of England's established church, the Puritans were severely persecuted by the English king Charles I and his archbishop, William Laud. Numerous Puritans went into hiding in England, while others fled into exile throughout Europe. Others escaped to the New World. Eventually, the Puritans who remained in England engaged in a civil war against the king. Under the Puritan leadership of Oliver Cromwell, King Charles I was executed, and Cromwell briefly took control of England (1649–60).

▶ MIGRATION TO THE NEW WORLD

In 1630, sailing on a ship called the *Arbella*, John Winthrop (1588–1649) led the first group of English Puritans to Massachusetts Bay in New England. Although they were among the first immigrants to come to America in search of a better life, they were not the "poor, huddled masses" known to later generations. Most were well-educated ministers, lawyers, merchants, and farmers, who enjoyed connections to religious and political leaders back in England.

The Puritans thought of New England as a place to experiment with new structures of church and state governments that could later serve as models for reform in England and other parts of the world. Winthrop, a founder and four-term governor of the Massachusetts Bay Colony, believed in **theocracy**—a form of government that combines the laws of church and state and emphasizes the greater good of the community over personal gain. Winthrop envisioned "a city upon a hill" that could serve as "a model of Christian charity." Other early Puritan leaders who embraced these beliefs included the ministers John Cotton (1584–1652); John Harvard (1607–38), founder of Harvard College (1638); Richard Mather (1596–1669); Richard's son Increase Mather (1639–1723); and Increase's son Cotton Mather (1663–1728). They and their followers established churches in Boston and Newtown (present-day Cambridge), in Massachusetts; Hartford and New Haven, in Connecticut; and other towns in New England.

RELIGIOUS BELIEFS

The Puritans borrowed many of their religious doctrines from the writings of the Protestant reformer John Calvin (1509–64), as did the Huguenots, a group of French Protestants whose beliefs were similar to those of the Puritans. Calvin believed in predestination, meaning that God had long since decided who would and who would not go to heaven. Good Puritans had to have faith that they would achieve salvation and had to examine their daily lives for signs of God's disfavor. For example, when the poet Anne Bradstreet's house burned down, she took it as a message from God to be stronger in her faith.

To help them develop their faith, the Puritans relied on three books: *The New England Primer*, which taught them the alphabet as well as moral lessons; *The Bay Psalm Book*, which offered English translations of the Psalms to be sung at church services; and the Bible. To help them understand and decode the Bible, the Puritans listened to hundreds of hours of sermons. At least twice each week, ministers would explain how scripture should be used both as a guide to daily living and as a way to predict future events.

The Puritans believed that the simple way was the quicker and better way to God. Ministers wrote their sermons in what is called the **plain style**, a way of writing and speaking without complicated words, distracting refer-

Many Puritans immigrated to New England, where they hoped to build a new life free from religious intolerance.

ences to unknown books, or quotations in foreign languages. They also favored plain, black garments over the fancy, colorful robes of the Catholic Church and held services in small white chapels instead of in elaborately decorated churches.

CONTROVERSY

The Puritans of New England experienced many conflicts almost from the moment they arrived in the New World. Several notable Puritan dissenters, including Roger Williams and Anne Hutchinson, were ordered out of the Massachusetts Bay Colony because they would not conform to the strict codes of the Puritan leaders. Certain others who failed to follow the rules of religion and society were put on trial as witches and sometimes executed, the most notable incident being the Salem Witch Trials of 1692. In addition, the Puritans warred almost continuously with Native Americans. It is one of the great curiosities of history that the Puritans—who had fled persecution in England—would themselves establish a rigid and intolerant society in New England.

PURITAN LEGACIES

Although strict Puritanism died out in the mid-1700s, many of the ways and beliefs of the Puritans became a permanent part of the American culture. For example, the Puritans' resistance to centralized authority in favor of locally ruled towns and churches was a forerunner to American democratic principles. Today's immigrants still share the Puritan dream that life will be better for those who come to America. In addition, the Puritan work ethic continues to teach that hard work and discipline will earn both spiritual and material rewards.

MICHAEL KAUFMANN
Temple University

Jazz, a form of music that developed in the United States, is now played and enjoyed around the world. Characterized by its use of syncopated rhythms, blue notes, and improvisation, jazz can be played by large bands, small combos, and solo performers. *Clockwise from left:* the Count Basie Orchestra, pianist Chick Corea, the Modern Jazz Quartet.

JAZZ

"Jazz" is a word that has come to describe a variety of contemporary musical styles. But it was originally the name given to a music first played by African Americans in the early years of the 20th century. This early jazz was a type of folk music; that is, it was performed by people in a community simply for their own enjoyment. Since then, jazz has evolved into both a means of artistic expression and a form of commercial entertainment. It is now performed by people of all races and nation-alities and enjoyed by audiences around the world. It has influenced almost every other kind of music in the United States and Europe, and it has produced many of the world's most distinguished instrumentalists, composers, and singers.

Early jazz was a blending of musical elements from Europe and Africa. The first jazz musicians borrowed their ideas of melody and harmony, as well as the instruments they used, from European musical traditions. What made jazz sound different from any other kind of music played in the United States in

366

the early 1900s were certain elements assumed to be African in origin. Foremost among these was **rhythm**. All music makes use of rhythm; one way to think of it is as the element that moves a piece of music along from one note to the next. But jazz rhythm was more pronounced—it made people want to clap their hands or tap their feet.

What was African about this new approach to rhythm was **syncopation**. It means playing a game of sorts with the rhythmic pattern, stressing beats that normally would not be acccented. In other words, instead of ONE-two-THREE-four, the beat might be one-TWO-three-FOUR. Syncopation can be found in all kinds of music, but jazz syncopation had more in common with that found in some African music. In jazz, there was almost a beat between the beats: AH one-AND A two-AND A three-AND A four.

Another African element in jazz had to do with **pitch**—the relative highness or lowness of a musical tone. In jazz, as in the traditional music of Africa and that of many other non-European countries, the musician often seems to be "bending" certain notes as they are played or sung. That is, the note produced seems to fall in between two notes of a scale. These notes eventually came to be referred to as **blue notes**. They are a key element in jazz and in the many kinds of music that have been influenced by jazz.

The final new element in jazz that was perhaps more African than European in origin was the use of **improvisation**. To improvise means to make something up on the spot. Jazz improvisations may be based on the melody of the music being played, or they may be based on the chords to that melody. A chord is the tone produced when two or more notes are played at the same time. Chords are the sounds beneath a melody—what a friend would play on the piano as you sang the melody to a song. Jazz musicians, as they improvise, often ignore the melody and invent new melodies from those piano chords on the spur of the moment.

▶ **EARLY HISTORY**

Most of what we know about the origins of jazz is based on recordings. But jazz was not recorded until 1917, and by that time it had already existed for a decade or more. Another way to learn about the origins of jazz is

---

OUTSTANDING JAZZ RECORDINGS

A basic jazz collection should start with the following CD's:

- *The Smithsonian Collection of Classic Jazz* (Smithsonian Collection of Recordings SMI-CD-033)
- Louis Armstrong, *Portrait of the Artist as a Young Man* (Columbia/Legacy C4K-57176)
- *Jelly Roll Morton & His Red Hot Peppers* (Bluebird 6588-2)
- *The Fletcher Henderson Story: A Study in Frustration* (Columbia/Legacy C3K-57596)
- Bix Beiderbecke, *Volume 1, Singin' the Blues* (Columbia Jazz Masterpieces CK-46175)
- Duke Ellington, *The Blanton-Webster Band* (Bluebird 5859—2-RB); *The Far East Suite* (Bluebird 07863—66551-2)
- *The Essence of Billie Holiday* (Columbia/Legacy CK-47917)
- Count Basie, *The Complete Decca Recordings* (Decca/GRP GRD-3-611)
- Charlie Parker, *The Complete Dial Sessions* (Stash ST-CD567-70); *The Charlie Parker Story* (Savoy Jazz SVY-0105)
- Thelonious Monk, *Brilliant Corners* (Fantasy/Original Jazz Classics OJCCD-026)
- Miles Davis, *Birth of the Cool* (Capitol C21Y-92862); *Kind of Blue* (Columbia/Legacy CK-40579)
- John Coltrane, *Giant Steps* (Atlantic 1311-2); *A Love Supreme* (Impulse GRD-155)
- Ornette Coleman, *The Shape of Jazz to Come* (Atlantic 1317-2)
- World Saxophone Quartet, *Revue* (Black Saint 120056)

---

to examine two earlier forms of African American music: ragtime and the blues.

Ragtime took shape in St. Louis, Missouri, and other midwestern American cities in the late 1800s. A typical ragtime piece had several different melodies. Each would be played one after the other, with some repeats. More significantly, ragtime featured a high degree of rhythmic syncopation, thus anticipating jazz. An important difference between ragtime and jazz, however, is that ragtime allowed for very little improvisation.

Ragtime was usually played on piano, although there were also ragtime banjo players, and quite a few ragtime pieces were written for full orchestra. Its leading composer was Scott Joplin, who won fame for his piece "The Maple Leaf Rag" (1899). Ragtime caught on very quickly, becoming the 20th century's first popular music craze. The most famous popular song to use ragtime's synco-

ragtime

the blues

Profiles of some notable jazz musicians appear along this time line: Jelly Roll Morton, Duke Ellington, Django Reinhardt, Thelonious Monk, Ornette Coleman, and Wynton Marsalis.

Bessie Smith

pated rhythms was "Alexander's Ragtime Band" (1911), by Irving Berlin.

The Blues. The origins of the blues are even more mysterious than those of jazz. In 1912, W. C. Handy copyrighted a song called "Memphis Blues." Two years later, another of Handy's songs, called "St. Louis Blues," became such a big hit that it was soon followed by many other songs with the word "blues" in their titles. Yet even the people of that day knew that the blues was much older—it is a form of music that sounds as old as time. Some people say that the blues can be traced back to slavery. Others believe that it is something African slaves brought with them to America, but this seems very unlikely.

Like the earliest jazz, the earliest blues blended musical elements from different cultures. It was African in sound, but it borrowed its narrative structure—the way it told a story—from Anglo-Scots ballads. A song is not necessarily a blues just because it is slow and sad or because the singer complains about having the blues. The blues is a strict musical form, twelve measures in length. It is also a form of poetry. In a typical blues lyric, the opening line is sung twice, then followed by a third line that rhymes with it. Each line takes up four measures of music, for a total of twelve measures.

The blues probably originated in the Mississippi Delta in the early 20th century, about the same time that jazz was taking shape elsewhere. Like jazz, it uses blue notes. A blues performer who both sings and plays guitar often sounds as though he or she is carrying on both ends of a conversation, singing a line and then bending the strings of the guitar in such a way that the guitar seems to be singing, too. This is sometimes referred to as **call and response**, and it is a common feature in traditional African music. Just as blues guitarists often seem to be "talking" on their instruments, so do jazz horn players. It suggests that jazz and the blues sprang from the same roots.

The earliest blues performers tended not to be professional entertainers. Most of them were men, but by the 1920s, a number of popular women entertainers had incorporated the blues into their acts. It was these women who popularized the blues, singing both blues songs and their own versions of popular songs with jazz accompaniment. The greatest of these women singers was Bessie Smith, who influenced many jazz instrumentalists as well as many other blues singers.

▶ **NEW ORLEANS JAZZ**

Jazz was initially associated with New Orleans, the Louisiana city that many people still believe was the music's birthplace. In the early 1900s, New Orleans was perhaps the most multicultural city in the United States, a trade port with a mix of French, Spanish, and African American influences. Perhaps as a result of this, early New Orleans jazz was a mix of different cultural elements. It combined the deep emotion of the blues and African American spirituals with Spanish and Caribbean rhythms, along with elements of ragtime and European folk music.

The New Orleans style of jazz—nicknamed **Dixieland**, but not until much later—introduced a new style of improvisation. In addition to piano, banjo, drums, and bass or tuba, a typical New Orleans ensemble of the early 1920s included trumpet (or cornet), trom-

Louis Armstrong

Ferdinand "Jelly Roll" Morton (1885–1941), born in Gulfport, Louisiana, was one of the first great New Orleans jazz artists. He began his career as a ragtime pianist and later worked as a musician in several cities. He began recording in 1923, as a solo pianist and with his band, the Red Hot Peppers. Many of his compositions have become jazz standards.

bone, and clarinet. These three horns would often improvise on the melody all at once, with the trumpet or cornet player taking the lead and the trombonist and clarinetist weaving their improvisations around that.

However, the most important feature of New Orleans jazz may have been its new approach to rhythm. New Orleans rhythm was complex, but it was also very relaxed.

The most important musicians produced by New Orleans in the early days of jazz were trumpeter, cornetist, and singer Louis Armstrong and pianist and composer Ferdinand "Jelly Roll" Morton.

Armstrong first demonstrated his brilliance as a member of a New Orleans band led by cornetist Joseph "King" Oliver. Eventually he surpassed Oliver to become the first great jazz improviser. Armstrong moved away from the group improvisations of earlier New Orleans jazz. Instead, he favored improvisations by one player at a time, accompanied only by the rhythm section (usually piano, bass, and drums). Armstrong's most famous solos in-

clude those on "West End Blues," "Struttin' with Some Barbeque," and "Sweethearts on Parade." His fresh approach to melody and rhythm influenced other jazz musicians of the 1920s and 1930s and extended into popular music.

Jelly Roll Morton can be said to have practically invented the notion of jazz composi-

new orleans jazz

Jelly Roll Morton with the Red Hot Peppers

tion, by blending improvisation with written music. In this, he set an example for later jazz composers. His most important pieces were "King Porter Stomp," "Dead Man Blues," and "Black Bottom Stomp."

There were other important jazz musicians from New Orleans during this period, notably clarinetist and soprano saxophonist Sidney Bechet.

At a time when the music of African Americans was not being recorded, the first jazz recordings were made in 1917 by a white group from New Orleans who called themselves the Original Dixieland Jazz Band. It was this band's recordings that popularized the word "jazz" and started a craze for this kind of music. The commercial success of this band's recordings was the first sign that jazz could no longer be thought of as a folk music of significance only to one group of people. Jazz would soon be heard all over the world, and it would be played by white musicians as well as by African Americans.

JAZZ SINGERS

Jazz instrumentalists and singers have always influenced one another. Early jazz horn players often sounded as though they were talking or singing through their horns. As time went on, jazz singers began to attempt to improvise as though they were playing horns. Even when they were singing words, they wanted to be able to take as many liberties with a melody as a jazz instrumentalist might take. Many jazz singers **scat**. Scat singing is a form of vocal improvisation in which a singer departs from a song's words, offering instead his or her own version of the sounds a jazz horn player might make.

However, there are as many possible approaches to jazz singing as there are approaches to instrumental jazz improvisation. Billie Holiday (*pictured*), whom many people consider to have been the greatest jazz singer of them all, never scatted. She simply sang the melody, often completely reshaping it as she went along.

▶ THE RISE OF BIG BANDS

Historians used to say that jazz came up the Mississippi River from New Orleans, landing first in Chicago, Illinois, and then in New York City. There is some truth to this theory, if only because that was the route traveled by Louis Armstrong, who joined a band led by Fletcher Henderson after arriving in New York in 1924. But jazz was being played in New York long before Armstrong got there.

An early kind of New York jazz was Harlem "stride" piano, so named because the pianist's left hand often sounded like someone walking, or taking giant strides. Harlem stride owed much to ragtime but allowed for a much higher degree of improvisation.

New York was also the birthplace of the big-band style of jazz. Big bands included a greater number of instrumentalists than did New Orleans ensembles. Then, as now, a big band usually included three different instrumental sections: brass (trumpets and trombones), reeds (saxophones and clarinets), and rhythm (piano, guitar, bass, and drums).

The most influential of the early big bands was Fletcher Henderson's. In Henderson's band, as in others of the period, there was some improvisation, but a good deal of the music was arranged, that is, written down beforehand. Henderson and Don Redman, the band's chief arrangers, devised a way to pit one section of the

big bands

Duke Ellington with his band

band against another, using the same principle of call and response used in the blues. For example, the brass section might state a phrase and the saxophones would answer. This is still a characteristic big-band sound.

The Henderson orchestra also produced many of the most important soloists of the late 1920s and 1930s. In addition to Louis Armstrong, at various times its members included trumpeter Roy Eldridge, alto saxophonist Benny Carter, and tenor saxophonist Coleman Hawkins.

The Henderson band's white counterpart, at a time when jazz performance remained rigidly segregated, was the Paul Whiteman Orchestra. This was the band that introduced George Gershwin's *Rhapsody in Blue*, in 1924. Its outstanding soloists included trumpeter Leon "Bix" Beiderbecke, trombonist Jack Teagarden, guitarist Eddie Lang, and violinist Joe Venuti. Beiderbecke was especially important, bringing a quieter and more reflective sound to jazz improvisation.

Big bands caught on with the public in the late 1930s, and their popularity lasted through World War II (1939–45). People who danced to the big bands during that period are likely to remember it as the big-band era, but jazz historians tend to call these same years the **swing era**. Swing was the name given to a carefree style of jazz of the 1930s and 1940s,

one of America's greatest composers, writing over 1,000 jazz and non-jazz works.

With the help of his band members, Ellington combined composition and improvisation in especially imaginative ways. Instead of pitting the brass instruments against the reeds, as earlier big-band orchestrators had done, he grouped instruments together in unexpected and highly effective new ways. His best-known numbers are popular melodies like "Sophisticated Lady" and "Mood Indigo." But the works that best demonstrate his genius as a composer and arranger are instrumental pieces, such as "Ko-Ko" and "Concerto for Cootie."

▶ **MODERN JAZZ**

After big-band swing, the next significant development in jazz was bebop. Bebop and the styles that have followed it, including

swing

Edward Kennedy "Duke" Ellington
(1899–1974) born in Washington, D.C., was a pianist, bandleader, and one of the most important composers in jazz history. Ellington moved to New York in 1923; he and his orchestra were stars of Harlem's famous Cotton Club. Radio broadcasts from the club made him a national celebrity, while films, recordings, and European tours brought international fame.

Jean Baptiste "Django" Reinhardt
(1910–53) a guitarist born in Liverchies, Belgium, was the first important European jazz musician. Reinhardt, a Gypsy, lost the use of two fingers of his left hand in a caravan fire and as a result developed an unusual two-fingered playing technique. In 1934 he founded, with violinist Stephane Grappelli, the Quintet of the Hot Club de France.

Dizzy Gillespie

Django Reinhardt
with Stephane Grappelli

but it also refers to the almost indefinable sense of forward motion heard in practically all good jazz.

Some of the most popular big bands of the 1930s and 1940s were those led by Benny Goodman, Artie Shaw, Glenn Miller, Jimmy and Tommy Dorsey, Woody Herman, Jimmie Lunceford, Chick Webb, and Andy Kirk. Perhaps the greatest big band of all was the one led by pianist and composer Edward Kennedy "Duke" Ellington. Ellington was

"cool" and "hard bop," are sometimes referred to as modern jazz.

Bebop, a very adventurous form of music, has come to be associated with small groups rather than with big bands. A typical bebop ensemble includes trumpet, one or two saxophones, piano, bass, and drums.

However, the big bands—in particular, the one led by William "Count" Basie—prepared the way for what is usually called modern jazz. In tenor saxophonist Lester Young, the band had the most original and daring jazz improviser since Louis Armstrong. With Basie himself on piano, the band also featured a rhythm section that accompanied the soloists with a flowing feeling completely new to jazz.

The musicians who originated the style that was eventually named bebop did so, for the most part, at informal gatherings called **jam sessions**. Bebop was more harmonically complex than earlier styles of jazz had been. Bebop musicians improvised not so much on the melody of a tune, but on the tune's underlying chords. Even more important was bebop's rhythmic complexity.

Bebop quickly became associated with New York City, but its roots were in the southwestern United States, specifically Kansas City, Missouri. The Basie band had been formed there, and alto saxophonist Charlie Parker, the greatest of the bebop musicians, grew up there. Just as Louis Armstrong had twenty years earlier, Parker reshaped jazz in his own image. He improvised with a quickness and logic that astonished both audiences and his fellow musicians.

bebop

Thelonious Monk

Thelonious Monk (1917–82) was born in Rocky Mount, North Carolina, and raised in New York City. A gifted youth, he began playing piano professionally in 1935. As a composer and performer, playing in bands led by Coleman Hawkins and Dizzy Gillespie, he had a key role in the development of bebop. But Monk did not win widespread fame until he was in his 40's, when his compositions such as "Round Midnight," "Misterioso," and "Brilliant Corners" were recognized as masterpieces.

COMPOSITION IN JAZZ

A defining feature of jazz is its extensive use of improvisation, and an important job of the jazz composer is to present musicians with strong material on which to improvise. A jazz score might be as detailed as a classical music score, but it might also be just an outline. Jazz composers tend to be instrumentalists, and much of what qualifies as composition in jazz takes place in performance, with the composer as a full participant. In other words, the score is not completed until it has been performed. And the next time it is performed, it may sound very different.

Major jazz composers include pianists Jelly Roll Morton, Duke Ellington, and Thelonious Monk; bassist Charles Mingus (*pictured*); and, more recently, pianists Tadd Dameron, Carla Bley, and Toshiko Akiyoshi.

In addition to Parker, bebop's leading figures included trumpeter John Birks "Dizzy" Gillespie, trombonist J. J. Johnson, pianist Earl "Bud" Powell, vibraphonist Milt Jackson, bassist Ray Brown, and drummers Kenny Clarke and Max Roach. Pianist and composer Thelonious Monk was among the most important of the early bebop musicians, but his full significance did not become apparent until the 1950s.

Cool and Hard Bop. In the 1950s, bebop itself evolved into two different schools, one called cool and the other called hard bop. The trumpeter Miles Davis, who had started his career in Parker's band, helped set the rules for both styles. Cool introduced airy new textures to jazz. Along with Davis, its leading figures included trumpeter Chet Baker, tenor saxophonist Stan Getz, baritone saxophonist Gerry Mulligan, pianist Lennie Tristano, and arranger Gil Evans. Hard bop returned to jazz some of the fervor of the blues and of black church music. In addition to Davis, its leading figures included trumpeter Clifford Brown, tenor saxophonist Theodore "Sonny" Rollins, pianist Horace Silver, and drummers Art Blakey and Max Roach.

How can we tell if a performance is an example of bebop, cool, or hard bop? Often we cannot, because the three styles can be very similar.

Some people felt that jazz had reached a form of perfection with bebop and that there was no place else to go. But some jazz musicians began to look for other ways to improvise, and this search has continued to the present day.

Modal Jazz. Beginning in the late 1950s, some jazz musicians attempted to simplify jazz improvisation by improvising on scales rather than chords. (A scale is a series of ascending or descending notes.) In particular, they investigated **modes**, types of scales used in much of the world's music, including that of Africa and Asia. The album that first showed musicians the endless possi-

cool and hard bop

Charlie Parker

John Coltrane

free jazz

Ornette Coleman

Ornette Coleman (1930–   ), born in Fort Worth, Texas, is a saxophonist and composer who developed a highly individual approach to harmony and improvisation. Largely self-taught, Coleman began playing alto sax in his early teens. His album *Free Jazz* (1960) influenced many jazz artists of the 1960s. His later work reflects his explorations of other musical styles, including rock and the music of Morocco.

One musician, Miles Davis, was closely associated with each.

Davis led the most influential band of the 1950s. It combined elements of bebop, hard bop, and cool. But it also pointed to future developments in jazz. Its members included tenor saxophonist John Coltrane, who quickly emerged as the most influential figure in jazz since Charlie Parker. Davis led another influential band in the 1960s. It included tenor saxophonist Wayne Shorter and pianist Herbie Hancock, two other musicians who had a great impact on jazz in the decades that followed.

bilities of modal improvisation was Miles Davis's *Kind of Blue* (1959).

One of the musicians on that album was John Coltrane, who went on to record a number of influential modal pieces of his own. But Coltrane never completely gave up improvising on chords. He took this more traditional approach to an even greater complexity on "Giant Steps," perhaps his most famous recorded performance. He often combined both approaches, as on *A Love Supreme* (1964).

Free Jazz. Before his death in 1967, Coltrane also became a leading figure in what

Wynton Marsalis

Miles Davis

fusion

Wynton Marsalis (1961–), a trumpeter, was born in New Orleans, Louisiana. The son of a jazz pianist and teacher, he studied both jazz and classical music from an early age. In 1980, while still a student at New York's Juilliard School, he joined Art Blakey's Jazz Messengers. He quickly won acclaim for his brilliant technique and improvisational skills. In 1984 he became the first musician to receive Grammy Awards for both classical and jazz recordings.

is sometimes called free jazz. This style takes a number of different approaches to improvisation but is generally characterized by its free approach to rhythm. The traditional rhythm or accompanying instruments—including bass and drums—take a leading part in a performance, along with the horns.

But the key figure in free jazz was alto saxophonist Ornette Coleman, who is also the man who coined the phrase "free jazz." Coleman's approach to jazz was so original that when he first appeared on the scene in 1959, some other musicians accused him of not knowing how to play his horn. But Coleman's music communicates its own sort of beauty. His most famous performances include "Lonely Woman," "Ramblin'," and "Beauty Is a Rare Thing."

Fusion. Another trend in jazz since the late 1960s has been the attempt to combine elements of jazz with elements of rock and roll. This kind of jazz involves the use of amplified instruments. It is sometimes called fusion. Again, a key figure in this movement was Miles Davis. Some others include pianist Chick Corea, guitarist John McLaughlin, and the members of the group Weather Report.

▶ **JAZZ TODAY**

Since the 1960s, the most creative jazz musicians have begun to question the basic assumptions of jazz and to answer these questions in their own way. They have looked for new ways to combine improvisation and composition, and they have introduced new instruments into jazz ensembles. Among these musicians are pianist Anthony Davis, soprano saxophonist Steve Lacy, alto saxophonists Anthony Braxton, Julius Hemphill, and Henry Threadgill, tenor saxophonist David Murray, and the members of Air, the Art Ensemble of Chicago, and the World Saxophone Quartet.

It is important to remember that one style of jazz never simply replaces the style that came before it. Almost every kind of jazz is still being played somewhere. Perhaps the most famous living jazz musician is trumpeter Wynton Marsalis, who was still in his teens when he began to make a name for himself in the early 1980s. Marsalis has demonstrated that not all the possibilities of earlier forms of jazz have been exhausted. He has helped bring younger audiences to jazz.

Today jazz is heard in the world's leading concert halls, as well as in dark, smoky nightclubs. The audience for jazz is international. Many of the world's leading jazz festivals take place in Europe or Japan. The first important foreign-born jazz musician was the guitarist Django Reinhardt, a Belgian Gypsy who was one of the most inventive soloists of the early 1940s. Current important foreign-born musicians include French violinist Stephane Grappelli, German trombonist Albert Mangelsdorff, South African pianist Abdullah Ibrahim, Belgian pianist Martial Solal, Dutch pianist Misha Mengelberg, and British bassist Dave Holland.

FRANCIS DAVIS
Contributing Editor, *The Atlantic Monthly*

LLAMAS

With their calm manner and quick intelligence, llamas make an ideal beast of burden. Sure-footed and strong, they can cover 20 miles (32 kilometers) a day carrying more than 100 pounds (45 kilograms).

Llamas are native to the Andes mountains of South America. They were domesticated by the Inca peoples at least 4,000 years ago and no longer live in the wild. Llamas belong to the camelid family, a group that also includes alpacas, guanacos, vicuñas, and camels. While camels live in Asia and northern Africa, all other camelids live in South America.

Used for thousands of years in mountainous regions of South America, llamas are highly social domestic animals.

▶ CHARACTERISTICS OF LLAMAS

Llamas are well suited to life high in the mountains. Adults stand about 4 feet (1.2 meters) tall at the shoulder and weigh 250 to 300 pounds (113 to 135 kilograms). Their feet have two toes, each with a long nail curving over the top. Soft pads provide traction on rough terrain. The llama's long silky hair insulates the animal against cold, wind, and moisture. Coat color may be brown, black, gray, white, or red, often with spots or other patterns.

Although llamas eat mainly hay, they also browse on a variety of shrubs and other plants. After eating, they slowly chew the **cud**, a wad of partly digested food. They swallow the cud again, and digestion is completed in the animal's three-chambered stomach. With this thorough digestive system, llamas can handle a poor-quality diet that other animals cannot.

Llamas communicate with sound and body language. When curious or disturbed, they hum, a sound something like human humming. If danger approaches, they will sound a high-pitched alarm call. Llamas also signal their mood through head and ear position. Ears forward mean the llama is relaxed, while ears pinned back and nose tilted up mean the llama is worried.

Spitting is the llama's way of saying "Stop it!" Females spit more often than males, usually to establish dominance in the herd or to fend off an unwanted suitor. A common belief is that llamas spit on people. In truth, only a llama that has been mistreated or raised improperly will spit on a person.

▶ THE LIFE OF LLAMAS

Female llamas are usually ready to breed at 2 years of age. They give birth to one youngster at a time, and pregnancy lasts 335 to 355 days. Baby llamas, often called **crias**, weigh 15 to 20 pounds (7 to 9 kilograms) at birth. Within half an hour they are up and walking. Young llamas spend much of their time playing with each other and prancing about. After 4 to 6 months they are weaned, and by age 4 they are fully grown. Most llamas live from 20 to 25 years of age.

The Incas first raised llamas for their meat, wool, and dung, which they used for fertilizer and fuel. Later, llamas became important pack animals, carrying silver ore, farm crops, and other goods over rough mountain trails. Known as ships of the Andes, they remained the main form of land transport until roads were built in the early 1900's.

Llamas were first brought to the United States in the late 1800's by zoos and private collectors. In recent years, llama breeding has become a growing industry.

Hikers and hunters may rent llamas to carry their gear. Llamas are also featured in parades and even as golf caddies. Craftspeople sell clothing, blankets, and rugs made of llama wool. Because they are so easy to care for, and because they get along well with people, llamas are likely to remain popular.

CARRIE DIERKS
Science Writer

375

HUMAN RIGHTS

Human rights are basic freedoms that all people are entitled to enjoy. They include civil and political rights, such as freedom of speech, religion, and assembly; the right to fair and equal treatment under the law; and the right to vote. Economic and social rights, such as the right to work or obtain an education, also fall under the banner of human rights.

The idea that people are entitled to human rights—regardless of age, nationality, race, religion, sex, or economic status—is relatively new. Many rights are viewed differently in various cultures. Even where human rights are acknowledged, people may not enjoy them equally. Individual rights are often violated in times of social upheaval, war, and revolution and by repressive governments that seek to silence opposition. Violations of human rights occur in all parts of the world. Slavery is outlawed throughout the world, yet it still exists in some places. News reports tell of pro-democracy protesters being arrested in China; prisoners being tortured in Iraq; and "ethnic cleansing"—an effort to drive out or kill an entire ethnic group—being carried out in Bosnia. Even in democratic countries like the United States, where human rights are valued, there are cases of police brutality and other abuses. Many societies deny equal rights to women. All of these and many other violations of human rights are a source of concern worldwide.

The Mothers of the Plaza de Mayo, a human rights group in Argentina, has demonstrated for years to obtain information about *los desaparecidos*, loved ones who disappeared in a military coup in 1976.

▶ **HUMAN RIGHTS IN HISTORY**

Until modern times, rights were generally viewed as privileges granted to people by their rulers. But beginning in the 1600's, a new idea took shape—the idea that people are born with natural rights that government must not take away. This idea formed the basis for the English Bill of Rights and for early state constitutions in America. It was at the heart of the American Declaration of Independence, which says that "all Men are ...endowed by their Creator with certain unalienable rights" and that "among these are Life, Liberty, and the Pursuit of Happiness."

This concept of individual rights is central to Western democratic systems. In a democracy, people consent to be governed, and in exchange, government is obligated to protect their rights. The U.S. Constitution guarantees the individual's freedoms and civil rights. But it took years for some Americans to actually gain those rights. Even after slavery was abolished at the end of the Civil War, African Americans were denied the right to vote and other basic freedoms. Women also had to struggle for basic rights. Thus many Americans did not have a chance to exercise their rights until well into the 1900's.

Also in the 1900's, a series of terrible events helped give rise to the view that people worldwide should be entitled to the same basic rights, regardless of the form of government they live under. These events included the massacre of millions of Armenians in the Ottoman Empire during World War I (1914–18), political executions and forced starvation in the Soviet Union in the 1930's, and the murder of 6 million Jews and others by German Nazis during World War II (1939–45).

After World War II, those who had been responsible for atrocities were brought before international war crimes tribunals. Among the charges against them were "crimes against humanity"—a new category of offenses that included murder, enslavement, extermination, deportation, imprisonment, torture, rape, and other acts committed against civilians. In the hope of preventing future atrocities, securing human rights became an international ideal.

THE UNITED NATIONS AND HUMAN RIGHTS

When the United Nations was founded after World War II, advancing human rights was among the goals set out in its charter. In the organization's early days, a committee chaired by former first lady Eleanor Roosevelt, the U.S. representative, drew up an international bill of rights. This Universal Declaration of Human Rights sets standards for human rights, but it is not legally enforceable. The United Nations has adopted many other measures to provide a legal basis for human rights. Among the most important are the Covenant on Civil and Political Rights and the Covenant on Economic, Social, and Cultural Rights. These international agreements were approved in 1966.

The U.N. Commission on Human Rights monitors abuses and seeks ways to end them. In recent years it has condemned discrimination, torture, and executions without a trial in many nations, including Iraq, Iran, Myanmar (Burma), and Zaïre (now the Democratic Republic of Congo). Sudan has been condemned for actions against the Nuba people, including executions, slavery, torture, and abuses against women and children. Cuba has been criticized for arbitrary arrests and beatings. Russia has been censured for using excessive force against rebels in Chechnya.

Such condemnation shines a spotlight on rights abuses and exposes them to public opinion. But the United Nations has no way to enforce human rights, and its actions have not always been effective. Many countries have refused to sign one or both of the

As the U.S. representative to the United Nations, former first lady Eleanor Roosevelt promoted the Universal Declaration of Human Rights, adopted by the United Nations on December 10, 1948.

SUMMARY OF THE UNIVERSAL DECLARATION OF HUMAN RIGHTS

All people are entitled to

- equal rights and freedoms, regardless of race, color, sex, language, religion, political or other opinion, national or social origin, property, birth, or other status;
- the right to life, liberty, and security of person;
- freedom from slavery or servitude;
- freedom from torture or cruel, inhuman, or degrading treatment or punishment;
- the right to equal protection of the law, without arbitrary arrest, detention, or exile;
- in criminal cases, the right to a fair and public hearing by an independent and impartial court, and the right to be presumed innocent until proved guilty;
- freedom from arbitrary interference with privacy;
- the right to seek asylum from persecution;
- the right to a nationality, including the right to change nationalities;
- the right to marry and found a family;
- the right to own property;
- the right to freedom of thought, conscience, and religion;
- the right to freedom of peaceful assembly and association;
- the right to take part in government;
- the right to social security and to essential economic, social, and cultural rights, including the right to work, to receive equal pay for equal work, and to enjoy decent working conditions;
- the right to form and to join a trade union;
- the right to education.

1966 covenants, even though they support human rights. (The United States has approved only the Covenant on Civil and Political Rights.)

▶ **OTHER EFFORTS**

The European Commission on Human Rights and the Organization of American States (OAS) are among other international organizations that work to promote human rights. Individual countries have also given high priority to this cause. To one degree or another, rights have been a focus of U.S. foreign policy since the early 1900's. In the 1970's, President Jimmy Carter promised that no American aid would go to nations that violated human rights. But interests such as national security, trade, and political alliances have often caused the United States to over-

NOBEL PEACE PRIZE WINNERS FOR WORK IN HUMAN RIGHTS AND RELATED FIELDS

1964 Martin Luther King, Jr., of the United States
1974 Seán MacBride of Ireland (co-winner)
1975 Andrei Sakharov of the Soviet Union
1977 Amnesty International
1980 Adolfo Pérez Esquivel of Argentina
1983 Lech Walesa of Poland
1984 Desmond Tutu of South Africa
1986 Elie Wiesel of the United States
1991 Daw Aung San Suu Kyi of Myanmar
1992 Rigoberta Menchú of Guatemala

look abuses. The same is true for other countries that champion human rights.

Private groups that have no national interests have often led the way in exposing violations of human rights. **Amnesty International**, founded in 1961 by Peter Benenson, a British attorney, is among the best-known groups, with more than one million members in 150 countries. Amnesty International organizes international protests, including letter-writing campaigns on behalf of victims of torture, political imprisonment, and other rights violations. It also promotes legal guarantees of rights and issues a yearly report cataloging abuses, in wealthy and powerful countries as well as developing nations. Organizations such as Human Rights Watch, Asia Watch, and thousands of local groups also monitor human rights worldwide.

The work of all these groups depends on the efforts of individuals. Many people who have fought for human rights have suffered for it, by being imprisoned or executed. Some have won international recognition. In the end, the future of human rights will depend on the willingness of individuals to stand up against repression.

ELAINE PASCOE
Author, *Freedom of Expression: The Right to Speak Out in America*

Profiles: Modern Crusaders

Iqbal Masih (1982–95), born in Muridke, Pakistan, was sold into bonded labor at the age of 4 by his father. Iqbal worked 12-hour days at a carpet factory, where he was beaten and chained to his workstation. Impassioned by revolutionaries of the Bonded Labour Liberation Front (BLLF), Iqbal took a bold stand by refusing to return to his "owner," and he began speaking out against bonded labor. Iqbal attracted international attention, and in 1994 he was awarded the Reebok Prize for Youth in Action. On April 16, 1995, Iqbal was shot and killed while riding his bicycle. Most agree that he was murdered by opponents of fair labor practices.

Craig Kielburger (1983–), born near Toronto, Canada, heard about Iqbal's fate and immediately took up his cause. At the age of 13, Craig founded Free the Children (FTC), an international youth movement dedicated to reducing "the poverty and exploitation of children throughout the world, especially those in bonded, hazardous, and exploitative child labor." Free the Children estimates that there are nearly half a billion children working in the world, many of them horribly abused. Kielburger and other FTC representatives have addressed many organizations to promote children's rights and to give them a voice on issues. For information on how to help, contact Free the Children, 16 Thornbank Road, Thornhill, Ontario, Canada L4J 2A2.

SUPPLEMENT

Deaths

Independent Nations of the World

The United States

    Senate

    House of Representatives

    Cabinet

    Supreme Court

    State Governors

Canada and Its Provinces and Territories

DEATHS

Bing, Sir Rudolf. Austrian-born former general manager of the New York Metropolitan Opera; died on September 2, at the age of 95. Bing established the Met as one of the world's premiere opera companies by drawing the finest international stars, designers, and directors to the organization. Bing's often controversial tenure at the Met lasted from 1950 to 1972.

Brennan, William J., Jr. Former U.S. Supreme Court Justice, died on July 24, at the age of 91. Noted for his powers of persuasion, Brennan served on the Supreme Court from 1956 to 1990. In the many landmark opinions that he wrote for the Court, Brennan upheld a liberal view of the Constitution with a strong emphasis on the rights of the individual.

Calment, Jeanne. French woman recognized as the oldest person in the world; died on August 4, at the age of 122. Born in 1875, Calment was the longest-living person in recorded history. She was a lifelong resident of the city of Arles, where she maintained an active lifestyle—which included riding a bicycle until the age of 100.

John Denver

William J. Brennan, Jr.

Cousteau, Jacques-Yves. French ocean explorer and environmentalist; died on June 25, at the age of 87. Cousteau's hugely popular books, films, and television programs, including *The Undersea World of Jacques Cousteau* (1968–77), introduced millions of people to the hidden wonders of the ocean world. He was a co-inventor of the Aqua-Lung, the first portable underwater breathing device.

De Kooning, Willem. Dutch-born American artist; died on March 19, at the age of 92. One of the most influential painters of the 20th century, de Kooning pioneered the art movement known as abstract expressionism. His artistic style, which influenced generations of artists, emphasized shape, color, and line to convey an impression of spontaneity.

Deng Xiaoping. Chinese leader; died on February 19, at the age of 92. Deng was one of the revolutionary leaders who founded Communist China. He became the paramount leader of the country in 1978, and instituted the economic reforms that opened China to the outside world. He was also responsible for ordering the use of force to put down the pro-democracy demonstrators in Beijing's Tiananmen Square in 1989. Although Deng formally retired from leadership that same year, he remained a powerful figure in China's government until his death.

Denver, John. American singer and songwriter; died on October 13, at the age of 53. Denver gained fame in the 1970s for his lyrical ballads that combined elements of country, folk, and pop music to celebrate the wonder of love and the beauty of nature. Among his best-known songs were "Take Me Home, Country Roads," "Rocky Mountain High," and "Sunshine on My Shoulders."

Diana, Princess of Wales. See pages 40–43.

Ginsberg, Allen. American poet; died on April 5, at the age of 70. Ginsberg first came to prominence in 1956 with the publication of his lengthy poem "Howl." He was a major figure in what was called the Beat Generation of writers. This movement was known for its unconventional writings that celebrated the freedom of the individual and challenged many traditional values.

Roy Lichtenstein

Ben Hogan

Hogan, Ben. American golfer; died on July 25, at the age of 84. Called Bantam Ben because of his slight figure and forceful playing style, Hogan was one of the most outstanding players in the history of golf. Between 1946 and 1953 he won nine major tournaments—four U.S. Opens, two Masters, two Professional Golfers' Association (PGA) championships, and one British Open.

Keith, Brian. American actor; died on June 24, at the age of 75. Keith was best known for playing gruff yet kindly Uncle Bill on the television series *Family Affair* (1966–71). He also starred in *Hardcastle & McCormick* (1983–86).

Kuralt, Charles. American television news reporter; died on July 4, at the age of 62. Kuralt gained lasting recognition for chronicling offbeat, often whimsical stories that he found as he traveled the back roads of America. His "On the Road" reports were broadcast on the *CBS Evening News* from 1967 to 1980.

Mother Teresa. Roman Catholic nun who devoted her life to helping the world's "unwanted, unloved, and uncared for" and came to be regarded by many as a "living saint"; died on September 5, at the age of 87.

Born Agnes Gonxha Bojaxhiu to Albanian parents in Macedonia, she joined a Roman Catholic order of Irish nuns when she was 18 years old. During the 1930s and 1940s, she taught at a Catholic high school in Calcutta, India. But after "receiving a calling from God," she left teaching in 1946 to devote herself to caring for the poor. In 1948, Mother Teresa founded the Order of the Missionaries of Charity, which four years later established the Home of the Pure Heart to help the dying destitutes of Calcutta. Her work was later extended to helping lepers and those who had contracted AIDS. By the time of her death, her order had established some 2,500 homes, schools, orphanages, and clinics in more than 120 countries.

For her work, Mother Teresa won the 1979 Nobel Peace Prize. After a state funeral on September 13, she was buried in Calcutta, where the poor revered her as the "Saint of the Gutter."

Lichtenstein, Roy. American artist; died on September 29, at the age of 73. A master of the 1960s Pop Art movement, Lichtenstein's signature works were inspired by comic strips. His large, cartoon-style paintings often displayed a tongue-in-cheek sense of humor.

Michener, James. American writer; died on October 16, at the age of 90. Michener was acclaimed for his monumental best-selling historical novels, including *Hawaii* (1959) and *Texas* (1985). His first book, *Tales of the South Pacific,* won a Pulitzer Prize in 1948. It became the basis for the 1949 Richard Rogers-Oscar Hammerstein Broadway musical *South Pacific.*

Mitchum, Robert. American actor; died on July 1, at the age of 79. The gruff, droopy-eyed Mitchum portrayed both memorable heroes and villains in a film career that began

Red Skelton

Jimmy Stewart (in *It's a Wonderful Life*)

Solti, Sir Georg. Hungarian-born classical music conductor; died on September 5, at the age of 84. Solti led the Chicago Symphony Orchestra to world renown during his directorship from 1969 to 1991. Known for his exciting and vigorous performances, Solti won more than 30 Grammy awards—more than any other classical or popular musician.

Stewart, Jimmy. American actor; died on July 2, at the age of 89. Famous for his slow drawl and engaging manner, Stewart was a beloved film star for five decades. Among his many classic films were *Mr. Smith Goes to Washington* (1939), *The Philadelphia Story* (1940), *It's a Wonderful Life* (1946), *Rear Window* (1954), and *Anatomy of a Murder* (1959). Stewart was also a much-decorated combat pilot during World War II.

Versace, Gianni. Italian fashion designer; died on July 15, at the age of 50. Versace was considered one of the world's leading fashion designers. His innovative and eye-catching designs were worn by many celebrities.

Gianni Versace

in the 1940s. His films included *The Night of the Hunter* (1955), *Cape Fear* (1962), and *The Big Sleep* (1978), in which he portrayed Philip Marlowe, Raymond Chandler's famous fictional private eye.

Shanker, Albert. American labor leader; died on February 22, at the age of 68. A respected educator, Shanker was the president of the American Federation of Teachers, the powerful national teachers' union, from 1974 until his death.

Skelton, Red. American comedian; died on September 17, at the age of 84. An elastic-faced clown known for his gentle humor, Skelton starred on radio, film, and televison. He was best known for creating a multitude of memorable comic characters, such as the Mean Widdle Kid, Clem Kadiddlehopper, and Freddie the Freeloader, on his popular television show, *The Red Skelton Hour* (1950–70).

INDEPENDENT NATIONS OF THE WORLD

NATION	CAPITAL	AREA (in sq mi)	POPULATION (estimate)	GOVERNMENT
Afghanistan	Kabul	250,000	20,900,000	The Taliban—Muslim fundamentalist group
Albania	Tirana	11,100	3,400,000	Rexhep Mejdani—president Fatos Nano—premier
Algeria	Algiers	919,595	29,200,000	Liamine Zeroual—president
Andorra	Andorra la Vella	175	71,000	Marc Forne Molne--premier
Angola	Luanda	481,354	11,200,000	José Eduardo dos Santos—president
Antigua and Barbuda	St. John's	171	66,000	Lester Bird—prime minister
Argentina	Buenos Aires	1,068,297	35,200,000	Carlos Saúl Menem—president
Armenia	Yerevan	11,500	3,800,000	Levon Ter-Petrosyan—president
Australia	Canberra	2,967,895	18,300,000	John Howard—prime minister
Austria	Vienna	32,374	8,100,000	Thomas Klestil—president Viktor Klima—chancellor
Azerbaijan	Baku	33,500	7,600,000	Geidar A. Aliyev—president
Bahamas	Nassau	5,380	284,000	Hubert A. Ingraham—prime minister
Bahrain	Manama	240	599,000	Isa ibn Salman al-Khalifa—head of state
Bangladesh	Dhaka	55,598	120,100,000	Mustafizur Rahman—president Sheik Hasina Wazed—prime minister
Barbados	Bridgetown	168	261,000	Owen Arthur—prime minister
Belarus	Minsk	80,154	10,200,000	Aleksandr Lukashenko—president
Belgium	Brussels	11,781	10,200,000	Albert II—king Jean-Luc Dehaene—premier
Belize	Belmopan	8,867	222,000	Manuel Esquivel—prime minister
Benin	Porto-Novo	43,484	5,500,000	Mathieu Kerekou—president
Bhutan	Thimbu	18,147	1,800,000	Jigme Singye Wangchuck—king
Bolivia	La Paz Sucre	424,165	7,600,000	Hugo Banzer—president
Bosnia and Herzegovina	Sarajevo	19,800	3,600,000	3-member presidency
Botswana	Gaborone	231,804	1,500,000	Ketumile Masire—president
Brazil	Brasília	3,286,478	157,900,000	Fernando Henrique Cardoso—president
Brunei Darussalam	Bandar Seri Begawan	2,226	300,000	Hassanal Bolkiah—head of state
Bulgaria	Sofia	42,823	8,500,000	Peter Stoyanov—president Ivan Kostov—premier
Burkina	Ouagadougou	105,869	10,800,000	Blaise Compaoré—president
Burma (Myanmar)	Rangoon	261,218	45,900,000	Than Shwe—head of government
Burundi	Bujumbura	10,747	6,100,000	Pierre Buyoya—president

NATION	CAPITAL	AREA (in sq mi)	POPULATION (estimate)	GOVERNMENT
Cambodia	Phom Penh	69,898	10,300,000	Norodom Sihanouk—king Ung Huot—prime minister
Cameroon	Yaoundé	183,569	13,600,000	Paul Biya—president
Canada	Ottawa	3,851,809	30,300,000	Jean Chrétien—prime minister
Cape Verde	Praia	1,557	396,000	Antonio Mascarenhas—president
Central African Republic	Bangui	240,535	3,300,000	Ange Patasse—president
Chad	N'Djemena	495,754	6,500,000	Idriss Deby—president
Chile	Santiago	292,257	14,400,000	Eduardo Frei—president
China	Beijing	3,705,390	1,238,400,000	Jiang Zemin—communist party secretary Li Peng—premier
Colombia	Bogotá	439,736	35,600,000	Ernesto Samper Pizano—president
Comoros	Moroni	838	632,000	Mohammed Taki Abdoulkarim—president
Congo (Zaire)	Kinshasa	905,565	46,800,000	Laurent Kabila—president
Congo Republic	Brazzaville	132,047	2,700,000	Denis Sassou-Nguesso—president
Costa Rica	San José	19,575	3,400,000	José María Figueres Olsen—president
Croatia	Zagreb	21,829	4,500,000	Franjo Tudjman—president
Cuba	Havana	44,218	11,000,000	Fidel Castro—president
Cyprus	Nicosia	3,572	756,000	Glafcos Clerides—president
Czech Republic	Prague	30,469	10,300,000	Vaclav Havel—president Vaclav Klaus—premier
Denmark	Copenhagen	16,629	5,300,000	Margrethe II—queen Poul Nyrup Rasmussen—premier
Djibouti	Djibouti	8,494	617,000	Hassan Gouled Aptidon—president
Dominica	Roseau	290	71,000	Edison James—prime minister
Dominican Republic	Santo Domingo	18,816	8,100,000	Leonel Fernandez Reyna—president
Ecuador	Quito	109,483	11,700,000	Fabián Alarcón—president
Egypt	Cairo	386,660	60,600,000	Mohammed Hosni Mubarak—president Kamal al-Ganzoury—premier
El Salvador	San Salvador	8,124	5,800,000	Armando Calderón Sol—president
Equatorial Guinea	Malabo	10,831	410,000	Obiang Nguema Mbasogo—president
Eritrea	Asmara	45,405	3,300,000	Afeworke Issaias—president
Estonia	Tallinn	17,413	1,500,000	Lennart Meri—president
Ethiopia	Addis Ababa	426,372	58,500,000	Negasso Ghidada—president
Fiji	Suva	7,055	797,000	Kamisese Mara—president
Finland	Helsinki	130,120	5,100,000	Martti Ahtisaari—president Paavo Lipponen—premier
France	Paris	213,000	58,400,000	Jacques Chirac—president Lionel Jospin—premier
Gabon	Libreville	103,346	1,100,000	Omar Bongo—president
Gambia	Banjul	4,361	1,100,000	Yahya Jammeh—head of state
Georgia	Tbilisi	27,000	5,400,000	Eduard Shevardnadze—president
Germany	Berlin	137,744	81,900,000	Roman Herzog—president Helmut Kohl—chancellor

NATION	CAPITAL	AREA (in sq mi)	POPULATION (estimate)	GOVERNMENT
Ghana	Accra	92,099	17,800,000	Jerry Rawlings—president
Greece	Athens	50,944	10,500,000	Costis Stefanopoulos—president Costas Simitis—premier
Grenada	St. George's	133	99,000	Keith Mitchell—prime minister
Guatemala	Guatemala City	42,042	11,000,000	Alvaro Arzu Irigoyen—president
Guinea	Conakry	94,926	7,500,000	Lansana Conté—president
Guinea-Bissau	Bissau	13,948	1,100,000	João Bernardo Vieira—president
Guyana	Georgetown	83,000	838,000	Janet Jagan—president
Haiti	Port-au-Prince	10,714	7,300,000	René Préval—president
Honduras	Tegucigalpa	43,277	6,100,000	Carlos Flores—president-elect
Hungary	Budapest	35,919	10,200,000	Arpad Goncz—president Gyula Horn—premier
Iceland	Reykjavik	39,768	271,000	Olafur Grimsson—president David Oddsson—premier
India	New Delhi	1,269,340	944,400,000	Kocheril Raman Narayanan—president Inder Kumar Gujral—prime minister
Indonesia	Jakarta	735,358	196,800,000	Suharto—president
Iran	Teheran	636,293	61,100,000	Ayatollah Ali Khamenei—religious leader Mohammed Khatami—president
Iraq	Baghdad	167,925	20,600,000	Saddam Hussein—president
Ireland	Dublin	27,136	3,500,000	Mary McAleese—president Bertie Ahern—prime minister
Israel	Jerusalem	8,019	5,700,000	Ezer Weizman—president Benjamin Netanyahu—prime minister
Italy	Rome	116,303	57,400,000	Oscar Luigi Scalfaro—president Romano Prodi—premier
Ivory Coast	Yamoussoukro	124,503	14,800,000	Henri Konan-Bédié—president
Jamaica	Kingston	4,244	2,500,000	Percival J. Patterson—prime minister
Japan	Tokyo	143,751	125,800,000	Akihito—emperor Ryutaro Hashimoto—premier
Jordan	Amman	35,475	5,600,000	Hussein I—king Abdel Salem al-Majali—prime minister
Kazakhstan	Almaty	1,049,000	16,500,000	Nursultan A. Nazarbaev—president
Kenya	Nairobi	224,959	31,800,000	Daniel arap Moi—president
Kiribati	Tarawa	264	80,000	Teburoro Tito—president
Korea (North)	Pyongyang	46,540	22,500,000	Kim Jong II—president Hong Song Nam—premier
Korea (South)	Seoul	38,025	45,500,000	Kim Dae Jung—president-elect Koh Kun—premier
Kuwait	Kuwait	6,880	1,700,000	Jabir al-Ahmad al-Sabah—head of state
Kyrgyzstan	Bishkek	76,641	4,600,000	Askar Akayev—president
Laos	Vientiane	91,429	5,000,000	Nouhak Phoumsavan—president Khamtai Siphandon—premier
Latvia	Riga	24,600	2,500,000	Guntis Ulmanis—president
Lebanon	Beirut	4,015	3,100,000	Elias Hrawi—president Rafik al-Hariri—premier

NATION	CAPITAL	AREA (in sq mi)	POPULATION (estimate)	GOVERNMENT
Lesotho	Maseru	11,720	2,100,000	Letsie III—king Ntsu Mokhehle—prime minister
Liberia	Monrovia	43,000	2,800,000	Charles G. Taylor—president
Libya	Tripoli	679,362	5,600,000	Muammar el-Qaddafi—head of government
Liechtenstein	Vaduz	61	31,000	Hans Adam—prince
Lithuania	Vilnius	25,174	3,700,000	Algirdas Brazauskas—president
Luxembourg	Luxembourg	998	412,000	Jean—grand duke Jean-Claude Juncker—premier
Macedonia	Skopje	9,928	2,200,000	Kiro Gligorov—president
Madagascar	Antananarivo	226,657	15,400,000	Didier Ratsiraka—president
Malawi	Lilongwe	45,747	10,100,000	Bakili Muluzi—president
Malaysia	Kuala Lumpur	127,317	20,600,000	Jaafar bin Abdul Rahman—king Mahathir Mohammad—prime minister
Maldives	Male	115	263,000	Maumoon Abdul Gayoom—president
Mali	Bamako	478,765	11,100,000	Alpha Oumar Konare—president
Malta	Valletta	122	373,000	Ugo Mifsud Bonnici—president Alfred Sant—prime minister
Marshall Islands	Majuro	70	57,000	Amata Kabua—president
Mauritania	Nouakchott	397,954	2,400,000	Maaoiya Ould Sid Ahmed Taya—president
Mauritius	Port Louis	790	1,100,000	Cassam Uteem—president Navin Ramgoolan—premier president
Mexico	Mexico City	761,602	96,600,000	Ernesto Zedillo Ponce de León—president
Micronesia	Colonia	271	126,000	Jacob Nena—president
Moldova	Kishiniev	13,000	4,200,000	Petru Licinschi—president
Monaco	Monaco-Ville	0.6	32,000	Rainier III—prince
Mongolia	Ulan Bator	604,248	2,400,000	Natsagiin Bagabandi—president
Morocco	Rabat	172,413	27,600,000	Hassan II—king Abdellatif Filali—premier
Mozambique	Maputo	309,494	17,800,000	Joaquím A. Chissano—president
Namibia	Windhoek	318,260	1,600,000	Sam Nujoma—president
Nauru	Yaren District	8	11,000	Kinza Clodumar—president
Nepal	Katmandu	54,362	21,100,000	Birendra Bir Bikram Shah Deva—king Surya Bahadur Thapa—premier
Netherlands	Amsterdam	15,770	15,500,000	Beatrix—queen Willem Kok—premier
New Zealand	Wellington	103,736	3,600,000	Jenny Shipley—prime minister
Nicaragua	Managua	50,193	4,200,000	José Arnoldo Aleman—president
Niger	Niamey	489,190	9,500,000	Ibrahim Bare Mainassara—president
Nigeria	Abuja	356,667	115,000,000	Sani Abacha—head of government
Norway	Oslo	125,056	4,400,000	Harald V—king Kjell Magne Bondevik—premier
Oman	Muscat	82,030	2,300,000	Qabus ibn Said—sultan

NATION	CAPITAL	AREA (in sq mi)	POPULATION (estimate)	GOVERNMENT
Pakistan	Islamabad	310,404	134,100,000	Farooq Leghari—president Nawaz Sharif—prime minister
Palau	Koror	192	17,000	Kuniwo Nakamura—president
Panama	Panama City	29,761	2,700,000	Ernesto Pérez Balladares—president
Papua New Guinea	Port Moresby	178,260	4,400,000	William Skate—prime minister
Paraguay	Asunciùn	157,047	5,000,000	Juan Carlos Wasmosy—president
Peru	Lima	496,222	23,900,000	Alberto Fujimori—president
Philippines	Manila	115,830	71,900,000	Fidel V. Ramos—president Joseph Estrada—vice-president
Poland	Warsaw	120,725	38,600,000	Aleksander Kwasniewski—president Jerzy Buzek—premier
Portugal	Lisbon	35,553	9,800,000	Jorge Sampaio—president Antonio Guterres—premier
Qatar	Doha	4,247	558,000	Hamad ibn Khalifa al-Thani—head of state
Romania	Bucharest	91,700	22,600,000	Emil Constantinescu—president Victor Ciorbea—premier
Russia	Moscow	6,600,000	147,700,000	Boris N. Yeltsin—president
Rwanda	Kigali	10,169	5,400,000	Pasteur Bizimungu—president
St. Kitts and Nevis	Basseterre	105	41,000	Denzil Douglas—prime minister
St. Lucia	Castries	238	144,000	Kenny Anthony—prime minister
St. Vincent and the Grenadines	Kingstown	150	113,000	James F. Mitchell—prime minister
San Marino	San Marino	24	25,000	Gabriele Gatti—head of state
Sao Tome and Principe	São Tomé	372	135,000	Miguel Trovoada—president
Saudi Arabia	Riyadh	830,000	18,800,000	Fahd ibn Abdul-Aziz—king
Senegal	Dakar	75,750	8,600,000	Abdou Diouf—president
Seychelles	Victoria	107	76,000	France Albert René—president
Sierra Leone	Freetown	27,700	4,300,000	Johnny Paul Koromah—president
Singapore	Singapore	224	3,000,000	Ong Teng Cheong—president Go Chok Tong—prime minister
Slovak Republic	Bratislava	18,933	5,400,000	Michal Kovac—president
Slovenia	Ljubljana	7,819	2,000,000	Milan Kucan—president
Solomon Islands	Honiara	10,983	391,000	Bartholomew Ulufa'alu—prime minister
Somalia	Mogadishu	246,200	9,800,000	no functioning government
South Africa	Pretoria Cape Town Bloemfontein	471,444	42,400,000	Nelson Mandela—president
Spain	Madrid	194,896	39,300,000	Juan Carlos I—king José María Aznar—premier
Sri Lanka	Colombo	25,332	18,300,000	C. Bandaranaike Kumaratunga—president
Sudan	Khartoum	967,500	27,300,000	O. Hassan Ahmad al-Bashir—president

NATION	CAPITAL	AREA (in sq mi)	POPULATION (estimate)	GOVERNMENT
Suriname	Paramaribo	63,037	432,000	Jules Wijdenbosch—president
Swaziland	Mbabane	6,704	938,000	Mswati III—king
Sweden	Stockholm	173,731	8,800,000	Carl XVI Gustaf—king Goeran Persson—premier
Switzerland	Bern	15,941	7,100,000	Flavio Cotti—president
Syria	Damascus	71,498	14,600,000	Hafez al-Assad—president Mahmoud Zubi—premier
Taiwan	Taipei	13,885	20,500,000	Lee Teng-hui—president Vincent Siew—premier
Tajikistan	Dushanbe	55,250	5,900,000	Yakhyo Azimov--premier
Tanzania	Dar es Salaam	364,898	30,800,000	Benjamin Mkapa—president
Thailand	Bangkok	198,457	60,000,000	Bhumibol Adulyadej—king Chuan Leekpai—premier
Togo	Lomé	21,622	4,200,000	Gnassingbe Eyadema—president
Tonga	Nuku'alofa	270	99,000	Taufa'ahau Tupou IV—king Baron Vaea—premier
Trinidad & Tobago	Port of Spain	1,980	1,300,000	A.N.R. Robinson—president Basdeo Panday—prime minister
Tunisia	Tunis	63,170	9,200,000	Zine el-Abidine Ben Ali—president
Turkey	Ankara	301,381	62,700,000	Suleyman Demirel—president Mesut Yilmaz—prime minister
Turkmenistan	Ashkhabad	188,455	4,600,000	Saparmurad Niyazov—president
Tuvalu	Funafuti	10	10,000	Bikenibeu Panieu—prime minister
Uganda	Kampala	91,134	20,300,000	Yoweri Museveni—president
Ukraine	Kiev	231,990	51,100,000	Leonid D. Kuchma—president
United Arab Emirates	Abu Dhabi	32,278	2,300,000	Zayd ibn Sultan al-Nuhayyan—president
United Kingdom	London	94,226	58,100,000	Elizabeth II—queen Tony Blair—prime minister
United States	Washington, D.C.	3,618,467	266,600,000	William J. Clinton—president Albert A. Gore, Jr.—vice-president
Uruguay	Montevideo	68,037	3,200,000	Julio Sanguinetti—president
Uzbekistan	Tashkent	172,750	22,900,000	Islam A. Karimov—president
Vanuatu	Vila	5,700	174,000	Jean Marie Leye—president
Vatican City	Vatican City	0.17	1,000	John Paul II—pope
Venezuela	Caracas	352,143	22,700,000	Rafael Caldera—president
Vietnam	Hanoi	128,402	75,200,000	Du Muoi—communist party secretary Phan Van Khai—premier
Western Samoa	Apia	1,097	171,000	Tanumafili Malietoa II—head of state
Yemen	Sana	203,849	15,900,000	Ali Abdullah Saleh—president Faraj Said bin Ghanim—premier
Yugoslavia	Belgrade	39,390	10,600,000	Slobodan Milosevic—president Radoje Kontic—premier
Zambia	Lusaka	290,585	8,300,000	Frederick Chiluba—president
Zimbabwe	Harare	150,333	12,000,000	Robert Mugabe—president

THE CONGRESS OF THE UNITED STATES

UNITED STATES SENATE
(55 Republicans, 45 Democrats)

Alabama
Richard C. Shelby (R)
Jefferson B. Sessions (R)

Alaska
Ted Stevens (R)
Frank H. Murkowski (R)

Arizona
John S. McCain III (R)
John Kyl (R)

Arkansas
Dale Bumpers (D)
Tim Hutchinson (R)

California
Barbara Boxer (D)
Dianne Feinstein (D)

Colorado
Ben Nighthorse Campbell (R)
Wayne Allard (R)

Connecticut
Christopher J. Dodd (D)
Joseph I. Lieberman (D)

Delaware
William V. Roth, Jr. (R)
Joseph R. Biden, Jr. (D)

Florida
Bob Graham (D)
Connie Mack (R)

Georgia
Paul D. Coverdell (R)
Max Cleland (D)

Hawaii
Daniel K. Inouye (D)
Daniel K. Akaka (D)

Idaho
Larry E. Craig (R)
Dirk Kempthorne (R)

Illinois
Carol Moseley-Braun (D)
Richard J. Durbin (D)

Indiana
Richard G. Lugar (R)
Daniel R. Coats (R)

Iowa
Charles E. Grassley (R)
Thomas R. Harkin (D)

Kansas
Pat Roberts (R)
Sam Brownback (R)

Kentucky
Wendell H. Ford (D)
Mitch McConnell (R)

Louisiana
John B. Breaux (D)
Mary L. Landrieu (D)

Maine
Olympia J. Snowe (R)
Susan Collins (R)

Maryland
Paul S. Sarbanes (D)
Barbara A. Mikulski (D)

Massachusetts
Edward M. Kennedy (D)
John F. Kerry (D)

Michigan
Carl Levin (D)
Spencer Abraham (R)

Minnesota
Paul Wellstone (D)
Rod Grams (R)

Mississippi
Thad Cochran (R)
Trent Lott (R)

Missouri
Christopher S. Bond (R)
John Ashcroft (R)

Montana
Max S. Baucus (D)
Conrad Burns (R)

Nebraska
Robert Kerrey (D)
Chuck Hagel (R)

Nevada
Harry Reid (D)
Richard H. Bryan (D)

New Hampshire
Judd Gregg (R)
Robert C. Smith (R)

New Jersey
Frank R. Lautenberg (D)
Robert G. Torricelli (D)

New Mexico
Pete V. Domenici (R)
Jeff Bingaman (D)

New York
Daniel P. Moynihan (D)
Alfonse M. D'Amato (R)

North Carolina
Jesse Helms (R)
Lauch Faircloth (R)

North Dakota
Kent Conrad (D)
Byron L. Dorgan (D)

Ohio
John H. Glenn, Jr. (D)
Mike DeWine (R)

Oklahoma
Donald L. Nickles (R)
James M. Inhofe (R)

Oregon
Gordon Smith (R)
Ron Wyden (D)

Pennsylvania
Arlen Specter (R)
Rick Santorum (R)

Rhode Island
John H. Chafee (R)
John Reed (D)

South Carolina
Strom Thurmond (R)
Ernest F. Hollings (D)

South Dakota
Thomas A. Daschle (D)
Tim Johnson (D)

Tennessee
Bill Frist (R)
Fred D. Thompson (R)

Texas
Phil Gramm (R)
Kay Bailey Hutchinson (R)

Utah
Orrin G. Hatch (R)
Robert F. Bennett (R)

Vermont
Patrick J. Leahy (D)
James M. Jeffords (R)

Virginia
John W. Warner (R)
Charles S. Robb (D)

Washington
Slade Gorton (R)
Patty Murray (D)

West Virginia
Robert C. Byrd (D)
John D. Rockefeller IV (D)

Wisconsin
Herbert H. Kohl (D)
Russell D. Feingold (D)

Wyoming
Craig Thomas (R)
Michael Enzi (R)

(D) Democrat
(R) Republican

UNITED STATES HOUSE OF REPRESENTATIVES
(228 Republicans, 204 Democrats, 1 Independent, 2 Vacancies)

Alabama
1. H. L. Callahan (R)
2. T. Everett (R)
3. B. Riley (R)
4. R. Aderholt (R)
5. B. Cramer (D)
6. S. Bachus (R)
7. E. Hilliard (D)

Alaska
D. Young (R)

Arizona
1. M. Salmon (R)
2. E. Pastor (D)
3. B. Stump (R)
4. J. Shadegg (R)
5. J. Kolbe (R)
6. J. D. Hayworth (R)

Arkansas
1. M. Berry (D)
2. V. F. Snyder (D)
3. A. Hutchinson (R)
4. J. Dickey (R)

California
1. F. Riggs (R)
2. W. Herger (R)
3. V. Fazio (D)
4. J. T. Doolittle (R)
5. R. T. Matsui (D)
6. L. Woolsey (D)
7. G. Miller (D)
8. N. Pelosi (D)
9. R. V. Dellums (D)
10. E. Tauscher (D)
11. R. Pombo (R)
12. T. Lantos (D)
13. F. H. Stark (D)
14. A. Eshoo (D)
15. T. Campbell (R)
16. Z. Lofgren (D)
17. S. Farr (D)
18. G. Condit (D)
19. G. Radanovich (R)
20. C. Dooley (D)
21. B. Thomas (R)
22. vacant
23. E. Gallegly (R)
24. B. Sherman (D)
25. H. McKeon (R)
26. H. L. Berman (D)
27. J. E. Rogan (R)
28. D. Dreier (R)
29. H. A. Waxman (D)
30. X. Becerra (D)
31. M. G. Martinez (D)
32. J. C. Dixon (D)
33. L. Roybal-Allard (D)
34. E. E. Torres (D)
35. M. Waters (D)
36. J. Harman (D)
37. J. Millender-McDonald (D)
38. S. Horn (R)
39. E. Royce (R)
40. J. Lewis (R)
41. J. Kim (R)

42. G. E. Brown, Jr. (D)
43. K. Calvert (R)
44. S. Bono (R)
45. D. Rohrabacher (R)
46. L. Sanchez (D)
47. C. C. Cox (R)
48. R. Packard (R)
49. B. Bilbray (R)
50. B. Filner (D)
51. R. Cunningham (R)
52. D. Hunter (R)

Colorado
1. D. DeGette (D)
2. D. Skaggs (D)
3. S. McInnis (R)
4. R. W. Schaffer (R)
5. J. Hefley (R)
6. D. L. Schaefer (R)

Connecticut
1. B. B. Kennelly (D)
2. S. Gejdenson (D)
3. R. DeLauro (D)
4. C. Shays (R)
5. J. H. Maloney (D)
6. N. L. Johnson (R)

Delaware
M. N. Castle (R)

Florida
1. J. Scarborough (R)
2. A. Boyd, Jr. (D)
3. C. Brown (D)
4. T. Fowler (R)
5. K. Thurman (D)
6. C. B. Stearns (R)
7. J. Mica (R)
8. B. McCollum (R)
9. M. Bilirakis (R)
10. B. Young (R)
11. J. Davis (D)
12. C. Canady (R)
13. D. Miller (R)
14. P. J. Goss (R)
15. D. Weldon (R)
16. M. Foley (R)
17. C. Meek (D)
18. I. Ros-Lehtinen (R)
19. R. Wexler (D)
20. P. Deutsch (D)
21. L. Diaz-Balart (R)
22. E. C. Shaw, Jr. (R)
23. A. L. Hastings (D)

Georgia
1. J. Kingston (R)
2. S. Bishop (D)
3. M. Collins (R)
4. C. McKinney (D)
5. J. Lewis (D)
6. N. Gingrich (R)
7. B. Barr (R)
8. S. Chambliss (R)
9. N. Deal (R)
10. C. Norwood (R)
11. J. Linder (R)

Hawaii
1. N. Abercrombie (D)
2. P. T. Mink (D)

Idaho
1. H. Chenoweth (R)
2. M. Crapo (R)

Illinois
1. B. Rush (D)
2. J. Jackson, Jr. (D)
3. W. O. Lipinski (D)
4. L. V. Gutierrez (D)
5. R. R. Blagojevich (D)
6. H. J. Hyde (R)
7. D. K. Davis (D)
8. P. M. Crane (R)
9. S. R. Yates (D)
10. J. E. Porter (R)
11. G. Weller (R)
12. J. F. Costello (D)
13. H. W. Fawell (R)
14. J. D. Hastert (R)
15. T. W. Ewing (R)
16. D. Manzullo (R)
17. L. Evans (D)
18. R. LaHood (R)
19. G. Poshard (D)
20. J. M. Shimkus (R)

Indiana
1. P. J. Visclosky (D)
2. D. McIntosh (R)
3. T. Roemer (D)
4. M. Souder (R)
5. S. Buyer (R)
6. D. L. Burton (R)
7. E. Pease (R)
8. J. Hostettler (R)
9. L. H. Hamilton (D)
10. J. Carson (D)

Iowa
1. J. Leach (R)
2. J. Nussle (R)
3. L. L. Boswell (D)
4. G. Ganske (R)
5. T. Latham (R)

Kansas
1. J. Moran (R)
2. J. Ryun (R)
3. V. Snowbarger (R)
4. T. Tiahrt (R)

Kentucky
1. E. Whitfield (R)
2. R. Lewis (R)
3. A. Northup (R)
4. J. Bunning (R)
5. H. Rogers (R)
6. S. Baesler (D)

Louisiana
1. R. Livingston, Jr. (R)
2. W. J. Jefferson (D)

3. W. J. Tauzin (R)
4. J. McCrery (R)
5. J. Cooksey (R)
6. R. H. Baker (R)
7. C. John (D)

Maine
1. T. Allen (D)
2. J. Baldacci (D)

Maryland
1. W. T. Gilchrest (R)
2. R. L. Ehrlich, Jr. (R)
3. B. L. Cardin (D)
4. A. Wynn (D)
5. S. H. Hoyer (D)
6. R. Bartlett (R)
7. E. E. Cummings (D)
8. C. A. Morella (R)

Massachusetts
1. J. Olver (D)
2. R. E. Neal (D)
3. J. McGovern (D)
4. B. Frank (D)
5. M. Meehan (D)
6. J. F. Tierney (D)
7. E. J. Markey (D)
8. J. P. Kennedy II (D)
9. J. J. Moakley (D)
10. W. D. Delahunt (D)

Michigan
1. B. Stupak (D)
2. P. Hoekstra (R)
3. V. Ehlers (R)
4. D. Camp (R)
5. J. Barcia (D)
6. F. S. Upton (R)
7. N. Smith (R)
8. D. A. Stabenow (D)
9. D. E. Kildee (D)
10. D. E. Bonior (D)
11. J. Knollenberg (R)
12. S. M. Levin (D)
13. L. Rivers (D)
14. J. Conyers, Jr. (D)
15. C. C. Kilpatrick (D)
16. J. D. Dingell, Jr. (D)

Minnesota
1. G. Gutknecht (R)
2. D. Minge (D)
3. J. Ramstad (R)
4. B. F. Vento (D)
5. M. O. Sabo (D)
6. W. Luther (D)
7. C. C. Peterson (D)
8. J. L. Oberstar (D)

Mississippi
1. R. Wicker (R)
2. B. Thompson (D)
3. C. W. Pickering, Jr. (R)
4. M. Parker (R)
5. G. Taylor (D)

Missouri
1. W. L. Clay (D)
2. J. Talent (R)
3. R. A. Gephardt (D)
4. I. Skelton (D)
5. K. McCarthy (D)
6. P. Danner (D)
7. R. Blunt (R)
8. J. Emerson (R)
9. K. Hulshof (R)

Montana
1. R. Hill (R)

Nebraska
1. D. K. Bereuter (R)
2. J. Christensen (R)
3. B. Barrett (R)

Nevada
1. J. Ensign (R)
2. J. Gibbons (R)

New Hampshire
1. J. E. Sununu (R)
2. C. Bass (R)

New Jersey
1. R. E. Andrews (D)
2. F. LoBiondo (R)
3. H. J. Saxton (R)
4. C. H. Smith (R)
5. M. Roukema (R)
6. F. Pallone, Jr. (D)
7. B. Franks (R)
8. W. J. Pascrell, Jr. (D)
9. S. R. Rothman (D)
10. D. M. Payne (D)
11. R. Frelinghuysen (R)
12. M. Pappas (R)
13. R. Menendez (D)

New Mexico
1. S. H. Schiff (R)
2. J. R. Skeen (R)
3. B. Redmond (R)*

New York
1. M. Forbes (R)
2. R. Lazio (R)
3. P. T. King (R)
4. C. McCarthy (D)
5. G. L. Ackerman (D)
6. F. H. Flake (D)
7. T. J. Manton (D)
8. J. Nadler (D)
9. C. E. Schumer (D)
10. E. Towns (D)
11. M. R. Owens (D)
12. N. Velazquez (D)
13. V. J. Fossella, Jr. (R)*
14. C. Maloney (D)
15. C. B. Rangel (D)
16. J. E. Serrano (D)
17. E. L. Engel (D)
18. N. M. Lowey (D)
19. S. W. Kelly (R)
20. B. A. Gilman (R)
21. M. R. McNulty (D)

22. G. B. Solomon (R)
23. S. L. Boehlert (R)
24. J. McHugh (R)
25. J. T. Walsh (R)
26. M. Hinchey (D)
27. L. W. Paxon (R)
28. L. M. Slaughter (D)
29. J. J. LaFalce (D)
30. J. Quinn (R)
31. A. Houghton, Jr. (R)

North Carolina
1. E. Clayton (D)
2. B. R. Etheridge (D)
3. W. Jones, Jr. (R)
4. D. E. Price (D)
5. R. Burr (R)
6. J. H. Coble (R)
7. M. McIntyre (D)
8. W. G. Hefner (D)
9. S. Myrick (R)
10. T. C. Ballenger (R)
11. C. H. Taylor (R)
12. M. Watt (D)

North Dakota
E. Pomeroy (D)

Ohio
1. S. Chabot (R)
2. R. Portman (R)
3. T. P. Hall (D)
4. M. G. Oxley (R)
5. P. E. Gillmor (R)
6. T. Strickland (D)
7. D. L. Hobson (R)
8. J. A. Boehner (R)
9. M. Kaptur (D)
10. D. Kucinich (D)
11. L. Stokes (D)
12. J. R. Kasich (R)
13. S. Brown (D)
14. T. C. Sawyer (D)
15. D. Pryce (R)
16. R. S. Regula (R)
17. J. A. Traficant, Jr. (D)
18. B. Ney (R)
19. S. LaTourette (R)

Oklahoma
1. S. Largent (R)
2. T. Coburn (R)
3. W. Watkins (R)
4. J. C. Watts (R)
5. E. J. Istook (R)
6. F. Lucas (R)

Oregon
1. E. Furse (D)
2. R. F. Smith (R)
3. E. Blumenauer (D)
4. P. DeFazio (D)
5. D. Hooley (D)

Pennsylvania
1. vacant
2. C. Fattah (D)
3. R. A. Borski (D)
4. R. Klink (D)
5. J. E. Peterson (R)

6. T. Holden (D)
7. W. C. Weldon (R)
8. J. Greenwood (R)
9. E. G. Shuster (R)
10. J. M. McDade (R)
11. P. E. Kanjorski (D)
12. J. P. Murtha, Jr. (D)
13. J. Fox (R)
14. W. J. Coyne (D)
15. P. McHale (D)
16. J. R. Pitts (R)
17. G. W. Gekas (R)
18. M. Doyle (D)
19. W. F. Goodling (R)
20. F. Mascara (D)
21. P. English (R)

Rhode Island
1. P. Kennedy (D)
2. R. A. Weygand (D)

South Carolina
1. M. Sanford (R)
2. F. D. Spence (R)
3. L. Graham (R)
4. B. Inglis (R)
5. J. M. Spratt, Jr. (D)
6. J. Clyburn (D)

South Dakota
J. Thune (R)

Tennessee
1. W. Jenkins (R)
2. J. J. Duncan, Jr. (R)
3. Z. Wamp (R)
4. V. Hilleary (R)
5. B. Clement (D)
6. B. J. Gordon (D)
7. E. Bryant (R)
8. J. S. Tanner (D)
9. H. E. Ford, Jr. (D)

Texas
1. M. Sandlin (D)
2. J. Turner (D)
3. S. Johnson (R)
4. R. M. Hall (D)
5. P. Sessions (R)
6. J. Barton (R)
7. W. R. Archer (R)
8. K. Brady (R)
9. N. Lampson (D)
10. L. Doggett (D)
11. C. Edwards (D)
12. K. Granger (R)
13. W. Thornberry (R)
14. R. Paul (R)
15. R. Hinojosa (D)
16. S. Reyes (D)
17. C. W. Stenholm (D)
18. S. Jackson-Lee (D)
19. L. Combest (R)
20. H. B. Gonzalez (D)
21. L. S. Smith (R)
22. T. D. DeLay (R)
23. H. Bonilla (R)
24. J. M. Frost (D)
25. K. Bentsen (D)
26. D. Armey (R)

27. S. P. Ortiz (D)
28. C. Rodriguez (D)*
29. G. Green (D)
30. E. B. Johnson (D)

Utah
1. J. V. Hansen (R)
2. M. Cook (R)
3. C. Cannon (R)

Vermont
B. Sanders (I)

Virginia
1. H. H. Bateman (R)
2. O. B. Pickett (D)
3. R. C. Scott (D)
4. N. Sisisky (D)
5. V. H. Goode, Jr. (D)
6. R. Goodlatte (R)
7. T. Bliley, Jr. (R)
8. J. P. Moran, Jr. (D)
9. F. C. Boucher (D)
10. F. R. Wolf (R)
11. T. Davis III (R)

Washington
1. R. White (R)
2. J. Metcalf (R)
3. L. Smith (R)
4. D. Hastings (R)
5. G. Nethercutt (R)
6. N. D. Dicks (D)
7. J. McDermott (D)
8. J. Dunn (R)
9. A. Smith (D)

West Virginia
1. A. B. Mollohan (D)
2. R. E. Wise, Jr. (D)
3. N. J. Rahall II (D)

Wisconsin
1. M. Neumann (R)
2. S. Klug (R)
3. R. Kind (D)
4. G. D. Kleczka (D)
5. T. Barrett (D)
6. T. E. Petri (R)
7. D. R. Obey (D)
8. J. Johnson (D)
9. F. J. Sensenbrenner, Jr. (R)

Wyoming
B. Cubin (R)

(D) Democrat
(R) Republican
(I) Independent

*elected in 1997

UNITED STATES SUPREME COURT

Chief Justice: William H. Rehnquist (1986)
Associate Justices:
  John Paul Stevens (1975)
  Sandra Day O'Connor (1981)
  Antonin Scalia (1986)
  Anthony M. Kennedy (1988)
  David H. Souter (1990)
  Clarence Thomas (1991)
  Ruth Bader Ginsburg (1993)
  Stephen G. Breyer (1994)

UNITED STATES CABINET

Secretary of Agriculture: Daniel R. Glickman
Attorney General: Janet Reno
Secretary of Commerce: William M. Daley
Secretary of Defense: William S. Cohen
Secretary of Education: Richard W. Riley
Secretary of Energy: Federico F. Peña
Secretary of Health and Human Services: Donna E. Shalala
Secretary of Housing and Urban Development: Andrew M. Cuomo
Secretary of Interior: Bruce Babbitt
Secretary of Labor: Alexis M. Herman
Secretary of State: Madeleine K. Albright
Secretary of Transportation: Rodney E. Slater
Secretary of the Treasury: Robert E. Rubin
Secretary of Veteran Affairs: Togo West
  (nominated, waiting for Senate confirmation)

In a close race in New Jersey, Governor Christine Todd Whitman, a Republican, was re-elected governor in 1997. She defeated Democrat James E. McGreevey by a razor-thin margin.

STATE GOVERNORS

Alabama	Forrest James, Jr. (R)	**Montana**	Marc Racicot (R)
Alaska	Tony Knowles (D)	**Nebraska**	Ben Nelson (D)
Arizona	Jane Dee Hull (R)***	**Nevada**	Bob Miller (D)
Arkansas	Mike Huckabee (R)	**New Hampshire**	Jeanne Shaheen (D)
California	Pete Wilson (R)	**New Jersey**	Christine Todd Whitman (R)**
Colorado	Roy Romer (D)	**New Mexico**	Gary Johnson (R)
Connecticut	John Rowland (R)	**New York**	George Pataki (R)
Delaware	Thomas R. Carper (D)	**North Carolina**	Jim B. Hunt, Jr. (D)
Florida	Lawton Chiles (D)	**North Dakota**	Edward Schafer (R)
Georgia	Zell Miller (D)	**Ohio**	George V. Voinovich (R)
Hawaii	Ben Cayetano (D)	**Oklahoma**	Frank Keating (R)
Idaho	Phil Batt (R)	**Oregon**	John Kitzhaber (D)
Illinois	Jim Edgar (R)	**Pennsylvania**	Thomas J. Ridge (R)
Indiana	Frank L. O'Bannon (D)	**Rhode Island**	Lincoln Almond (R)
Iowa	Terry E. Branstad (R)	**South Carolina**	David Beasley (R)
Kansas	Bill Graves (R)	**South Dakota**	William Janklow (R)
Kentucky	Paul Patton (D)	**Tennessee**	Don Sundquist (R)
Louisiana	Mike Foster (R)	**Texas**	George W. Bush (R)
Maine	Angus King (I)	**Utah**	Mike Leavitt (R)
Maryland	Parris N. Glendening (D)	**Vermont**	Howard Dean (D)
Massachusetts	Paul Cellucci (R)****	**Virginia**	James S. Gilmore III (R)*
Michigan	John Engler (R)	**Washington**	Gary Locke (D)
Minnesota	Arne Carlson (R)	**West Virginia**	Cecil H. Underwood (R)
Mississippi	Kirk Fordice (R)	**Wisconsin**	Tommy G. Thompson (R)
Missouri	Mel Carnahan (D)	**Wyoming**	Jim Geringer (R)

*elected in 1997   **re-elected in 1997   ***succeeded F. Symington, who resigned from office   ****succeeded W. Weld, who resigned from office
(D) Democrat (R) Republican (I) Independent

CANADA

Capital: Ottawa
Head of State: Queen Elizabeth II
Governor General: Romeo LeBlanc
Prime Minister: Jean Chrétien (Liberal)
Leader of the Opposition: Preston Manning (Reform Party)
Population: 30,286,600
Area: 3,851,809 sq mi (9,976,185 km²)

PROVINCES AND TERRITORIES

Alberta
Capital: Edmonton
Lieutenant Governor: H. A. Bud Olson
Premier: Ralph Klein (Progressive Conservative)
Leader of the Opposition: Grant Mitchell (Liberal)
Entered Confederation: Sept. 1, 1905
Population: 2,847,000
Area: 255,285 sq mi (661,188 km²)

British Columbia
Capital: Victoria
Lieutenant Governor: Garde Gardom
Premier: Glen Clark (New Democratic Party)
Leader of the Opposition: Gordon Campbell (Liberal)
Entered Confederation: July 20, 1871
Population: 3,933,300
Area: 366,255 sq mi (948,600 km²)

Manitoba
Capital: Winnipeg
Lieutenant Governor: Yvon Dumont
Premier: Gary Filmon (Progressive Conservative)
Leader of the Opposition: Gary Doer (New Democratic Party)
Entered Confederation: July 15, 1870
Population: 1,145,200
Area: 251,000 sq mi (650,090 km²)

New Brunswick
Capital: Fredericton
Lieutenant Governor: Marilyn Trenholme Counsell
Premier: J. Raymond Frenette (Liberal)
Leader of the Opposition: Bernard Lord
  (Progressive Conservative)
Entered Confederation: July 1, 1867
Population: 762,000
Area: 28,354 sq mi (73,436 km²)

Newfoundland
Capital: St. John's
Lieutenant Governor: Arthur Max House
Premier: Brian Tobin (Liberal)
Leader of the Opposition: Loyola Sullivan
  (Progressive Conservative)
Entered Confederation: March 31, 1949
Population: 563,600
Area: 156,185 sq mi (404,517 km²)

Nova Scotia
Capital: Halifax
Lieutenant Governor: J. James Kinley
Premier: Russell MacLellan (Liberal)
Leader of the Opposition: John Hamm (Progressive
  Conservative)
Entered Confederation: July 1, 1867
Population: 947,900
Area: 21,425 sq mi (55,491 km²)

Ontario
Capital: Toronto
Lieutenant Governor: Hilary M. Weston
Premier: Mike Harris (Progressive Conservative)
Leader of the Opposition: Dalton McGuinty (Liberal)
Entered Confederation: July 1, 1867
Population: 11,407,700
Area: 412,582 sq mi (1,068,582 km²)

Prince Edward Island
Capital: Charlottetown
Lieutenant Governor: Gilbert R. Clements
Premier: Patrick Binns (Progressive Conservative)
Leader of the Opposition: Keith W. Milligan (Liberal)
Entered Confederation: July 1, 1873
Population: 137,200
Area: 2,184 sq mi (5,657 km²)

Quebec

Capital: Quebec City
Lieutenant Governor: Lise Thibault
Premier: Lucien Bouchard (Parti Québécois)
Leader of the Opposition: Daniel Johnson (Liberal)
Entered Confederation: July 1, 1867
Population: 7,419,900
Area: 594,860 sq mi (1,540,700 km^2)

Saskatchewan

Capital: Regina
Lieutenant Governor: John N. Wiebe
Premier: Roy Romanow (New Democratic Party)
Leader of the Opposition: Ken Krawetz (Saskatchewan Party)
Entered Confederation: Sept. 1, 1905
Population: 1,023,500
Area: 251,700 sq mi (651,900 km^2)

Yukon

Capital: Whitehorse
Premier: Piers McDonald (New Democratic Party)
Leader of the Opposition: John Ostashek (Yukon Party)
Commissioner: Judy Gingell
Organized as a Territory: June 13, 1898
Population: 31,600
Area: 186,299 sq mi (482,515 km^2)

Northwest Territories

Capital: Yellowknife
Commissioner: Helen Maksagak
Government Leader: Don Morin
Reconstituted as a Territory: Sept. 1, 1905
Population: 67,500
Area: 1,304,896 sq mi (3,379,684 km^2)

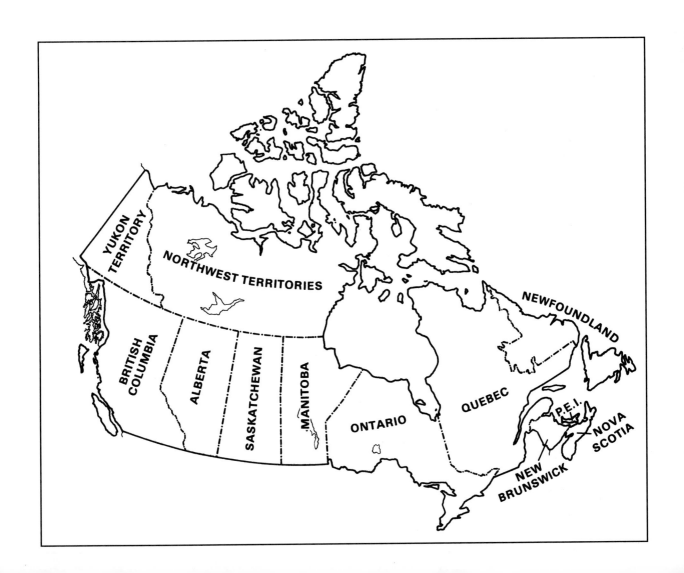

INDEX

A

Academy Awards 248; pictures 249
  record-holding movie, picture 197
Accidents and disasters
  airplane crash, Indonesia 37
  air-polluting heavy haze, Southeast Asia 37
  car crash, France 13, 30-31, 40, 43
  earthquakes, Iran 18, 24
  El Niño-related 128
  ferry capsize, Haiti 32
  fire, Saudi Arabia 22
  floods, Canada 23
  floods, United States 16, 23; picture 20
  hurricane, Mexico 34
  mass suicide, California 20
  tornadoes, United States 20, 24
Afghanistan 384
Africa
  ceremonial masks 242; picture 243
  edible insects 84; picture 85
  ethnic violence 54-55
  North African terrorist attacks 53-54
  see also specific countries
African Americans
  Kwanzaa stamp 136
  Medal of Honor recipients 62
  Museum of African American History, picture 255
  Robinson, Jackie 140, 181
Ahern, Bertie, prime minister of Ireland 26
Air Force One, movie 262
Air pollution
  Southeast Asia 37
Akhenaton, Egyptian pharaoh 187
Akira, Japanese *anime* movie 272
Alarcón, Fabián, president of Ecuador 18-19
Alaska
  Iditarod Trail Sled Dog Race 179
  Yupik ceremonial masks 243; picture 244
Albania 384
  leadership change 21, 29
Alberta, province, Canada 394
Albright, Madeleine K., American government official
  appointment as secretary of state, picture 60
Algeria 384
  civil war violence 53-54
Allen, Paul, American entrepreneur
  Microsoft founding 226
Ambroise, Valerie, American student
  namer of *Sojourner* space rover, picture 237
AmeriCorps, government volunteer program, picture 50
Anderson, Gillian, actress, picture 265
Andorra 384
Angola 384
Animals 130-31
  cloned sheep 106-09

edible insects 84-85
  environmental changes affecting 128, 130-31
  Iditarod Trail Sled Dog Race 179
  llamas 375
  newsmakers, pictures 90-95
  rain-forest inhabitants 116, 117, 118, 119
  rat trained for Internet wiring, picture 111
  record holders as slowest and fastest, pictures 203
  shrimp 78-79
  snow monkeys 74, 86-89
  stamps 136-37, 138
  tongues 80-83
  Yellowstone National Park wildlife preserve 31
Animation
  Bugs Bunny stamp 136; picture 137
  Hercules movie, picture 263
  Japanese *anime* films 272-73
Aniston, Jennifer, American actress, picture 256
Annan, Kofi, Ghanian UN secretary general, picture 61
Anniversaries 39
  Bell, Alexander Graham, 150th birthday 214-16; picture 184-85
  Cabot, John, landing on North American coast 286
  Constitution, U.S.S., picture 28
  Earhart, Amelia, attempted round-the-world flight 64
  Edison, Thomas Alva, 150th birthday 185, 214, 216-17
  Jell-O centennial, picture 21
  Roswell Incident 27
  stamps, first U.S. 136
  "there is a Santa Claus" newspaper editorial 33
  Tutankhamen tomb discovery, Egypt 186-91
  Yellowstone National Park 31
Antarctica
  first solo trek across, picture 196
Anteater 80
Antigua and Barbuda 138, 384
Ants
  edible 85
  rain-forest habitats 118
Apes
  laughter 76, 124
Arafat, Yasir, Palestinian leader 53
Archeology
  dinosaur fossil, Argentina 24
  fossil ground, China, picture 22
  pirate ship wreck 204, 207; picture 206
  tool find, Ethiopia 17
  Tutankhamen tomb, 75th anniversary, Egypt 186-91
  Viking settlement, Greenland, picture 19
Argentina 384
  dinosaur fossil discovery 24
Arizona
  governor's fraud conviction and resignation 32
Arkansas
  tornadoes 20
Armenia 384
Arms control
  campaign against land mines 32-33, 35
  poison-gas weapons ban treaty 22
Arteaga, Rosalia, president of Ecuador 19
Artrain, traveling museum in a train, picture 210

D

E

G

H

M

N

O

P

S

X-Y

Z

ILLUSTRATION CREDITS AND ACKNOWLEDGMENTS

The following list credits or acknowledges, by page, the source of illustrations and text excerpts used in this work. Illustration credits are listed illustration by illustration—left to right, top to bottom. When two or more illustrations appear on one page, their credits are separated by semicolons. When both the photographer or artist and an agency or other source are given for an illustration, they are usually separated by a slash. Excerpts from previously published works are listed by inclusive page numbers.

6   © J. H. Carmichael, Jr./Bruce Coleman, Inc.; © DIC Entertainment, L.P.; © 1991 F&W Publications, Inc. Used by permission of North Light Books, a division of F&W Publications, Inc.

7   Fritz Hasler/NASA Goddard Lab for Atmospheres-Data from NOAA GOES 9; © Boltin Picture Library © Alan DeJecaion/ Gamma Liaison

12– © Andrew Murray/Sygma
13

13   © John Stillwell/Reuters/Archive Photos

16   © Doug Mills/AP/Wide World Photos

17   © Mary Burkus/AP/Wide World Photos

19   © Jette Arneborg/The National Museum of Denmark; The Granger Collection

20   © Phil Masturzo/Akron Beacon Journal/ AP/Wide World Photos

21   Corbis-Bettmann; © Globe Photos

22   © David S. Bubier/Vireo

23   © Martin Mejia/AP/Wide World Photos

25   © Washington Stock Photo

26   © Gehring/Gamma Liaison

27   © Rod Rolle/Gamma Liaison; ©Chip Simons

28   © Jim Bourg/Gamma Liaison

29   © Jeffrey Aaronson/Network Aspen

30   © Tim Grahman/Sygma

31   © Milton Rand/Tom Stack & Associates

32   © David Brauchli/Sygma

33   © NYT Pictures; The Granger Collection

34   © Reuters Archive Photos

36   © Wide World Photos/NBC News; Jeff Stahler reprinted by permission of Newspaper Enterprise Association, Inc. 200 Madison Avenue New York, NY 10016

37   © Bernama/ Wide World Photos

38   © Joan Marcus

40   © Cherruault/Sipa Press

41   © Gamma Liaison; © Tim Graham/Sygma

42   © Cherruault/Sipa Press

43   © Pool/FSP/Gamma Liaison

44   © Cynthia Johnson/Gamma Liaison

46   © Ian Jones/FSP/Gamma Liaison; © Lenhof-Rat/Gamma Liaison

47   © Fred Chartrand/Canapress

48   H. Rumph, Jr./AP/WideWorld Photos; © Stephen Savoia/AP/Wide World Photos

49   © Eddie Adams

50   © Toby Talbot/AP/Wide World Photos; © Jonathan Kirn/Gamma Liaison

51   © 1997 Creators Syndicate, Inc./Richmond Times Dispatch

52   © Jassim Mohammed/AP/Wide World Photos

53   © Reuters/Jim Hollander/Archive Photos

55   © P. Robert/Sygma

56   © Jeffrey Aaronson/Network Aspen

57   © Nate Thayer/Tom Keller & Assoicates

58   © J. Scott Appleswhite/AP/Wide World Photos

59   © Baldev/Sygma

60   © David Karp/AP/Wide World Photos

61   © A. Tannenbaum/Sygma; © Acey Harper/People Weekly

62   AP/Wide World Photos; © Reuters/Rick Wilking/Archive Photos; © Saurabh Das/AP/Wide World Photos

63   © Mike Nelson/AP/Wide World Photos; Sygma

64   © Kim Kulish/Saba

65   © Chuck Harrity/U.S. News and World Report; Office of Congressman Harold Ford, Jr.

66– © Tim Davis/Davis/Lynn Images
67

68   © Bill Everitt/Tom Stack & Associates

69   © Alan & Sandy Carey

70   © S. Michael Bisceglie/Animals Animals

71   © Gary W. Griffen/Animals Animals

72   © Stan Osolinski/Oxford Scientific Films © David Fritts/Tony Stone Images

74   © Leonard Lee Rue III/Animals Animals

75   © Tim Davis/Photo Researchers, Inc.; © C. Greg Gilman/FPG International

76   © Miriam Austerman/Animals Animals; © Frans Lanting/Minden Pictures

77   © Norbert Rosing

78   © Doug Perrine/Innerspace Visions; © Fred Bavendam

79   © F. Stuart Westmorland/Photo Researchers, Inc.; © Fred Bavendam

80   © J. H. Carmichael, Jr./Bruce Coleman Inc.

81   © Del Mulkey/Photo Researchers, Inc.; © David T. Roberts/Photo Researchers, Inc.

82   © Jane Burton/Bruce Coleman Inc.

82– © Joe McDonald/Bruce Coleman Inc.
83

83   © Ron Garrison/Zoological Society of San Diego

84   © Peter Menzel

85   © Anthony Bannister; © Peter Menzel

86   © Mitsuaki Iwago/Minden Pictures

87   © Francois Gohier/Photo Researchers, Inc.

88   © Mitsuaki Iwago/Minden Pictures

89   © Werner Forman Archive/Art Resource

90   © Wildlife Images

91   © Jeffrey Lowe/People Weekly; © Gerald Kooyman/Scripps Institution of Oceanography

92   © J. M. Lammertink; © Ron Austing/ Cincinnatti Zoo

93   Courtesy, Zoo Atlanta

94   © AP/Wide World Photos; © R. Ian Lloyd

95   © Paul Donahue

96– © Bruce Fier/Gamma Liaison
97

98   © Frank Zullo/Photo Researchers, Inc.

99   © Chip Simons/People Weekly

100 Courtesy, The Space Sciences Laboratory Center for Science Education

101 The Granger Collection

102 © Chad Slattery

103 © Randy Duchaine/The Stock Market; © Chad Slattery

104 © Chicago Sun-Times

105 © Chad Slattery

106 © Reuters/Ho/Archive Photos

107 © Stephen Rountree/U.S. News & World Report

108 © Reuters/John Chadwick/Archive Photos

109 © Joyce Mejia Ingram/Sygma

110 © James D. Wilson/Gamma Liaison

111 © Susan Ragan/AP/Wide World Photos

112 © Chris Usher Photographs; © Becky Underwood

113 © William Mercer McLeod

114 © Michael Melford; © Dick Keen/ Visuals Unlimited

115 © Michael Melford

117 © Frans Lanting/Minden Pictures; © Michael Fogden/Bruce Coleman, Inc.

118 © J. C. Carton/Bruce Coleman, Inc.; Tim Laman/National Geographic Society

119 © Jonathan Doster

120 © JPL/NASA/Gamma Liaison

121 Space Telescope Science Institution

122– Johnson Space Center
123

124– Artist, Vince Caputo
127

128 Fritz Hasler/NASA Goddard Lab for Atmospheres-Data from NOAA GOES 9

129 © Noah Portiz/Photo Researchers, Inc.; © Pat Anderson/Visuals Unlimited

130 © Robert Yin/Gamma Liaison

131 © Douglas Faulkner/Photo Researchers, Inc.; © AP/World Wide Photos/Minnesota Pollution Control Agency; © L. West/ Photo Researchers, Inc.

132– Designed and created by Jenny Tesar
135

140 SOLUTION: Brooklyn Dodgers

142– © 1991 F&W Publications, Inc. Used by
143 permission of North Light Books, a division of F&W Publications, Inc.

144 © Jim Corwin/Photo Researchers, Inc.

145 © B. Daemmrich/The Image Works; © Michael Newman/Photo Edit

146 © Dana White/Photo Edit; © Ken Lax/ Photo Researchers, Inc.

147 © Mary Kate Denny/Photo Edit; © David Young-Wolff/Photo Edit

148 © Ken Lax/Photo Researchers, Inc.

149 © Steve Chenn/Westlight

152– From Many Friends Cooking: An
153 International Cookbook for Boys and Girls, by Terry Touff Cooper and